THE COMPLETE PRACTICAL HANDBOOK OF
GARDEN BULBS

THE COMPLETE PRACTICAL HANDBOOK OF
GARDEN BULBS

HOW TO CREATE A SPECTACULAR FLOWERING GARDEN THROUGHOUT THE
YEAR IN LAWNS, BEDS, BORDERS, BOXES, CONTAINERS AND HANGING BASKETS

KATHY BROWN

southwater

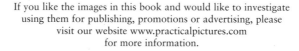

This edition is published by Southwater, an imprint of
Anness Publishing Ltd, Hermes House, 88–89 Blackfriars Road,
London SE1 8HA; tel. 020 7401 2077; fax 020 7633 9499

www.southwaterbooks.com; www.annesspublishing.com

If you like the images in this book and would like to investigate
using them for publishing, promotions or advertising, please
visit our website www.practicalpictures.com
for more information.

UK agent: The Manning Partnership Ltd; tel. 01225 478444;
fax 01225 478440; sales@manning-partnership.co.uk
UK distributor: Grantham Book Services Ltd;
tel. 01476 541080; fax 01476 541061;
orders@gbs.tbs-ltd.co.uk
North American agent/distributor: National Book Network;
tel. 301 459 3366; fax 301 429 5746; www.nbnbooks.com
Australian agent/distributor: Pan Macmillan Australia;
tel. 1300 135 113; fax 1300 135 103;
customer.service@macmillan.com.au
New Zealand agent/distributor: David Bateman Ltd;
tel. (09) 415 7664; fax (09) 415 8892

Publisher: Joanna Lorenz
Editorial Director: Judith Simons
Executive Editor: Caroline Davison
Project Editors: Molly Perham and Sarah Uttridge
Designer: Nigel Partridge
Production Controller: Wendy Lawson
Editorial Readers: Rosie Fairhead and Jay Thundercliffe

ETHICAL TRADING POLICY
Because of our ongoing ecological investment programme, you,
as our customer, can have the pleasure and reassurance of
knowing that a tree is being cultivated on your behalf to
naturally replace the materials used to make the book you are
holding. For further information about this scheme, go to
www.annesspublishing.com/trees

A CIP catalogue record for this book is available
from the British Library.

Previously published as *The Gardener's Guide to Bulbs*

Contents

Introduction

This book is bursting with ideas on how to use bulbs in your garden, whether you want to grow them in beds or borders or more naturally in open grass or shady orchard or woodland situations. It describes not only how to plant bulbs, but in which situation they will thrive best, with regard to soil moisture, drainage, acidity and alkalinity, sun or shade. It also includes details on how to look after flowering bulbs, with advice on pests and diseases, feeding, staking, and, in the case of exotic varieties, how to cope with winter protection. Propagation is another major consideration with helpful information on which varieties can be easily grown from seed, whilst others may be more readily propagated from cuttings.

An entire section is devoted to outdoor containers showing how it is possible to enjoy inspirational arrangements throughout the year whether they are small, medium or large, with ideas for long-term planting as well.

Another major chapter of the book deals with bulbs as houseplants with ideas for growing and displaying many different varieties for mid-winter pleasure as well as spring and summer bringing scent and colour right into your home.

A comprehensive bulb directory provides information on the origins, hardiness and cultivation of over sixty key genera, and includes a useful at-a-glance bulb planner to help you to create a spectacular display of colour throughout the year.

Cannas provide some of the most dramatic foliage of all, with their wide tapering leaves, sometimes bronze and occasionally variegated, often with distinctive veining.

What is a bulb?

The word bulb is used in this book as an umbrella term for all those plants that have a root system that has been adapted to withstand long periods of drought by storing food reserves beneath ground. It includes not only true bulbs but also corms, tubers and rhizomes, as well as plants with fleshy roots.

Crocosmias, dahlias and lilies join forces to add splendour to the summer border, where earlier narcissus and tulips played centre stage.

Countries of origin

The bulbs we grow in our gardens today originated from around the world. Countries such as Spain, France, Italy, Greece and Turkey, which border the Mediterranean Sea, are home to a host of species daffodils, blue and white anemones, tiny scillas and chionodoxas, dainty *Galanthus* (snowdrop) and *Leucojum* (snowflake). California is the source of yellow calochortus, while South Africa is the home of colourful gladioli, stately agapanthus, shapely *Zantedeschia* (arum lily), scented freesias, pretty watsonias and gorgeous gloriosa, to name but a few. Central Asia provides brilliantly coloured tulips, tall eremurus (foxtail lily) and scented lilies. Other, more tender plants, such as dahlias and *Tigridia* (tiger flower), are native to Mexico and Central America, while many of the begonias come from the Andes of Peru and Bolivia. Hippeastrums, sometimes known as indoor amaryllis, are native to Central and South America.

Bulbs for all seasons

Wonderful flowers for every season of the year can be grown from bulbs. As soon as midwinter has passed *Eranthis hyemalis* (winter aconite) thrusts up its shoots, together with snowdrops, early crocuses, anemones and *Iris danfordiae*. Spring welcomes daffodils, hyacinths and tulips, fritillaries and *Hyacinthoides* (bluebell). More irises follow in early summer, along with all the alliums. Then it is time for gladioli, begonias, lilies, agapanthus, eremurus and dahlias. As summer turns to autumn, dahlias are still in flower, and they are joined by a beautiful array of nerines, crinums, colchicums and cyclamen.

Choosing a site

There are bulbs for everywhere in the garden. Most prefer a sunny position and well-drained soil, with tulips and gladioli being notable examples. Others, such as bluebells and trilliums, will enjoy a shadier home. But some genera, such as alliums, are more diverse. Certain members of the family, including *A. karataviense*,

Species tulips such as *Tulipa tarda* and *T. urumiensis* will give great pleasure in a hanging basket for more than one season.

Freesias make wonderful plants for a conservatory, where they may continue to thrive for many years.

love sun, while *A. triquetrum* prefers the shade. They also vary widely in height. Short species, such as anemones and crocuses, are best near the front of a border or in a rock garden, while tall eremurus and stately lilies are usually better in the middle or back of the border. However, these rules can all be broken, for most bulbs will grow successfully in different garden settings. Lilies are an excellent example: some are so wonderfully flamboyant and beautifully scented that they deserve several homes in the border or to be planted next to a path or in a pot near a door.

In Europe in the 16th century some bulbs were so valuable that they were displayed far apart from each other in the garden so that they

Blue grape hyacinths and Double Early tulips combine to provide a sumptuous display and even the container is colour-co-ordinated.

were easy to cultivate and could be appreciated individually. Sometimes a single tulip was the only occupant of an entire bed. Today, commercial propagation allows us to buy most bulbs relatively cheaply, so that ten might be planted in one group or perhaps in a single container. Sometimes double that number may be planted in a large container, especially if small bulbs, such as crocuses, *Muscari* spp. (grape hyacinth) or anemones, are used to underplant taller ones, such as hyacinths, early tulips or daffodils. There are so many possibilities that you should experiment and enjoy the results, but, whatever you do, be sure only to buy commercially cultivated bulbs. Never plant any bulbs that have been taken from the wild.

Dahlias are a brilliant choice for a sunny summer border where they will be valued for the long period of flowering and their colours.

The botany of bulbs

The word "bulb" is often used to describe true bulbs, corms, tubers, rhizomes and plants with fleshy root systems that can cope with long periods of drought by storing food reserves beneath ground. There are, however, clear differences between these five types of plant.

True bulbs

The inside of a true bulb consists of stems and fleshy leaves that have been modified for storage. In tulip, hyacinth and daffodil bulbs the modified leaves are layered closely around each other, with the outer leaves, which are often dry and brown, forming a tunic around the bulb. In other bulbs the leaves are not wrapped around each other but overlap, producing a far more succulent bulb. These bulbs are known as scaly bulbs, and the lily is one of the best-known examples.

Individual bulbs usually survive for many years in the ground, during which time the old ones will produce offsets or "daughter" bulbs and thus create small groups. Some tulip bulbs are unlikely to produce flowers for a second year, but the bulb will form replacement bulbs, which then flower the following year.

Corms

Inside all corms there is a stem that is swollen and adapted to store food. This forms the base of the new shoots. Unlike true bulbs, corms appear solid throughout. After flowering, a new corm, formed at the base of the new stem, will grow on top of the old one and the old corm will die. Each corm, therefore, has only one season in which to produce a flower. Small young corms will also form on the basal plate, which is slightly concave. Crocosmias, gladioli and crocuses are all cormous plants.

Rhizomes

A rhizome is a swollen underground stem, from the ends of which shoots, then foliage and flowers emerge, while roots grow on the underside of the rhizome. Side branches will form each year, typically after flowering has occurred, enabling the plant to spread. Cannas and zantedeschias are typical rhizomatous plants.

Chasmanthe (top left and right) has a wide corm, while freesias (bottom left) are smaller and, for their size, relatively elongated. Those of gladioli (bottom right) are more rounded.

Cannas (top) produce many fairly large, elongated rhizomes each season, and these can be severed to produce new plants. Zantedeschia rhizomes (bottom) can be treated in the same way, although the rhizomes are squatter and more rounded.

Tubers

A tuber is a swollen underground root or stem, but it is not the base of the stem, as in the corm. It is usually fleshy and rounded and may be covered with scaly leaves or with fibrous roots. Buds usually develop on top of the tuber and produce stems. Tubers get larger with age and can live for years. Dahlias, cyclamen and some types of begonia and anemone are tuberous plants.

Fleshy root systems

This last group is of plants that make leaf and root growth when the soil and atmosphere around them is moist, come into bloom and then undergo a period of dormancy during the summer drought. Such

In this group of summer- and autumn-flowering true bulbs, the crinum (top) has a long, tapering neck, while the lilies (middle) and smaller tulips (bottom) are more compact.

Begonia tubers (top left) are compact, with a hairy, round base and a concave top from which tiny pink shoots appear. Dahlias (top right) have a clutch of large, fat tuberous "legs", while ranunculus (bottom left) have thin, claw-like legs. If the legs break off they will not produce new plants. Anemones (bottom right) are hard and knobbly, and it is from these protuberances that the new growth appears.

plants come mainly from regions of the world where winters are cool and moist and summers are hot and dry.

Families, genera, species and cultivars

True bulbs, corms, tubers and rhizomes belong to a relatively small number of plant "families" based on similarities in the reproductive organs within the flower rather than on the appearance of the flower or the storage organ itself. Most true bulbs and corms belong to only a few families. The family Amaryllidaceae includes well-known genera such as *Narcissus* (daffodil), *Nerine*, *Sternbergia* and *Galanthus* (snowdrop). Iridaceae embraces the genera *Freesia*, *Schizostylis*, *Tigridia*, *Gladiolus* and *Iris*, and Liliaceae includes *Lilium* (lily), *Fritillaria* and *Tulipa* (tulip).

Tuberous and rhizomatous plants have more widespread family connections. Cyclamen are part of the family Primulaceae, *Begonia* of Begoniaceae, *Sinningia* of Gesneriaceae and *Dahlia* of Compositae.

Genera are distinct plant groups within the larger family, yet some have a strong family resemblance. For example, some bulbs of the Hyacinthaceae family, as well as the flowers, show marked similarities. The genera *Muscari*, *Chionodoxa*, *Scilla*, *Hyacinthus* and *Hyacinthoides* from Europe and the Middle East have a similar appearance to *Camassia* bulbs, which come from North America.

Each genus usually contains more than one species. These might be regarded as extremely close relatives with many common characteristics. Within the genus *Narcissus*, for example, there are about 50 species. Sometimes species vary naturally, and the resulting plants are known as varieties. A well-known example is *Narcissus poeticus* var. *recurvus*, which has been grown for centuries and is known as pheasant's eye.

Nurserymen often breed from a species, and the results are referred to as cultivars. Hence, the species *Narcissus cyclamineus*, with its distinctive swept-back petals, has been used to produce popular cultivars such as N. 'February Gold', 'Jetfire' and 'Peeping Tom'. As a result, we now have thousands of cultivars from around 50 species of *Narcissus*. They flower at different times, vary in height and colour and have different flower structures.

The Hyacinthaceae family is represented here by five genera: *Camassia* and *Hyacinthus* are the larger bulbs at the back, with *Muscari* (grape hyacinth), *Hyacinthoides* (bluebell) and *Scilla* (squill) from left to right at the front.

This cross-section shows that corms, such as that of the gladiolus (bottom), have a more solid appearance, while true bulbs, such as those of lilies (top), are made up of stems and fleshy, scaly leaves.

Of all these narcissus bulbs only *Narcissus poeticus* var. *recurvus*, the one with the long tapering noses, is a species growing wild in the mountains of central and southern Europe. The others are cultivars bred for the trade.

The history of bulbs

Plant hunters risked their lives to bring the bulbs that we know today from their native habitats, and sometimes it has taken several attempts to introduce them successfully to the gardens of the West. Fashion has also played a major role in their history. Tulips, for example, became almost beyond price in the heady days of the 1630s, but now they are available in their thousands and are used in spring bedding schemes right around the world.

Tulips

Of all bulbs, the tulip has one of the most colourful histories. Its principal homelands were Persia (now Iran) and Turkey, where even in the 12th and 13th centuries poets sang its praises. When Süleyman I, the Magnificent, became sultan in 1520, the Ottoman Empire stretched from the Crimea in the east to Egypt and beyond in the west, and it covered large parts of the Balkans. City gardens were well established, and tulips were one of the most popular flowers. The

The beauty of tulips and other flowers that were being discovered was captured by artists in detailed drawings and prints.

period even became known as the Tulip Age. Regular tulip festivals were held, and the flower was used to decorate tiles and pottery as well as clothes.

These tulips were introduced to Europe in the middle of the 16th century. Conrad Gesner (1516–65), the Swiss scholar and humanist, recorded how he saw a red tulip growing in a garden in Augsburg, Bavaria, in 1557. The garden belonged to Johannis Heinrich Herwart. Also important in tulip history was the part played by the Flemish ambassador Ghislain de Busbecq (1522–91), who was the representative in Constantinople of the Habsburg emperor, Ferdinand I. In 1529 the city of Vienna had withstood a siege by Ottoman forces, but the emperor was keen to maintain trading links with the Ottoman Empire and so continued to send ambassadors to the sultan. Busbecq, who was sent as Ferdinand's emissary in 1554, greatly admired the tulips he saw growing in the gardens of Constantinople. He was able to obtain seeds and bulbs at a great price, and he eventually sent them back to the imperial gardens in Vienna, where they were grown under the care of Carolus Clusius (Charles de L'Écluse; 1526–1609).

Clusius was curious to know how the bulbs tasted and asked an apothecary to preserve them in sugar in the same manner as orchids. He ate them as sweetmeats and said he preferred them to orchids. Fortunately he survived, but eating bulbs is not recommended.

The bulbs travelled with Clusius from Vienna to Frankfurt and eventually to the Netherlands, where he was appointed Professor of Botany at Leiden University in

Conrad Gesner, Swiss scholar and humanist, recorded the first tulip growing in Europe in Augsburg in 1557.

1593. There he was given the opportunity of laying out a new botanical garden. As the tulips came into flower, interest in the unusual bulbs escalated, and people wanted to buy them. Clusius was continually obtaining bulbs from new suppliers, and through his extensive network of contacts throughout Europe he was responsible for tulips reaching many new areas. He demanded high prices for his stocks, and such a precious commodity was clearly vulnerable. On many occasions bulbs were stolen and then grown on and traded, becoming the original stock of the Dutch bulb industry.

Soon, absurdly high prices were being demanded for a single bulb. To begin with the tulip was a status symbol among the aristocracy. The length and strength of the stalk, the size and shape of the flower and even the colour of the stamens were remarked upon. Each tulip was regularly afforded a lot of growing space, and sometimes a single specimen was given an entire bed in which to be shown off. Tulips came to be desired by the growing

Nico Jungman (1872–1935) painted these Dutch tulip fields near Haarlem in 1909. Born in the Netherlands, he later moved to London where he was a landscape and figure painter as well as an illustrator and painter of travel books.

merchant classes in the Netherlands. Prices rose from hundreds of florins (a florin was worth two shillings) for a specific cultivated variety to 3,000 florins in the 1620s. Such was the interest in the trade – as distinct from interest in the actual plant – that a "futures" market developed, by which bulbs were paid for in instalments between the time of lifting in early summer and the time of planting in mid-autumn. During that time the same bulb might be bought and sold several times, as each merchant tried to make a profit on the deal. A dry bulb could not show the colour or quality of the flower it was going to produce, so the whole business depended on trust.

As demand increased, the trade grew and all levels of society became involved, including landowners, farmers, sailors, artists, weavers and servants. In 1636 tulips were traded on the London Exchange. They were also traded in Scotland, but there was little interest.

Not all the bulbs were expensive. White- and red-flowered tulips, for example, could be bought for only 12 florins a pound weight, but a single bulb of the 'Viceroy' tulip fetched 4,600 florins when it was sold at auction in 1637. The 'Viceroy' was a Violette, which had flowers with wonderful, streaked purple markings on a white background. There is a story that one 'Viceroy' changed hands for 12 fat sheep, 4 fat oxen, 8 fat pigs, 2 loads of wheat, 4 loads of rye, 2 hogsheads of wine, 4 tons of beer, 2 tons of butter, 1,000 pounds of cheese, a silver drinking horn, a suit of clothes and a complete bed! The total value of this single bulb, which was probably recorded by one of the pamphleteers campaigning against the evil and misery caused by gambling, was 3,500 guilders, a fortune at a time when the average annual income was only 150 florins and a first-class house was worth 5,000 florins.

In February 1637 the bubble burst, and when the crash came many people in the Netherlands suffered. Local authorities and growers tried to stabilize the market, but it was

many years before people could pay off their debts. Nevertheless, Dutch soil was ideal for growing tulips, and, because the flowers were appreciated across Europe, trade continued. In the 1630s and 1640s at least 650 varieties were still being grown. A list of those cultivated in the gardens of the Margrave of Baden-Durlach in Karlsruhe in 1730 contained almost 2,400 names; three years later he grew nearly 4,000. At the beginning of World War II, just before the German invasion, the Netherlands was exporting 100 million tulip bulbs to the United States annually. Today, there are about 5,000 cultivars in the trade.

The word "tulip" is thought to have derived from Busbecq's original description of the plant, which he wrote after first seeing it in the gardens near Constantinople around 1554. He recalled that Turkish people called them *tulipam* because of the similarity of the shape of the open flowers to a turban. In fact, the Turkish word for turban is *tulbend*, but, whatever its origin, the name tulip has stuck ever since.

Tulips still form one of the largest groups of bulbs sold each year, and they are still centred on the Dutch bulb fields.

This picture of the lesser daffodil was painted in 1786 and appeared in William Curtis's *Botanical Magazine*, volume 1, in 1793.

Narcissi

Most species of *Narcissus* are found in the countries bordering the Mediterranean, and they have long been appreciated as garden plants. There are many references to them in classical and more recent literature.

There has long been confusion about the difference between daffodils and narcissi. Today all daffodils fall into the genus *Narcissus*. The popular old names of daffodil, daffodilly and daffadowndilly are thought to be corruptions of the word asphodel or asphodelus, while the old name Lent lily refers to the season in which they flower – that is, the 40 days leading up to Easter.

Both names – narcissus and daffodil – have been used in popular poetry and literature. In the early 1800s the poet William Wordsworth and his sister Dorothy were captivated by them. She poignantly described the scene in her diary as they walked in the woods beside Ullswater in the English Lake District:

April 15th 1802
We fancied that the lake had floated seeds ashore, and that the little colony had so sprung up. But as we went along there were more and yet more; and at last, under the boughs of the trees, we saw that there was a long belt of them along the shore, about the breadth of a country turnpike road. I never saw daffodils so beautiful. They grew among the mossy stones about and about them; some rested their heads upon these stones, as on a pillow, for weariness; and the rest tossed and reeled and danced, and seemed as if they verily laughed with the wind that blew upon them over the lake; they looked so gay, ever glancing, ever changing.

Dahlias

Originating from the mountain ranges of Mexico and south to Colombia, the dahlia was probably used in medicine and as fodder by the Aztecs before the Spanish conquest. In 1789 a handful of seeds was sent by Vincente Cervantes of the Botanical Gardens in Mexico City to his friend Abbé Cavanilles, who was in charge of the Botanical Gardens at Madrid. The Abbé later named this Mexican flower after the Swedish botanist, Dr Anders Dahl (1751–89). The plant was known not so much for its single flowers and rather poor stems but for its edible root, which was introduced to Europe as an alternative to the potato. Dahlia roots came to be eaten in France and parts of the Mediterranean coast, but their peculiar, sharp flavour prevented their adoption as a staple food.

One of the keys to its success as a garden plant was the interest taken in it by the Empress Josephine (1763–1814), wife of Napoleon Bonaparte, who kept the garden at Malmaison near Paris, France. She grew dahlias and guarded the roots jealously, refusing to give any away. One of her ladies-in-waiting, Countess de Bougainville, wanted to grow some for herself. She hatched a plan with her lover, a Polish prince, who went to the gardener at Malmaison and offered money to obtain the tubers. The gardener

The popular old English names of the daffodil were daffodilly and daffadowndilly, and it is still known as Lent lily. Socrates called it "Chaplet of the infernal Gods" because of its narcotic effects.

This miniature of Empress Josephine, the wife of Napoleon Bonaparte, was painted by J.B. Isabey. The Empress grew some of the first dahlias in Europe in her garden at Malmaison near Paris.

deceived his mistress and apparently sold a hundred plants for one gold louis each. When the empress found out what had happened she was furious. She sacked her gardener, banished both the lady-in-waiting and the prince and thereafter refused to show any more interest in dahlias.

Several attempts were made to introduce the dahlia tubers to Britain. In 1789 the Marchioness of Bute visited Spain and sent one of the tubers home, but it died. A few years later Lady Holland, who scandalized polite society by divorcing Sir Godfrey Webster and eloping with Lord Holland, who was ambassador to King Philip of Spain, went to Spain and saw a dahlia in bloom. Captivated by the flower, she too sent plants home. This time they thrived, and so Lady Holland can be credited with introducing the dahlia to Britain. Nurserymen began experimenting with its form, and within a short time the single-flowered variety had been dropped in favour of a double "globular" form, which became all the rage and was known as the globe dahlia. These were the precursors of the double "show" and "fancy" types, valued respectively for their single colours and mixed hues. At one time it was recorded that as many as 10,000 varieties were available.

Nerine

Flamboyant nerines also travelled a long way to reach Europe, for these bulbs are native to South Africa. In 1652 the first 500 colonists arrived at Table Bay to join the new settlement that the Dutch East India Company had established there. Among them were two gardeners, whose task was to grow fruit and vegetables for the community and, no doubt, for all the ships that sailed to destinations in the Pacific and those returning to Europe. They were also commissioned to collect any wildflowers that might be valuable to the Dutch at home. They were successful in their work, and seven years later crates of nerines were among a cargo to be shipped to the Netherlands in one of the Dutch East India Company's vessels.

Sadly, the ship was wrecked in the English Channel, off the island of Guernsey. The nerine bulbs were washed ashore and some took root in the sand. Over the years they spread inland and eventually produced brilliant pink flowers, which local gardeners sent to the London flower market. They became commonly known as the Guernsey lily, a name that has been used for nerines ever since.

The islanders assumed that the bulbs were native to Japan, and it was more than 100 years before the error was realized, when in 1774 Francis Masson, the first ever official to be sent out as a plant hunter by Kew Gardens, England, saw the same flower, *Nerine sarniensis*, growing on the slopes of Table Mountain in South Africa.

Nerines first found their way to Europe on a boat that was shipwrecked near the island of Guernsey, where the bulbs have since naturalized.

Easter lily and regal lily

Like other plants, bulbs were sometimes unsuccessful when they were first introduced to the gardens of western Europe. This may have been because the season was inclement, the winter was particularly harsh or the cultural conditions were unsuitable. The lily is one such plant. A German doctor, Philipp von Siebold (1796–1866), first sent the lily we now know as the Easter lily from Japan to the Botanical Garden in Ghent in 1830, and it was reintroduced in 1840.

It was, however, a storm in the Atlantic that really changed the course of its history. Sometime in the 1860s a missionary was returning home to Europe from the coast of China. Among his possessions were a few bulbs of the same lily that von Siebold had previously tried to introduce. The stormy weather caused his vessel to take refuge in the shelter of St George's harbour on the island of Bermuda. The missionary was looked after there by the Reverend Roberts, and, as thanks for his hospitality, he gave the rector some of his special bulbs, which were planted in the rectory garden. The lilies enjoyed the mild climate and shallow limestone soil and soon became well established on their new island home. By the end of the 19th century more than three million bulbs were exported from Bermuda each year, but disease ravaged the stock and ruined it.

The plant hunter E. H. Wilson records that it was Mr Harris, an American nurseryman from Philadelphia, who first brought the bulbs to the trade. Captivated by their elegant, pure white blooms and heavenly scent, which is just like orange blossom, Harris realized that if they could be forced into flower for Easter, he would have a valuable flowering commodity to fill the church vases. He launched his find under the name *Lilium harrisii*, a name by which it is still sometimes known today, although the correct name is now *Lilium longiflorum* var. *eximium*, commonly known as the Easter lily.

Wilson was an expert in lilies from eastern Asia, and he thought he had found one that would surpass the Easter lily. His great quest was the *Lilium regale*, which grew in the remote Min valley, where western China borders on Tibet. He had first discovered it in 1903 and the following year had dispatched 300 bulbs to Veitch & Sons, the sponsors of his expedition. He tried again in 1908, but on neither occasion did he succeed in getting them established.

In 1910 Wilson set out yet again, this time working for the Arnold Arboretum in Boston, Massachusetts. His driving ambition was to introduce the lily to the gardens of the West. He recognized its great potential, for it could withstand very cold winters and extremely hot summers and thrived despite high

E. H. Wilson's epic journey to the Min valley in western China in 1910 resulted in the successful introduction of *Lilium regale* to Western gardens.

Lilium longiflorum, or Easter lily, is still used to decorate churches on Easter Day.

winds. His journal describing the expedition reveals a story of great courage and determination. He left Boston, Massachusetts, at the end of March 1910 for Europe and from there travelled on the Trans-Siberian Railway, reaching Peking in early May. He had to navigate 2,900km (1,800 miles) up the Yangtze river, and northwards up its tributary, the Min, for another 400km (250 miles) until he at last reached the remote region between China and Tibet which he described as a "no man's land".

He gathered supplies at the town of Sungpang Ting (Songpan) and travelled for seven consecutive days down the endless gorge of the Min river. The path was winding and difficult, with few passing places. Wilson walked for most of the day, although he also had a light sedan chair made of rattan which was an outward sign of importance and respectability, crucial in those far-off places where Western travellers were rare and treated with great suspicion. His dog always went with him. On the eighth day, Wilson decided to make a base camp from which to explore the area and arrange for the autumn collection of bulbs.

Wilson was in the heart of the Min valley and, although the district was barren and desolate, it was here that he found the lilies growing, clinging to the windswept hillsides. The first flowers began to open in late spring, along the banks of the river some 760m (2,500ft) above sea level. As summer advanced, the band of white trumpets rose up the mountain, so that by midsummer lilies were blooming at 1,830m (6,000ft). From his camp Wilson arranged for between 6,000 and 7,000 lily bulbs to be lifted in autumn. The bulbs were to be encased in clay, before being packed in charcoal and sent to America.

Although tired after many months travelling, it was, he recorded, with a "light heart" and "satisfied mind" that he began his long homeward journey. As before, the road was tortuous, and he was travelling in his sedan chair when disaster struck: a rock fall started down the hillside. One of the stones hit his chair; another struck his right leg and broke it in two places. He eventually managed to get up and rode in his boy's chair with his leg lashed to the right pole. It was an agonizing three days before they reached the missionary post at Chengdu. In spite of the threat of amputation, three months later Wilson was able to get about on crutches. He hired a boat to take him eastwards to Shanghai and on to America. He was able to walk again, although with a limp.

Just a few days after his return, the huge shipment of bulbs arrived. He found them in excellent condition and they were planted the following spring. Since then millions of them have been raised and planted, and they have become one of the most popular lilies in cultivation today.

E. H. Wilson recorded in his diary that he found lilies growing "not in two or threes but in hundreds, in thousands, aye, in tens of thousands".

Gardening techniques

Work in the bulb garden changes as the seasons unfold. From the initial excitement of choosing and buying a selection of bulbs in the autumn comes the pleasure of planning where to plant them, whether this is in grassland, woodland, borders or in containers. As soon as they sprout into growth, the process of caring for the bulbs begins in earnest. Sometimes taller bulbs such as dahlias need staking, while many will need protection from pests and diseases. Some require a scant diet, while others are gross feeders. Some bulbs, such as snowdrops, hyacinths, daffodils and lilies, may be left in the ground year after year, while others, such as dahlias, cannas and begonias, require an annual lifting to avoid freezing winter temperatures. This may seem like an onerous task, but these are among the most flamboyant of all garden plants and so certainly well worth the extra effort.

Most spring-flowering bulbs, tubers, corms and rhizomes should be planted as dry bulbs in autumn. There is a wonderful choice, including these *Hyacinthus* (hyacinth) and *Muscari* (grape hyacinth).

Buying and planting bulbs

Obtain bulbs from mail-order suppliers or buy them as soon as they become available in the garden centres, when the range on offer will be at its maximum. Keep the bulbs in cool, dry conditions and plant them in the garden when weather conditions are favourable.

For summer colour, tuberous begonias, fuchsias and aeoniums replace tulips and wallflowers.

Choosing bulbs

Only plant bulbs that are firm to the touch and show no sign of damage. Storage of *Eranthis hyemalis* (winter aconite), *Iris reticulata*, little *Anemone blanda* and *Galanthus nivalis* (snowdrop) can cause drying, which in turn will impair their flower production. Buy bulbs as soon as they are available in the garden centre and plant as soon as possible. Alternatively, purchase them as growing plants "in the green".

Other storage problems can arise when the bulbs have been lifted too early, which typically happens when tulip bulbs are lifted before the leaves have died down. The result will be a chalkiness and hardness of the bulb, which will look dull and feel solid to the touch. It is not worth planting bulbs like this. Mail-order companies normally take great

care, and these problems are less likely to arise. In garden centres you can often select bulbs from an open display unit. Choose the plumpest and biggest, and those that show no signs of damage.

Storing bulbs

You will be able to plant some bulbs immediately after you have purchased them. However, you may have to keep others until weather

conditions are more suitable or until a new bed is ready. While you are waiting, it is important to keep bulbs in cool, dry, well-ventilated conditions, away from predators, such as mice or squirrels. If the air is damp and they are kept in enclosed bags, even paper bags, bacterial infections can set in, leading to a blue mould on the outer parts. Avoid planting any bulb that shows signs of this disfigurement.

Here are two plump and two dried-out *Iris reticulata* corms. Plant with care, discarding any that are shrivelled or damaged.

Blue mould on lily bulbs has been caused by poor storage. Do not plant.

Planting times

There are two main seasons for buying bulbs: autumn and late winter. Spring-flowering bulbs and corms, such as daffodils, tulips, hyacinths and crocuses, should be planted in autumn. These are all hardy plants and can withstand winter frosts. In late winter summer-flowering bulbs, corms, tubers and rhizomes of plants such as crinum, gladioli and begonias are available. These are not necessarily hardy and are best planted outside in spring. Indeed, begonias are half-hardy and thrive only in warm summer conditions. The tubers are brought into growth indoors and moved outside only after all risk of frost has passed. Dahlia tubers are usually treated in a similar way, although in

Some narcissus bulbs are particularly large, but must still be planted at three times their depth.

less frost-prone areas they can be planted deeper than normal, with the eye bud 10–15cm (4–6in) deep, then left as a permanent planting with a thick mulch in winter.

How to plant

Most bulbs, corms, tubers and rhizomes have a rounded bottom or base from which the old roots grow, and these are sometimes still attached to the bulb. They may also have a pointed or tapering nose at the top, from which the first shoots emerge. The general rule for planting is that the rounded base sits on the soil while the nose points upwards.

The planting depth is normally determined by the size of the bulb, and the general rule is that a bulb should be planted at a depth of three times its own size. Thus, if a bulb measures 5cm (2in) from nose to base, there should be 15cm (6in) of soil on top of it. This means that the hole required for planting is actually 20cm (8in) deep. There are a few exceptions to this rule –

nerines and crinums, for example, should be planted close to the surface of the soil, as should *Lilium candidum* (Madonna lily), which should be planted at a depth of about 2.5cm (1in).

Snowdrops "in the green"

Some bulbs, such as *Galanthus* (snowdrop), do not like being out of the ground too long in late summer before autumn planting. They are among the first to flower in the new year and like to make their root growth early. Many do not adapt well to the drying-out process to which most bulbs are subjected. An alternative method, therefore, is to buy snowdrops "in the green", which are available in late winter in pots or as a loose clump of plants with the leaves still attached to the bulbs. Plant them in border soil, where they will spread quickly, or in turf, where they will spread more slowly but will still naturalize well. Plant in groups of between eight and ten, spacing the individual plants about 7.5cm (3in) apart.

The correct planting tool

The size of the bulb also usually determines the tool used for planting. A dibber or trowel may be used for small bulbs, such as crocuses and anemones, but larger ones, such as *Lilium* (lilies), *Narcissus* (daffodils), or tulips need a sharp-edged spade to make a deep hole.

Planting in borders

Techniques for planting bulbs vary according to the season, to the style of garden, and to the effect you want to create in the borders.

Informal groups

Planting informal groups of the same bulb can be highly effective and, depending on the size of the border, the groups may be repeated a number of times, with bedding plants or other herbaceous perennials between them. Groups of tulips may be surrounded by *Myosotis* (forget-me-not) or *Viola* (pansy). Groups of alliums may be grown through nearby *Erysimum cheiri* (wallflower), while groups of gladioli might appear behind penstemons or earlier flowering poppies.

Extra drainage

Lilies are extremely hardy bulbs and can be planted in autumn or in late winter, whenever they become available to buy. However, they strongly dislike sitting in wet ground, much preferring well-

Allium hollandicum 'Purple Sensation' and *Lilium regale* grow side by side and in both cases the seedheads can be left intact to encourage self-seeding, but also to be enjoyed in their own right.

drained soil. If your soil is naturally heavy add a generous layer of grit in the bottom of the hole as you plant lily bulbs. This will improve the growing conditions, so they can remain in the soil for many years.

Fritillaria imperialis (crown imperial) is another large bulb that dislikes too much moisture at its

base. Use extra grit here, too, and plant the bulbs slightly tilted to ensure that moisture does not drain into the open, funnelled tops from where the shoots emerge.

Pre-planting in pots

It is possible to lift spring-flowering bulbs in summer, after flowering is over, and replace them with other seasonal bulbs or bedding. Simply dig them up with a spade (take care not to slice them in half) and move them elsewhere while their life-cycle is completed. Alternatively, plant them in a perforated plastic pot that can be buried in the border. This makes lifting much easier and allows the bulbs to complete their growth cycle without any root disturbance. Special wide bulb-savers can be used, which control the planting area and make lifting straightforward. Simply dig a hole that is wide enough to bury the bulb-saver in the ground, at the required depth, using a layer of gravel if necessary to make a level base. Position the bulbs and fill in with soil. If bulbs are not required for the following year, lift after

USING A BULB-SAVER

1 A bulb-saver allows bulbs to be located easily at lifting time. Dig down to the required depth, level off the hole and place the bulb-saver within it.

2 Arrange bulbs in the bulb-saver and cover with soil. Lift bulbs after flowering if they are not wanted for another year or wait until the leaves have died back before lifting.

PLANTING IN A BURIED POT

1 Dig a hole deep enough to contain a large, black, plastic pot. Fill the pot with a 2.5cm (1in) layer of drainage material.

2 Add loamy compost (soil mix), and sit the bulbs 15cm (6in) below the rim of the pot. Cover with more compost.

3 Bury the pot in the hole and cover the top with a thin mulch of cocoa shells or compost to keep weeds at bay.

4 Enjoy the flowers, then remove the pot. Dry off the bulbs and fill the space with summer plants.

flowering. If they are required, allow them to complete their life-cycle and only then lift and store.

Pre-planting in pots is also a useful technique for dealing with summer-flowering bulbs that cannot survive frosty, damp conditions and are best planted in the garden only after all risk of frost has passed. Bulbs planted in containers the previous autumn, such as *Ornithogalum dubium*, or earlier in spring, such as freesias, can be transferred to the garden in early summer when they are already well into growth. Similarly, they can be lifted in autumn before the onset of wintry weather.

Planting for a succession of spring colour

Although an individual group of bulbs will enhance any border, it is possible to plant several types together at the same time in the autumn. This will create an enormous impact and give colour for many weeks. Choose from any of the dwarf early daffodils, such as *Narcissus* 'February Gold', 'Tête-à-tête', 'Topolino', 'Jumblie' or 'Jetfire', for example, and any of the early tulips, including *Tulipa* 'Shakespeare', 'Heart's Delight' or 'Stresa'. You can then interplant with crocuses, chionodoxas or *Muscari* spp. (grape

hyacinth). These can be followed by another grouping nearby of mid-season daffodils, such as *N.* 'Pipit' or 'Thalia', and tulips, such as *T.* 'White Dream' and 'Attila'. For late-spring blooms choose tulips such as *T.* 'Queen of Night' and 'Blue Heron' and late daffodils, such as *N. poeticus* var. *recurvus* (pheasant's eye). Choosing bulbs from within these three seasonal groups will give great pleasure throughout early, mid- and late spring. Plant pansies, violas, polyanthus, primroses, forget-me-nots or wallflowers on top to add extra colour.

Planting for spring and summer

A bulb border can have summer as well as spring interest, and a single planting session in autumn can give six months of delightful colour. In a formal box-hedged border, for example, a spring planting of tulips, anemones and fritillaries might give way in summer to groups of *Allium hollandicum* 'Purple Sensation' and white *Lilium regale* (regal lily). All these bulbs can be left in the ground year after year, but it would be possible to lift the tulips and plant summer bedding (annuals) to enhance the alliums and lilies.

Bulbs for borders

Late autumn to late spring	Early summer to mid-autumn
Anemone blanda	Amaryllis
Camassia	belladonna
Crocus	Begonia
Eranthis hyemalis	Crinum x powellii
Eremurus	Crocosmia
Erythronium	Eremus
Fritallaria	Galtonia
Galanthus nivalis	Hedychium
Hyacinthus	Lilium
Narcissus	Nerine
Tulipa	Tigridia

Planting in grass

Many of the bulbs that flower in late winter, early spring and mid-spring, such as *Galanthus* (snowdrop), *Eranthis hyemalis* (winter aconite), crocuses, anemones, most daffodils and some *Erythronium* (dog's tooth violet), thrive in grass, coming up year after year and self-seeding themselves. These robust bulbs can withstand competition from grass roots and are much more suitable for this type of planting. Early in the year, when the grass is short and competition for light is not a problem, the pointed shoots cut through the turf quite easily.

Late spring and summer flowering bulbs

Some of the late-flowering spring bulbs can also be grown successfully in this way. *Hyacinthoides non-scripta* (English bluebell) and *H. hispanica* (Spanish bluebell), as well as *Ornithogalum nutans*, *Narcissus poeticus* var. *recurvus* (pheasant's eye) and the camassias, such as *Camassia leichtlinii*, make attractive additions to grassy areas in meadow gardens or between orchard trees. Tall blue camassia flowers look particularly pretty with the fallen petals of apple blossom. A number of late-flowering tulips can also be used in these situations, but

Bulbs for planting in grass	
Anemone blanda	*Eranthis hyemalis*
Camassia (many)	*Erythronium*
Chionodoxa	(several)
(several)	*Fritillaria*
Colchicum spec.	*meleagris*
'Album'	*Galanthus nivalis*
Crocus (many)	*Narcissus*
Cyclamen coum	(many)
Cyclamen	*Ornithogalum*
hederifolium	*nutans*

most species will need to be replanted every second or third year, and it will be difficult to know where previous bulbs have been planted.

By mid- to late summer the choice is more restricted because by this time the grass presents too much competition for most bulbs, and most gardeners are, in any case, anxious to cut the grass regularly and keep it neatly mown. It is better to rely on the earlier periods of the year for the extra colour that naturalized bulbs bring.

To ensure successful displays of flowers in future years, bulbs that are planted in grass need to complete their growing cycle before the grass can be mown and the bulbs' leaves cut off. This usually takes about six weeks after flowering. Camassias

Crocus vernus naturalized in grass.

and late daffodils should not be mown until midsummer is past or even later.

Protecting bulbs

Sometimes newly planted bulbs are discovered by squirrels and mice. Be sure to replace the turf firmly to make it more difficult for the bulbs to be found. Crocus corms will be especially at risk. Later in the year sparrows might peck out the flowers. Crisscross the area with black thread to deter them, but make sure that the supporting pegs are clearly visible or it might prove a hazard to humans as well as the birds.

PLANTING BULBS INDIVIDUALLY

1 Throw the bulbs on to the turf in a random fashion and plant accordingly, but try to allow a distance of about 7.5–20cm (3–8in) between each one.

2 Dig a deep, square hole, of about a spade's width and about 25cm (10in) deep, depending on the size of the bulb. You may need to go deeper than one spade's depth.

3 Plant the bulb, base down and the neck or nose pointing upwards. Cover the bulb with loose soil and replace the top divot. Firm down gently.

PLANTING BULBS IN LARGE GROUPS

1 Dig a trench a spade's width and fold the turf backwards on itself. Use a trowel or dig down to a depth of about 25cm (10in).

2 Plant *Narcissus poeticus* var. *recurvus* with *Camassia leichtlinii*, placing them alternately about 20cm (8in) apart.

3 Fill in with loose soil so that the tops of the bulbs are covered. Replace the turf and firm down well with the heel of your boot.

Planting individually

When you are planting small bulbs a special metal bulb dibber is ideal. Because you should be planting the bulbs to a depth three times their own height, check to see if there are any markings up the side of the dibber to indicate how far down to press. Choose the spot, push the dibber into the turf, twist slightly and pull it out. This action will remove a small clod of earth. Drop the little bulb or corm into the hole, nose upwards, and break off a little of the base soil from the clod so that it gently covers the bulb or corm before you replace the divot of earth.

Larger bulbs, such as daffodils, are better planted with a spade. Throw the bulbs down at random and plant them where they fall, although you should try to allow a distance of at least 15–20cm (6–8in) between each one. The space allows the bulbs to multiply below ground and over the years to create a much greater display. Some daffodil bulbs are large, more than 6cm (2¹/₂in) high, and so need more than one spade's depth. In fact, the hole may need to

be nearly 25cm (10in) deep. Plant a group of 10 to 20 bulbs or even more in this way so that you create a good show for spring.

Planting larger groups

Where larger planting areas are planned, it can be easier to remove a whole section of turf with a spade and plant several bulbs in one hole. The step-by-step sequence shows the planting of late-flowering *Narcissus poeticus* var. *recurvus* (pheasant's eye) with *Camassia leichtlinii* in a trench. They were planted to create an outer row of bulbs that would flower in

late spring, flanking an area of two lots of earlier flowering daffodils, which were planted formally in rows between cherry trees. In this way, there is a succession of flowering from early to mid-spring through to late spring.

Leaving the grass

Although it will look untidy, allow six weeks to pass after flowering before cutting the grass where bulbs have been growing. This will ensure good results for the following year. The grass will soon recover.

Drifts of daffodils look wonderful in spring grassland where they will multiply over the years.

Planting in the eye of a tree

Some trees and situations will be more suitable than others. The soil around the trunks of most evergreen trees is too dry for the planting of bulbs to be successful, while many conifers have comparatively shallow roots. Deciduous trees, such as apples, pears, ornamental crab apples or cherry trees and magnolias, on the other hand, are ideal. The borders can be any shape you choose, but an area about 90cm (36in) long and 60cm (24in) from the centre of the tree trunk is easiest for a lawn mower to get around.

Selecting suitable bulbs

Choose bulbs that will flower before the trees come into leaf and block out all the sunlight. All the early spring-flowering dwarf daffodils are perfect, and if you combine them with *Anemone blanda, Muscari armeniacum* (grape hyacinth), scillas and tulips, as well as earlier flowering *Galanthus* (snowdrop), cyclamen and *Eranthis hyemalis* (winter aconite), you can have a succession of flowering that will be a delight

Muscari armeniacum (grape hyacinth) will start into flower in late winter or very early spring. Here it is planted beneath *Magnolia stellata*, producing a gorgeous blue haze.

year after year. Herbaceous plants can be used as well. Hellebores, *Tanacetum parthenium* 'Aureum' (golden feverfew), *Lunaria annua* (honesty), *Myosotis* (forget-me-not) and *Galium odoratum* (sweet woodruff) make excellent bedfellows.

The choice of bulb will depend to some extent on the shape of the tree and its position in the garden. Where an ornamental tree with low branches such as *Magnolia stellata* or one of the soulangeana hybrids

Plant a large group of blue *Muscari armeniacum* (grape hyacinth) about 5cm (2in) apart. Cover with soil so that their tips are about 5cm (2in) below soil level.

features as a centrepiece of a formal lawn in a front or back garden, for example, low-growing bulbs are appropriate. *Muscari armeniacum* (grape hyacinth) would be perfect, massed up on their own or mixed rather more formally with short pink Double Early tulips, such as *Tulipa* 'Peach Blossom'. In this type of situation either informal or formal would be appropriate and effective. You might have to replant the tulips every two years, and eventually you would have to extend the size of the eye as the tree expanded its branches with age, but there would be no need to buy more grape hyacinths. You could simply divide the ones already established closer to the trunk.

A gnarled old apple tree on the fringes of the garden or in the orchard suggests a natural look, using species bulbs or cultivars that are close to the species. A sheet of blue or white *Anemone blanda* would look exquisite; so would a single planting of *Narcissus* 'Topolino' or *N.* 'February Gold'. But whatever you do, avoid the split corona narcissi, such as *N.* 'Cassata' or garish *N.* 'Professor Einstein', which are much less likely to do well in future years in these circumstances and

Narcissus 'February Gold' is one of the best of all the early dwarf daffodils. Lustrous in colour, it is early to flower, sturdy, long lasting and elegant in shape. Planted en masse, it creates a generous splash of yellow beneath an old cherry tree.

would not be in keeping with the spirit of the planting. If you want a display that will reliably flower for many years to come N. 'February Gold' is a great stalwart and easy to find. It is sturdy, long lasting and makes a wonderful show for several weeks in early spring, lasting for much longer than many of the mid-spring varieties.

Another excellent choice for a long-lasting and long-term display is *Anemone blanda*. The tubers are relatively inexpensive to buy and can be planted liberally and allowed to self-seed. Available in many shades of blue and mauve, and also in white, the anemones will eventually form a sea of colour beneath the tree, completely covering the eye border and even expanding into the grass beyond if allowed to do so. The lumpy tubers should be soaked in water overnight to rehydrate them before they are planted, about 5cm (2in) deep and 5cm (2in) apart. It is sometimes difficult to tell which is the top and which is the bottom of the tubers, but if you can detect any hairy roots you will know they are growing from the bottom. Plant them on their own or mix in the

Anemone blanda makes a wonderful display beneath an apple tree, starting its display in late winter and lasting until mid-spring.

An eye-shaped border, 90cm (36in) long and 60cm (24in) in width from the centre of a deciduous tree, is ideal for a lawnmower to get around. It can look splendid planted with early, mid- or even late spring bulbs.

company of wild primroses, golden feverfew and clumps of dwarf daffodils such as *Narcissus* 'February Gold' or 'Tête-à-tête'.

Late summer- and early autumn-flowering bulbs

Allow bulbs and corms to complete their cycle of growth before clearing away the old leaves in midsummer. By then these borders will be in heavy shade and little else will grow successfully, except perhaps a few *Digitalis* (foxglove) and a rambling rose. Just as the fruit is turning ripe a range of late summer- to early autumn-flowering bulbs will come into flower. One lovely example is *Colchicum speciosum* 'Album' (autumn crocus), whose white, goblet-shaped flowers open before the foliage appears, giving rise to the common name, naked ladies. The leaves may, in fact, dwarf any spring-flowering

bulbs planted close by. *Cyclamen hederifolium* is another autumn and winter subject for this position. It, too, often flowers before producing leaves, welcome for their distinctive shape and intricate markings.

Bulbs for planting in the eye of a tree

Anemone blanda	Hyacinthus
Anemone	orientalis
nemerosa	Muscari
Arum italicum	Narcissus
Chionodoxa	'February Gold'
Colchicum	Narcissus
speciosum	'Hawera'
Crocus	Narcissus
Cyclamen coum	'Jumblie'
Cyclamen	Narcissus
hederifolium	'Segovia'
Eranthis hyemalis	Narcissus 'Tête-
Galanthus nivalis	à-tête'
Hyacinthoides	Narcissus
non-scripta	'Topolino'

Planting in large containers

If you are planting a large container in autumn to give a spring display, you have a wide choice of medium to tall daffodils, hyacinths and tulips, which can be underplanted with polyanthus, violas, pansies, forget-me-nots or wallflowers. Combine any of these with bronze or bright golden foliage and you will have a masterpiece.

Planning

It is important to plan before you plant. Think of the overall shape you want to achieve and consider the height and spread of the plants in relation to the depth of the container. Dwarf daffodils or tulips are best for a hanging basket, but a large half-barrel will accommodate taller plants, including the mid-season tulips and daffodils, which grow to 30–40cm (12–16in). If there is room, include a shrub or conifer in the centre to give added structure, or use *Hedera* (ivy) or *Vinca* (periwinkle) to soften the edges of the container and make a pleasing shape as they trail.

Consider also when you would like the container to look its best. If you want an explosion of colour in mid-spring, use daffodils or tulips with pansies. For a later splash of colour, use late-flowering tulips with pansies, forget-me-nots or wallflowers,

Bulbs for large containers

Late autumn to late spring	Early summer to mid-autumn
Anemone blanda	Begonia
Crocus	Canna
Hyacinthus	Dahlia (small to
Iris reticulata	medium)
Muscari	Eucomis
Narcissus 'Actea'	Hedychium
Narcissus 'Pipit'	Lilium
Narcissus	Nerine
'Salome'	Tigridia
Tulipa (many)	Tulbaghia

A DAFFODIL HALF-BARREL

1 Drill six drainage holes in the base of the half-barrel. Line the base and sides with a bin liner (trash bag) or black plastic. Cut slits in the liner to match the drainage holes. Add a 7.5cm (3in) layer of drainage material, such as pieces of polystyrene (styrofoam). Fill to about two-thirds full with potting compost (soil mix).

2 Position the central shrub (the cornus) so that it sits just below the rim. Plant the daffodil bulbs, base down, nose up, close to the edge of the barrel, so that the tips of the bulbs will be at an eventual depth below soil level of three times their own height, allowing for a 5cm (2in) gap at the top of the container.

3 Add more compost, then plant the skimmias and heucheras on opposite sides of the barrel.

4 Fill in the gaps with more compost to within 2.5cm (1in) of the rim. Plant the pansies around the edge. Water well.

which are available in a wide range of colours that complement almost any choice of tulip. Although they will not start flowering until mid-spring, they will provide greenery, and once they start to flower the show will last for many weeks.

Summer containers

Wonderful summer containers can be achieved by using lilies, begonias, eucomis, cannas and dahlias. Begonias combine well with many bedding plants and look spectacular with some fuchsias, while lilies and triteleias make simple and effective partnerships. Dahlias might team up with a fringe of lobelia, but cannas and eucomis are usually best kept as a single-species planting.

A long-lasting display

If you want colour and interest from the time of autumn planting through to mid- or late spring, you will have to choose a range of plant material. Winter-flowering pansies and violas will flower on and off from the time of planting right through to early summer, depending on the temperature and how much sun the container receives. The sunnier the spot, the better the display will be.

Coloured bark on shrubs adds drama and interest, particularly as the winter progresses and the colours deepen. *Cornus alba* 'Sibirica' (red-stemmed dogwood), with its glistening rich red stems, is an excellent choice. Evergreen shrubs can be selected to provide foliage, coloured berries, buds or flowers. *Viburnum tinus* (laurustinus) is a great favourite, or choose *Skimmia japonica* 'Rubella', which has dark red flower buds throughout the winter months, opening to white flowers in spring. It makes a dramatic association with red-stemmed dogwoods. Add a purple-leaved heuchera and mahogany-red pansies as a wonderful backdrop for the spring bulbs.

Crocuses would extend the display in spring, together with various irises or *Anemone blanda*, which could be followed by later-flowering daffodils or tulips. Any bulb with a coppery or pink colour variation will look stunning with red and bronze foliage. *Narcissus* 'Rose Caprice', with rosy salmon-pink cups, 'Salome', with pinkish-orange cups, or 'Rainbow', with coppery pink cups, would all make lovely combinations. The coppery pink hues of lilies, such as *Lilium* 'Pink Tiger', would tone well in midsummer.

Drainage

All containers need to be given adequate drainage, but you must take extra care with winter containers to avoid damaging the bulbs. Choose a soil-based potting compost (soil mix) or use a peat-based compost (soil mix) and add extra grit, in the ratio of approximately three parts compost to one part grit. Before planting place a layer of broken pots

A TULIP AND WALLFLOWER TERRACOTTA POT

1 Cover the drainage hole with broken pots or pieces of polystyrene (styrofoam) and add a layer of compost, with extra grit mixed in if using peat-based compost (soil mix).

2 Add sufficient compost so that when the tulip bulbs are planted, base down, nose up, they will be at a depth below soil level of three times their own height.

3 Wallflowers are often sold in bunches of ten. Separate them, choosing those with the best root systems.

4 Plant seven or eight of the wallflowers around the top of the container. Firm them down into the compost. Water well.

or polystyrene (styrofoam) at the base of the container, which will help to give extra drainage in periods of continued wet weather. The drainage layer will also help to prevent the roots of the plants from blocking the drainage holes, which are sometimes too small in relation to the size of the pot.

Wooden containers will eventually rot. To slow down the process, add a lining of plastic sheeting, which will retain the moisture in the compost and keep the wood dry on the inside. Make holes in the base of the plastic to match the holes in the container base. The lining also helps minimize

moisture loss through evaporation in late spring when the container may be in danger of drying out.

Tulipa 'Blue Heron' and orange wallflowers make a vibrant combination.

Planting in small containers and window boxes

Shorter flowering bulbs, tubers and corms are more suitable for small containers and window boxes than for medium to large containers.

Choosing suitable bulbs

There are many bulbs to choose from, including all the dwarf daffodils, such as *Narcissus* 'February Gold', 'Jack Snipe', 'Jetfire', 'Jumblie', 'Topolino', 'Tête-à-tête' and 'Peeping Tom', and the later-flowering 'Hawera'. Dwarf tulips also look wonderful in pots. All the early-flowering singles, such as *Tulipa* 'Heart's Delight', 'Shakespeare' and 'Stresa', and the doubles, such as 'Peach Blossom' and 'Willemsoord', can be used. Hyacinths also make excellent container bulbs and are

available in a wide range of colours including blue (*Hyacinthus orientalis* 'Delft Blue' and 'Blue Magic'), white ('L'Innocence'), yellow ('City of Haarlem'), pink ('Lady Derby') and salmon-pink ('Gipsy Queen'). This is just a small selection: there are many others.

Four planting schemes

These main three types of spring bulb – daffodils, tulips and hyacinths – can be treated in four ways. First, plant them on their own, in generous numbers, and wait for them to flower. Second, add some bedding plants – pansies, violas, primroses or polyanthus, for example – to extend the season of colour so that there is interest before the main bulb display.

Bulbs for small containers

Late autumn to late spring	Early summer to mid-autumn
Anemone blanda	Begonia (cascade
Chionodoxa	pendulous, or
Crocus	Non-Stop)
Hyacinthus	Begonia 'Picotee'
Iris reticulata	Dahlia (small
Muscari	varieties)
Narcissus	Eucomis 'White
'Bellsong'	Dwarf'
Narcissus	Lilium (short
'Hawera'	varieties)
Scilla peruviana	Tigridia

Third, adopt a two-tier planting scheme and add another type of lower-growing corm, bulb or tuber, which will flower at the same time. The white or blue star-shaped flowers of *Anemone blanda* make a lovely carpet of colour, as do late Dutch crocuses (forms of *Crocus vernus*), *Muscari armeniacum*, *M. neglectum*, *M. latifolium* or *M. botryoides* 'Album' (grape hyacinths in various shades and combinations of blue, almost black and white), *Chionodoxa* (blue or pink) and, to a lesser extent, scillas. These all have the advantage of being relatively inexpensive and are often sold in packets of ten or twenty. Try, for example, combining *Narcissus* 'February Gold' and large Dutch crocus; hyacinths with white *Anemone blanda*; Double Early tulips with *Muscari armeniacum*; or *Narcissus* 'Segovia' with pale blue *Muscari armeniacum* 'Valerie Finnis'.

The fourth approach is to adopt the two-tier planting scheme and then add a few violas or primroses. Avoid planting the bedding plants directly above the bulbs because the shoots of the bulbs are sharp and will force their way between the roots of the bedding plants, lifting them out of the compost (soil mix).

PLANTING A SMALL CONTAINER

1 Cover the base of the pot with a 2.5cm (1in) layer of drainage material. Add 5cm (2in) of a soil-based compost (soil mix).

2 Add four handfuls of grit to give extra drainage. This is important because hyacinths do not like to be too wet in winter.

3 Plant the bulbs so that their bases sit firmly on the grit, spacing them so that they do not touch each other or the sides of the container. Cover with more compost until their tips are just showing.

4 Plant the primroses in a circle between the outer bulbs. Top up with more compost, bringing the level to within 2.5cm (1in) of the rim of the container. Water well and add more compost if necessary.

Planting depths in winter containers are sometimes less than in the ground, especially when small pots or shallow containers are used. This is usually acceptable as long as the bulbs are not expected to remain as a long-term planting scheme and the pots are put in a sheltered spot during the winter.

Drainage

One of the major problems for bulbs that are overwintered outdoors is inadequate drainage. If possible, use a soil-based compost (soil mix) with plenty of grit mixed in. If you prefer to use a peat-based compost (soil mix), add extra grit in the ratio of three parts compost to one part grit. When you are planting sensitive bulbs, such as hyacinths, add an extra layer of grit beneath the bulbs. This will improve the drainage still further and avoid their roots sitting in cold, waterlogged soil.

Colour combinations

For late spring and summer colour try *Anemone coronaria*, using the single flowers in the De Caen Group or the double flowers of the St Bridgid Group. Both types are available in a range of vibrant colours. An all-white colour scheme using *A. coronaria* De Caen Group 'The Bride' would look stunning, or you might prefer a mix of red and rich blue.

If you prefer a mid- to late-summer display that lasts into autumn, Non-Stop and trailing begonias are hard to beat for length of flowering and range of colours. Start the tubers into growth in a greenhouse, placing them hollow side up on the top of the compost. You could combine Non-Stop and trailing begonias in the same display or use the Non-Stops with bedding plants such as dark blue lobelia to soften the edge.

PLANTING A WINDOW BOX

1 Cover the base of the window box with a 2.5cm (1in) layer of drainage material, such as small pieces of polystyrene (styrofoam) or broken pots.

2 Add about 5cm (2in) of soil-based compost (soil mix), or a peat-based compost with extra grit (in the ratio of three parts compost to one part grit).

3 Plant the daffodil bulbs in two rows, spacing them so that they do not touch each other or the sides of the container. Cover with more soil so that just the tips show.

4 Bring the soil to within 2.5cm (1in) of the rim and add the bedding plants. Here, two cinerarias are planted in the middle with three *Anemone* and three white violas on either side.

The window box looks stunning with the yellow and white spring flowers set off by the silver-grey foliage of *Senecio cineraria*.

Planting in hanging baskets

Whether you choose a sophisticated white and gold colour scheme or opt for a daring riot of bright colours, you will find that spring and summer hanging baskets make a delightful addition to a house wall or patio.

Spring hanging baskets

For spring colour, hanging baskets can be planted with a wide range of bulbs, including all the dwarf daffodils, dwarf tulips and hyacinths, together with an underplanting of crocus, *Anemone blanda, Muscari armeniacum* (grape hyacinth), chionodoxa, scillas and so on. Scale is the important factor here, so avoid

any that grow more than 30cm (12in) high. *Hedera* (ivy) is a simple but effective edging plant to clothe the sides of a spring hanging basket. The main problem comes in mid- to late winter, when cold winds dry out the leaves, turning them brown and ragged. If you are using a wire basket, take a tip from Victorian gardeners and use small wires to fix the ivy trails in to the moss lining. The effect is to create a ball of ivy, where the trails stay close to the sides of the basket and do not get spoiled by the wind. By the time spring arrives, dwarf daffodils and grape hyacinths, for example, will be

in full flower. Meanwhile, the ivy will have started to root in the moss and within a season you will have an ivy ball, which will make summer and next winter's planting easy. It will dry out quickly in summer so hang the basket in a shady place where evaporation will be less of a problem. Add some shade-tolerant bedding plants in the top so that you remember to water the basket. Keep pegging in the ivy trails as they grow. After the second season, the ivy will need pruning both at its growing tips and roots or it will take over completely. Empty the basket, save some ivy trails and replant along with the bulbs in fresh soil.

Severe winter weather can spoil autumn-planted, spring-flowering baskets because neither moss nor wicker lining provides much insulation. In extremely cold or windy conditions, put the basket in a porch or garage. Never water in frosty conditions. It is better to keep all containers on the dry side in freezing weather as long as you keep the compost (soil mix) just moist. More moisture will be required in spring, when growth is taking place. If you have used bedding plants, such as pansies, apply a liquid feed in early spring to encourage a good display to coincide with the bulbs.

Summer hanging baskets

Sumptuous summer baskets can be filled with Non-Stop or trailing begonias. Start the begonias into growth in a greenhouse, planting the tubers on top of the compost, hollow side up. Three or four trailing begonias with a Non-Stop bushy begonia for the centre will make a wonderful display in a 35–40cm (14–16in) diameter basket. For something different try *Begonia* 'Picotee', a cultivar with an upright

The tulips and muscari are long lasting and make a wonderful contrast among the violas and pansies in this colourful hanging basket (see steps on page 33).

habit but large, heavy flowers, which create a natural fountain effect providing colour all round the margins of the basket as well as in the centre. Like all the tuberous begonias it will provide colour from midsummer through to late autumn. But be sure to take the basket down off its hook before the first autumn frosts and take it to the shelter of a frost-free greenhouse. Remove the topgrowth as the compost dries out and the stems break off from the tubers, and leave dormant tubers until growth buds appear in spring when watering can begin again.

Autumn and winter baskets

You can give structure to autumn and winter schemes by adding *Hedera* (ivy) or the low-growing *Euphorbia myrsinites* around the edges. Include a central herbaceous plant, such as the purple form of wood spurge, *Euphorbia amygdaloides* 'Purpurea'. Alternatively, a young shrub, such as the tree heath, *Erica arborea* 'Albert's Gold', or a rosemary with its flush of pale blue spring flowers. The variegated Japanese spindle, *Euonymus japonicus* 'Aureus', is excellent for its golden touch, or use bushy *E. fortunei* 'Emerald 'n' Gold'. If you prefer a silver and white display, include *E. fortunei* 'Silver Queen' with its white-edged leaves or *Viburnum tinus*, which is not only evergreen but has white flowers as well. Even the buds are colourful, being tinged with pink. The viburnum is a good evergreen choice, offering colour and interest through the winter months. White or pink winter-flowering heathers can be planted at the sides to soften the edges. Devise your own colour scheme by introducing pansies, violas, primroses and daisies. When the display is over, plant the shrubs in the garden and allow them to grow on.

A COLOURFUL HANGING BASKET

1 Cover the base of the basket with a generous amount of moss and line with a piece of plastic sheeting. Cut some 2.5cm (1in) slits in the bottom. Add a layer of compost (soil mix) to a depth of 5cm (2in).

2 Plant three violas, spacing them widely, on top of the moss wall with their roots firmly in the compost. Plant three of the pansies between them.

3 Tuck a large handful of moss around the shoulders of each plant so that no gaps remain. Bring the moss wall two-thirds up the sides of the basket.

4 Plant the top tier so that a viola sits above a pansy and vice versa. Add more moss around each plant, bringing the wall 2.5cm (1in) above the rim.

5 Plant the tulip bulbs in outer and inner circles. Cover with soil until just the tips of the bulbs show. Add the *Muscari armeniacum* and add more soil to completely cover all the bulbs.

6 Plant the remaining violas and pansies, making sure they do not cover any of the bulbs. Water well, and hang the basket in a sunny sheltered spot.

A long-term hanging basket

Euphorbia amygdaloides (wood spurge), a hardy herbaceous perennial, might seem an unusual choice for a hanging basket, but it has many qualities, the chief of which is that it provides interest all year round. The cultivar 'Purpurea' has dark reddish-purple stems, which deepen as the weather gets colder in late autumn, then from mid-spring to early summer it comes to life with lime-green flowers. The stems need cutting right back after flowering to encourage new growth from the base to produce the following season's flowers. Apart from this, it needs little extra attention. A simple planting of ivy around the edge of the basket provides an evergreen frill. There are many ivies to choose from, but *Hedera helix* 'Glacier' has the added attraction of its variegation, and planted with the purple spurge it, too, takes on russet, purple tones in cold winter weather. Planted alongside are a few violas. These are

from the Princess Series, chosen for their compact habit and pretty colours. But there are many others to choose from, so you can replace them each autumn. The crowning glory is the dwarf daffodil, *Narcissus* 'Hawera', which flowers for many weeks spanning the season between mid- and late spring. Each stem bears up to five dainty canary yellow blooms, an effective partner for the flowering spurge. Hardy and reliable, it is a good choice for a long-lasting display both in its first season and in following years.

Winter hanging baskets

The ivy ball is just one idea for a winter hanging basket that lasts for more than one season. There are many other possibilities for using bulbs mixed with young shrubs and heathers or herbaceous perennials. If you are using a dense planting scheme, choose a lined wicker basket, rather than a wire-framed one, because this will give more planting room and will retain moisture better, both in winter and, more importantly, throughout the following summer. As with the ivy ball, plant a summer bedding plant in a gap where a pansy or viola has been flowering in winter and spring. This will add freshness to the arrangement as well as reminding you to keep the container moist through the summer.

Bulbs for hanging baskets

Late autumn to late spring	Early summer to mid-autumn
Anemone blanda	*Begonia* (cascade
Crocus	pendulous, or
Hyacinthus	Non-Stop)
Iris reticulata	*Begonia* 'Picotee'
Muscari	*Tigridia*
Narcissus	*Tulipa clusiana*
'Bellsong'	'Lady Jane'
Narcissus	*Tulipa* 'Honky
'Hawera'	Tonk'
Tulipa	*Tulipa* 'Tinka'
'Shakespeare'	*Tulipa urumiensis*

PLANTING A LONG-TERM HANGING BASKET

1 Plant *Euphorbia amygdaloides* 'Purpurea' in the centre surrounded by ten *Narcissus* 'Hawera' bulbs.

2 Alternate three *Viola* x *wittrockiana* (pansy) from the Princess series and three *Hedera helix* 'Glacier' ivies around the edge.

3 Deadhead the narcissi and remember to apply a liquid feed to strengthen the bulbs for next year's display.

4 Trim the euphorbia in midsummer, cutting right back to the base so that new growth will emerge for next season's flowers. Replace the violas with summer bedding. In autumn replace with new violas.

PLANTING A LINED WICKER BASKET

1 Cut slits, 2.5cm (1in) long, in the plastic lining of a 40cm (16in) lined wicker basket.

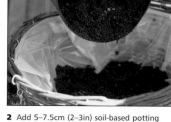

2 Add 5–7.5cm (2–3in) soil-based potting compost (soil mix).

3 Plant *Euonymus fortunei* 'Emerald 'n' Gold' towards the back, teasing out the roots.

4 Plant two *Erica carnea* 'Springwood White' on either side of the euonymus, close to the edge of the basket.

5 Plant ten *Narcissus* 'Hawera' bulbs around the central shrub and cover with soil so that just the tips of the planted bulbs show.

6 Plant small groups of *Tulipa* 'Tinka' and *Muscari* 'Valerie Finnis' in the next layer between the heathers and the central shrub.

7 Add more soil, particularly around the edge of the basket so that the heathers are well surrounded. Plant four *Viola* x *wittrockiana* (pansy), making sure they do not cover any of the bulbs, and fill in any gaps with soil. Firm in the plants, water well and hang up in a sheltered spot in sun or partial shade.

8 Keep the soil in the basket moist, especially in the spring growing season, and apply a liquid feed. Trim the heathers back after flowering. Keep watered throughout the summer and enjoy the show another year, clipping back the euonymus if necessary and replacing the pansies in the autumn.

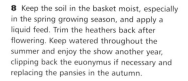

Care and maintenance

The most widely grown spring-flowering bulbs, including daffodils, tulips and hyacinths, are fully hardy and will cope with frosty weather, but some summer- and autumn-flowering plants, such as crinums and nerines, are only borderline hardy. In extreme winter weather they will benefit from a protective layer of dry peat, bracken or sacking.

Some sites may be too windy for certain bulbs, and if you cannot find a sheltered corner, it would be better to choose plants that can cope with the conditions in your garden. For example, large-flowering, mid-season daffodils are often planted in grassland. Some will be fine planted in this way, but those with weak stems are best avoided. Instead, select shorter, earlier flowering daffodils with small flowers that will stand up to the buffeting of spring winds.

Staking
Some plants – cannas, large dahlias, most lilies and some gladioli, for example – grow tall in summer and should be grown in sheltered positions where gusts of wind will not cause damage. Dahlias in particular, which put on bushy as well as high growth, must be staked. Use metal plant supports or wooden stakes with string to contain the growth in early to midsummer. This might look unsightly at first, but the supports will soon be hidden by foliage. Smaller patio dahlias do not need staking, nor do the single-flowered forms with wiry stems, such as *Dahlia* 'Dark Desire'.

Lilies with large trumpet-shaped flowers might also need support. The stems are often strong and wiry and will not break, but the weight of the flowers can pull the head down and the display is less impressive. A single metal stake with a ring support positioned behind the plant is ideal because it allows some movement and is not intrusive. A bamboo cane and string are good alternatives. Tall gladioli should be supported in the same way. *Crocosmia* 'Lucifer' is a tall plant producing large flowerheads and providing support early in the growing season will enhance the flowering display.

Drainage
Some plants, notably lilies, hate having their roots constantly in wet soil, so it is a good idea to plant lily bulbs on a layer of extra grit to aid drainage. This is true whether they are grown in pots or in garden soil. If you have clay soil in your garden, treat hyacinths in the same way.

Watering
Newly planted bulbs need adequate moisture to allow their roots to grow in autumn. Watering is important throughout the year, not just in summer. Bulbs planted in garden soil do not normally need extra watering, but it is important that the compost (soil mix) in containers is kept moist. This is most important in spring, when rainfall may miss hanging baskets and window boxes that are in the rain shadow cast by the house. In summer additional and regular watering is vital, particularly in dry spells. Some plants, notably begonias, are easily spoiled if water is allowed to splash on to leaves and petals and left when the sun is shining. The scorch marks that

Metal ring supports should be placed around dahlias as soon as growth begins to get above about 30cm (12in).

Early staking is important, especially for plants that bear large flowers, to protect them in windy weather.

It is important to add a layer of grit to aid drainage when planting lilies in a container or in the garden.

result are not only unattractive but may harm the plant itself. Always direct water to the soil, rather than watering from above the plant.

Feeding

Providing additional nutrients will help most bulbs, especially those with long-flowering displays, such as cannas and dahlias, which may be described as gross feeders. They respond well to a liberal dressing of well-rotted manure or a granular fertilizer when they are planted out in spring. A spring feed for tulips, daffodils and hyacinths, applied when the leaves are still green, will help next year's show, but it is even more important to allow the foliage to remain intact until it has died down naturally, thus allowing all the goodness from the foliage to be used in forming the basis of the following year's display. Resist the temptation to pull the leaves off tulips in the herbaceous border until they have really withered and come away easily in your hand. Allium leaves look untidy when the flowers begin to appear, but do not be tempted to tidy up at this stage. Instead, hide them by putting a herbaceous plant in front of the bulbs.

Deadheading and seedheads

Many bulbs, including fritillaries, *Eranthis hyemalis* (winter aconite), *Hyacinthoides* spp. (bluebell), lilies, *Anemone blanda* and alliums, can be propagated by seed if it is gathered before nature disperses it. Some of these bulbs have attractive seedheads – the rosette that appears on the winter aconite is especially appealing.

Much larger seedheads appear after the alliums have flowered, and those of *Allium hollandicum* 'Purple Sensation' are often used in dried-flower arrangements. Gather the

Remove foliage from daffodils only after it has died back naturally and pulls away easily.

Dry allium seedheads upside down and use them later in an indoor flower arrangement.

seedheads while they still have some purple colouring and hang them upside down in a well-ventilated spot. Those left in the border can be enjoyed for many weeks.

Some flowers are best deadheaded long before seed production is allowed to take place, especially if you want to encourage more flowers. Dahlias, cannas and begonias all benefit from thorough, regular deadheading, which will ensure an

abundance of flowers until autumn. You should also deadhead daffodils, tulips and lilies, where removing the flowers prevents the plant from wasting energy in seed production.

Deadhead *Hyacinthoides hispanica* (Spanish bluebell) rigorously to prevent self-seeding and cross-fertilization with the native *H. non-scripta* (English bluebell). Spanish bluebells are more vigorous than the native plant and difficult to control.

Dahlia 'Dark Desire' produces a wealth of small flowers. Deadhead regularly to keep the display looking good.

Remove the flowerheads of daffodils before the seed has time to develop, to preserve the energy needed for rebuilding the bulb.

Dormancy and winter treatment

Where they are grown in border setting tender summer-flowering plants, such as dahlias, begonias, cannas and gladioli should be lifted in autumn and brought into growth again in spring if they are to flower once more in the summer.

The tubers and corms of these plants should be lifted, dried and stored in dry, cool, frost-free conditions. Begonias, gladioli and watsonia are stored dry; dahlias and cannas should be stored in barely moist peat or coarse vermiculite. Most bulbs and tubers should be lifted before the first frosts. Dahlias, however, will benefit if the foliage is actually killed by frost. When this happens, the leaves become blackened. If your dahlias have stopped flowering but there have still been no autumn frosts, lift them anyway.

In some mild areas it is possible to cut off the dahlia foliage and leave the tubers in the ground, protecting them with a mulch of grit with a layer of leaf mould or bark chipping, in the same way that nerines, crinums and the hardier types of agapanthus are left in the ground. Dahlias treated in this way are always at risk,

Dust damaged bulbs with a fungicide, such as yellow or green sulphate of ammonia.

LIFTING AND REPLANTING DAHLIAS

1 When the dahlia has finished flowering, use secateurs (pruners) to remove the foliage and trim back the stems, leaving about 20cm (8in) of each stem.

2 Fork gently around the plant, leaving a radius of 25–40cm (10–16in) from the main stem, depending on the amount of growth it has made. Gently lift the root, taking care not to damage the tubers.

3 Place the plant upside down in a box so that any moisture can drain down the hollow stems. Remove the soil from the tubers once it has dried off. Store in a dry, frost-free place in boxes of barely moist peat.

4 In late spring or early summer prepare a planting hole, approximately a spade's depth. Add some well-rotted manure or a long-term granular feed, and mix well into the soil.

5 Carefully lower the dahlia into the prepared hole and add more compost (soil mix) as necessary to bring to soil level.

6 Gently firm in the plant with your hands or feet. Water well.

especially if the winter happens to be severe. When green shoots begin to emerge on lifted dahlias in spring, water sparingly to keep the compost moist. Then in late spring or early summer, after all risk of frost has passed, choose a sunny, sheltered spot and prepare a planting hole.

Cannas should be treated in the same way as dahlias, except that the stalks of cannas are not hollow and it is not necessary to hang them upside down to drain. Moreover, cannas produce rhizomes, not tubers, and these are easily separated in spring when the new shoots start to

emerge to produce new plants. Each rhizome will make a substantial show of colour in one summer, so it is a great opportunity to propagate.

Lift begonia plants in autumn and remove all foliage, leaving about 7.5cm (3in) of stem. When the soil has dried, clean the tubers and remove the stems. Store in a dry, frost-free place at a minimum temperature of 7°C (45°F). In early spring plant the begonia tubers and keep them in a warm place until the little pink buds start to expand. Water more frequently as the leaves emerge. Plant out when all risk of frost has passed.

In early spring, plant begonia tubers, hollow side up, on barely moist compost (soil mix).

LIFTING AND REPLANTING CANNAS

1 Lift cannas when they have finished flowering in the autumn, before any hard frosts. Dig round their roots with a fork and lift the entire clump. Place the clump in a large wooden box.

2 Using secateurs (pruners), carefully remove all the foliage and cut back the stems to about 7.5cm (3in).

3 Allow the soil to dry off around the rhizomes before cleaning them and storing in barely moist peat or vermiculite. Treat any damaged rhizomes with a fungicide, such as yellow or green sulphate of ammonia.

4 In spring, the clumps can be divided. Where the rhizome is severed, dust with the same fungicide as before. Pot up into moist compost (soil mix).

5 In late spring or early summer, after all risk of frost has passed, choose a sunny spot and prepare a large planting hole. Mix in a long-term granular feed or well-rotted manure.

6 Plant the canna in the prepared hole and firm in gently. Water in well.

Container-grown plants

If they are grown in containers, all bulbs that might be described as 'summer exotics' – begonias, dahlias, cannas, tulbaghias and eucomis – will need frost-free conditions at a minimum temperature of 7°C (45°F) to survive the winter. Take action before the first frosts are threatened in the autumn, or as soon after as practicable.

You must allow the plants to dry off naturally. Then carefully clean away the soil from corms, tubers, rhizomes and bulbs before storing them in cool, dry conditions. If you do not have a frost-free greenhouse, a frost-free garage or shed will be appropriate or even somewhere indoors, as long as it is not too warm. It is important that the bulbs do not start into growth too early. Replant the bulbs in fresh compost in spring.

Alternatively, the plants can be left in their container and the whole pot or basket moved into a frost-free greenhouse. Here, they will remain dormant through the darker, cold days of winter and burst into life

Use electric or paraffin heaters to maintain minimum frost-free conditions inside the greenhouse, but open the door in milder weather to allow air to circulate.

TIDYING UP BEGONIAS

Remove hanging baskets containing begonias from their brackets before the first frost.

If the basket is relatively dry you might find that whole stems come away easily, in which case simply remove them for composting. Otherwise, cut back stems to within 8cm (3in) of the base. Allow the soil to dry out and soon the base of the previously cut stems will fall away from the top of the tuber.

Move pots containing begonias into the greenhouse. This one is also planted with *Fuchsia* 'Thalia'. Leave the arrangement intact and only tidy away dead leaves. Later, when it has dried off, the begonia stems will come away easily. Early next spring both fuchsia and begonia will start into growth once more.

when the longer, warmer days return in spring. When temperatures fall close to or below freezing, heat the greenhouse with a thermostatically controlled electric heater, which will turn on automatically at a pre-set temperature. If you do not have electricity in your greenhouse, use a paraffin heater, relit every day as necessary. When temperatures rise above freezing in the daytime, open the greenhouse door to allow air to circulate and remove any build-up of moisture.

Although pots can be moved outside in late spring, during the daytime, cold evening temperatures mean that they are best brought back into the shelter of the greenhouse. Only leave containers outside all day and all night once all risk of frost has gone.

Watering in the greenhouse

In winter the watering of pots and baskets can be tricky. Sunny weather encourages us into the greenhouse to inspect the plants and maybe then we think of watering. For most of the plants regular watering will not be needed during the winter months; the soil needs just to be kept barely moist. Occasional light watering might be necessary as the compost will inevitably dry out where the greenhouse catches lots of sunshine. But clear skies in the daytime are often followed by frosty nights, so it is better not to water on bright sunny days. Wait for cloudy conditions when temperatures will remain slightly higher during the night.

By early to mid-spring signs of new growth will be evident, with tiny pink buds on the begonias, spiky new shoots on the cannas and leafy green tufts on the eucomis. At this stage, it is a good idea to increase the watering programme gradually.

TIDYING UP TULBAGHIAS

1 Tulbaghias will survive in the greenhouse or a potting shed. Tidy away flowering stalks and dead foliage for simple good husbandry.

2 The leaves are evergreen, so remember to water occasionally during the winter and more frequently once spring has arrived.

POTTING ON EUCOMIS

1 Eucomis will survive in the greenhouse or a potting shed. Only remove the dry leaves as they die back naturally.

2 Now the top of the pot is clean it reveals small seedlings. These can be removed and potted up.

OVERWINTERING CANNAS

1 Cannas in pots should be moved into the greenhouse for protection. Do not water the compost at this stage.

2 Cut down the canna's stems and remove the foliage, along with any snails or slugs that are lurking there. Keep the compost barely moist throughout the winter.

If possible, move containers close to a south-facing house or garage wall where they will have extra protection from extreme temperatures. In severely cold weather it may be better to move them inside the garage or porch.

Use a soil-based compost or a peat-based compost, both with added grit. A well-drained soil will provide better protection than over-wet compost, which may freeze around delicate roots.

Choosing hardy winter- and spring-flowering bulbs

Winter- and spring-flowering bulbs are hardy, but they will be more sensitive to the cold if they are planted in exposed containers, where they lack the insulation that is provided by the garden soil in borders or grasslands. The smaller the container, the less protection the bulbs will have against the cold.

Normal frosty weather should not be a problem, especially if sensible precautions are taken. Only plant bulbs that you know to be fully hardy in a container.

If you choose to plant daffodils, avoid the indoor-flowering types, such as 'Paper White Grandiflorus', which owe their parentage to *Narcissus papyraceus*. This species is native to the warmer climates of south-eastern France, south-western Spain and Portugal, where it flowers outdoors in winter. All other species of spring-flowering daffodils should be safe, however.

Siting containers

The siting of pots and baskets is crucial. Avoid placing pots in exposed sites, such as a windy corner of the house. A passageway would be even worse, because it will act as a wind tunnel. A position near a house or garage or a wall will be warmer than one in an exposed site in the middle of the garden. Remember that you can always move the containers away from the house and into a border once spring arrives. If you have a choice, a sunny, south-facing wall where the pots will have a chance to warm up during the day is preferable to a cold, north-facing, sunless wall.

Drainage

Make sure that all containers have adequate drainage holes in the base. After a deluge of rain you want to be certain that all excess water can run quickly out of the bottom. Half-barrels are often sold without drainage holes. Always check before planting and, if necessary, drill several holes in the base.

Always add plenty of drainage material, such as broken pots, small stones or pieces of polystyrene (styrofoam), to the bottom of a container and plant into a freely draining compost (soil mix) for all autumn and winter planting schemes.

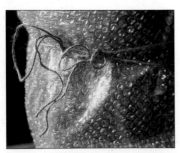

If pots are too heavy to move, use bubble wrap as a protective coat. Tie it securely in place with string.

This container has good holes at the base, which will allow adequate drainage. Always add plenty of drainage material.

Pieces of polystyrene (styrofoam), broken pots, stones or grit can be used as drainage material, depending on the container's size.

Move hanging baskets to temporary shelter in freezing weather.

Tulipa 'Tinka' has happily survived the winter outdoors and is partnered by violas, heuchera and *Millium effusum* 'Aureum'.

Weather warning

Although the compost needs to be kept moist, never water when frost is forecast, and be careful about watering on a sunny winter's day — clear night skies cause temperatures to plummet. Water on damp, dank days when cloud cover will mean less extreme temperatures. It is better to allow the compost to stay on the dry side in cold weather. In freezing conditions containers will benefit from some protection. Remove hanging baskets from their brackets to a garage, porch, greenhouse or outbuilding. Small and medium-sized pots could be placed on a level windowsill or next to the house wall. Larger containers may be wrapped in hessian (burlap) or bubble wrap. If possible, take these measures before extreme conditions have begun so that the bulbs will not be so badly affected by dropping temperatures.

A sunny windowsill affords good protection for small pots of bulbs, especially in severe winter weather.

Propagating bulbs

If you empty out a container of daffodils in summer you will find that the old bulbs are still intact but have now formed offsets, each one capable of growing on to produce flowering stems and offsets of its own.

Self-propagation

Look at the old bulbs of a *Muscari armeniacum* (grape hyacinth). They will have increased in size and produced several tiny ones, each clinging to the parent. In years to come, these will each grow on and become flowering bulbs in their own right. If left undisturbed, they will form clumps of bulbs and in time produce a beautiful carpet of bright blue flowers. Meanwhile, the flowers will have produced a generous crop of viable seeds. No wonder they naturalize so well. The same is true of alliums, which produce copious quantities of seed. The leaves spring up, looking like chives around the parent plant in spring, each little leaf with a miniature bulb at the base. Grow them on and they will produce flowers within three or four years.

Hyacinthoides spp. (bluebell) are prolific self-seeders. If you wanted to plant a new bluebell wood, you would no doubt be impatient for the

This daffodil has produced three excellent offsets in just one season's growth. It is this facility that makes daffodils such good naturalizers in grass or borders.

results, but if you had them growing in your garden borders, you would probably be waging war on the new patches of bulbs before too long. Avoid planting *Hyacinthoides non-scripta* (English bluebell) near *H. hispanica* (Spanish bluebell), because cross-fertilization will occur with a dilution of the natural stock of English bluebells, which are less vigorous than the Spanish plant.

Lifting and storing

Because bulbs multiply underground by producing daughter bulbs around the parent, sooner or later clumps become congested. Some species,

Muscari spp. (grape hyacinths) multiply surprisingly quickly. Separate the bigger bulbs and replant 7.5cm (3in) apart. The smaller ones can be grown on for another year.

Lilium regale seeds

Lilium regale will produce lots of seeds. If uncollected, these may self-seed beneath the parent plant. Alternatively, gather the seedpods, empty the contents and sow the seeds thinly in pots or trays filled with a moist, sieved, gritty compost, ready to grow on.

SELF-SEEDING ALLIUM

1 *Allium hollandicum* 'Purple Sensation' produces generous quantities of seed and will self-seed beneath the parent plant.

2 Within a short time, small bulbs have grown that can be carefully harvested in the autumn.

3 Replant the small bulbs in a pot or directly into border soil where you would like a display in the future.

such as nerines, flower better when they are congested, and these are best left alone for many years until flowering dwindles. When this happens, it is time to lift and divide the bulbs. Clumps of other bulbs, such as alliums, *Muscari* spp., narcissi, tulips and tulbaghia, are best divided every three years or so. Where they have become well established you will be amazed by the proliferation that has occurred. Lift the bulbs during the summer dormancy and tease them apart carefully, replanting the largest bulbs as needed.

All seedlings, whether they are *Galanthus* (snowdrop), *Eranthis hyemalis* (winter aconite), *Muscari* spp. (grape hyacinth) or bluebells, do better in border soil than in turf, where there is too much competition from dense, coarse grasses for the young plants to establish themselves, but these species will still multiply in grass, albeit more slowly. For best results, choose an area with fine grass, where competition will be less intense.

SEEDING EUCOMIS

1 *Eucomis bicolor* produces many small black seeds. These may be sown into pots ready to be grown on for a year before being potted on the following year. They should flower within two years of sowing.

2 Alternatively, eucomis may self-seed in the pots in which they are growing. Remove the tiny new plants and grow them on in a pot in gritty compost for a year. Then repot into individual pots to flower the following summer.

Bulbils

Lilies have another way of propagating themselves. As well as forming offsets and seeds, some lilies will produce bulbils at leaf axils up their stems. These fall off in time and form new plants when they root into the soil at the foot of the parent plant, where they will soon develop. These miniature bulbs can be lifted in autumn and potted on ready for planting out 18 months later. This type of propagation occurs most commonly on *Lilium lancifolium* (syn. *L. tigrinum*; tiger lily) and many of the Asiatic hybrids.

Another method of propagation is to collect the bulbils themselves, detaching them carefully from the stem, and plant them into small pots. Grow on for two years before planting out in the garden.

Seeds from tulbaghia may be collected and sown in small pots for a year until they may be potted on into new permanent containers.

Allium cristophii produces lots of seeds which can be sown in pots. It also multiplies quickly by offsets, which can be dug up in the autumn and moved to another spot in the garden. To make the most of their metallic sheen, try to place some where they will catch the warm evening light.

Propagating rhizomes, corms and tubers

One of the wonderful attributes of rhizomes, corms and tubers is that they are successful self-propagators, by creating both new growth below ground and seeds above.

Rhizomes

Anyone who has planted a canna from what seems like a small rhizome in late winter will be amazed at the sheer quantity of root material that can be dug up the following autumn after just one summer's growth – a mass of rhizomes all waiting to be divided and propagated. If that was not enough, some cannas are also generous producers of seed.

Corms

With corms the story is different. After flowering the old corm dies, and a new one forms on top of the old one, with clusters of cormlets around the sides. In this way some cormous plants, such as crocosmia, are able to form quite large clumps, which need to be divided every three years or so to prevent overcrowding and congestion. Cormous plants can also propagate themselves by seed – *Crocus tommasinianus*, for example, naturalizes well in late winter grassland where the grass is fine.

Begonias can be started from cuttings taken from over-wintered tubers in early- to mid-spring. They make excellent bedding plants for containers and borders, offering a wide range of colours.

Tubers

Plants grown from tubers are also great survivors. Individual tubers grow to quite large proportions – surprisingly large compared with the tiny tubers on offer in the shops – and also produce generous quantities of seeds and shoots, which can be propagated. Leave a few *Anemone* *blanda* tubers planted in the eye of an old apple tree and within a few years it will be a mass of blue flowers as the seeds form new plants and the tubers plump up and grow. Cyclamen and *Eranthis hyemalis* are also generous seeders, both enjoying a position beneath deciduous shrubs or trees, where they will get plenty of

PROPAGATING TUBERS

1 Take a sharp knife and cut the tuber (in this case a begonia tuber) through the middle so that each part has a shoot.

2 Dust the open cuts with a fungicide such as yellow sulphur powder. Prepare two small pots with moist potting compost (soil mix).

3 Plant both halves so that they sit firmly on top of the compost. Keep the compost moist and plant on when new growth is apparent.

TAKING BEGONIA AND DAHLIA CUTTINGS

1 Gently pull a young begonia stem away from the tuber. A small piece of rooting material may well have come away at the base of the shoot.

2 Plant the new cutting into a pot of moist compost (soil mix) and grow on in warm conditions, out of direct sunlight, until the new plant can be planted out.

3 For dahlias, slice through the bottom of a stem and plant the cutting in moist compost. Place on a windowsill, out of direct sunlight, covered with a clear plastic bag until rooted.

moisture in winter. *Eranthis hyemalis* is usually quick to establish. Scatter seed in mid-spring and within just a few years you will have sheets of golden flowers in midwinter. For best results, soak cyclamen seeds for up to ten hours before sowing.

Begonia tubers can be divided in late winter or early spring if two shoots are seen on one tuber. They can also be propagated from cuttings taken from small shoots that have grown from the tuber in late winter or early spring. Dahlias can also be propagated from cuttings taken from new growth during the same periods.

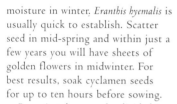

Canna rhyzomes can be propagated in early spring by cutting into short sections, leaving an eye from which new growth will be made.

Started from cuttings, dahlias will make very large plants even in just one summer's growth. Here Dahlia 'Bishop of Llandaff' makes a great show with its brilliant red flowers.

Pests, diseases and other problems

Earwigs may spoil dahlia flowers, vine weevil might damage begonia tubers, snails might attack lily shoots, and pollen beetles will seek out narcissus. Help is at hand in all these cases.

PESTS

Aphids

How to identify Clusters of tiny greenfly will infest emerging bulb buds and foliage, especially tulips and hyacinths. Blackfly are also an occasional problem. Tulip bulb aphids mainly attack stored bulbs.
Damage Unsightly and, in the extreme, deforming.
Control Encourage garden-friendly wildlife, such as ladybirds and the larval stages of both hoverfly and lacewing, which are all voracious eaters of aphids. You might choose to apply a soapy water spray as soon as the aphids appear, or an appropriate insecticide. Stored tulip bulbs should be dusted with an insecticidal powder.

Earwigs

How to identify Slender, dark, glossy creatures with pincers, which feed mainly at night on both leaves

and flowers. During the daytime they hide in dark places.
Damage Particularly noticeable on dahlias. Both leaves and flowers will show rounded indentations where the earwigs have been at work. On a small scale they can be ignored, but if an infestation builds up the holes can be disfiguring.
Control Stuff small plant pots with straw or newspaper and spike them on to canes pushed into the ground close to the dahlias. They will act as a dark daytime retreat. Empty out each morning and kill the trapped earwigs. On the same principle, apply an insecticide dust on to the newspaper, thereby destroying any earwigs automatically, or simply use the dust directly on the plant.

Gladiolus thrips

How to identify From mid- to late summer, in hot dry conditions, the sap-feeding insects (*Thrips simplex*) live in the flower buds and at the base of the leaves.
Damage. The foliage develops a fine, pale mottling with tiny black excrement spots. Flowers have a pale flecking and in some cases will fail to open.

Lily beetles have become far more prevalent in recent years with devastating effects on lilies and fritillaries in particular.

Control Spray with bifenthrin, but avoid treating plants in sunny weather. Store corms in a cool, frost-free place.

Lily beetle

How to identify The adult beetle is bright red; the humpbacked, maggot-like larvae are covered with black excrement. The adults feed on the foliage of lilies and fritillaries from early spring onwards, then in midsummer they will be joined by the larvae.
Damage Severe destruction of emerging shoots and flower buds.
Control Pick off adults by hand and wash off larvae with a water spray, but where infestations are heavy, use an appropriate insecticide. This will be more effective on the grubs than the adult beetles.

Mice, squirrels and voles

How to identify These animals will eat dry-stored bulbs and those planted in the ground, especially in winter when food is scarce.
Damage Part-eaten bulbs may remain in the ground as evidence, otherwise gaps in the planting displays are an eventual sign. Crocuses are particularly susceptible.

Blackfly on dahlias can quickly multiply and spoil the appearance, especially on new growth tips below flowering buds.

Greenfly on tulips can look very unsightly where large infestations occur. Soapy water or an insecticide spray will solve the problem.

Saxifraga × urbium (London pride) will create a dense mat on top of bulbs, and this will inhibit squirrels and mice finding bulbs planted below. Cover with fine mesh in the first year, while the saxifrage is getting established, or transfer mature plants from elsewhere in the garden.

Pollen beetles are especially attracted to yellow flowers in mid- to late spring and may be found on yellow-flowered narcissi.

Control Keep stored bulbs in rodent-proof containers. Use bait or traps where pets and other wild animals will not be affected. For bulbs or corms in containers, add a top layer of bedding or foliage plants, thus avoiding bare soil. Press the soil down firmly around newly planted bulbs in the garden to make it more difficult for the bulbs or corms to be found and dug up. Bulbs that are already established will be less likely to be affected.

Narcissus bulb fly

How to identify The adult flies resemble bees, but you are more likely to find the larvae, which resemble white maggots and feed on narcissus or hyacinth bulbs.
Damage Total destruction by the larvae at the centre of the bulb.
Control Destroy all affected bulbs to limit the future spread of the fly. Individual narcissus and hyacinth bulbs can be dusted with insecticide before planting.

Narcissus eelworm

How to identify Above ground this eelworm causes stunted and distorted foliage and flower stems.
Damage Visible brown rings or arcs through a transverse section of the bulb.
Control Destroy all affected bulbs and do not replant with fresh bulbs for at least three years as the infestation will continue.

Pollen beetles

How to identify Small, shiny, black insects, which are also known as rape beetles because they are associated with oil seed rape crops. They are strongly attracted to yellow flowers, especially those of yellow narcissi.
Damage In extreme infestations the flowers will be eaten and disfigured.
Control Difficult, but spraying with water should help. If flowers are picked for display indoors, shake and leave them in a darkened place outside, where the beetles will fly off in search of the light.

Slugs and snails

How to identify Slugs will mainly attack underground, while snails will do most damage above ground, devouring allium leaves and lily shoots as well as attacking fritillaries, tulips and many other bulbs.
Damage Disfigurement or total destruction.
Control Garden-friendly wildlife should be encouraged. Song thrushes will eat snails, while devil's coach horse beetles and hedgehogs will eat slugs. Biological controls, such as nematodes, are available or simple traps, such as upturned grapefruit.

Mainly night-time feeders, slugs will severely damage young foliage on dahlias, as seen here, as well as many other plants.

Slugs can do great damage to tulip buds. Even a small nibble will be disfiguring, but often the effects are much greater.

Guard against vine weevil damage to begonia tubers by watering the container in autumn and again in spring to give six months' treatment. Use nematodes *(Steinernema kraussei)* or imidacloprid, which acts as a systemic insecticide.

Rabbits

How to identify The tops of the plants are eaten.

Damage Stalks of flowering bulbs will remain but the flowers will have been eaten. Tulips and *Fritillaria meleagris* are especially favoured.

Control Rabbit-proof netting has to be 1.2–1.5m (4–5ft) high and with an extra 30cm (12in) below ground level to be effective. Narcissi are not palatable to rabbits, so are safe.

Sparrows

How to identify House sparrows will attack crocus blooms, destroying the flowers and scattering them on the ground around the plants. Yellow crocus seem to be a favourite choice, but other colours are sometimes eaten as well.

Damage The flowers will be shredded.

Control The old-fashioned method was to crisscross the vulnerable area with black cotton thread to create a barrier to stop them feeding. Otherwise there is little to be done, except to plant early flowering narcissus nearby or among them so that the sparrows have less of a monoculture attraction.

Vine weevils

How to identify Cream-coloured vine weevil larvae live below soil level and eat roots and tubers. Begonias are a favourite. The adults are dull black with a hard, defensive back. Each female lays up to 1,000 eggs in the soil, which hatch into larvae in two to three weeks. Larvae are destroyed in temperatures below -6°C (21°F), which means that they are far more widespread in areas with milder winters. They are primarily a problem for the container gardener but, in some regions, they will overwinter in garden soil.

Damage The adults feed mainly at night on foliage, making small notches on the edges of leaves. The larvae are more destructive, particularly in spring and autumn, although they may attack at any time in a conservatory or greenhouse. They eat root systems, wreaking havoc with cyclamen, sinningia and begonia tubers to the point that the whole plant will collapse, almost overnight.

Control Be constantly vigilant and destroy any adults on sight. They are mainly night-time movers (they cannot fly, but will climb). During the day they take refuge in dark places, so check under pots and leaf debris. Special traps can be laid, such as a roll of dark corrugated paper. Apply a liquid drench of beneficial nematodes *(Steinernema kraussei)* in spring and late summer to control the larvae. They will not be effective on clay or dry soils, or where the soil temperature is less than 5°C (41°F) Alternatively, apply a soil drench of imidacloprid, which acts as a systemic insecticide. Apply barrier glue around the tops of containers to deter adult vine weevils from getting into the pots to lay eggs. Burn any tubers that have been eaten by them.

Vine weevil larvae look like cream-coloured, C-shaped maggots.

Botrytis appears as grey mould on the leaves or stems of affected plants. The foliage may be disfigured.

Lily disease has produced distorted growth on this *Lilium regale*. However, the bulb may remain healthy and grow well next year.

DISEASES

Basal rot

How to identify Bulbs are soft and there may be mould around the base. **Damage** The leaves are usually yellow and tend to wilt. Narcissus bulbs are most likely to be affected. **Control** Lift and destroy affected plants. Avoid replanting in contaminated soil.

Botrytis (grey mould)

How to identify Fluffy grey mould on the leaves and dying flowers. It can also cause spots on the leaves and flowers, as in the case of miniature cyclamen from the F1 Miracle Series.

A narcissus with stunted growth displays the symptoms of basal rot.

Damage Disfigurement of the foliage and bulb rot. **Control** Lift and destroy if the bulb is affected, otherwise remove affected parts and spray with systemic fungicide. Prevention is possible through dry storage conditions. Take care to remove the soil and decayed outer bulb parts, and dust with a fungicidal powder before storing.

Snowdrop grey mould

How to identify The fungus *Botrytis galanthina* produces numerous spores, which cause fuzzy grey mould on the leaves and stems. It may be seen on the leaves when they first appear. **Damage** Disfigurement of the foliage and bulb rot. **Control** Lift and destroy affected bulbs. Do not replant *Galanthus* in the same place for at least five years.

Storage rots

How to identify Stored dahlia tubers may start to rot, with fungal growth on the surfaces. It may be caused by a range of fungi and bacteria, either as primary pathogens entering on sound tissue or as a secondary infection on previously damaged parts.

Damage Softening of the tissue. **Control** Remove and destroy affected tubers. Dust any injured parts of flowers with sulphur before storing.

Dry rot of bulbs and corms

How to identify Foliage will turn brown and then die, often with a specific dark discoloration just above soil level. Narcissi, crocuses, gladioli and crocosmias may be affected. **Damage** The bulbs and corms will show tiny black dots or fungal fruiting bodies. **Control** Remove and destroy affected bulbs and corms. Do not replant in contaminated soil.

Lily disease

How to identify The fungus *Botrytis elliptica* produces numerous spores, which cause dark green spots to develop on the foliage. The leaves then turn brown and wither from the base of the stem upwards. **Damage** Flower buds become distorted. The plant may topple over, but the bulb may remain healthy. **Control** Remove debris to avoid the fungus persisting from year to year. Bulbs may be kept if they show no signs of rotting.

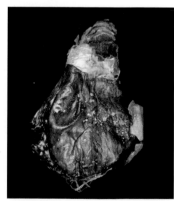

Dry rot storage disease may be evident on newly purchased bulbs. Discard diseased bulbs.

Leaf scorch, caused by a fungus, has damaged this narcissus foliage. The problem begins at the tips and spreads down the leaves.

Distorted leaves are a sign of tulip fire, which is a serious fungal problem. Affected plants must be dug up and then destroyed.

Narcissus leaf scorch

How to identify The fungus *Stagonospora curtisii* causes the leaf tips to become brown and scorched as they emerge. The problem spreads down the length of the leaves. Flowers may occasionally be attacked.

Damage Affects narcissi, crinums, hippeastrums, nerines and snowdrops.

Control Remove and destroy affected leaf tips or other affected parts.

Tulip fire

How to identify The leaves are distorted and the shoots and flowers show stunted growth. In moist conditions the leaves are covered with a grey mould with black fruiting bodies. Small, black scales develop on the outer scales of the bulbs, which may rot.

Damage Flower buds may fail to open and, if they do, they may show small bleached spots on the petals. The flower stems may topple over, and in wet weather the whole plant may rot.

Control Dig up and burn affected plants. Do not plant tulips in the same soil again for at least three years. Late planting may decrease the chance of this disease causing significant problems.

Tulip grey bulb rot

How to identify In some cases no growth appears above ground at all. Any shoots that do appear are distorted and will soon die. Alliums, amaryllis, chionodoxas, colchicums, crocuses, eranthis, fritillarias, gladioli, hyacinths, irises, lilies, narcissi, snowdrops and scillas may be affected in addition to tulips.

Damage Infected bulbs turn dry and grey as they rot. The basal plate and roots may be all that remain.

Control Dig up and burn affected plants. Do not replant in contaminated soil for five years.

Tulip viruses

How to identify Although viruses themselves are invisible, the symptoms include streaked flowers, streaked or mottled foliage, stunted growth and distorted leaves. Sap-sucking aphids transfer viruses from one plant to another. Bought bulbs might already be infected. Tulip-breaking virus also causes problems on lilies, so avoid planting lilies and tulips close to each other.

Damage Not necessarily serious, although it can be. The virus leads to a weakening of the stock.

Control Dig up and destroy any seriously affected plants. Spray against aphids to limit new infections and therefore possible damage.

OTHER PROBLEMS
Drought

How to identify The leaves will start to emerge, then turn yellow and stunted. Flowering will be impaired.

Damage Container-grown plants are susceptible, particularly those with spring bulbs that have been kept too dry in autumn when the roots are being formed.

Control Check that the soil is kept moist at all times (and water if necessary except in frosty weather). Window boxes and hanging baskets may be particularly at risk if they are in the rain shadow of a building. An easy way to recognize the symptoms is to plant some bedding plants, such as violas or primroses, on top of the bulbs. If these show signs of wilting and drought, it indicates that the bulbs might be suffering too.

Frost damage

How to identify The foliage will collapse or blacken.

Damage This could occur in the autumn when tender plants such as

Tulip virus will cause streaking on flowers and mottled foliage, weakening the plants and causing potential spread elsewhere.

dahlias are grown outside and are affected by frosty weather. The foliage will turn black. But it could also occur in late spring when the tubers have been brought into growth under glass and planted out in their summer bedding positions. It might also be seen when borderline hardy bulbs are left outside for the winter, and despite mulches protecting the bulb itself, newly emerging leaves can be affected by late frosts.

Control The autumn frost is not a problem: simply remove the topgrowth and bring tubers inside or cover with a mulch. The late-spring frost will not kill the tubers but it will damage the foliage and delay flowering. Avoid the problem by planting out only after all risk of frost has gone or be prepared to cover with horticultural fleece if frost threatens.

Leaf scorch

How to identify The foliage will show scorch marks and become desiccated.

Damage This is most likely to occur under glass on a sunny day in late spring when tender plants, such as begonias, are in strong early growth and water has been splashed on their

Cyclamen are susceptible to overwatering and dislike being watered from above. It is best to allow them to soak up moisture from below, but never leave them standing in water for long.

A late spring frost has caused the newly emerging leaves of this *Crinum x powellii* to blacken.

leaves. It could also happen if the begonias are grown outside in a sunny spot and watered from above in the middle of the day. The scorch marks will impair growth, although they will not cause the plant to die.

Control Best to avoid watering when the sun is directly on the plants.

Overwatering

How to identify The leaves will turn yellow, then flop and the whole plant will collapse.

Damage Cyclamen are particularly susceptible if grown indoors.

Control Plant in a container with adequate drainage holes, omit the drainage material and use a specially formulated indoor bulb compost.

Water only when the leaves begin to flag and then only from the base by standing the pot in a saucer of water for a short time until the moisture has been absorbed from the bottom.

Poor drainage

How to identify The leaves will turn yellow and flowering will be impaired.

Damage Particularly affects plants that prefer drier conditions, such as hyacinths, nerines and tulips.

Control Make sure that containers have good drainage holes at the base. Add a layer of drainage material so that holes do not get blocked and to provide a free-draining base to the soil area. Use a freely draining soil-based compost mixed with extra grit.

The bulb garden

The bulb garden changes constantly with the seasons. *Galanthus* (snowdrop) and *Eranthis hyemalis* (winter aconite) are the first signs of life in the winter garden, and the first daffodils are also just beginning to show themselves like daggers through the ground. Soon the garden will be filled with their golden heads waving in spring sunshine. Colourful tulips and stately *Fritillaria imperialis* (crown imperial) will take centre stage, while in woodland areas the little *Anemone nemorosa* (wood anemone) and swaths of *Hyacinthoides* spp. (bluebell) will have their moments of glory. Grasslands will be filled with camassias, and in the borders the elegant Dutch irises and rounded alliums add an air of exuberance. Summer borders are filled with lilies, begonias and gladioli, with dahlias and cannas joining the summer ranks and following on into autumn, when nerines, colchicums and cyclamen are at their best. There is so much to choose from and to enjoy.

Various alliums, including dark purple *Allium* 'Purple Sensation', and slightly later Dutch iris create a wonderful display beneath wisteria arches following on from earlier tulips.

Mid- to late winter gallery

This is always a quiet period in the garden, with short, cold days and long, frosty nights. However, some plants have adapted well to the conditions and produce exquisite flowers, even in the bleakest of environments. Given the low light levels, cold temperatures and often windy conditions, it is not surprising that most winter-flowering bulbs and corms are short in height.

Several winter bulbs, such as *Eranthis hyemalis* (winter aconite) and *Galanthus* (snowdrop) show their flower buds at ground level, lengthening their stems only gradually as the daylight increases. Even so the stems will remain relatively short, but planted en masse the displays will be marvellous.

Crocus flowers vary considerably from the palest blue to soft lavender blue to rich deep purple, often revealing a delicate veining.

About 15 different species of snowdrop are found in Europe, from Spain to western Russia, the Crimea and Turkey, their flowering times ranging from early to late winter, and many having slightly different markings or variations in flower size. From these species many, many cultivars, each with their own distinctive characteristics, have been developed.

The winter gallery also includes early crocuses, dwarf irises, tiny cyclamen and low-growing *Anemone blanda*. Only the earliest daffodils, such as *Narcissus* 'January Gold', are significantly taller than the low-growing snowdrops and aconites, and even they still reach only 25–30cm (10–12in) in height.

Most snowdrops begin to flower from midwinter onwards, becoming more and more impressive as the days begin to lengthen.

Galanthus nivalis (common snowdrop) is the most familiar of all the snowdrop species grown in gardens. It is found widely throughout Europe, from Spain to western Russia, and also in Britain. It occurs naturally, both with single and double white flowers, all with a sweet honey scent.

Narcissus 'Rijnvelds Early Sensation' (syn. N. 'January Gold') is one of only a few daffodils that flower at this time of year. It grows to 30cm (12in) high, with the large, golden flowers borne on relatively short stems, which stand up well to buffeting winds. The blooms should last three, four or even five weeks.

Eranthis hyemalis (winter aconite), which grows to 5–7.5cm (2–3in) high, produces a tightly formed yellow cup. Each cup struggles against the cold earth to meet the winter air and unfurl its golden petals. As the stems lengthen, a frill of green leafy bracts acts as a ruff beneath each flower.

Galanthus 'Atkinsii', one of several clones of G. nivalis (common snowdrop), grows to 20cm (8in) high. This comparatively tall, early flowerer is highly scented and elegant in its poise and makes an attractive addition to the winter garden. Enjoy the flowers as they open wide in the sunshine.

Iris danfordiae, which grows to 10cm (4in) high, is one of several dwarf irises that flower in late winter. A beautiful shade of yellow, it is often sweetly perfumed and intricately marked. The slightly taller Iris reticulata, 10–15cm (4–6in) high, is violet in colour with a yellow ridge to the falls.

Crocus tommasinianus is a hardy and reliable plant from Hungary, the Balkans and Bulgaria. It grows to 7.5–10cm (3–4in) high and is tolerant of sun or partial shade. It is a prolific self-seeder, and, in time, the narrow, pale silver-lilac flowers will create a delicate carpet of colour.

Cyclamen coum emerges with broad, heart-shaped leaves displaying a variety of attractive grey or silver markings. These are followed by tiny but enchanting white, pale pink or rose-pink flowers, which bring a welcome splash of warmer colour to the winter garden.

Crocus chrysanthus 'Blue Pearl' is one of the best of all the early crocuses. It grows to 7.5cm (3in) high, and its exquisite pale blue outer colouring, silvery inside and bronze base makes it the perfect choice for many displays, both in borders and in containers.

Anemone blanda grows to a height of 10–15cm (4–6in) and is a rewarding flower for both the winter and early spring garden, as it blooms for six weeks or more. The blue flowers are shy to begin with, but they gather strength as the sun begins to warm the earth.

Mid- to late winter borders

The bulbs that flower in late winter, such as *Galanthus* (snowdrop), cyclamen and early daffodils, can be used alone or in combinations of two or three different types to produce welcome colour in the winter border. Remember to plant them close to a path or within view of your window – it is more comfortable to admire the brave little flowers from indoors than outside in the cold winter garden.

Key plants for the border

Snowdrops look stunning in small individual groups. The most widely grown plant is *Galanthus nivalis*, in either the single or double form. The single flower is more poised and elegant, particularly in the cultivar *G.* 'S. Arnott', which has long stems and beautifully rounded, drop-like flowers. On warmer days the petals open wide, revealing a labyrinth of green veins. It is worth bending down and looking right into each flower to enjoy its intricacies to the full. As a bonus, you will also find that it is wonderfully scented.

The various shades of pink *Cyclamen coum* make an exquisite combination with pure white snowdrops, the whole enhanced by the silver marking on the cyclamen foliage.

Blue-flowering *Anemone blanda* self-seeds with alacrity over a period of just a few years, so that soon the area beneath a tree, for example, would be completely filled with them. The foliage provides an attractive green carpet above which the pretty daisy-like flowers are poised ready to open in the winter sunshine.

Snowdrops associate happily with many other bulbs. They make a remarkably warm and welcome grouping with the tiny pink flowers of *Cyclamen coum*, which is further enhanced by the often intricate silver veining on the cyclamen leaves. The fly-away petals of the cyclamen flower are easily recognizable, and there is a darker stain around the nose of each flower. After flowering the seedhead is pulled down to the ground by the coiled stem so that it comes to rest on the surface of the soil. In early summer the pods burst open, and the sticky seed is ready to be propagated.

In their turn, cyclamen make a pretty partnership with the purple and violet shades of the dwarf Reticulata irises, such as *Iris* 'Pauline', 'Hercules' and 'J.S. Dijt'. Although small, they are packed with colour and vibrancy. *I.* 'George' is a fine example of a Reticulata: the gorgeous purple with yellow on its falls is just enough to lift the eye and bring out the lovely pink background of the cyclamen.

Another favourite at this time of year is the bright yellow *Eranthis hyemalis* (winter aconite), which will form generous groups once it has established itself. It is an excellent choice for a damp border beneath deciduous shrubs, where it will have shade in summer but receive more light in winter when it flowers. It associates well with white snowdrops or the little irises, and looks lovely with other herbaceous plants, such as the dark bronze-leaved bugle *Ajuga reptans* 'Atropurpurea' or the lime green *Helleborus foetidus* (stinking hellebore).

The powerful colouring of *Iris* 'George', a Reticulata iris, looks striking against a background of *Cyclamen coum*.

Planting in the eye of a tree

The area beneath deciduous trees and shrubs – the eye – will usually look bare in midwinter, but then the colour will begin to appear. When moisture and light reach the soil a whole array of plant associations is possible. Late winter- and spring-flowering bulbs, corms and tubers can take advantage of the sparse canopy above to flower and complete their lifecycles before the leaves that exclude moisture and sunlight.

Similar to the snowdrop, *Leucojum vernum* (spring snowflake) has rounder flowers with six equal petals (snowdrops have three long and three short petals). They are native to France, central and eastern Europe and have become naturalized in parts of Britain, where they are easy to grow in shade or semi-shade in moist soil. *L. vernum* var. *carpathicum*, a handsome variant with yellow tips at the ends of the petals, is native to Romania and Poland. The greener, broader leaves are larger than those of snowdrops and make a happy association with winter aconites.

Daffodils and anemones

The first daffodils are in flower at this time of year. *Narcissus* 'Rijnvelds Early Sensation' (syn. *N.* 'January Gold') is one of the earliest, and the golden cupped flowers last for several

Eranthis hyemalis (winter aconite) can be planted to great advantage in front of *Helleborus foetidus* (stinking hellebore).

Leucojum vernum var. *carpathicum* makes an admirable association with the golden flowers of *Eranthis hyemalis* (winter aconite).

weeks. It is an excellent choice for planting in borders generally or in the eye beneath a deciduous tree, where later-flowering daffodils can continue the spring display. 'February Gold' will soon follow, spanning the period between late winter and early spring. By this time the first flowers of *Anemone blanda* are beginning to open in the sunshine to reveal the bluest of daisy-like flowers,

the dainty petals fluttering in the winter breeze. White varieties are more expensive, but by far the cheapest are mixtures of mauve, pink, blue and white. Anemones make a glorious display on their own, but when they are planted with a few primroses and dainty early daffodils the momentum of the display can be carried forward in the most delightful way.

Mid- to late winter naturalized bulbs

Galanthus (snowdrop), *Leucojum* (snowflake), *Eranthis hyemalis* (winter aconite), *Anemone blanda* and the earliest daffodils, as well as a wide range of crocuses, create a sparkling display when they are naturalized in borders, grassland and woodland. Do not be surprised, however, if the bulbs, corms and tubers in the borders, which do not have to compete with grass and tree roots, multiply more quickly. Some genera adapt well to both meadow and woodland conditions, although be prepared for the naturalization process to take longer.

Positions in open grassland or light shade will suit early-flowering crocus species such as *Crocus tommasinianus*, *C. chrysanthus* and *C. vernus*, which are all good for naturalizing.

Grassland

Both *Galanthus nivalis* (common snowdrop) and *Leucojum vernum* (spring snowflake) will grow well in grassed areas, where winter and spring moisture are paramount and summer drought is avoided. Ideal conditions are the grassy swards between deciduous shrubs and around fruit trees, where other, later-flowering bulbs are grown so that the grass is not cut short until after

This group of mixed crocuses, which includes *Crocus tommasinianus*, *C. chrysanthus* and *C. vernus*, forms a carpet of colour.

midsummer. The same is true for *Eranthis hyemalis* (winter aconite) and *Anemone blanda*. To make the most of the display cut the grass in late autumn or early winter so that it is short enough for the mid- to late winter flowers to be appreciated.

Of the many crocus species, *Crocus tommasinianus* and its cultivars are among the most successful in grass, whether grown in sun or semi-shade. This crocus will self-seed extensively, and although each flower is narrow and delicate, a well-established group will create a broad sheet of blue when the sun shines and the petals open. *C. flavus* subsp. *flavus*, with its golden petals, will enjoy similar conditions. It will not self-seed, but will mass up in clumps as the corms multiply below ground. *C. chrysanthus*, which is native to the Balkans and Turkey, has scented, creamy yellow flowers and will compete well in winter grassland. *C. c.* 'Cream Beauty', with creamy yellow flowers, 'Ladykiller', with blue, white-edged flowers, and 'Zwanenburg Bronze', with pale yellow and bronze flowers, are popular, widely available cultivars.

Deciduous shrubs and woodland

The ground beneath deciduous shrubs and areas of woodland offers a convivial home to early snowdrops, cyclamen, daffodils and *Eranthis hyemalis* (winter aconite). The winter tracery of bare branches allows maximum light and moisture to reach early-flowering bulbs, corms and tubers, enabling them to

Aconites and mixed single and double snowdrops look glorious together, providing a tapestry of colour for several weeks.

complete most of their lifecycle before the canopy of leaves appears later in spring. For best results with snowdrops and – if possible – with aconites and cyclamen too, buy growing bulbs "in the green" so that they get off to a good start.

Galanthus nivalis (common snowdrop) will naturalize large areas of deciduous woodland, where they will revel in the cool, damp conditions if they are given a bed of moist leaf mould. Over many years, in these conditions they will create spectacular displays, providing a wonderful sight from mid- to late winter, especially with the added drama of the winter sun penetrating the naked canopy of the trees to highlight the tracery of the branches and the virginal sheet below. Plant single and double varieties in neighbouring groups. Although majestic on a large scale, even 20 clumps will give huge pleasure on the edge of a woodland area or small copse in a domestic setting.

Eranthis hyemalis (winter aconite) colonize with the same effect, and if they are planted with snowdrops wonderful swirls of yellow and white will form on the woodland floor. For the greatest impact, plant in groups distinct from the snowdrops and then allow a few clumps to intermingle. The aconites produce lots of seed. When they are ripe give nature a helping hand and spread them around the woodland floor. Before long you will be richly rewarded.

Elsewhere *Cyclamen coum*, enjoying the damp leaf mould of late winter, will naturalize generously, creating a broad pink carpet, softened by the silver veining of the rounded leaves. Choose a selection from the Pewter

The leaves of *Cyclamen coum* are variably patterned with intricate silver veining or blotches. These create the perfect background for the tiny flowers, which appear in many appealing shades of light and dark pink.

Group, which has plants with leaves predominantly silver-grey above with a dark green margin, and from the Silver Group, with their predominantly grey-marked leaves. Mix them with earlier flowering *Cyclamen hederifolium*, the leaves of which will persist through winter.

Galanthus 'Magnet' has taller, larger flowers than *Galanthus nivalis* (common snowdrop). Here, it forms a marvellous carpet beneath the witch hazel *Hamamelis x intermedia* 'Pallida'.

Early spring gallery

As the days begin to lengthen, the garden starts to come alive and suddenly an array of different bulbs is in flower. This is the main season for all the many types of dwarf daffodil, including old favourites such as *Narcissus* 'February Gold' and 'Tête-à-tête', whose short, sturdy stems enable them to withstand blustery spring winds.

The little *Anemone blanda* flowers have now opened their starry faces to greet the spring sunshine. They are one of the most valuable plants in the garden, lasting for six weeks or more and spreading easily to create a dense carpet of colour. This is also the time for *Crocus* 'Large Dutch Purple', *Scilla siberica* (Siberian squill), *Chionodoxa* (glory of

Double Early tulips flower at the same time as *Muscari armeniacum* (grape hyacinth), providing ideal partners for borders or pots.

the snow) and early single, Kaufmanniana-type tulips, such as *Tulipa* 'Shakespeare', 'Stresa' and 'Heart's Delight'. All of these will happily mix and match to provide endless associations with each other.

As the weeks progress, the first gorgeous blue flowers of *Muscari armeniacum* (grape hyacinth) begin to emerge. These look superb with any of the Double Early tulips or with ordinary bedding hyacinths. The exotic blue of grape hyacinths is stunning with yellow *Tulipa* 'Mr Van der Hoef' and with 'Peach Blossom'. Violas, pansies, primroses and polyanthus act as fine bedfellows with any of these bulbs, producing wonderful planting combinations which can be changed each year to provide different colour effects.

Once established, *Anemone blanda* will soon naturalize to form large carpets.

Narcissus 'February Gold' grows to a height of 25cm (10in). It is short, sturdy and one of the longest flowering of all the dwarf daffodils. It has a long, golden trumpet with swept-back petals, so reminiscent of its parent *N. cyclamineus*. It looks lovely underplanted with white or purple large Dutch crocus.

Crocus 'Large Dutch Purple' reaches a height of 10cm (4in) and is a pivotal player in the spring garden, providing a carpet of bright colour for the early dwarf daffodils. Night-time frosts are to be expected and endured, but as the flowers open in the morning sun, they reveal their gorgeous orange stamens.

Narcissus 'Jetfire', with a height of 25cm (10in), is similar in shape to 'February Gold', having the same fly-away petals. But the trumpet is more orange (rather than yellow), making it a perfect partner for any late purple crocus as well as all the streaked orange Kaufmanniana tulips.

Double Early *Tulipa* 'Orange Nassau' reaches a height of 20cm (8in) and has a mass of vibrant orange-red petals, a bold combination wherever it grows, whether in borders or containers. This tulip is excellent with blue or yellow hyacinths, red, orange, yellow or blue primroses or with polyanthus.

Double Early *Tulipa* 'Peach Blossom' reaches a height of 20cm (8in) and is one of the most popular of all the early dwarf tulips. It has such a delicate combination of colours in its myriad of petals and looks stunning with blue grape hyacinths, a combination which will last for many happy weeks.

Double Early *Tulipa* 'Kareol' grows to a height of 20cm (8in) and is one of several early double tulips, all of which are lovely in garden borders and containers. Early to flower, sturdy and long lasting, they have wide flowering heads which make them a valuable ingredient where planting space is limited.

Scilla siberica (Siberian squill) grows to 15cm (6in) in height and can be used in pots, but it looks best where it has been planted in garden borders and allowed to colonize. Its nodding, rich blue flowers look much stronger en masse than as individuals or small groups.

Muscari armeniacum (grape hyacinth) will flower for many weeks from early to mid-spring. It grows to 20cm (8in) high and provides a memorable underplanting to many tulips, hyacinths and daffodils, both in containers and in the border.

Chionodoxa forbesii 'Pink Giant' grows to a height of 15cm (6in) and provides racemes of four or more star-shaped flowers, pale pink around the edge, white within. They make a pretty association with early spring bulbs, such as dwarf daffodils and hyacinths.

Early spring borders

Plant groups of single types of bulb beside each other or plant more densely, allowing the taller subjects to be underplanted with shorter ones. In this way, early dwarf daffodils and Kaufmanniana tulips can be associated with or underplanted by purple or white late-flowering Dutch crocuses, starry blue, mauve and (slightly later) white *Anemone blanda*, blue or pink chionodoxas, rich blue scillas and bright blue *Muscari armeniacum* (grape hyacinth). The strong yellow and blue makes a vibrant contrast.

Planting partnerships

Seasons vary, and some flowers will last longer than others, depending on the temperature and moisture, but there is usually quite an overlap between all these plants, with the exception only of the late-flowering Dutch crocuses. These flower with the early dwarf daffodils and Kaufmanniana tulips but will not usually last long enough to partner hyacinths and Double Early tulips, which will be in bloom slightly later

'Heart's Delight' is a Kaufmanniana tulip that looks lovely with blue *Chionodoxa luciliae*, *Anemone blanda* or *Muscari armeniacum*.

Narcissus 'February Gold' and the elegant *Tulipa* 'Stresa', a Kaufmanniana tulip, make a striking combination.

and flower on into mid-spring as well. It is safer to plant these with chionodoxas, grape hyacinths, scillas and *Anemone blanda*. A favourite partnership is pink hyacinth with the simple starry flowers of blue *Anemone blanda*, a combination that should flower well year after year.

Violets, violas, pansies, double daisies, primroses and polyanthus play their supportive roles in the

early spring border. Among the prettiest sights now are groups of primroses and violets with clumps of early dwarf daffodils among them. There is little to match the sheer delicacy of *Narcissus* 'Topolino', with its white petals and pale yellow cup, seen above a fragrant bed of tiny white violets. A similar effect can be achieved with the other yellow and white bicoloured daffodils, such as dainty *Narcissus* 'Minnow' underplanted with the little white grape hyacinth, *Muscari botryoides* 'Album'. You might also like to try 'Jack Snipe', or the even smaller 'Canaliculatus' or 'Little Beauty', planted with creamy white violas or *Primula vulgaris* (wild primrose).

For strength and warmth of colour, plant the brighter, more richly coloured tulips and grape hyacinths among vibrant red, orange or blue polyanthus and primroses or amid the blues and purples of violas and pansies. Plan the borders in autumn and reap the rewards next spring. You can build on your successes, adapting them if needed each season by including, for example, a selection of different

Narcissus 'Tête-à-tête' with its tiny golden heads has become deservedly popular. Like many of the early dwarf daffodils, it associates beautifully with vibrant blue *Muscari armeniacum* (grape hyacinth).

violas or primroses. New forms and colours come on the market each year, offering slightly different shades, markings, sizes and shapes. The results will be well worth the care taken over planning.

Planting in the eye of a tree

The early spring season is perfect for the border "eye" around the base of a deciduous tree. Here, the canopy of leaves will not yet have emerged, which means that sunlight and moisture will still be able to reach the ground beneath the crown. The area could be filled with just one sort of bulb – *Narcissus* 'February Gold', for example – or a massed planting of, say, scillas, chionodoxas and *Anemone blanda*.

If you have more than one suitable tree you can create a variety of effects. In just a few years, all these bulbs will multiply, providing colour and interest. Add a few primroses or *Tanacetum parthenium* 'Aureum' (golden feverfew), and you will have a miniature garden that is at its best in spring but that can lie dormant

Tulipa 'Oranje Nassau' is a fiery mixture of orange and red, which looks extremely vibrant with red polyanthus (primrose). Plant close to *Tanacetum parthenium* 'Aureum' (golden feverfew) or other bright green herbaceous plants.

for the rest of the year, except for the odd *Digitalis* (foxglove) or rambling rose. In the dry, shady summer months, the bulbs will lie dormant, waiting for the cooler autumn rains to bring them back into growth.

Anemone blanda are wonderful for this type of situation where they can be left to colonize undisturbed. Not only will they spread by seed, but their tubers will increase in size and provide a wealth of flowers. Plant them beneath an old apple or pear tree and enjoy the sea of blue in the spring sunshine. *Anemone blanda* is sold in autumn as small, hard, knobbly tubers. They can be difficult to establish in the first year, because the tubers can become too dry in the storing process between lifting and autumn sales. It is a good idea to soak them overnight before planting. They will expand noticeably and will be ready to plant the next day. From small beginnings in the garden centres in autumn, the tubers will increase in size over the years to 2.5cm (1in) across and may grow to as much as 7.5–10cm (3–4in) in size. Once established, they can be transferred to another part of the garden in autumn or winter.

Hyacinthus orientalis 'Pink Pearl' is splendid with blue *Scilla siberica* (Siberian squill). All other hyacinths would work well here.

The little white grape hyacinth, *Muscari botryoides* 'Album', bridges the season between early and mid-spring.

Early spring naturalized bulbs

Spring grasslands are transformed by early-flowering daffodils, which are generally quite short by nature, while scillas will create a wonderful woodland display.

Grassland

Generous clumps of daffodils can be planted in grass, but make sure that you allow a distance of 7.5–20cm (3–8in) between each one so that the bulbs have space to multiply around the original planting as well as by self-seeding.

Some species narcissi will spread extremely well if the conditions are favourable. *Narcissus bulbocodium* (hoop-petticoat daffodil), for instance, with its wide-spread cup, which is native to western France, Spain, Portugal and North Africa, seems to prefer peaty, acidic or sandy soils. The sandy conditions of the Alpine Meadow at the Royal Horticultural Society Gardens at Wisley, England, seem to be ideal – perhaps it is the slope that is vital or the natural spring water that seeps through or perhaps it is a combination of both factors.

N. pseudonarcissus, sometimes known as the Lent lily, looks delicate with its soft primrose petals and yellow cup, but it is a tolerant plant, thriving in a range of habitats, including meadows, woodland or rocky hillsides. *N. obvallaris*, formerly known as *N. pseudonarcissus* subsp. *obvallaris* and commonly known as the Tenby daffodil, is similar in size but has deep yellow petals and cup. Both naturalize well in grass, and the Tenby daffodil will cope particularly well with shady conditions. Of all the miniature trumpet daffodil cultivars, 'Topolino' must rank as one of the best for naturalizing in grass. It looks so delicate, with its white petals and pale yellow cup. A clump of primroses or violets close by would be perfect.

N. cyclamineus, which is native to north-western Spain and Portugal, enjoys damp river banks and valley bottoms rather than the higher mountain slopes, as do the many modern cultivars that have been developed from it. With its swept-back petals and long, narrow cup, this is one of the easiest of the

A bank of *Scilla bithynica* looks marvellous in the dappled sunlight beneath a broad deciduous tree.

species narcissi to identify. Although the species itself is quite difficult to purchase, its progeny is vast, and widely available garden cultivars include 'February Gold', 'Peeping Tom' and 'Jack Snipe'. Like the parent, these appreciate damp conditions but are tolerant of any well-drained soil.

The little *Narcissus bulbocodium* (hoop-petticoat daffodil) has been allowed to naturalize in the Alpine Meadow at Wisley, in England. It may not prove as prolific in all conditions.

Scilla siberica, often known as the Siberian squill, is at home in sun or shade but prefers well-drained soils. Here it makes a charming picture in short grass with wild primroses.

Narcissus cyclamineus has distinctive reflexed petals and a long, narrow cup. Here it is growing with *Iris unguicularis* 'Mary Barnard'.

Chionodoxa sardensis from Turkey has deep clear blue flowers and naturalizes well beneath deciduous shrubs or in grassland.

daffodils or other bulbs have finished flowering. Only then will they have had the chance to complete their lifecycles. By this stage the leaves will have died down and all the nutrients will have gone back into the bulbs ready for new growth in autumn. If the leaves are removed inadvertently the bulbs may well be blind – that is, without flowers – the following year.

Woodland

Some daffodils, such as *Narcissus obvallaris* (Tenby daffodil), and nearly all scillas thrive in the light shade found in deciduous woodland, and they will adapt well to shady places in the garden, where they may be grown under deciduous trees or shrubs. When you plant, leave a generous space between each bulb so they can multiply readily. Primroses and hellebores are their natural companions, with *Hyacinthoides non-scripta* spp. (English bluebells) following in mid- to late spring.

All dwarf daffodils associate well with chionodoxas, which thrive in a sunny position but will also cope with partial shade, as long as the soil is free draining. Golden daffodils look splendid with groups of vibrant blue chionodoxas nearby, while the pastel bicolour daffodils, such as 'Jack Snipe', associate well with the pinker forms. The blues and pinks of *Anemone blanda* also make good partners for daffodils, while the taller and slightly later *A. blanda* 'White Splendour' looks superb with those dwarf daffodils that bridged the gap between early and mid-spring. So much depends on the season!

Low-growing *Anemone blanda* and *Scilla siberica* (Siberian squill) will do better if they are planted where finer grasses are growing, such as between shrubs or beneath deciduous trees. *S. siberica* will cope with sun or shade, and it prefers a light, sandy soil. *A. blanda*, on the other hand, is at home in full sun or light shade, but it must have well-drained soil. Either

looks pretty in a small group beside violets or wild primroses.

As with all spring bulbs grown in grassy areas it is vital to remember that the grass should not be cut until at least six weeks after the

Chionodoxa forbesii 'Pink Giant' is another member of the chionodoxa family that is native to western Turkey and that will cope well with spring grassland.

Mid-spring gallery

The spring bulb garden reaches its zenith with mid-season tulips and daffodils flowering together, creating one of the most colourful tapestries imaginable.

The late-winter and early-spring bulbs are nearly all dwarf forms, but many of the mid-season varieties, including *Leucojum aestivum* (summer snowflake), most of the daffodils and almost all tulips, are much taller, growing to 35–60cm (14–24in). Meanwhile *Fritillaria imperialis* (crown imperial) rises to a stately 1.2m (4ft) or more, making it one of the most statuesque of all bulbs. The grape hyacinths, including *Muscari armeniacum*, *M. botryoides* 'Album' and *M. latifolium*, *Anemone nemorosa* (wood

Fritillaria meleagris is one of the most beautiful spring bulbs with flowers gracefully poised and petals intricately marked.

anemone), *Hyacinthoides* spp. (bluebell) and *Erythronium dens-canis* (dog's tooth violet) are shorter, at 15–30cm (6–12in). There are also some shorter daffodils, such as *Narcissus* 'Thalia', 'Silver Chimes', 'Segovia' and 'Hawera', and some small species tulips, such as the lilac *Tulipa saxatilis* and diminutive *T. tarda*.

While tulips and grape hyacinths prefer to bask in spring sunshine, several of the fritillaries, including *Fritillaria meleagris* (snake's head fritillary), and nearly all daffodils are happy in sun or partial shade. Others, such as wood anemones, dog's tooth violets and summer snowflakes, enjoy light shade, in damp grass or woodland. Here the first bluebells will be starting to flower.

Tulipa :'Apricot Beauty' looks beautiful in the mid-spring border, beside scented *Viburnum* 'Anne Russell'.

Leucojum aestivum grows to 45–60cm (18–24in) high and likes damp conditions, where it soon multiplies to create a large clump of tall, graceful, white flowers, each petal tipped with a distinctive green blotch. It is called summer snowflake to distinguish it from its earlier-flowering relative L. vernum.

Typical of mid-season daffodils, Narcissus 'Romance' grows to about 50cm (20in) high. It is a beautifully proportioned white daffodil with a rich pink trumpet, and it looks stunning backlit with spring sunshine. It is excellent for borders near the lime-green foliage of newly emerging herbaceous plants.

The Lily-flowered Tulipa 'West Point', which grows to 50cm (20in), bridges the seasons between mid- and late spring. The vivid yellow petals are exquisitely pointed, and the flowers look dramatic with strong yellows, red or blues but also look wonderful with soft grey foliage plants, such as Senecio cineraria.

Erythronium dens-canis (dog's tooth violet) is native to woodlands throughout Europe. It grows from an elongated bulb that looks rather like a dog's tooth. It adapts well to conditions in a partially shady border. The flowers have attractive, fly-away petals, while the leaves are sometimes densely mottled.

Fritillaria meleagris (snake's head fritillary) is a wildflower of European meadowlands, and it adapts well to damp, grassy spots in the garden as well as to borders. It is a plant with many common names, including snake's head fritillary and ginny-hen floure, because the petals are patterned like guinea hen feathers.

Muscari latifolium is an unusual later-flowering species of grape hyacinth. It has urn-shaped flowers in shades of blue, violet and black, and its leaves are wider than those of the widely grown M. armeniacum. Growing to 20cm (8in) tall, the species is native to the open pine forests of north-western Turkey.

With a flowering height of about 30cm (12in), Narcissus 'Pipit' is one of the loveliest daffodils to flower in mid-spring. It produces two or three flowers on each stem, each flower being a strong lemon yellow suffused with white streaks.

Tulipa 'New Design' is a beautiful pink tulip growing to 50cm (20in). It is particularly pretty with the light behind it, when the petals have a translucent quality. Its leaves are edged with white, making it a favourite with garden designers.

The tall Fritillaria imperialis (crown imperial), which can achieve a height of 1.2m (4ft) or more, has been a favourite bulb for more than 400 years. Inside the giant cups large drops of nectar collect above the long stamens, which glisten in the sunlight.

Mid-spring borders

This is one of the most exciting times of year in the bulb garden, and it is rewarding to admire what has been planted the previous autumn, especially if some new designs have been introduced.

For example, one or more strongly coloured tulips, such as deep purple 'Attila', beetroot 'Negrita', burgundy and yellow 'Gavota', red 'Cassini', or orange and purple 'Princes Irene', will allow you to develop eye-catching schemes with *Myosotis* (forget-me-not), *Bellis perennis* (double daisy), pansies and *Erysimum cheiri* (wallflower) in rich shades of deep blue, orange, gold, red, black and purple. You will have wonderfully showy borders, no matter what the weather.

Meanwhile, the pastel-toned tulips, including salmon-pink *Tulipa* 'Apricot Beauty', shell pink 'Esther', double satin pink 'Angélique', 'White Dream' and the lovely cool, creamy white and green 'Spring Green',

Muscari latifolium bears a mixture of dark blue and lighter blue flowers on each stem.

call for a softer colour scheme, incorporating the paler tones of polyanthus, double *Bellis* (daisy), pansies and violas, forget-me-nots and wallflowers with combinations of primrose yellows, pale pinks, creams and pale blues. Foliage plants can be used to great advantage too. The cheery golden foliage of *Tanacetum parthenium* 'Aureum' (golden feverfew), the silver variegations of *Silybum marianum* (blessed Mary's thistle) and the soft seedlings of *Nigella damascena* (love-in-a-mist) are all valuable spring-time partners: the effect is subtle but beautiful.

Formal and informal styles

So many different styles, both formal and informal, can be adopted. Where there is a strong design with clipped box hedging, the formal lines of tulips are most appropriate. The bright green of the new growth on *Buxus* (box) looks good with scarlet tulips, but a different type of

The flowers of *Tulipa* 'Apricot Beauty' are an exquisite mixture of shades of apricot, peach and tangerine. It looks especially striking next to the biennial *Silybum marianum*, which has prominent white-veined leaves.

Tall *Fritillaria imperialis* make striking displays with their large bell-shaped flowers associating well with shorter daffodils. Sometimes the leaves are variegated and edged in gold, as in *F. imperialis* 'Aureomarginata', or white, as in *F. imperialis* 'Argenteovariegata'.

formality can be achieved if tulips are interplanted with co-ordinated bedding plants, whether you choose a vivid or a subtle approach.

A more informal scheme might use different types of bulb within a large herbaceous border. A few clumps of daffodils, some *Muscari latifolium* (grape hyacinth), two or three *Fritillaria imperialis* (crown imperial) and three or four groups of tulips will create a wonderful effect, informal but full and colourful. It might look haphazard, but in reality it will have been carefully thought out. You might want to use the height of the *Fritillaria imperialis* to form a bold grouping at the back of the border, placing shorter tulips or daffodils in front. These tall fritillaries come from southern Turkey to Kashmir and may be various shades of orange, red or yellow. They can grow to 1–1.5m (3–5ft) in height and have as many as six or even eight bell-

shaped flowers, often displaying an enticing drop of nectar at the end of the stamens. The distinctive cluster of green, leaf-like bracts gives the plant its common name. Plant the large bulbs on their sides so that moisture does not collect in the central gully, which will cause the bulbs to rot, and add a layer of grit or sharp sand beneath them to improve drainage. These plants like deep, well-drained, fertile soil and a position in full sun. Both the bulbs and flowers have a foxy smell, so are best planted away from paths.

If you have a sunny, well-drained site, try other dramatic fritillaries, including *F. persica*, which comes from southern Turkey and has a flowering spike to 1m (3ft) tall with bloomed, green to purple bell-shaped flowers, and the even taller *F. persica* 'Adiyaman', which has brown-purple flowers. These can be more tricky to establish, but when conditions are just right they will look stunning.

A minimalist garden

In recent years a minimalist style has become fashionable where bulbs are planted in gravel or among different coloured stones or bark, with few other plants around.

This mid-spring garden is just awakening, with the white-barked birch *Betula utilis* var. *jacquemontii* 'Jermyns' underplanted with *Narcissus* 'Salome', ornamental grasses and perovskia, and the broad, grey-green leaves of *Allium karataviense* beginning to emerge.

Fritillaria imperialis has a tuft of distinctive bract-like leaves emerging from the crown. The orange form has a dark bronze stem.

A longer-term planting scheme

For gardeners who want to experiment and are willing to change their spring borders regularly, the choice of colour and the range of bulbs is vast. If you prefer a simpler approach with a longer-term planting scheme, you also have an enormous choice but bear in mind that some bulbs are more reliable than others, and there is little doubt that some bulbs naturalize in borders better than others. Remember, too, that your success with bulbs will depend on soil conditions and factors such as proximity to tree roots or hedges, and the aspect and rainfall in your garden. Sometimes it is difficult to determine why crown imperials grow exuberantly in some gardens for many years, but in others they will hardly flower at all after the first year. The same is sometimes true of the highly bred split corona daffodils, such as *Narcissus* 'Cassata' and 'Mondragon'.

Most daffodils will establish themselves well. They form good clumps and have a more natural appearance than bold, highly coloured tulips. So, if you like informality, grow daffodils. *Narcissus* 'Pipit' is a favourite choice, long in flower, a good naturalizer and with beautiful lemon yellow flowers streaked with white. At 30cm (12in) or just a little taller, it is a real winner.

Tulips will naturalize best in well-drained soil rather than in heavy clay. For best results be sure to plant bulbs at a depth of at least three times the size of the bulb. Among the best tulips to naturalize on loam or clay is 'Apeldoorn' and its close relatives. 'Apeldoorn' itself was introduced after World War II and is still one of the bestselling cultivars because of its vigour, boldness and reliability. Look out for bright yellow 'Golden Apeldoorn', orange-flushed 'Blushing Apeldoorn', the original scarlet red 'Apeldoorn' and 'Apeldoorn's Elite', which has red flowers edged with yellow. Any one of these – or a combination of several – will add vibrancy to your borders for many years. They associate well with self-seeding blue forget-me-nots, golden feverfew, purple-leaved heuchera and colourful primulas, all of which will naturalize.

A cottage-garden border

For a mixture of tulips and daffodils that will last for many years, try a combination of *Tulipa* 'Orange

Narcissus 'Romance' offers an attractive pink and white theme, with white petals and a warm pink cup. It naturalizes well.

Narcissus 'Pipit' is one of the best daffodils for naturalizing, combining elegance with reliability.

Mid-spring border case study

This vibrant mid-spring border combines *Tulipa* 'Orange Emperor' and 'Golden Apeldoorn' with the bicolour daffodil *Narcissus* 'Tahiti'. Meanwhile white *N.* 'Thalia' echoes the bridal wreath *Spiraea* 'Arguta' in the background. With peonies, irises and herbaceous delphiniums, and then lilies, crocosmias and dahlias to follow, this makes an excellent cottage border for spring and summer colour using bulbs, corms and tubers to great effect. Only the dahlia will need winter protection (either by lifting and storing or adding a mulch).

Earlier in the year winter-flowering aconites *Eranthis hyemalis* and snowdrops *Galanthus nivalis* had both made a welcome appearance.

Tulipa 'Orange Emperor'

Tulipa 'Golden Apeldoorn'

Narcissus 'Thalia'

Narcissus 'Tahiti'

Emperor', which is an excellent and reliable plant, flowering just before, and overlapping with, *T.* 'Golden Apeldoorn'. Clumps of yellow and orange-red *Narcissus* 'Tahiti' make a valuable addition in linking the two colours of tulips. As an alternative arrangement, try a single yellow narcissus such as *N.* 'Pipit', along with an orange tulip, *T.* 'Beauty of Apeldoorn', which is particularly beautiful and very reliable.

Flowering spring viburnums such as 'Anne Russell' or 'Park Farm Hybrid' and *Spiraea* 'Arguta' (bridal wreath) would add height and substance to the spring border. Both have white flowers, providing a

lightness of touch and an excellent background to any spring bulbs.

For a more vibrant colour theme, try the vivid red *Tulipa* 'Apeldoorn' planted alongside yellow, red or orange wallflowers, which will start to flower by mid-spring and continue blooming for several weeks, bridging the gap between spring and early summer. The tulips may be planted in straight lines or grouped in clumps to give a more cottage garden feel. The wallflowers will provide delicious fragrance, especially after a shower of rain. They will have to be replaced each year, but the tulips can be left in the soil where they will multiply well.

Otherwise, to keep the straight lines in future years, the tulips will have to be thinned. Lift them about six weeks after flowering, when all the foliage has died back.

The original *Tulipa* 'Apeldoorn' is vibrant red with dark, almost black interior.

Mid-spring naturalized bulbs

The fledgling canopy of deciduous trees, as yet immature, still allows shafts of sunlight to reach the ground at this time of year, allowing many grassland or woodland bulbs to flourish, including *Anemone blanda*, *Erythronium dens-canis* (dog's tooth violet), *Leucojum aestivum* (summer snowflake), *Anemone nemorosa* (wood anemone) and trilliums.

Grassland

One of the real stars of mid-spring is the delicate *Fritillaria meleagris* (snake's head fritillary). Their white or lilac heads hang demurely among the short grass, each flower an exquisite chessboard pattern of intricate veining. Their season overlaps with the early dwarf daffodils and primroses, but the fritillaries will continue to flower with the later bulbs and cowslips. They associate beautifully with pure white *Narcissus* 'Thalia' and starry *Anemone blanda* 'White Splendour'. They like sunny, damp conditions,

Narcissus 'Thalia' grows about 35cm (14in) tall and produces two or three flowers on each stem, each one pure white with a characteristic twist to the petals.

Anemone blanda 'White Splendour' seems to be bigger and slightly later flowering than the blue form, and it always looks wonderful with *Fritillaria meleagris* (snake's head fritillary).

and if they are really happy they will multiply quite naturally. Even a handful in a small patch of turf is well worth trying. Unfortunately, rabbits rather like them, so only plant them if your garden is a rabbit-free zone.

Many daffodils will naturalize in grass, such as the yellow Large-cupped *Narcissus* 'Carlton', and the Trumpet daffodil 'King Alfred'. Others have white petals, including the well-known Large-cupped 'Ice

Follies', with its white petals and broad, creamy white cup, or the simple white 'Mount Hood', with its well-proportioned trumpet. Another favourite is 'Actaea', again with white petals but this time with a distinctive, small, red-tipped cup, rather similar to *N. poeticus* var. *recurvus* (pheasant's eye), which will flower a few weeks later. Some daffodils have so-called pink cups, which are really a soft salmon-pink that darkens with age. 'Salome' and 'Rainbow' will grow

successfully in grass. Another
bicolour to look out for is golden
'Pipe Major', which has an orange-
red corona. Some of the multiheaded
types are excellent in borders,
particularly white 'Thalia' and 'Sir
Winston Churchill' and the primrose
yellow 'Yellow Cheerfulness'.

Several other types of bulb will
grow in grassy places. *Ornithogalum
nutans*, with its nodding green and
white flowers, will survive well if the
soil is well drained; it will also grow
among shrubs.

Woodland

Hyacinthoides spp. (bluebell), which
can be white or pink as well as blue,
prefers the cool, damp shade near
a hedgerow or the leafy soil in a
deciduous wood, especially among
beech trees. It starts to flower in
mid-spring, but its main season is
late spring.

Erythronium dens-canis (dog's tooth
violet) prefers sparse grass, although
it, too, will grow in the shade of
shrubs or deciduous trees. It is one

Narcissus 'Yellow Cheerfulness' naturalizes
well in grass or borders. It looks especially
lovely near the fresh foliage of the mock
orange *Philadelphus coronarius* 'Aureus'.

Tolerant of sun or shade, *Ornithogalum
nutans* will produce many pendent green and
white flowers on each stem. It is worth
seeking out for its quiet presence.

of the prettiest of the spring flowers,
with its delicate, swept-back petals in
white, pink or lilac. *Leucojum aestivum*
(summer snowflake) likes damp soil
where it has a good moist root run
and will form a lovely graceful clump
in grass or woodland.

Another wonderful naturalizer is
Anemone nemorosa (wood anemone),
which is at its best in a deciduous
wood or beneath shrubs. It will soon
spread to form a dainty white carpet,
looking perfect with a clump of
dog's tooth violets or a group or two
of bluebells. Try it beneath a spring-
flowering tree or in the light shade
of summer-flowering shrubs, where
it will thrive with a good mulch
of leaf mould. *A. nemorosa* 'Allenii' is
one of several blue forms, and
'Robinsoniana' is a lighter blue.

Trilliums also like the shade. They
are found in the woodlands of the
Appalachian Mountains in eastern
North America where they revel in
the damp humus, especially near
mountain streams. They prefer either
neutral or acid soil. The best-known
species is *Trillium grandiflorum* (wake
robin, wood lily), which has white
flowers that turn pink as they age.
Black fruits are formed, which ants
take away to their nests, eating the
pulp but leaving the seed and so
helping to propagate the plants.

Narcissus 'Pipe Major', which reaches 45cm (18in) in height, is a distinctive bicolour with its
yellow petals and orange-red cup. It is a colour combination that works well in grass.

Late spring to early summer gallery

Although most of the daffodils and many of the tulips are now over, there is still a wealth of other bulbs to enjoy at this time of year.

Late-flowering tulips are among the most exciting, both in colour and shape. Parrot tulips produce superb buds, with the petals tightly wrapped around each other, before opening to reveal sumptuous, full-bodied flowers, with streaks of secondary colours. One of the best of all the late tulips is the Fringed *Tulipa* 'Blue Heron', which is not blue at all but more a warm lilac. The Single Late 'Queen of Night', a mysterious shade of dark purple verging on black, is a great performer, whether it is grown in a formal bedding scheme, a cottage border or a container.

Dutch iris 'Sapphire Beauty' combines a sumptuous mix of deep blue and gold and looks splendid beside the dusky poppy, *Papaver orientale* 'Patty's Plum'.

The tall *Camassia* (quamash) from North America, also known as Indian lily or American bluebell, is useful for sunny borders or grassland. The flowers may be blue or white, and both forms associate well with the last of the daffodils, *Narcissus poeticus* var. *recurvus* (pheasant's eye).

At the front of a sunny border *Anemone coronaria* hybrids will make a real splash of colour with their brilliant red, white or blue flowers. Cheap and cheerful, they are also suitable for containers. For best results, just remember to soak the tubers overnight before planting. Meanwhile, alliums provide rich colours, from white to lilac and purple, and they will be joined by shapely Dutch irises, in beautiful shades of purple to gold and yellow.

Tall *Allium giganteum* and shorter *Allium hollandicum* are just poised, waiting to bloom.

Tulipa 'Blue Parrot' grows to 55cm (22in) and is a full-bodied, lilac-blue tulip, which flowers at the same time as blue forget-me-nots, red or purple aubrieta and purple- or rose-coloured wallflowers. In maturity, its large blooms are sumptuous, and make perfect cut flowers for a table decoration.

Tulipa 'Queen of Night', a tall tulip at 60cm (24in), is described as satin black but is really a deep, dark purple. It looks lovely with pale blue forget-me-nots or with tall, purple alliums, with which it overlaps for a fleeting moment. Perhaps the best of all partners, however, are orange wallflowers.

Allium cristophii grows to 60cm (24in) high and has round, open heads, about 20cm (8in) across, with large, star-shaped, amethyst-blue flowers. The leaves are long and strappy and appear early, before beginning to dry off as the flowers open. The huge seedheads are useful in dried-flower arrangements.

Anemone coronaria De Caen Group 'Die Braut' ('The Bride') is a beautiful, pure white, single-flowered anemone, with a contrasting apple-green centre. Best planted near the front of a sunny border, it grows to 25cm (10in) and associates well with almost any other plant. It does well in containers, too.

Allium karataviense grows to 20cm (8in) high and has rounded umbels, 5–8cm (2–3in) across, of small, pink, star-shaped flowers. Its broad, grey, almost elliptical leaves are a special feature. The flowerheads dry well and look attractive throughout the summer. Left in place, self-seeding will soon occur.

Iris 'Purple Sensation' grows to 45cm (18in) and is one of the many bulbous Dutch irises that are useful for bridging the gap in sunny borders between the late tulips and taller alliums. They look lovely in small groups beneath wisterias or laburnums and are pretty with pale yellow wallflowers.

Camassia leichtlinii subsp. *suksdorfii* Caerulea Group is a good subject for borders or damp grassland, where it will multiply and create large groups of tall blue flower spikes up to 75cm (30in) high. The flowering period is all too short, but the impact is magnificent.

Tall *Tulipa* 'Blue Heron' grows to 60cm (24in) and is a strong, elegant tulip, with fringing around its lilac petals. Grow it in the border or in large pots underplanted with orange or primrose yellow wallflowers or 'Ivory and Rose Blotch' winter-flowering pansies.

Allium schubertii grows to 40cm (16in) and has flowerheads about 30cm (12in) across, with an inner compact ball of flowers and an outer sphere shooting off like fireworks. It is certainly a talking point, both when in flower and when seen as a dried specimen.

Late spring to early summer borders

Late-flowering tulips bridge the seasons between mid- and late spring, enjoying the longer days and warmer temperatures.

This group includes some of the most sensational tulips of all, particularly the Parrot types, with their full-bodied, curvy petals. *Tulipa* 'Fantasy' is a mixture of salmon-pink and reds, with flushes of yellow and green, and it looks wonderful when it is grown with lime-green or deep bronze foliage plants. 'Blue Parrot' is more lilac than blue, and it looks marvellous with many spring bedding plants, including rose-pink or purple wallflowers, rose-pink or pale blue pansies and various shades of aubrieta.

Of the so-called black (actually dark purple) tulips, look out for shapely 'Black Parrot', with its dark, twisted petals, or the tall double 'Black Hero', which has a wonderful glossy sheen, as does the double, rather more purple than black, 'Blue Diamond'. Among the singles, 'Queen of Night', 'Paul Scherer' or 'Black Swan' will still be in flower, as will 'Recreado', which is another

Tulipa 'Black Parrot' is a sensational Parrot tulip with sculptured, almost black petals.

choice deep purple tulip. Planted in nearby groups or used as dot plants, they will certainly make a strong statement and add drama to the late spring garden. Blue forget-me-nots make a simple but glorious partnership with any of these dark coloured tulips.

If you want a black and white theme a good white double tulip is 'Mount Tacoma'. 'New Dawn' is tall, single, white with purple feathering at the sides of the petals. 'White Triumphator' is definitely one to look out for, with its tall, sturdy

Tulipa 'Paul Scherer', one the darkest of all tulips, has velvety maroon flowers.

stem and elegant, lily-shaped flower. Over the years it has become a firm favourite. For a more subtle effect, add to the black, purple and white theme by planting a touch of dreamy lilac with 'Lilac Perfection', which has broad, peony-type flowers, or add a group of pastel lilac Fringed tulips, such as 'Blue Heron'. Growing to 60cm (24in), this is a tall but sturdy and shapely tulip, which is one of the last to flower.

You might want to forget subtlety altogether and throw some vibrant reds into the borders. Orange-red

Tulipa 'Blue Parrot' can be used in a massed bedding display with *Aubrieta* 'Royal Red", which provides a profusion of carmine red flowers beneath the lilac pink tulips.

Tulipa 'Lilac Perfection' is a peony-flowered tulip with broad double flowers.

Camassia leichtlinii subsp. *suksdorfii* Caerulea Group is another candidate for mass bedding.

A group of the Dutch iris 'Symphony' creates a lively and refreshing picture. Fine and shapely in figure, no wonder they make such a popular cut flower.

'Ballerina' and 'Pieter de Leur' are both lily-flowered tulips with attitude. They can make a border come alive even on a dull day.

Architectural camassias

The tall and slender camassias, with their tapering flower spikes, are white, rich blue or pale blue. These are versatile bulbs and adapt well to the border and to unmown grassy areas as long as the soil is damp and the site is sunny. A spot beside a garden pond would be ideal, but they look just as attractive in a clump in a herbaceous border or in formal bedding patterns partnered by wallflowers. If you want to leave them in the ground for a number of years, add blue forget-me-nots, which are sure to self-seed and will avoid the need for replanting. The all-blue scheme will be enchanting.

Colourful Dutch irises

Dutch irises provide colour year after year, spanning the seasons between late spring and early summer. They vary in colour from white through to yellow, blue and purple, and sometimes a mixture of more than one colour. Each of the flowers has intricate veining. Grown from small bulbs, for a short period they will be in flower at the same time as alliums, and together they make an exciting partnership. Indeed, alliums and Dutch irises have a host of suitable homes, including the mixed herbaceous border, the cottage-style garden or beneath arches of wisteria, laburnum or *Robinia hispida* (bristly locust, rose acacia). Wherever they are planted they will provide a brilliant display for years.

Tulipa 'Pieter de Leur' is a dramatic lily-flowered tulip with elegant pointed petals.

Dutch iris 'Oriental Beauty' is a superb combination of lilac blues, silvers and gold, adding a touch of majesty to any border.

Medium to tall alliums with large drumstick flowerheads

Among the tallest of all alliums, reaching 1.2m (4ft) or more, is *Allium* 'Mount Everest' with its large grapefruit-sized flower heads. Its ivory white florets show up well against the darker foliage of a yew hedge or among other brighter colours. Kicking at its heels is lilac-purple *Allium giganteum*, with deep purple *A. hollandicum* 'Purple Sensation', and 'Globe Master', at 90cm (36in), close behind. All are strong and sturdy and together they make a popular choice for garden borders. *A. nigrum*, with its ivory white flowers and bold black ovaries, normally reaches 70cm (28in) high and is slightly later to flower than the purple and lilac forms. It looks lovely with silver *Cynara cardunculus* (cardoon) and *Hesperis matronalis* var. *albiflora* (the white form of sweet rocket). The pale lilac *A. hollandicum* (syn. *A. aflatunense*) has a flowering height of 60cm (24in). Rather than just choosing one or another, plant a mixture that will associate very well together, provide a long period of

The densely rounded heads of *Allium hollandicum* 'Purple Sensation' contrast beautifully with the tall spires of foxgloves.

flowering and a wonderful pattern of tiered planting. All white alliums mix happily with purple and lilac forms and together look stunning beneath all shades of wisteria whether pink, white or blue. They also associate well with yellow laburnum and white or pink *Clematis montana*.

The only drawback to most alliums is the leaves, which apppear well before the flower buds emerge,

and by the time the flowers open they look very untidy. It is best to grow some other leafy plant nearby to conceal the mess. Biennial or perennial wallflowers are a perfect foil providing both foliage and contrasting or complementary flower colour. Japanese anemones are also excellent bedfellows. Their leaves soon grow up to hide the allium leaves and in turn their flowers will provide colour in the border from late summer to autumn. Large grey-leaved hostas also make good companions, giving the alliums a strong visual base and at the same time hiding their foliage. Foxgloves make another great partner, their large basal leaves easily hiding the bulb foliage while their spires of flowers, either pink or white, offer an architectural contrast to the rounded heads of the alliums.

Later-flowering species

Allium cristophii, at around 60cm (24in) high, has a very large open flower which makes it one of the most popular of all garden alliums. Its flowers have a metallic quality

Deep purple *Allium hollandicum* 'Purple Sensation' lives up to its name as the buds open and the flowers emerge.

Allium hollandicum 'Purple Sensation' flowers well beneath an arch of honeysuckle and combines beautifully with Dutch iris.

The white *Allium nigrum* is slightly later to flower and is 70cm (28in) tall. The term *nigrum* refers to the dark green ovaries.

Allium cristophii has large heads, which take on a vibrant metallic sheen in the evening sunlight. They contrast well with hostas, hesperis and Iceland poppies, and go on to make a lasting contribution with their round dramatic seedheads.

which makes them look stunning in the evening when the warmer light seems to bring them even more to life. Many of the Dutch irises make good companions offering a contrast in shape of flower and often in colour. Meanwhile all the early roses, whether pink, purple, white or yellow, make super partners as well. *A. schubertii*, at 40cm (16in), is slightly shorter but its flower heads are even wider. Two circles of flowers appear creating an inner and outer ring which creates the effect of a firework in mid-explosion. They can reach 30–45cm (12–18in) across in a sunny warm spot. Their leaves are early to grow. Both these alliums are a little later to flower than the taller drumsticks mentioned opposite, thus they help to bridge the seasons between late spring and early summer. Their untidy leaves are less noticeable for they will flower with poppies, herbaceous geraniums and hesperis, whose foliage by then is well grown, providing a valuable foil for the long strappy leaves.

Alliums look marvellous as a mass planting beneath arches dripping with wisteria, early honeysuckle, early-flowering clematis, laburnum or *Robinia hispida*. Here they are just beginning to flower, with buds ready to burst open.

All these allium flowers are notable additions to the garden, and their seedheads will last for many weeks to be enjoyed either in the garden or in the house in a dried flower arrangement. Where they have multiplied, either by natural massing of the bulb below ground or by self-seeding, the seedheads will create a noteworthy mass display. Few other bulbs can claim such a long period of interest.

Slender and shorter

Though undoubtedly tall, *Nectaroscordum siculum* is also both slender and graceful and is very happy in sun or partial shade so long as the soil is neither dry nor waterlogged. Though strictly no longer called an allium, *Nectaroscordum siculum* is of the same family and grows from a similar rounded bulb and in most bulb catalogues will be found in this section. The name is derived from Greek *nektar*, which refers to its large ovaries, and *skorodon*, which reflects the fact that the whole plant smells of garlic when crushed. It comes from France and Italy where it is known as the Sicilian honey garlic. Its flower stems reach up to 1.2m (4ft), producing bell-shaped flowers suitable for an informal cottage style of border. They are creamy white, flushed with pink and dark red, with green at the base, creating a charming combination of subtle colours. Like many alliums, it is much favoured by bees. After their visit, the seedpods become erect making this a most distinctive plant both before and after flowering.

Allium unifolium has delightful pretty pink flowers which show up well here against the blue-green slate mulch. Self-seeding is common in a sunny spot.

By contrast, many alliums are much shorter and are either suitable for growing in containers where their scale is matched, or at the front of a herbaceous border where they are not dwarfed by taller more vigorous plants. They are also a bonus in the modern garden, mulched by gravel, granite chippings or slate. Here they can live close to the path, either alone or in partnership with others.

Allium unifolium bears pretty pink flowers about 30cm (12in) high (although can be taller); its leaves are erect and though not particularly attractive, are not untidy either. Good planting partners are later-flowering herbaceous plants such as pink echinaceas, which will then fill the gap after the allium has finished its main display. These in turn associate well with ornamental grasses. All these plants look striking against a blue-green slate mulch. An alternative bulb for the gravel garden could be *A. flavum*, again only 30cm (12in) high. It has attractively coloured blue-green leaves and contrasting yellow flowers with up to 60 tiny bells on each stem. It too loves a sunny spot and will self-seed easily. Another choice could be *A. caeruleum* with its rich blue drumstick-type flower heads, only 2.5cm (1in) across, borne on slender stems in early summer. The leaves die back completely before flowers appear. All three alliums could be planted in close alliance for a late spring and early summer display.

The buds of *Nectaroscordum siculum* (syn. *Allium siculum*) are about to burst into flower.

The flowers are creamy white flushed with pink and dark red, and are loved by bees.

Unlike many alliums, foliage is a positive asset in the case of *A. karataviense*, which grows around 20cm (8in) high. Each bulb produces a pair of broad grey leaves, held almost horizontal, which have a metallic sheen. This allium is suitable for a minimalist style of gardening, and looks most effective against a carpet of gravel or red granite chippings, either of which provides a sharp, clean background. It needs a sunny spot to do well and will enjoy the additional warmth of the surrounding gravel or stone which will encourage it to self-seed with ease. The individual flowers are small but numerous, star-shaped, white to pale pink, borne in umbels 5–7.5cm (2–3in) across.

Shade lovers

There are just a handful of alliums that actually prefer shade and, like many plants which grow in these conditions, they are both white in bloom. They include *Allium triquetrum* with its loose flower heads and unusual triangular stems. It is often called the three-cornered leek. Growing to around 38cm (15in), it thrives in damp shade but, being a native of southern Europe, is only borderline hardy although it has now naturalized in several parts of the British Isles. Meanwhile, its slightly shorter relation, *A. ursinum*, is native to wide regions of northern Europe into Russia and is fully hardy. It revels in damp woodland conditions where it can become invasive. It is

Here *Allium karataviense* looks very snug with the newly emerging foliage of another sun lover *Eryngium bourgatii,* whose intricate leaf shape provides a foil as the foliage of the allium dies back.

colloquially known as wild garlic on account of its smell, and like the domesticated garlic, *A. sativum*, it has many medicinal properties. Its leaves and flowers are used to flavour salads and soups.

Allium karataviense thrives in a sunny position and combines well with other sun-loving plants such as *Eryngium bourgatii* and *Perovskia*.

Late spring to early summer naturalized bulbs

Both *Hyacinthoides non-scripta* spp. (English bluebells) and camassias will naturalize where the conditions suit them, but bluebells prefer a cooler, shadier site, whereas camassias prefer a sunnier location.

Both plants, however, like moisture-retentive soil. Camassias are ideal partners for *Narcissus poeticus* var. *recurvus* (pheasant's eye), which is the last of the daffodils. Both plants flower in late spring and provide colour long after many of the spring bulbs have finished. This daffodil originates from the deep mountain valleys of Switzerland, where it flowers after snowmelt. Its delicacy of flower and lateness make it one of the most popular of the genus. However, the principal drawback of

The white form of *Hyacinthoides non-scripta* spp. (English bluebell) offers an alternative to the more commonly known bluebell. Pink forms are also known in the wild. Clumps of all three colours would look attractive in a woodland setting. The native English bluebell has flowers on one side only of a tall raceme.

naturalizing these late-flowering bulbs is that you have to delay the time when you can cut the grass. Resist the temptation to get out the lawnmower. Wait for at least six weeks after the bulbs have finished flowering before you cut the grass. By then, the bulbs will have completed their lifecycles and will be resting until root growth starts again in autumn.

A carpet of bluebells

Not many gardeners are lucky enough to have an entire woodland to plant with beautiful bluebells, but the blue carpet can still look extremely pretty on even a relatively modest scale, such as when it is confined to an orchard or beneath a mixed deciduous hedge. Both the larger *Hyacinthoides hispanica* (Spanish bluebell) and the more delicate *H. non-scripta* (English bluebell) are available in white and shades of blue

Narcissus poeticus var. *recurvus* (pheasant's eye) and camassias are a major feature of the spring garden. They will naturalize in grass and give years of pleasure. Buttercups add further colour to the picture.

The Spanish bluebell, *Hyacinthoides hispanica*, produces flowers all the way round its flower spike, which remains upright. Shades of blue, pink and white flowers are all available.

The woodland is a wonderful picture now that the *Hyacinthoides non-scripta* spp. (English bluebells) are in full flower, a vast sheet of blue beneath a canopy of emerging oak leaves. They have a sweet, heady perfume, which can be overpowering on a large scale. They self-seed freely.

and pink, and both species will settle down with ease and multiply – and this may cause a problem, for if they are planted close together they will interbreed, and the seedlings will show characteristics of both parents. While this may not be an issue in your garden, it does have wider ramifications. If bees have taken nectar from Spanish bluebells and the next generation of mixed bluebells in your garden and then fly off and take nectar from native English bluebells growing in the hedgerows or woods, the result will be a diminution of the precious and dwindling native stock. If possible, avoid the thuggish (though attractive) *H. hispanica* and remove any that are growing in your garden, including any mixed Spanish and English seedlings. Choosing the more delicate *H. non-scripta* will help to sustain numbers of one of the most evocative and beautiful of all British wildflowers. Plant bulbs of English bluebells in groups in the autumn (cut and allow them to self-seed), or buy them as growing plants in the green in late spring. Plant immediately on purchase and allow them to self-seed.

Camassia cusickii bears long racemes of cup-shaped, pale blue flowers. It will cope with quite shady positions in grass or borders.

Mid- to late summer gallery

The summer gallery contains many glorious lilies, including familiar border species, like *Lilium regale* (regal lily), as well as a host of cultivated forms, in white and all shades of pink, orange, yellow and salmon-pink. Some lilies are now bred without stamens to help people who are allergic to pollen, and these are generally sold as "Kiss" lilies.

Many summer bulbs and corms produce tall plants, but exceptional among them are the cardiocrinums, which can grow to 2–4m (6–12ft) in height. With their long, scented, trumpet-shaped flowers, they are a spectacular choice for a shrubbery or woodland area. Shorter, but still tall, are the creamy white *Galtonia candicans*

The luscious white blooms of this tall gladiolus are quite at home among the softer shapes of *Cosmos* 'Sonata Pink' and *Astrantia major* 'Ruby Wedding'.

(Cape hyacinth) and *Crocosmia* 'Lucifer', whose flowering stems, bearing rich red flowers, might need support. Gladioli are another feature of the summer border, the colourful flowers borne on long, thrusting stems. Both exuberant and elegant, white, pink or yellow zantedeschias make a bold statement at this time of year as well with their exotic, funnel-shaped, perpendicular flowers.

Begonias also flower throughout summer and well into autumn; they may be upright in habit or trailing, with single or double red, yellow, orange, white or pink flowers, which are sometimes two-toned. Always sumptuous in appearance, they are a mainstay of summer containers, and look lovely in borders, too.

Agapanthus are available in many shades of pale and rich blue and provide a fabulous display where they are well established.

Gladiolus 'Seraphin', which is a tender, early-flowering, butterfly-type cultivar, grows to 70cm (28in). It bears ruffled, pink flowers, each with a creamy white throat, and it looks especially good near lime green or yellow. Plant in spring in the herbaceous border to provide colour from mid- to late summer.

Crocosmia 'Lucifer' is a graceful plant, originally from South Africa, growing to 90cm (36in) with exotic sprays of deep orange flowers on tall, arching stems, which may need support in a windy spot. Plant the corms in spring, in sun or partial shade, and soon they will become established in large clumps.

Gladiolus 'Charming Beauty' is a hardy cultivar, growing to 60cm (24in). The small, rose-coloured, funnel-shaped flowers have delicate pointed petals. Plant the corms when they are available in autumn or spring. An ideal site would be a south-facing border beneath a sunny wall.

Agapanthus praecox subsp. *maximus* 'Albus' grows to 60–90cm (24–36in) tall. It forms bold clumps, bearing rounded umbels of large, white, trumpet-shaped flowers. Grow in a sunny border beneath a south-facing wall. If your garden is exposed, grow in containers in a potting compost (soil mix).

Zantedeschia aethiopica 'Crowborough', the hardiest of the arum lilies, grows to 90cm (36in) and is suitable for a damp border or near a pond. The rhizomes can be treated as an aquatic plant and grown in a planting basket in heavy loam. The distinctive funnel-shaped flowers appear in summer.

Galtonia candicans (Cape hyacinth) grows to 1.1m (3ft 6in) and bears tall spikes of creamy white, pendent flowers. Plant bulbs in early spring in bold groups towards the back of the herbaceous border, where the flowers will add height and grace. They show off particularly well against a dark background.

Growing to 60–90cm (24–36in), *Lilium lancifolium* (syn. *L. tigrinum*; tiger lily) has vibrant orange flowers, marked with maroon spots, the same colour as the anthers. Plant the bulbs in autumn or in late winter to early spring as soon as they are available.

Lilium regale (regal lily), which grows to 60–180cm (2–6ft), does well in containers. It bears large, white, scented, trumpet-shaped flowers that are streaked with maroon on the outside. Plant bulbs in autumn or late winter to early spring as soon as they are available.

Begonia 'Picotee' is a vigorous plant, growing to 20cm (8in) and producing large double flowers, which are suitable for centre stage in a summer bedding border, in hanging baskets or in window boxes. The tubers should be planted indoors in late winter or early spring.

Mid- to late summer borders

The mid- to late-summer border is rich in both colour and variety, with the choice of great swaths of red, orange or yellow crocosmias and brilliant blue agapanthus punctuated by tall spires of eremurus, lilies and gladioli. Large clumps of ornamental grasses offer a strong contrast.

Agapanthus and eremurus

A sunny border is perfect for rich blue or white agapanthus, which look best crowding together near the front of the border, basking in the heat, alongside the bold, tapering spikes of kniphofias and elegant watsonias. Meanwhile sand-coloured eremurus could dominate the back of the border, along with the spires of gladioli and galtonias. Groups of yellow, pink, white or orange lilies could create more focal points along the way, all planted to provide the magical highlights of this time of year. Apart from tender gladioli and watsonias, and borderline galtonias, all can be left to mature and multiply for another year. Agapanthus and eremurus do not fall into any of the

The strappy leaves of agapanthus look good with tall grasses. Blue *Agapanthus* 'Ben Hope' forms a wonderful large grouping in front of the frothy masses of *Chionochloa conspicua* (plumed tussock grass).

four main categories of bulbs, corms, tubers and rhizomes, but they have developed thick, fleshy roots to combat the annual droughts they experience in their native habitats. For this reason, they are generally considered under the wider umbrella of bulbs.

There are many agapanthus to choose from, including tall *Agapanthus* 'Bressingham White', which grows to 90cm (36in), and dark blue *A.* 'Ben Hope', flowering at 1.2m (4ft), both blooming from mid- to late summer and slightly later. Taller still, to 1.5m (5ft), is

Agapanthus 'Loch Hope' produces dense heads of broadly trumpet-shaped flowers, which are an impelling deep blue. This is a great favourite if space is not at a premium.

Agapanthus 'Loch Hope' is one of the more robust cultivars, making a strong statement on the corner of this border where it relishes its sunny position.

A. 'Loch Hope', which is also deep blue but flowers from late summer to early autumn, making a huge display. *A.* 'Lilliput' is much smaller, its deep blue flowers growing to only 40cm (16in), and it is an ideal choice for a sunny gravelled area near steps or a path. These varieties are all deciduous plants and classed as hardy, although it is safer to mulch well in winter.

There is also a good choice of eremurus, although you will succeed with these plants only if you can provide lots of space around their roots, which spread out a long way like black tentacles and do not respond well to being disturbed. Their untidy leaves might be regarded as another drawback, but the flowers more than make up for either of these factors. Known as the foxtail lily, the spectacular flower spikes can reach between 1.2 and 2.4m (4–8ft), each spike consisting of several hundred individual flowers. Plant them in rich, well-drained soil, in a sunny but sheltered spot where wind will not do damage, otherwise they will need support. Mulch in winter with coarse material, such as grit or ashes, to deter slugs and help protect them from frost and damp. Several fine cultivars are available, including pinkish-brown 'Oase', salmon 'Romance', coppery rose 'Cleopatra' and towering white 'Joanne'.

Red-hot poker

Another tall, bold plant is *Kniphofia* (red-hot poker), which produces tapering spikes of red, yellow, orange and sometimes green. They grow from rhizomes. Like agapanthus, flowering extends from midsummer to autumn, depending on the species. 'Buttercup,' 'Bees' Sunset' and 'Fiery Fred' are all early flowerers.

Eremurus 'Oase' forms a dense mass of flower spikes, about 1–1.2m (3–4ft) high, which are perfect at the back of a sunny herbaceous border, where a dark green background can show them off to full advantage.

Galtonia candicans

Yet another tall, tapering plant is *Galtonia candicans*, which bears tubular white flowers on leafless stems that can reach to 1–1.2m (3–4ft) high. This is best treated as a back-of-the-border plant, where its flowers can

Gladiolus 'Seraphin' is a tender butterfly gladioli with ruffled pink flowers and a creamy white throat. It associates well with lime green or yellow, including the pubescent tall spires of *Solidago* (golden rod).

Kniphofia rooperi syn. *K.* 'C. M. Prichard' exhibits the typical fiery colours that give this plant its common name of red-hot poker. However, this species has unusually broad elliptical racemes.

be seen but its strappy leaves are well hidden. Beware slugs, which love to feast on them. The bulbs may be left in the ground with a winter mulch or lifted and stored in a frost-free place.

Gladioli

The corms of gladioli are generally sold dry in late winter for planting in spring on a bed of sand. Choose a sunny border and grow them in rows or clumps. The colours range from shades of lilac and pink to cream, yellow and white. Some of the taller types grow to more than 1m (3ft) high, but there are also shorter ones, growing to about 70cm (28in), and even smaller gladioli, known as the Nanus Group, grow to 60cm (24in). Depending on their height, they can be mixed with other summer annuals, such as crimson, pink or white cosmos, or planted in front of bronze *Atriplex hortensis* (orache). Meanwhile, many herbaceous plants, such as sidalcea, golden rod and aconitum, would make excellent companions.

Watsonia 'Tresco Dwarf Pink' grows about 35cm (14in) high and is best planted in a large group or dotted among ornamental grasses. It associates well with low-growing, silver-leaved plants.

Zantedeschia aethiopica 'Crowborough' provides an outstanding display where it has been allowed to mature in moist soil. The tall spathes look wonderful beside a reflecting pool.

Watsonia

Like gladioli, watsonias also have sword-like leaves, grow from corms and, in frost-prone areas, need to be planted each spring and lifted in autumn. But they are a more delicate plant, with spires of dainty, trumpet-shaped flowers symmetrically grown and pleasing to the eye. They like a sunny spot in well-drained soil and can be classed as hardy in only the warmest maritime areas of Britain, where *Watsonia* 'Best Red' is regarded as one of the most robust cultivars. However, there are many pretty colours to choose from, including sugar pink *W.* 'Tresco Dwarf Pink', which grows to about 35cm (14in). Plant them in a drift at the front of a sunny border or among ornamental grasses in a gravel garden. In either case, they will make a lovely display.

Borders in sun or partial shade

Grown from a rhizome, *Zantedeschia aethiopica* produces a succession of white spathes from early summer through to midsummer. It thrives best in moist soil in full sun or partial shade. It can be grown as an aquatic plant on the margins of a pond, but it is a robust grower and may reach up to 1m (3ft). The cultivar 'Crowborough' is perhaps the most reliable, while 'Little Gem' is only half its height. It is usually treated as hardy, but mature, established plants will survive cold winters much better than younger specimens.

Crocosmia

Crocosmias also like moist soil, but it must be well drained. They grow from corms and flower from mid- to late summer and sometimes on into early autumn. *Crocosmia* 'Lucifer' is one of the best-known cultivars, with its magnificent long stems and joyous red flowers, and even the early pointed leaves and later seedheads are attractive. But, growing to 1–1.2m (3–4ft) or more, its size does mean that it is rather unruly. In sunny spots it will associate well with yellow achilleas and with bold canna leaves, dahlias and yellow lilies. Smaller cultivars,

such as *Crocosmia* 'Emberglow', *C.* 'Jackanapes' and *C.* 'Emily McKenzie', grow to 40–60cm (16–24in) high, flower in mid- or late summer and may be better suited to a smaller garden. They are regarded as borderline hardy, surviving best where the soil is well drained. Again, older clumps seem to winter best, so mulch well in early years.

Dahlias

While they love the sun and thrive in a sunny spot, dahlias will cope with shade for part of the day. They have a long season of flowering, from midsummer right through to the first frosts of autumn. Heights range from over 1.2m (4ft) to 30cm (12in) for the newer patio types.

Lilies

Most lilies enjoy sunshine on their flowers, but many like to have roots in the shade and are happy to have half the day in sun and half in shade. For midsummer flowers those from the Golden Splendour Group are hard to beat for their strong stems and scented, trumpet-shaped flowers. Growing to 1.2–1.8m (4–6ft) high, they add lightness to the summer borders and contrast well with tall

Dahlia 'Bishop of Llandaff' is prized for its single red petals surrounding an open centre with yellow anthers, and its dark foliage.

Crocosmia 'Lucifer', which flowers at the same time. Alternatively, place them beside the golden-variegated foliage of *Hedera* (ivy), *Euonymus* or *Elaeagnus*, for example, or match the maroon staining on the reverse of the flower with the dark purple leaves of *Cotinus*.

Another attractive choice is *Lilium superbum* (American 'Turk's Cap' lily), which originates in the eastern United Sates, where it grows best in moist, acid soil. It grows to 1.5–3m (5–10ft) so is best suited to the back of a border, preferably where it will be sheltered by taller shrubs or trees, against which it will show up well. Its orange flowers are unscented but attractive, with their deeply recurved, orange petals with maroon spots. They appear in late summer and last until early autumn.

Lilium regale will cope with full sun or partial shade. It will also tolerate a wide range of soils, making it not only one of the most beautiful lilies but also one of the easiest to grow.

Lilium martagon (martagon lily) grows 1–1.8m (3–6ft) tall and has attractive, but unscented, glossy, pinkish-purple, pendent flowers with darker spots.

Lilium Bellingham Group thrive in dappled shade beneath deciduous trees or between shrubs. They have great poise and an exquisite palette of colour.

Staking lilies

First position the metal stake 15cm (6in) away from the emerging stem. Release one side of the ring and carefully trap the lily stem within. Clip the second end of the ring into the hole provided on the metal support. The lily now has freedom to move but cannot stray too far.

The flowers have a strong, heady perfume that hangs on the evening air. Grow it in formal borders, behind box hedges, next to the path where the scent can be fully appreciated or try it beside deep red roses, picking up the colour of the outside petals. It can reach to 1–1.2m (3–4ft) and may need staking when its flowerheads are fully open and weighing it down. *Lilium regale* 'Album' is pure white, without the subtle extra flush of maroon on the species.

Martagon lilies will also tolerate almost any well-drained soil, in sun or partial shade, and will even cope with quite deep shade if necessary, although flowering might not be as effusive as when they receive some sunlight. From early to midsummer these lilies will produce tall stems, 1–1.5m (3–5ft) high, with up to 50, though usually fewer, turkscap-shaped flowers in shades of pink to purplish-red with darker spotting. They have a rather unpleasant smell, but this is nevertheless a choice

plant for a refined colour scheme.

Although many lilies will cope with light shade, hybrids in the Bellingham Group positively thrive in these conditions, but they do like acid soil. They flower from early to midsummer producing racemes of beautifully poised turkscap flowers, ranging from red to orange and yellow with darker spots.

The large, trumpet-shaped flowers of *Lilium regale* associate beautifully with *Rosa* 'Sander's White Rambler'.

Plants for dappled shade

Not all garden borders are in a sunny
location. Most will be in some shade
for at least a few hours of the day,
and many plants will flourish in
these conditions, including some
lilies, veratrum and begonias.

The giant lily *Cardiocrinum
giganteum* will thrive in dappled shade
all day long but dislikes dry or
waterlogged conditions. It originates
in the forest and scrub of the
Himalayas and enjoys a sheltered,
shady spot among shrubs and trees.
Though hardy, it will benefit from a
deep winter mulch and plenty of leaf
mould mixed in the soil at the time
of planting. The bulbs need to be
planted just beneath the surface.
They take several years to reach

Veratrum album grows from a rhizome and
has large, bold, pleated leaves and unusual
starry green flowers, which are borne on
freely branched panicles.

maturity, and after flowering die,
but by then several offsets will have
been produced to continue the
species. The flower spikes reach a
massive 1.5–4m (5–12ft) in height
and produce many trumpet-shaped,
white flowers, which are well scented.
The basal leaves are large and glossy
but unfortunately they are very
attractive to slugs.

Veratrum album (false hellebore) is
a spectacular plant, which grows
from black, poisonous rhizomes. It
likes a rich, deep soil that does not
dry out and, in these conditions, will
cope with a sunny site or one in
partial shade. A shrubbery would be
ideal, as long as you can keep the
slugs away, for its bold, pleated
leaves are one of the great

The flower spikes of *Cardiocrinum giganteum* can reach a massive
1.5–4m (5–12ft) and produce many well-scented, trumpet-shaped white
flowers. The resulting display is a real show-stopper.

White begonias offer a simple solution to a shady or partially shaded
spot in the garden, where they show up so well, especially in the
evening when they appear almost luminescent.

Mid- to late summer border case study

This is a border where the house casts deeper afternoon shadow as the summer lengthens. Earlier in the year tulips and daffodils flowered against a backdrop of white bridal wreath *Spirea* 'Arguta'. Now fiery red crocosmias take centre stage with their long pleated strappy leaves and stunning red flowers held on strong slightly arching stems. They have multiplied quickly, producing a striking display for several weeks from mid- to late summer. One of the loveliest of the summer lilies from the Golden Splendour Group is blooming just behind them, producing a beautiful contrast to the red crocosmias, while to one side *Dahlia* 'Lemon Cane' has survived the winter in situ with a covering of mulch.

Lilium Golden Splendour Group

Dahlia 'Lemon Cane'

Crocosmia 'Lucifer'

characteristics of this plant. In early and midsummer it produces tall panicles of pale green flowers, reaching up to 1.8m (6ft). The black form, *Veratrum nigrum*, produces dark reddish-brown flowers, though the pleated leaves are still green.

Begonias will cope with sun, partial sun or shade, but thrive best when not baked by sun all day long. Water splashed on their broad leaves will cause scorch in sunny weather, so water them at ground level, beneath the leaves, or before or after sunset when it is cooler. In many

gardens tuberous begonias are planted out in early summer to create brilliant splashes of colour through summer and early autumn, a show that will last for months, not weeks, as is the case with most of the plants described so far. Available in self-colours of white, yellow, red, pink and orange, as well as bicolours (as trailing plants, compact bush and taller doubles), begonias can be used for formal patterns of contrasting or matching shades with other summer bedding plants, such as nasturtiums, fuchsias and lobelias, depending on

aspect. They will not tolerate frost, so be sure to lift them before sub-zero temperatures damage them.

Begonia 'Picotee' produces outstanding golden-yellow flowers, edged with deep orange.

Autumn gallery

Autumn borders are an absolute delight, with exotic dahlias and cannas vying for attention with strident colours and bold foliage.

Cannas need to be lifted before winter, and so do dahlias, unless a protective mulch is given in late autumn. Other autumn-flowering bulbs, such as eucomis, nerines, sternbergias, crinums and schizostylis, are all borderline hardy and will survive the winter best in very well-drained soil beneath the protection of a wall where they can remain undisturbed for many years.

Eucomis have stout spikes of starry pink or green flowers, with a tuft of leaves at the top that gives rise to the common name, pineapple flower. This is also the time when

Growing to a height of only 15cm (6in) *Sternbergia lutea* is also known as autumn daffodil, autumn crocus or Mount Etna lily.

nerines bear their large heads of frilly, bright pink, trumpet-shaped flowers, which bloom on naked stems, with the leaves appearing later. Other highlights include the diminutive sternbergias, with their bright yellow, crocus-like flowers, giant crinums, which produce an array of large, pink, funnel-shaped flowers, and schizostylis, available in pink or red.

Some autumn-flowering bulbs can be left in the open ground and are regarded as fully hardy. Colchicums are found in shades of lilac and pink as well as white and will grow in sun or partial shade. They are often referred to as autumn crocuses because of the shape of their flowers. In fact, several true crocuses flower in autumn. *Crocus sativus* (saffron crocus) is probably the best known.

Drama is easily achieved in the autumn border using bold *Canna* 'Striata' with their broad variegated leaves and brightly coloured flowers.

Eucomis bicolor has a flowering height of up to 60cm (24in). The flower spike is dense, with small, starry, waxy flowers, each tinged with pink. It can be grown singly in a small pot or as a group in a large container. Alternatively, try a clump of three or five at the front of a sheltered, sunny border.

Crinum x *powellii* 'Album' grows to about 1m (3ft) and produces a rosette of broad, bright green, fleshy leaves. These are followed by a stout stem with pretty, funnel-shaped, white flowers. It is a focal point of the autumn garden but requires thoughtful lower planting companions to hide the untidy leaves.

Nerine bowdenii produces its flowers before the leaves. Growing to 45cm (18in), it likes a sunny, sheltered spot – beneath a south-facing wall is ideal. Make sure that it is at or near the front of the border so that other larger plants do not cast shade on it, as it will only thrive in a sunny position.

Canna 'Rosemond Coles' is a robust plant with large green leaves that produce long racemes of brightly coloured flowers with yellow-spotted throats. The petals themselves are red edged with yellow, producing a vibrant and distinctive colour scheme. Expect it to grow to around 1.5m (5ft) tall.

Dahlia 'Clair de Lune' grows to about 1.1m (3ft 6in) high. A Collerette dahlia, the flowers have an open centre, surrounded by a collar of short, flat petals or florets, as they are known, and a single outer row of florets. The light yellow colouring shows up well in the border, particularly in the evening light.

Canna 'Wyoming' is a tall-growing rhizome with broad bronze leaves and large, flamboyant, orange flowers. It must be lifted before any severe autumnal frosts. Plant near other orange flowers, such as dahlias, or in front of silver-leaved plants such as *Eucalyptus gunnii* (cider gum).

Colchicum 'The Giant' sounds tall but actually grows to only 20cm (8in) rather than the 10–15cm (4–6in) stature of its many close relatives. Each corm produces a succession of up to five purplish-violet goblet-shaped flowers. The leaves follow after flowering.

Schizostylis coccinea 'Major' loves a sunny moist position where it is best left undisturbed. In time it will multiply to create a large clump producing 6–10 flowers per stem to a height of 60cm (24in), thus making a very welcome contribution to the autumn border.

Cyclamen hederifolium is a carpeting plant, growing to only 10cm (4in) tall, which produces its tiny blooms either before or at the same time as the leaves. It prefers well-drained soil in light shade beneath a group of trees or shrubs or in the eye of a fruit tree.

Autumn borders

Some late-flowering bulbs need the warmth of a wall to help them produce their best flowers and give them protection through the autumn and the winter cold.

Many eucomis are grown in pots so that they can be given winter protection. However, planted at the foot of a wall, they should survive the winter if they are well mulched. *Eucomis pallidiflora* has long flower spikes, to 75cm (30in), topped with a large tuft of leaf-like bracts which give it its common name, giant pineapple flower.

A warm south-facing wall will favour *Crinum x powellii*, which produces many tall stems up to 1.5m (5ft), bearing widely flared, pink flowers, creating a sumptuous display in late summer and early autumn. The flowers of *C. x powellii* 'Album' are white. At half the height, *Amaryllis belladonna* produces bright pink flowers in autumn without any foliage to set it off; the strappy, fleshy leaves follow after flowering.

Amaryllis belladonna, which is native to South Africa, produces stout stems with trumpet-shaped flowers about 60cm (24in) high. The foliage emerges after the flowers.

Like the crinum, it is an exceptionally beautiful bulb.

Nerines are another example of a pink-flowering autumn bulb, and they, too, bloom before the leaves have developed. The frilly flowers are funnel shaped and vary mainly in their shade of pink, their crinkly

Nerine bowdenii 'Blush Beauty' is an excellent specimen plant for the autumn border with its fine deep pink flowers.

margins and overall width. They are slightly shorter, usually reaching only 45cm (18in). Mulch all these bulbs to help guard against frost damage.

Dahlias

Grown from tubers, dahlias put on their main growth in summer, so by early autumn they are fully grown and at their best. They are available in a wide range of colours from

Eucomis pallidiflora produces its tall flowers in late summer. The leaf-like bracts give it its common name, giant pineapple flower.

Nerine bowdenii 'Silver Smith' is an arresting sight in the autumn border but it needs to be allowed to settle in for a few years before massing up. Like other nerines, it will flower much better when the bulbs are congested.

Dahlia 'Dark Desire' is a recently introduced cultivar that has been immediately admired for the delicacy of its foliage, stems and flowers. Its deep dark chocolate blooms are also a particularly winning feature.

Dahlia 'Yellow Hammer' makes an exciting association with lime-green grasses or other golden foliage plants. It would also look dramatic mixed with purple *Verbena bonariensis*.

yellow, orange, red, through to white, pink, mauve and purple, with some displaying two tones of colour or even more. And if that was not enough to choose from, you have all the different shapes of flowers, from spiky cactus, to giant decorative, to neat pompon and small patio dahlias, to name but a few.

The taller cultivars will need staking, and it is better to do this when the dahlias are first planted out so that they grow into well-shaped plants. By late summer it will be too late and at the first hint of stormy weather the stems will have been bent or broken.

An additional distinction between dahlias is the foliage colour. Usually it is an unexciting mid-green, and if you are lucky it has not been eaten by slugs! But the recent fashion has been to enjoy dark bronze foliage, as exhibited by bright red 'Bishop of Llandaff' and others, such as gold 'Elise', dark pink 'Giselle', salmon-orange 'Poeme', 'Rosamunde', which has deep rose-pink flowers, and white 'Swanlake'. These dahlias are all about 1m (3ft) high and would be suitable for the middle or back of a border, though exceptions can always be made for one of these

exciting specimens by placing it in the forefront to catch the attention. 'Poeme' is only 50cm (20in) tall, so would be ideal beside a path or next to a patio. Golden 'Yellow Hammer' is even shorter, at 45cm (18in).

Another range of dahlias offers a move away from heavy flowers and overpowering foliage. It concentrates instead on rather more open, irregularly shaped flowers, slender but sturdy wiry stems, which are often dark red, and foliage that is sometimes described as filigree. *Dahlia* 'Dark Desire' is a stunning

dark chocolate-purple with contrasting golden stamens, which help to lift the brooding effect of both flower and dark green foliage. It will reach around 1m (3ft) high and suits a raised bed where the foliage and stems can be admired as much as the flowers. Planting it next to a bronze aeonium augments the drama. It looks just as good in a traditional ground-level border too. 'Ragged Robin' and 'Royal Blood' are similar. Prolific in flower, there is no need to stake these dahlias, which are an exciting development.

Dahlia 'Bishop of Llandaff' was named in 1924 after Bishop Hughes, whose ecclesiastical chair was in Llandaff Cathedral, Cardiff, Wales. Within four years it had won the prestigious RHS Award of Garden Merit. It has recently enjoyed a revival and is now a popular cultivar in designer gardens as well as the garden centre stores.

Canna 'Black Knight' associates well with yellow abutilons and orange kniphofias, both acting in their supporting role to the star performer.

'Bishop of Llandaff'. Another favourite is *C.* 'Tropicanna', which is admired for its deep bronze, pink-striped foliage and orange flowers. *C.* 'Striata' has green-striped yellow leaves and orange flowers. Either would look marvellous besides *Dahlia* 'Nargold'. *Canna* 'Rosemond Coles' is attractive too with its bright red flowers edged in gold. All these cannas thrive in sunny conditions, but they will also grow well in boggy soils, and associate well with waterside planting. They will need to be lifted before the first frosts and stored in a frost-free place before starting into growth again the following spring. One small tuber will put on tremendous growth in just one season.

Winter protection

The autumn garden is full of contrasting shapes and colours. The tall, slender flower spikes of cannas rise above the large, oval leaves, sometimes with brilliant colouring, which spiral around the stem. Tall

Canna 'Black Knight' is dramatic in both bloom and foliage. The leaves are striped, dark bronze and the large, deep red flowers are stunning. Excellent as a specimen canna or for mass plantings, it grows to a height of up to 1.2m (4ft).

flower spikes are also seen from late plantings of gladioli, but here the foliage is shaped like swords. In contrast, begonias and dahlia have round flowers, varying in size and colour but always making a strong contribution until the first frosts, both fully mature now after the long growing season throughout the summer months. All these plants are from hot climates and need to be given protection before winter, but with proper care many will live for years and can be easily propagated.

Cannas seek great heights in autumn, as they reach up to the skies after a full summer's growth, loving the sunshine and creating a magnificent spectacle in the borders with flowering grasses, abutilons, colourful dahlias and towering kniphofias for company. There are many varieties to choose from, including dark red *Canna* 'Black Knight', which is sumptuous in flower and has dark-striped foliage. It would look awesome beside *Dahlia*

Bold planting schemes

Kniphofias, commonly called red-hot pokers or torch lilies, are native to grasslands or by streams in southern Africa, and, like cannas, they grow from rhizomes. They like a sunny spot with moist but well-drained soil. *Kniphofia* 'Percy's Pride' grows

Canna 'Tropicanna' is a recent sport of Canna 'Wyoming', which has bronze leaves and tangerine orange flowers. 'Tropicanna' has similar orange flowers, but the foliage is electrifying: vibrant pink veins run through the leaves. It is an outstanding cultivar.

The autumn border becomes architectural with sculptural *Cortaderia* (pampas grass), warmed by hot cannas.

about 1.2m (4ft) tall and produces racemes with green to canary-yellow flowers in late summer and early autumn. The species *K. rooperi* (syn. *K.* 'C. M. Prichard') flowers from early to late autumn with orange-red flowers, eventually changing to orange yellow. It is unusual among the family in that its flowers are more oval than torch shaped: definitely one to look out for. All of these cannas and kniphofias can be placed with great effect in close proximity, either right next to each other or separated by some neutral plant such as an ornamental grass.

Any *Miscanthus* and *Cortaderia* (pampas grass) will make useful partners to the autumn border, adding further textural contrast and softening the otherwise strong colours of the exotics. This is a time when bold planting schemes can work even on a modest scale.

Kniphofia rooperi (syn. *K.* 'C. M. Prichard') flowers from early to late autumn, producing blooms that are a mixture of autumnal shades of orange and yellow. This hardy, evergreen perennial has dark green, strappy leaves.

Dahlia 'Nargold' was introduced in 1994. It is a cactus dahlia with fimbriated petals and gorgeous tangerine yellow colouring. It makes an excellent colour association with any of the orange or yellow cannas and kniphofias.

Autumn naturalized bulbs

Both autumn grasslands and woodlands can be rich with flowers. Colchicums, for example, which are happy in sun or partial shade, will grow in grass or lightly shaded woodland areas.

Where a new display is required, buy the corms in late summer or early autumn just prior to flowering and be sure to plant immediately. The flowers will then be produced followed by root growth that is made as the leaves are produced in late winter and the spring. By then they will have settled in ready to create a good display for years to come.

Grassland

Colchicum autumnale is a native of western and central Europe and can tolerate temperatures down to –20°C/-4°F. It has a rather weak tube to support the flower, and sometimes flops over after a shower. Grow it in grass, where the heads may be supported by the grass itself. *C. a.* 'Alboplenum' is double white, while *C. a.* 'Plenum' is double lilac-pink. *C. bivonae* is a sturdier plant

Colchicum 'Violet Queen' is a beautiful shade of violet-pink, and it associates well with low-growing incised foliage plants, which create a foil for its naked stems.

and again easily grown, although it is susceptible to frost in severe winters, so choose a sheltered site. *C. speciosum* is a good strong-growing plant, from north-east Turkey and Iran. Here it has to cope with very cold winter temperatures and is

almost as hardy as *C. autumnale*. It can be grown in grass in the shade of a shrub or even in a sunny border so long as the soil is moist. Its goblet-shaped flowers are pinkish purple and show up well at around 18cm (7in) high. *C. speciosum* 'Album' has thick white flowers which stand up well to autumn weather.

One of the characteristics of colchicums is that the tall strappy leaves appear after the flowers. In severe winter conditions this may be as late as spring, while in milder climates they may surface in late winter. They will grow about 18–25cm (7–10in) long and must not be prematurely removed.

Many cultivars exist which offer slightly different shades of rose pink, lilac and white, some tessellated, some double. *C.* 'Violet Queen' is another beautiful choice colchicum producing fragrant pinkish violet flowers, similar to *C.* 'The Giant', while 'Lilac Wonder' is slightly pinker.

Colchicum 'Lilac Wonder' is caught by autumn sunshine as it peeps out beneath *Heuchera micrantha* var. *diversifolia* 'Palace Purple'.

Colchicum speciosum 'The Giant' has purplish-violet blooms. Together with white-flowered 'Album', it is one of the most popular cultivars.

Cyclamen hederifolium has variable leaf shape and colouring. Some forms, notably the Silver Leaved Group, are remarkable for their silver foliage, which makes such a valuable contribution to autumn and winter borders.

Woodland

Cyclamen also enjoy the partial shade of a shrubbery or woodland and will spread with ease to create an attractive autumnal carpet. *Cyclamen hederifolium* has wonderful marbled foliage which just emerges as the flowers are fully out. The flowers vary in shades of pale and deeper pink, some are white, but they have conspicuous maroon rimmed mouths. They are sweetly scented. This cyclamen grows from small dark brown tubers which are rounded below and flattened above. The roots are produced both from the apex and sides. It is a humble little plant growing only 10cm (4in) high but it is easy, reliable, stands up well to autumn weather and as winter advances produces handsome leaf formations echoing the shape of ivy leaves from which its species name is derived. Plant a group alongside *C. coum* which will flower in the following months and together will provide many months of interest.

For milder climates, there is an autumn-flowering snowdrop called *Galanthus reginae-olgae*, which is very similar to the common snowdrop *G. nivalis* but flowers three months earlier. It comes from Sicily, Greece and south-west Turkey and is best planted in a dry spot where it will flourish and naturalize well. Milder winters are changing the boundaries of some of these borderline hardy plants and in recent years this snowdrop has established well at the National Trust Gardens at Anglesey Abbey in Cambridgeshire, UK.

Cyclamen hederifolium is a diminutive plant, but it will spread to become a wonderful carpet of colour, both when it flowers in mid- to late autumn and when it is in leaf throughout late autumn and winter.

The container garden

Many bulbs make excellent container plants and even in inexperienced hands there is a very good chance of great results as all the new bulbs have, at the time of purchase, the flower bud already formed within them like a wrapped parcel waiting to be opened. Plant daffodils, tulips and hyacinths in autumn and you will reap rewards in spring with a host of pretty flowers. Plant begonias, cannas and dahlias in early spring and you will have flowers all summer long.

Looking after the bulbs year after year is slightly more of a problem. With hardy hyacinths, daffodils and grape hyacinths the show will go on for many years, especially if you divide and replant on a three-year cycle. Tulips will rarely give such long-term rewards, although the smaller, later-flowering species are more reliable than the larger cultivars.

Meanwhile the summer bulbs will last for many years if they are correctly looked after through the winter period. Lilies need little extra attention, but exotic begonias, cannas and dahlias all require frost-free conditions either still planted in their containers or dried off and kept in cool, dry conditions indoors. Nerines, tulbaghia and *Pelargonium* 'Schottii' all need winter protection as well.

This shallow stone trough of spring bulbs includes *Narcissus* 'Hawera' and 'Bell Song', *Fritillaria meleagris* and several types of *Muscari*.

Mid- to late winter containers

The weather in mid- to late winter is often cold and inhospitable for both gardeners and plants, but if you choose carefully you will find several gems to bring welcome colour, even on the dullest days.

Galanthus (snowdrop), *Leucojum vernum* (spring snowflake), dwarf irises, *Eranthis hyemalis* (winter aconite), *Anemone blanda* and the early daffodils in containers will all flower at this time. Position them in a sheltered spot outside the house and enjoy them as you enter or leave. Or simply hang them in a basket close to a window so that you can admire and appreciate them from indoors.

If you want an instant container, buy two or three pots of *Cyclamen coum*, transfer them to a little wicker basket or shallow pot with a few trails of ivy and enjoy immediately.

Snowdrop bulbs and the lumpy tubers of winter aconites are sold as small, dry specimens in autumn, and it is a sad fact that, because they are over-dried and kept out of the ground for too long, only a small number will produce leaves and

flowers. Once established, however, they will flower and multiply well, massing up underground as well as by self-seeding. Instead of trying to have a container display from new bulbs and tubers bought in autumn, buy them as growing plants at flowering time in late winter, pot them on into a larger container and keep them in an out-of-the-way corner for the following year, by which time they should be nicely established. Alternatively, if you already know that you have some growing in the garden but would like to try them nearer the house in small pots, dig them up out of the ground in late autumn and plant them immediately into a well-drained, soil-based compost (soil mix). This advice also holds true for *Leucojum vernum* (spring snowflake). Treat them as single specimens in containers, and they will look simple but charming.

Mixed plantings

Instead of planting individual pots of bulbs, corms and tubers, try mixing them with winter-flowering

This winter-flowering hanging basket contains lots of different evergreen plants, including variegated ivies and *Euphorbia myrsinites*. The blooms of the winter-flowering heathers and *Viburnum tinus* add extra interest, but the highlight of the basket is the little *Iris* 'Pauline', which combines beautifully with all its bedfellows.

shrubs and herbaceous plants. Winter-flowering *Viburnum tinus* (laurustinus) makes an excellent centrepiece for a winter container or,

FROM THE BORDER TO A POT

1 *Eranthis hyemalis* (winter aconite) may be quite hard to find in border soil because at first they just look like lumps of earth. By late autumn the buds will be showing, and where tubers have grown on and matured they can be 3–4cm (1¼–1½in) across.

2 Prepare a small pot with some drainage material, such as pieces of polystyrene (styrofoam) or broken pots, and a potting compost (soil mix) and replant one large tuber 5cm (2in) below the surface. Cover with more soil and water well.

3 Place the pot outdoors on your windowsill or in a group with other winter-flowering specimens on a patio table where they will give welcome colour to the winter garden. After blooming, they can be replanted in the garden borders or in short grass.

POTTING UP SNOWDROPS

1 Dig up a clump of snowdrops from your garden, divide and return half to the border where it came from, first splitting it into two or three smaller clumps.

2 Divide the remaining half and plant in small containers in well-drained soil-based compost (soil mix). After the flowering season return them to a new part of the garden.

3 Snowdrops make a wonderful display on a windowsill where they will flower from mid- to late winter with no worries about frosty or snowy weather.

if it is a relatively small plant, for a hanging basket. It is hardy, evergreen and produces a mass of pink-tinged buds, which open to white flowers any time from late autumn through to spring. White, mauve or purple winter-flowering heathers can be planted around the sides so that when they come into bloom, just after midwinter, they will soften the edge of the basket and give extra colour. Choose large specimens with plenty of flower buds. Trailing ivies can also be planted around the edge. As they cascade over the sides, peg them into the moss to stop them spoiling in the winter wind. As they touch the moss, they will take root and within a season you will have a

With their intricate patterning and sweet scent, snowdrop flowers deserve close inspection. Enjoy the varied but distinctive green markings.

well-established ivy ball. Another excellent hardy foliage plant is the evergreen *Euphorbia myrsinites*, with its long, architectural, grey trail, which produce bright yellow flowers in early spring.

For the highlight of a winter container or hanging basket, plant some specimen bulbs, corms or tubers. You might dig up a clump of snowdrops or snowflakes from your own garden (never from the wild) or just a few winter aconites. However, if you want to start with new bulbs, try some dwarf irises. *Iris danfordiae*, with its golden-yellow flowers, shows up brilliantly, but there are lots of irises to choose from, including all the Reticulata irises, such as 'Harmony' and 'Joyce', both of which have sky-blue flowers with yellow on the falls, and 'Pauline', which is a marvellous dusky violet with flecks of white on the falls. They will flower from late winter to spring, doing best in a sunny position. Planted in a hanging basket, the flowers can be enjoyed at eye level, and at this height they can also be appreciated for their lovely sweet scent. Hang the basket in a sunny, sheltered spot, but in severe weather take it off its bracket and keep it in a porch or garage. Keep the soil moist but never water in

frosty conditions. To extend the season of interest, you might like to plant early dwarf tulips or daffodils to follow on in early spring.

Mid- to late winter bulbs for containers

Anemone blanda
Crocus chrysanthus
Crocus tommasinianus
Cyclamen coum
Eranthis hyemalis
Galanthus nivalis
Iris danfordiae
Iris 'Katharine Hodgkin'
Iris 'Pauline'
Leucojum vernum
Narcissus 'Rijnveld's Early Sensation' syn. *N.* 'January Gold'

Planting partners
Erica arborea 'Albert's Gold' (tree heather)
Erica carnea 'Springwood White' (winter-flowering heather)
Euonymus fortunei 'Emerald 'n' Gold'
Euonymus japonicus 'Albomarginatus'
Euphorbia myrsinites
Hedera (ivy)
Helleborus foetidus (stinking hellebore)
Helleborus niger (Christmas hellebore)
Primula vulgaris (primrose)
Viburnum tinus
Viola

Early spring containers

Nearly all the early spring bulbs are extremely easy to grow in confined conditions and, because many of them are dwarf by nature, they have the perfect proportions for growing in containers of all descriptions.

Growing bulbs in containers is a wonderful opportunity to show plants off as specimens in their own right. When they are grown in a pot or urn that is sited on a wall or on the patio table, the plants become features in their own right, to be admired and enjoyed. A simple pot of crocus can look stunning just on their own, basking in the sun with their petals opened and orange style exposed. A small pot of hyacinths can give untold pleasure, seen at close quarters, when the intricate nature of the bells can be admired and the sweet scent enjoyed.

Double-planting

Although the planting space in a small- to medium-sized pot may be limited, it is possible to double-plant

Instead of allowing crocuses to get spoiled in bad weather, when the flowers remain closed, keep them on a windowsill indoors.

Dwarf early multiheaded daffodils, such as *Narcissus* 'Tête-à-tête', are excellent in pots and hanging baskets.

the bulbs, thereby achieving a much greater impact at flowering time. It is, for example, possible to plant six bulbs of *Narcissus* 'February Gold' in a lower layer in a small glazed ceramic pot, 20cm (8in) across and 18cm (7in) deep, with, after the addition of a little more soil, six more on their shoulders. Crowded by garden standards, this is not important for container-grown bulbs, which will be grown in these

circumstances for only one season. White crocuses, planted in a smaller matching glazed pot, could be planted to flower at the same time, so that their yellow stamens would provide the perfect partnership for the golden-yellow daffodils.

After flowering, transfer the contents to the garden where they should be carefully separated and planted at three times the depth of the bulb.

DOUBLE-PLANTING BULBS

1 Double-planting in autumn helps to create impact in a relatively small pot. Add drainage material, such as pieces of polystyrene (styrofoam) or broken pots, and a small covering of well-draining compost (soil mix). Plant the lower layer of bulbs, close to each other, but not touching. In this case, the bulbs used are *Narcissus* 'February Gold'.

2 Add more soil so that just the noses of the bulbs show, and plant the second layer on the shoulders of the first. Again, they should be close but not touching. Cover with more soil, bringing the level to within 2.5cm (1in) of the rim of the pot.

3 Plant a smaller, similarly coloured pot with crocus bulbs. Add a layer of drainage material and soil before placing the bulbs close together, but not touching. Depending on the number of bulbs in the package, single- or double-plant them.

A small pot of blue grape hyacinth *Muscari armeniacum* 'Heavenly Blue' would look good with the pots of narcissi and crocuses.

Other schemes could include N. 'Jetfire', which is another of the cultivars of *N. cyclamineus* with its characteristic swept-back petals, although here the trumpet is golden orange. N. 'Jenny' has a similar form but with a creamy white flower. A small pot of blue grape hyacinth *Muscari armeniacum* would provide a fitting contrast to either of them, both in colour and form; so would a planting of *Scilla siberica*. Alternatively, try a simple collection of pastel violas or primroses, which

could be planted up either in the autumn or in early spring to make an instant arrangement.

Front to back

Another idea to maximize space is to plant the front of a pot with early spring-flowering bulbs and the back half with mid-spring bulbs. When the first show is over, turn the pot round and enjoy the next display.

Narcissus 'February Gold' flowers at the same time as the delicate *Crocus sieberi* 'Albus' (formerly known as 'Bowles' White') or any of the large white, purple or blue Dutch crocuses. The result is a glorious early spring association.

Early spring bulbs for containers

Anemone blanda
Chionodoxa
Crocus (large Dutch flowered)
Hyacinthus (hyacinth)
Narcissus cyclamineus cultivars (daffodil)
Narcissus 'Jumblie'
Narcissus 'Rip Van Winkle'
Narcissus 'Tête-à-tête'
Narcissus 'Topolino'
Muscari armeniacum (grape hyacinth)
Muscari botryoides 'Album'
Scilla siberica
Tulipa Kaufmanniana hybrids
Tulipa Double Early

Planting partners

Bellis perennis (double daisy)
Erica arborea 'Albert's Gold' (tree heather)
Erica carnea 'Springwood White' (winter-flowering heather)
Hedera (ivy)
Helleborus foetidus (stinking hellebore)
Helleborus niger (Christmas hellebore)
Euonymus fortunei 'Emerald 'n' Gold'
Euonymus japonicus 'Albomarginatus'
Euphorbia myrsinites
Primula vulgaris (primrose)
Saxifraga x urbium 'Variegata'
Sedum acre 'Aureum' (golden stonecrop)
Tanacetum parthenium 'Aureum' (golden feverfew)
Viburnum tinus
Viola

Narcissus 'Quince' associates well with blue *Anemone blanda* and the creamy variegations of the ivy leaves.

An excellent daffodil for inclusion in a hanging basket, *Narcissus* 'Quince' has a sturdy, short stem and a flowering height of only about 15cm (6in). It produces several flowers on each stem, and each one has delicate pale yellow petals and a miniature broad golden cup.

Multiheaded daffodils

Dwarf, multiheaded daffodils are an excellent choice if impact is needed but space is limited. *Narcissus* 'Tête-à-tête' is a justifiably popular daffodil, for one bulb will provide two or three, well-proportioned flowers on each stem, each with a golden head and cup to match. *N.* 'Jumblie' may be less well known, but it too will provide a mass of flowers. The cups are slightly longer and appear to look in all directions, hence its name. Another great favourite is the cultivar 'Quince', which has pale yellow petals and a broad golden cup. All three are short, sturdy growers, and these qualities make them excellent choices for early spring pots, window boxes and, especially, hanging baskets.

Plant the daffodils with *Anemone blanda*, in white or shades of blue or mixed colours, underplant them with large crocuses, such as *Crocus vernus* 'Remembrance', or with single tulips, such as the Kaufmanniana *Tulipa* 'Shakespeare'. Together these bulbs can create a beautiful early-spring picture. Violas, double *Bellis perennis* (daisies) and primroses, combined with winter-flowering heathers and ivies, will make pretty partners.

Evergreen trails of ivy can be used to clothe the outside of an early spring basket. Use a few wire staples to peg the ivy into the moss sides and encourage it to make a complete ball of greenery to form the basis of the spring bulb display. This has an added advantage of preventing the ivy from being tossed about in cold winter winds, which will damage the tip ends. Plant the basket in autumn, choosing one with a diameter of 35cm (14in). Use three ivies and a mixture of 15 dwarf multiheaded daffodils, such as dainty *Narcissus* 'Quince', and 15 pretty blue *Anemone blanda*.

Maintaining hanging baskets

All hanging baskets that are outside in late winter to early spring should be hung in a sunny, sheltered position. Check that the soil is kept moist, especially in autumn and spring, but never water in frosty conditions. Although all the plants are hardy, play safe and, when severe weather is forecast, take the basket off the bracket and keep it in a less exposed position on the ground or in a porch or garage for a day or two, until milder conditions return.

Double Early tulips

As the days lengthen the Double Early tulips begin to flower. They have wide heads, full of vibrantly coloured petals. Short and sturdy, these tulips make good subjects for a container standing on the ground as well as for a hanging basket. They can be purchased as single colours, including red, orange, yellow, white and pink, or in mixed bags or boxes. *Tulipa* 'Peach Blossom' is one of the prettiest, with flowers that start as a pale pastel pink, sometimes revealing streaks of green or red. It always makes a winning combination when it is grown with blue *Muscari* (grape hyacinth), but any blue violas and pansies would look equally attractive.

These hybrids of *Narcissus cyclamineus*, with their swept-back petals, look beautiful with an underplanting of crocuses. Here, the fiery orange cups of *N.* 'Jetfire' bend as if to caress the bright orange stamens of *Crocus tommasinianus* 'Ruby Giant'.

Chionodoxa forbesii 'Pink Giant' has been planted with Double Early *Tulipa* 'Peach Blossom'. The blue *Muscari armeniacum* (grape hyacinth) in the background is yet to come into its full glory.

For an eye-catching hanging basket plant a mixture of Double Early tulips with grape hyacinths, surrounded by a frill of bedding plants, such as violas and pansies. The bedding plants will provide a certain amount of colour, even in autumn, but by the time the bulbs flower in early spring they will be in full array, providing a lively and colourful background. Give this basket a sunny, sheltered position. The more sheltered the position, the better the bedding plants will thrive.

Hyacinths

By now hyacinths are in flower, too. Many beautiful shades — pink, blue, amethyst, yellow and white — are available, and all the colours seem to have their equivalent or contrast in primroses, with which they associate so well. Strong on impact and perfume, hyacinths also associate beautifully with other bulbs, such as the rich blues of *Scilla sibirica* and *Muscari armeniacum* (grape hyacinth),

as well as all the Double Early tulips. A lovely combination would be white hyacinths such as *Hyacinthus orientalis* 'L'Innocence' or 'Ben Nevis' with dwarf yellow Double Early *Tulipa* 'Monte Carlo' and small white *Muscari botryoides* 'Album'. Creamy violas or primroses alongside *Tanacetum parthenium* 'Aureum' (golden feverfew) would make wonderful bedfellows underlining the fresh white, cream and yellow theme. There are so many beautiful associations possible with these groupings. Imagine salmon pink *Hyacinthus orientalis* 'Gypsy Queen' with orange Double Early *Tulipa* 'Nassau' planted in a trough with a carpet of rich blue *Muscari armeniacum* 'Heavenly Blue'. The addition of two-toned blue and violet violas or primroses would provide a strong contrast — the possibilities are endless. This is one of the joys of container gardening and bulbs provide one of the most important contributions for they are so varied in colour and form.

Mid-spring containers

Many of the short daffodils can be used in mid-spring containers. Although they are not all as dwarf as those that flower in early spring, there are several that are suitable for growing in hanging baskets, window boxes and tubs.

Some of the short daffodils are multiheaded and are valued by gardeners for providing a beautiful display where planting space is at a premium. *Narcissus* 'Hawera' is one of the most delicate of all, and the tiny, lemon-yellow flowers seem to last and last. Although there may be three or five flowers per stem, it is dainty in appearance, and its wiry, sturdy stem will withstand strong winds. This lovely little daffodil, which grows only 25cm (10in) high, is excellent in hanging baskets, window boxes and small pots.

The cultivar *Narcissus* 'Segovia' is another winner with its pure white petals and creamy little centre. It, too, grows only 25cm (10in) high. It should be used more, extending

the season and offering a purity of flower that is to be treasured.

Daffodils such as the glistening white *Narcissus* 'Thalia', white 'Silver Chimes' and the fresh-faced, white-streaked, lemon-yellow 'Pipit' are, perhaps, rather too tall for a hanging basket, but they are perfect for pots, window boxes or troughs. They would look charming with heathers, such as *Erica carnea* 'Springwood White' or *E. arborea* 'Albert's Gold', and winter-flowering pansies.

Mid-season tulips

There are so many mid-season tulips that it is hard to know where to begin. Most of them grow to 35–50cm (14–20in) in height and are best suited to medium-sized or large containers. All the Apeldoorn varieties, for example, with their mainly yellow, orange and scarlet blooms, are excellent, being strong in growth, reliable and long lasting. The Fosteriana tulips, such as *Tulipa* 'Orange Emperor', 'Yellow Emperor' and 'Red Emperor', are also firm

Narcissus 'Segovia' always looks fresh with its glistening white petals. Here it is planted in a hanging basket with *Tulipa saxatilis* Bakeri Group 'Lilac Wonder' and *Viburnum tinus*.

Both teacup and teapot are planted with *Narcissus* 'Hawera', which is a neat little daffodil with a multitude of dainty lemon-yellow flowers.

1 Cover the base of the pot with a 5cm (2in) layer of drainage material, such as broken pieces of polystyrene (styrofoam) or old pots. Half-fill the pot with a soil-based compost (soil mix) containing lots of grit.

2 If preferred, use a peat-based compost (soil mix) with a layer of grit mixed thoroughly in the bottom half. The advantage is that the pot will be slightly easier to move planted in this way.

The Single Early *Tulipa* 'Christmas Marvel' looks cheerful in its blue pot with the silver-grey foliage of *Senecio cineraria* 'Silver Dust'. It is perfect in a container in its own right or used as an extra in the herbaceous border to add height and focus to the forget-me-nots.

3 Plant ten tulip bulbs in two circles, spacing them so that they are not touching each other or the sides of the pot.

4 Bring the compost level to within 2.5cm (1in) of the top of the pot. Plant four blue winter-flowering pansies.

favourites. They do not grow quite as tall as the Apeldoorn group, but they are still suitable for medium to large pots. Pansies, which are available in a vast range of rich tones, including deep blue, golden yellow, yellow and red or purple, will make an excellent carpet beneath the strongly coloured blooms. The ever-reliable *Tanacetum parthenium* 'Aureum' (golden feverfew), polyanthus or *Erysimum cheiri* (wallflower) will also make good planting partners.

If pink is your preferred colour, consider the pretty *Tulipa* 'Gordon Cooper' or cherry-pink 'Christmas Marvel'. For a more subtle effect, try 'Ester', which looks charming in association with delightful *Dicentra spectabilis* in a large container or in separate pots. Another excellent choice would be the glorious, double, pink 'Angélique', which is very long

lasting in flower, spanning the season into late spring. The soft blues and whites of violas, pansies and polyanthus as well as pale blue *Myosotis* (forget-me-not) will make ideal companions for these tulips. If you can find pansies with distinctive markings, they will add extra interest to the scheme. The silver foliage of *Senecio cineraria* 'Silver Dust' will make an attractive partner. A pair of carefully co-ordinated pots, arranged symmetrically, could be especially striking, or place a planted pot in the middle of a border where dahlias or cannas might be planted later.

5 The result is a spring triumph of glorious soft pink tulips and winter-flowering pansies in shades of blue.

Late spring to early summer containers

With a little careful planning, late-flowering tulips can look sensational in large pots underplanted with forget-me-nots or pansies.

Any of the Parrot tulips are excellent treated in this way. Look out for *Tulipa* 'Apricot Parrot', which could be combined with mahogany-brown pansies, or *T.* 'Black Parrot', which could be planted with white or black pansies. *T.* 'Fantasy' looks charming with a true blue pansy. The two dark, late-flowering tulips, 'Queen of Night' and 'Black Hero' always look attractive with forget-me-nots, whether blue, pink or white.

Tulips and wallflowers

Late tulips can also look excellent with old-fashioned red, yellow, orange, purple, rose-pink or white *Erysimum cheiri* (wallflower). Some brilliant colour schemes can be devised, with both bright, eye-

Orange-coloured varieties of wallflower are among the most strongly scented. By late spring they are joined by the *Tulipa* 'Blue Heron' – tall, strong and beautifully shaped, with fringed petals.

catching plants and gentler, more subtle shades. The Fringed tulip 'Blue Heron', which has lilac-coloured petals, creates a strong contrast, for example, with rich

orange wallflowers, whose scent is welcome on a warm sunny evening. A more restful colour scheme could be achieved by substituting a pale primrose-coloured wallflower or even a rose-pink or purple form.

Wallflowers are usually treated as biennials – that is, they are sown in late spring one year and the flowers are seen the next. They are normally sold in autumn, either as growing plants in bedding boxes or in bunches of eight or ten with just a little soil attached to their bare roots. They should be thoroughly watered and planted as soon as possible in a sunny position, where they will start to flower the following spring. Once they begin to flower the show will continue for many weeks, contributing an informal, cottage-garden style to your pots and containers.

For a combination of tulips and wallflowers, prepare the container in the usual way, using drainage material and a soil-based potting compost (soil mix). Plant ten tulip bulbs so that their eventual depth

Tulipa 'Fantasy' is one of the delightful Parrot tulip group. Here it has been simply underplanted with the blue pansy, *Viola* x *wittrockiana* 'True Blue'.

Late spring to early summer bulbs for containers

Allium neopolitanum
Allium oreophilum
Allium schoenoprasum (chives)
Allium unifolium
Anemone coronaria De Caen and St Bridgid Groups
Narcissus poeticus var. *recurvus*
Scilla peruviana
Tulipa batalinii 'Bright Gem'
Fringed Tulips
Parrot Tulips
Viridiflora Tulips

Planting partners
Bellis perennis (double daisy)
Erysimum cheiri (wallflowers) with the taller tulips
Heuchera with the taller tulips.
Myosotis (forget-me-not)
Pansy
Polyanthus
Saxifraga x *urbium* 'Variegata' (variegated London pride)
Sedum acre 'Aureum' with the alliums
Tanacetum parthenium 'Aureum' (golden feverfew)
Viola

below soil level is about three times their own height, allowing for a 5cm (2in) gap at the top of the container. Plant seven or eight wallflowers in a wide circle, choosing those plants with the best root systems – discard the rest. Firm in the plants and water well. Place the container in a sunny, sheltered position.

Plantings of anemones

Anemone coronaria cultivars, with colours ranging from brilliant red to rich blue and pure white, also make excellent container displays, and they can be used to produce many different effects. *A. coronaria* De Caen Group 'Mr Fokker' has attractive blue petals, and 'Die Braut' ('The Bride') has pure white flowers. *A. coronaria* St Bridgid Group 'Lord Lieutenant' has deep blue, double flowers. The fern-like foliage of these anemones is attractive in its own right. Judicious planting at intervals in spring and early summer will give a succession of blooms, while planting two or three pots at the same time will give a sumptuous display. The knobbly tubers are best

Some anemones are blue, including the multi-petalled *Anemone coronaria* St Bridgid Group 'Lord Lieutenant'.

rehydrated by being soaked overnight before planting. Plant so that the buds point upwards and at a depth of about 7.5cm (3in) and 7.5cm (3in) apart, and allow at least three months between planting and early-summer flowering.

An earlier planting in late winter will take longer to produce blooms. Allow the tubers to dry off completely after the lifecycle is complete, ready for flowering again the following year.

A DISPLAY OF ANEMONES

1 The knobbly hard tubers of *Anemone coronaria* benefit from being soaked overnight in a tumbler of water to plump them up before planting.

2 Where possible, plant the anemone tubers with their protruding knobs pointing upwards (this is not apparent on all of them), 7.5cm (3in) deep and about 7.5cm (3in) apart.

3 Enjoy the brilliant colour of *Anemone coronaria* St Bridgid Group 'The Governor'. Succesive plantings of tubers will provide colour for weeks on end.

Planted as a single specimen, *Scilla peruviana* makes a wonderful container plant with its glorious flowers. Its leaves may be untidy at this stage, but the intense blue colouring makes up for this.

Long-term arrangements

Scilla peruviana is a glorious bulb to grow in a raised container where its brilliant blue flowers can be isolated and enjoyed to the full. It is only borderline hardy so it needs a cool winter refuge away from frost, but if you can manage to protect it, you will be rewarded year after year by a show-stopping display, which will be perfect for a sunny spot on a patio table or besides the door. Linnaeus was misled, because the bulb did not originate in Peru, as the specific name suggests, but from Portugal, Spain, Italy and North Africa. It is almost evergreen, with new basal leaves developing in autumn as the old ones fade. In late spring the leaves are quite large and strappy, but then the large bud begins to open and by early summer the gorgeous conical heads of up to a hundred starry flowers are revealed. You might have only one flower or be lucky and have two as the bulb matures in years to come. There is a white form, *S. peruviana* f. alba, but unless you are planning an all-white scheme, the blue is hard to beat.

Although it is shallow, a raised sink or trough can be planted as a long-term arrangement with a succession of interest and colour. Fortunately, many miniature bulbs are suitable for this purpose. Late-flowering species tulips will bridge the gap between mid- and late

In sun or partial shade *Hyacinthoides hispanica* (Spanish bluebell) will create a splash of colour, but do not grow them where they could cross-pollinate with *H. non-scripta* (English bluebell).

Tulipa tarda, with its starry white and yellow flowers, is a good companion for *T. urumiensis*, which has yellow flowers with bronze-green undersides. Both are multiheaded and are excellent in a trough or hanging basket.

The seedheads of *Allium unifolium* provide extra interest even after flowering, especially when they are seen at close quarters in a raised sink or trough. Like many alliums, it will self-seed readily.

In a raised trough the distinctive white flowers of *Allium neopolitanum* Cowanii Group (syn. *A. cowanii*) can be enjoyed at waist level.

Planted in a raised trough edged with golden marjoram and strawberries, the dainty flowers of *Saxifraga* x *urbium* (London pride) provide a pretty foil for the bright pink flowers of *Allium schoenoprasum* (chives).

spring, to follow on from the miniature daffodils, *Fritillaria meleagris* (snake's head fritillary) and *Muscari* spp. (grape hyacinth), which have already flowered. Any daffodil seedheads should be removed, but those of the fritillaries and grape hyacinths can look attractive as they mature and finally show off the seeds. With luck, they will self-seed and the display will multiply.

Later-flowering varieties

For later flowering include dainty yellow and white *Tulipa tarda*, which is native to Central Asia, or bronze-green and yellow *T. urumiensis*, which is native to north-eastern Iran. Both tulips look attractive in bud as well as in flower, and because they are multiheaded you will have a pretty display from even one or two bulbs planted in the middle of the trough or around the sides.

For a further succession include some little alliums. *Allium neopolitanum* Cowanii Group (syn. *A. cowanii*), which originated in southern Europe and North Africa bears loose umbels of pure white flowers on slim stems about 30cm (12in) high. Just a little shorter, *A. unifolium* has papery, clear pink flowers, and shorter still, at only 15cm (6in), *A. oreophilum* (syn. *A. ostrowskianum*) bears a profusion of

dainty carmine pink flowers. Meanwhile, *A. schoenoprasum* makes another easy and attractive option. Commonly known as chives, it is native to a wide area in Europe, Asia and North America, and both its leaves and flowerheads can be used in cooking. It is worth noting that planted in the restricted soil of a

container the foliage will not be as prolific as in border soil, but there will still be plenty of both flowers and leaves for the kitchen. A white-flowered form is also available. Like the earlier bulbs, the allium flowers look beautiful when they are seen raised up in the trough, and they all have attractive seedheads.

Mid- to late summer containers

Many hardy summer-flowering bulbs make excellent container plants and they will perform well year after year. *Zantedeschia* (arum lily), agapanthus, lilies and triteleia can all be grown in containers and are best planted in a gritty, soil-based compost (soil mix).

Container-grown lilies

Lilies can remain in the same container for many years if they are potted on into new compost every

Lilium 'Sweet Kiss' is a double lily, which is sterile. Because it produces no pollen it is the perfect choice for gardeners who suffer from pollen allergies.

two or three years; repot in autumn. *Lilium regale* (regal lily) does really well in containers, as do some of the Asiatic hybrids, such as 'Enchantment'. The Oriental lily hybrids, which are derived from *L. speciosum* and *L. auratum* (golden-rayed lily), are later flowering and make brilliant pot plants too. 'Star Gazer', which has deep red petals, is especially suitable for a container. The double-flowered 'Kiss' lilies are suitable for gardeners who are allergic to pollen. Their flowers are not as elegant as the singles, but they are prolific in bloom and great naturalizers, so they will create a great massed effect in a large container.

Plant three lily bulbs together to create a good display and, for extra colour and contrast, underplant with gorgeous blue triteleias. These look particularly attractive with yellow lilies. Choose a larger pot for medium to tall lilies, at least 30cm (12in) deep, and use a well-drained growing medium. Some lilies require acid soil, and for this group, which includes 'Star Gazer' and the other Oriental hybrids, use a ericaceous compost (soil mix) and extra grit (two-thirds compost, one-third horticultural grit).

Lilium 'Star Gazer' has deep red, white-edged flowers, and although they are not fragrant, this is one of the most popular lilies, flowering in midsummer.

Many lilies tolerate a wide range of conditions, including alkaline soils. This group includes the species *L. henryi*, *L. martagon* and *L. regale*, the Asiatic hybrids and the 'Kiss' hybrids. For these, use a soil-based compost and add a handful of extra grit beneath the bulb itself.

All lilies will respond to a low-nitrogen but high-phosphate and high-potash feed, applied for six to eight weeks from the first opening of buds. Deadhead and allow the leaves to die back before removing

A DISPLAY OF LILIES

1 *Lilium* 'Sweet Kiss' is of medium height and is ideal for containers where it needs no support. It multiplies well to form clumps in just a few years. Tidy stems in autumn.

2 Several small bulbs will form on top of the soil. Remove these carefully so as not to disturb the roots and carefully separate the little bulbs.

3 Transplant the bulblets to a small pot, so that you can move them on later to another container or plant them out to enjoy them elsewhere in the garden.

A WICKER BASKET WITH *HIPPEASTRUM*

1 In spring plant three *Hippeastrum* 'Yellow Goddess' in a wicker basket, with just their necks showing above the soil-based compost.

2 Plant three young *Sutera cordata* 'Snowflake' (syn. *Bacopa* 'Snowflake') plants around the edge of the basket.

3 The hippeastrum flowers are creamy yellow with striking lime green throats. There may be four to a stem, opening in succession and prolonging the display.

the stem. Lilies are hardy but need extra protection in severe winters when they are grown in containers. Move the pots into a sheltered spot and wrap them in bubble wrap if necessary to protect the rootball. Do not entirely cover the pot or condensation may lead to rot.

If arum lilies are grown in water, use an aquatic soil and an aquatic planting basket, with perforations around the outside and plenty of gravel on top.

Ornithogalum dubium

Available in white or orange form, *Ornithogalum dubium* can be planted in autumn and kept in frost-free conditions over winter, in which case

it will flower in midsummer, or it can be purchased and planted in mid- to late spring to flower in late summer. Whichever approach you prefer, this bulb makes a long-flowering specimen for a small to medium-sized pot, and despite the rather untidy leaves it makes a valuable contribution to the patio.

Hippeastrum

Like the bulbs of *Ornithogalum dubium*, those of *Hippeastrum* may also be available until late spring, when they, too, can be planted to flower in midsummer. Buy firm bulbs and plant them as soon as possible in soil-based compost. These plants (often, but wrongly, known as

amaryllis) are familiar flowers for indoor containers in midwinter, but their natural flowering time is closer to spring than midwinter, and by planting late the flowering can be delayed so that they can be grown outdoors in wicker baskets, window boxes or pots. Plant them with summer bedding plants, grasses or exotics, overwinter in frost-free conditions while they are dormant and enjoy for years to come.

A POT OF *ORNITHOGALUM DUBIUM*

1 *Ornithogalum dubium* bulbs are suitable for a small to medium container. Choose firm plump bulbs and if any are soft simply discard them.

2 Don't forget to put a layer of drainage material in the base of the pot. Add gritty, soil-based compost and plant four or five bulbs in each pot.

3 Place the pot in a sunny position where a succession of flowers will provide many weeks of colour. Allow to dry off after flowering and keep frost-free until the following spring.

Triteleia laxa 'Koningin Fabiola' is a useful summer-flowering corm to add in autumn to a spring-flowering bulb display with daffodils, for example. The narrow, grass-like leaves appear before the blue blooms. Here *Helleborus foetidus* will act as an excellent anchor plant, not only to show off the daffodils, but also the dainty blue *Triteleia* flowers. *Triteleia* also make a delightful display under dwarf yellow lilies. Both partnerships can remain in the container for several years.

Begonias

Tuberous begonias are probably the most colourful and versatile of all summer container plants, and they are ideal for pots, hanging baskets, wall-pots and window boxes. Although they are usually available as growing plants in early summer, you will have a much wider choice of colour if you select tubers in late winter, and plant them in late winter or early spring so that they are ready to plant out after the frosts have finished in early summer. Look out for *Begonia* 'Picotee', which makes a magnificent plant that looks beautiful in a hanging basket. Also in this group are *Begonia* 'Picotee Lace Pink' and 'Picotee Lace Red', both of which have flowers with distinctive white ruffled edges. The cultivar 'Picotee Lace Apricot' makes a memorable partnership as an

A BEGONIA HANGING BASKET

1 Line the basket with moss and plastic sheeting. Cut slits for drainage. Add potting compost (soil mix), mixed with water-retaining crystals and a long-term pelleted feed.

2 Plant the upright begonia in the centre of the basket.

3 Plant the trailing begonias and yellow *Bidens* around the edge. Top up with compost. Choose a sheltered site in sun or partial shade.

4 Water every other day, or every day in hot weather, taking care not to splash the leaves if the sun is shining, otherwise they scorch.

5 The hanging basket is splendid in its summer glory. Easy to look after and very colourful, all the tubers can be saved for next year with or without the need for a greenhouse.

Begonia 'Picotee Lace Apricot' has ruffled, rich apricot flowers dusted with white. It makes an excellent underplanting to orange Fuchsia 'Thalia'.

underplanting to orange or salmon fuchsias, such as *Fuchsia* 'Thalia'.

If you decide to save the tubers for the next year, before the first frost of autumn lift the plant and move it into a frost-free place. Gradually withhold water and allow the foliage to die down. After two or three weeks, remove the tubers and store them in a dry, cool place until the following spring, when they can be brought into growth once more. Alternatively, if you have a greenhouse, move the entire container under cover. As the compost dries out and the stems die off, the tubers can remain in the compost with no further disturbance

necessary. This is ideal for hanging baskets or for arrangements in which begonias are planted with fuchsias. They will break into growth in the spring when watering begins again.

Begonia tubers are especially susceptible to being eaten by vine weevil larvae in early autumn. To avoid this, use a natural predator, such as beneficial nematodes, or a systemic insecticide, called imidacloprid, which stops the grubs maturing. Nematodes have to be watered into warm compost, and spring and late summer are ideal times for carrying out the treatment. Such action will ensure flowers the following year.

Begonia 'Giant Flowered Pendula Yellow' is an excellent choice for a summer hanging basket. It flowers from midsummer to early autumn and has 20cm (8in) long trails.

Early to mid-autumn containers

As late summer turns to autumn the begonias will still be at their best, with all their glorious reds, oranges and yellows creating an explosion of fiery colours. By now the cannas, too, will be in full flower, revealing a mixture of orange, yellow, red and salmon, but their large, paddle-shaped leaves can be as exciting as the flowers, showing vivid combinations of glowing green and gold or brilliant bronze and pink. To capitalize on the drama, position the pots in a sunny position where they will be backlit by the sun.

Container-grown cannas

Canna rhizomes can be purchased in garden centres in late winter and planted into a smaller pot for starting into growth in spring. They can be potted on in early summer into their permanent summer containers. Coleus and dark blue

Canna 'Tropicanna' (syn. *C.* 'Phaison', *C.* 'Durban') has striking deep bronze-purple leaves, which are veined with pink, making this an exciting foliage plant for a container.

The flowers of *Canna* 'Tropicanna' are a bonus to the drama of the leaves, which they fully complement. They are a warm orange, and open in succession.

Trailing yellow and orange begonias flourish throughout the summer and early autumn in a shady spot. Exotic *Begonia* 'Marginata Crispa' enhances the picture with its yellow and red-edged flowers together with nasturtiums and *Fuchsia* 'Thalia'.

Early to mid-autumn bulbs for containers

Agapanthus
Begonia
Canna
Cyclamen 'Miracle Series'
Cyclamen 'Silverado'
Dahlia (especially short patio
  varieties)
Eucomis bicolor
Eucomis comosa 'Sparkling Burgundy'
Nerine bowdenii 'Blush Beauty'
Nerine bowdenii 'Mark Fenwick'
Nerine bowdenii 'Pink Triumph'
Pelargonium 'Schottii'
Tulbaghia

Planting partners

By now the bulbs etc. are fully grown, with little extra room for secondary partnerships, though *Coleus* associates well with begonias and *Canna* 'Tropicanna' while *Fuchsia* 'Thalia' will still look wonderful with orange and apricot begonias lobelia make good plant associations depending on whether you like single or mixed planting schemes.

By midsummer cannas will need daily watering when the weather is hot. Deadheading will encourage further flowering. The plants grow rapidly, so be prepared to divide the rhizomes the following spring or pot them on into a bigger container. This task will be easier if your pot is flared or has straight sides; because canna rhizomes can grow so large, avoid containers with narrow necks, which are difficult to empty and replant. Move the pots into a heated greenhouse as soon as frost threatens and leave them there until early summer temperatures are safe for them to be moved outside once more. The longer they grow on under cover of glass in late spring to early summer, the sooner they will come into flower.

Canna 'Striata' has large green leaves which are veined with gold, creating an eye-catching combination. The flower spikes have plum-coloured stems, and the flowers themselves are orange.

Early autumn containers can be filled with cannas, begonias and eucomis as well as fuchsias, aeoniums and felicias. Soon they will all have to be moved into a frost-free place, but for now they make a major contribution to the garden.

Canna 'Rosemond Coles' has large green leaves and vibrant red flowers edged with yellow. It makes an impressive container plant.

Pelargoniums

There are a few *Pelargonium* species that have tuberous roots and that may die back completely in winter, coming into life again in the warmer spring weather. *Pelargonium* 'Schottii' (syn. *P. x schottii*) is one of the most beautiful, and although it is tuberous, it remains evergreen throughout the winter. Its foliage is softly hairy, giving it a grey-green appearance that complements the simple wine-coloured flowers, with their dark purple stripes, which are borne from midsummer through to mid-autumn. Treat it as a specimen plant, alone in an attractive container. A porch or veranda would be an ideal situation. The foliage and flowers tend to create a dome shape, with blooms semi-prostrate rather than upright. Move the container indoors before the first frost and keep it on a sunny windowsill where you can continue to enjoy the blooms for a while at least.

The tuberous-rooted *Pelargonium* 'Schottii' has velvety grey-green foliage and attractive wine-coloured petals with dark purple stripes.

Eucomis

Bulbs of eucomis are generally available in late winter and should be planted in a soil-based compost (soil mix) immediately on purchase or in early spring if they can be stored in dry, frost-free conditions. They look good as single specimen plants but also look wonderful in groups of three, five or seven or even more if you have a large enough container. They produce long, strap-like leaves, which are sometimes wavy at the edges. From the centre of the leaves emerges a tall flower spike, covered with starry flowers all the way to the top, and this is crowned by a group of leafy bracts, which is why the plant is commonly called pineapple lily. It is an easy bulb to grow in a container, providing weeks of interest from the attractive leaves, then the flowers and, finally, the fleshy seedheads. Cut and brought inside these will continue to give pleasure through the winter. A drawback is that the flowers have quite a strong foetid smell, but this is only discernible close to. Once they have gone to seed, there is no smell.

Eucomis are borderline hardy, and in cold climates they will need the protection of a frost-free area through the winter months. Move

AN ARRANGEMENT OF EUCOMIS

1 Appearing in late summer and autumn, the tall stem of *Eucomis bicolor* bears racemes of pale green flowers with purple margins, topped with a crown of pineapple-type bracts. The stems are flecked with maroon, and the lower leaves are attractively wavy.

2 In early to mid-autumn, cut off the old flower stems of eucomis that have now been pollinated. The seedpods at the top will be fat, green and fleshy, while those at the bottom of the spike will be ripe, with shiny, round seeds visible inside.

3 Place the flowered stems in water and use them as an indoor arrangement. Once the water has been absorbed, enjoy the seedheads as a dry arrangement. Any seeds can be potted up and will produce flowering bulbs in just two or three seasons.

the pots into the shelter of a potting shed or greenhouse before or immediately after the first frost. Here they can remain dry until growth begins in the spring, when watering should begin again. Give only a little water at first, then more regularly as the leaves begin to grow. The large leaves lose water through transpiration, so when they are in full growth these are thirsty plants. Their native habitat is near streams in southern Africa, and as well as moisture-retentive soil, they prefer a position in partial shade.

There are many types of eucomis to choose from. *Eucomis bicolor* has green flowers edged with maroon or purple and blotches of a similar colour on the stem. *E. bicolor* 'Alba' has greenish-white flowers. *E. comosa* exhibits a wider variation in its colouring; it has a purple-spotted flower stem but the flowers are pinkish-purple and the leaves may be striated with purple, varying to intense deep purple. It does not have such a distinctive set of bracts at the top of its flower spike.

Nerines

For outdoor containers nerines are a good choice or, if you choose the less hardy cultivars or the late-

For an outdoor container, try *Nerine undulata* or choose one of the cultivars of *Nerine bowdenii* that flowers in early or mid-autumn.

flowering forms, they may be grown in a conservatory. For an outdoor container try *Nerine bowdenii* or any of its cultivars that flower in early or mid-autumn before the first frosts. In a container, even these nerines will be only borderline hardy and will need the shelter of a greenhouse in winter.

Winter protection

As autumn nights get colder, the summer exotics will be at risk from frost, so all the containers in which you have been growing begonias, cannas, dahlias, eucomis, tulbaghias and nerines will need to be moved to a greenhouse. Of these, the begonias will be most at risk, so act as soon as frost is likely. The first frost may blacken or damage the foliage of dahlias and cannas, but it will rarely damage their tubers and rhizomes, so they can remain outside for a little longer while there is still a chance to enjoy the last flowers.

The greenhouse will provide protection for all these plants from warmer climates, which cannot cope with freezing winter temperatures.

Move pots of tulbaghias into the greenhouse, together with cannas, begonias and eucomis, as soon as autumn frosts are forecast.

During periods of severe frost provide warmth in the greenhouse with a thermostatically controlled electric heater or a paraffin heater.

Late autumn to early winter containers

The weeks of late autumn to early winter are not the easiest for showy bulb containers, especially after the wealth of colour that has been seen in the garden in early autumn. However, there is a vast choice of bulbs that can be planted for late winter and spring flowering, with a wide choice of accompanying foliage to provide interest throughout the whole autumn and early winter.

Many bulbs are available for planting in autumn, including small crocuses, irises, grape hyacinths, chionodoxas and scillas. The rewards will come a few months later, with both bulbs and bedding plants in full flower.

Cyclamen Miracle Series

In recent years breeding programmes have been undertaken with *Cyclamen persicum*, which is best known for its use as a winter indoor plant, to produce a miniature cyclamen that will flower throughout autumn and early winter and will be hardy enough to withstand just light frosts. The result is the aptly named Miracle Series, which can be planted out in borders as well as used to great effect in containers. The flower colour varies from white, to white with a carmine pink mouth, wine red,

A POT OF *IRIS RETICULA* WITH A VIOLA

1 Choose a small pot and place some drainage in the base, top up with 5cm (2in) of soil-based compost (soil mix) and plant bulbs of *Iris reticulata* 'Katherine Hodgkin' with their noses pointing upwards.

2 Cover the bulbs with a little more soil and, for extra interest, add a viola, which will also remind you when the pot needs watering. *Viola* 'Hobbit Pippin Took' is a perfect colour match for this *Iris reticulata*.

rose, purple, salmon and scarlet. They are sweetly scented plants, but the best fragrance seems to emanate from the white forms. The leaves have different amounts of silvery mottling, but most, if not all, exhibit some degree of veining. The combination of flowers and foliage makes this little plant a winner. It lends itself to many lovely planting arrangements, being suitable for

wall-pots, window boxes, troughs and hanging baskets. A more recent introduction, *Cyclamen* 'Silverado' is slightly taller, at 20cm (8in), and makes a greater mound of foliage.

Weather protection

On frosty nights in late autumn the leaves of both *Cyclamen* Miracle Series and 'Silverado' will go limp, but by midday, as the temperature

Late autumn to early winter bulbs for containers

Cyclamen Miracle Series
Cyclamen 'Silverado'

Planting partners
Ajuga reptans 'Burgundy Glow'
Euphorbia myrsinites
Hedera (ivy)
Senecio cineraria 'Silver Dust'
Skimmia japonica
Stipa tenuissima

Miniature cyclamen are excellent subjects for a container or hanging basket display along with ivies and other foliage plants.

Viburnum tinus, winter-flowering heather and grasses provide year-round foliage interest while the bulbs are not in flower.

rises, the leaves should revive and show no ill-effects. Cyclamen planted in containers on an outdoor windowsill will be slightly protected by the building, but those in a hanging basket will be more exposed, and if prolonged periods of frost are forecast it may be safer to cover the plants with newspaper or move the basket to a cool, sheltered place, such as an outbuilding, garage, porch or even indoors. They will often survive the entire winter outdoors, but there is always an element of risk for plants in exposed containers, especially hanging baskets, where the rootball does not have the same protection as plants growing in deep garden soil.

Freezing temperatures present one type of problem. Another difficulty is posed by wet conditions. These cyclamen do not relish heavy rainfall, and the tell-tale sign that something is amiss will be pink blotches on the flowers where botrytis has become established. Extreme wet will also affect the tubers, causing rot. The shelter afforded by the house or even by a nearby tree may be sufficient

Some cyclamen have particularly attractive leaves. The silver markings on his plant look striking besides the lacy, almost white, leaves of *Senecio cineraria* 'Silver Dust'. It is ideal for a sheltered veranda or porch.

Euphorbia myrsinites makes an architectural partner for this little pink cyclamen, which shares its grey-green foliage. This pot has an underplanting of *Fritillaria michailovskyi*, which will flower in spring.

protection, but the more these plants are protected from frost and rain, the longer they will last.

Planting partners

Despite the potential problems, these small cyclamen have a great deal to offer early-winter containers.

Plants in the *Cyclamen* Miracle Series have richly coloured flowers, including pink, purple and red as well as white.

They mix well with a host of other foliage and flowering plants and make excellent companions for ivies, particularly those with silver variegations. Another perfect partner is *Euphorbia myrsinites* with all its strange spirals, or, for a softer look, *Senecio cineraria* 'Silver Dust' with its silver intricacy. For an altogether different type of arrangement, plant *Ajuga reptans* 'Burgundy Glow' with its glossy, dark red leaves. Even the wispy leaves of *Stipa tenuissima* and the bronze buds of *Skimmia japonica* 'Bronze Knight' make handsome companions. Plant scarlet red cylamen with a selection or all of these and you will have a container full of interest for months on end.

Apart from the cyclamen, all the other plants mentioned here are fully hardy, so you can simply replace the cyclamen in late winter with pot-grown daffodils, such as *Narcissus* 'Tête-à-tête' or 'Hawera'. They will give your container an instant spring face-lift and it will still look charming.

The indoor bulb garden

The range of bulbs available for growing indoors is extensive, with the opportunity to develop flower displays that are widely spread throughout the year.

Colour in the cooler months is achieved by maintaining frost-free conditions and providing gentle heat for a wonderful range of miniature and fringed cyclamens, as well as gorgeous *Hippeastrum* (amaryllis). Meanwhile, by growing *Narcissus papyraceus* (syn. *N.* 'Paper White') and commercially prepared hyacinth bulbs, we can enjoy colour and scent in the middle of winter.

In the hotter, brighter months, indoor planting schemes can produce exotic results with the climbing *Gloriosa superba* 'Rothschildiana', shapely eucomis, colourful achimenes and *Sinningia* syn. Gloxinias. Yet more plants can be grown either inside or outside in summer, such as freesias, the St Bridgid or De Caen hybrids of anemones, begonias, cannas and *Zantedeschia* (arum lily).

Available in many different colours, freesias multiply well over the years and soon provide a fantastic array of colour.

Growing techniques

Packets of commercially prepared crocuses, hyacinths, hippeastrums (amaryllis) and *Narcissus papyraceus* (syn. *N.* 'Paper White') are common sights in garden centres and supermarkets in autumn, inviting us to buy one to take home and plant.

These bulbs have been specially treated to flower early, providing indoor colour in mid- to late winter. They can also be purchased by mail order, and will withstand the rigours of the postal service. This resilience is one of the reasons why they have been so successfully marketed over the centuries.

Providing protection

Some species of bulb do require careful treatment. *Pleione* bulbs, for example, must be handled gently because they can sometimes send up shoots even before planting, and they are, therefore, usually sold individually in packets, surrounded by wood shavings. Completely

Although sturdy in physique, hyacinth bulbs are susceptible to virus diseases and fungus problems. They are, therefore, often treated with a special chemical to maintain their health. Touching the bulbs can produce a mild allergic reaction, so people who have susceptible skins should wear gloves when they handle them.

different to look at are the poisonous tubers of *Gloriosa superba* 'Rothschildiana', which are long and tapering and could be easily damaged in transit. They are often wrapped in tissue. The rhizomes of achimenes are not only brittle but tiny, so are often sold in little plastic pots surrounded by peat.

Choosing a container and compost

Many indoor containers do not have drainage holes at the base of the pot, which makes it essential that the type of compost (soil mix) and the frequency of watering are carefully monitored. With most displays of winter bulbs it is advisable to use a specially formulated indoor bulb compost, which will help to maintain the balance of the soil and prevent souring. This is particularly true when you use one of the containers that are sold especially for forcing crocus, hyacinths and daffodils but that have no drainage holes.

Containers with drainage holes make it possible to grow a wide range of bulbs, corms and so forth and to use different kinds of compost. They are ideal for plants that prefer a well-drained soil, such as freesias and nerines. Use a growing medium such as a soil-based potting compost (soil mix) with plenty of grit added for good drainage. Remember to put a glazed or plastic tray beneath the pot so that water seeping through does not spoil the windowsill or furniture.

Where it's necessary to combat summer drought, use a container without drainage holes and find a lightweight plastic pot that does have holes that will fit inside. Put some gravel in the base of the outer container so that the inner pot sits at the right height and add a shallow

Hyacinths cope with a shallow container, only 7.5cm (3in) deep, although they are happy with a deeper root run.

layer of gravel to the surface of the inner one. This way the plant will have its own water reservoir, although care will still be needed not to over- or underwater. A soil-based compost or peat-based compost, depending on the plant, can be used in these circumstances.

The choice of container gives rise to a number of other considerations, the chief of which is the size of the container you should use. The tall, midwinter-flowering daffodils, such as *Narcissus papyraceus* (syn. *N.* 'Paper White'), make a lot of root growth and need a container that is at least 15cm (6in) deep. However, hyacinths can cope with shallower containers, needing a minimum of 7.5cm (3in), although they will also be happy with a deeper root run.

Stem-rooting lilies need a much deeper container, so choose a pot that is at least 20–25cm (7.5–10in) deep. When you are choosing a container, consider the overall height and width of the fully grown plant and make sure that the container's dimensions are in proportion to the size of the plant.

GROWING CROCUSES INDOORS

1 These crocus corms are specially prepared to bloom indoors. Each of the many shoots will produce flowers.

2 The corms are planted in special indoor bulb compost. White chippings add interest to the top of the compost.

3 The pretty Dutch bowl has no drainage holes, but this is not a problem if you do not overwater.

Getting started

Once planted, crocuses, hyacinths and the later flowering daffodils, such as *Narcissus* 'Cragford' or *N.* 'Bridal Crown', need cool conditions and a period of darkness when they will make root growth, not topgrowth. This simulates the conditions they would experience outside, where they would be growing buried in soil, and though they will not appreciate freezing temperatures, they should

Special glass hyacinth vases with an upper cup mean that the bulb can sit above the water.

be kept in cool conditions at around 7–10°C (45–50°F). Eventually, shoots will begin to emerge, and after about ten weeks they should be around 12cm (4¹/₂in) long. At this stage the plants can be moved into the light and into warmer conditions. Do not, however, put them in a position next to a radiator or on a south-facing windowsill.

Narcissus papyraceus (syn. *N.* 'Paper White') and its close relatives 'Omri' and 'Ziva' will grow on immediately they are given moisture, being quick to make root growth as well as topgrowth. They need light and warmth, but avoid extremes of either. *Hippeastrum* (amaryllis) needs warmth to get started, so a warm airing cupboard is ideal, the degree of light or darkness being irrelevant.

Growing on water

Although compost can always be used, hyacinths, *Narcissus papyraceus* and hippeastrums can be grown on top of water with no compost at all. This is possible only with bulbs that are quick to produce their flowers and only if you do not wish to use the bulbs for a second flowering the following year, because all the food reserves will have been used up and not replenished.

Hyacinths have been grown in this way for many years, and special glass hyacinth vases are available. These have an upper cup in which the bulb is held so that it does not sit actually touching the water. The taller plants, such as *Narcissus papyraceus* and hippeastrums, need the addition of small stones in the water to help anchor the roots and stabilize the plants. Many colours of gravel and chippings are available for landscaping and for use in fish tanks, and these are suitable for use with all bulbs grown on water, as are coloured glass nuggets.

Narcissus papyraceus (syn. *N.* 'Paper White') grows well on water as long as it is given the support of a few stones.

Finishing touches

Moss or coloured stones can be added over the surface of the growing medium at the time of planting or once the bulbs have started to shoot, to give the bowl that final finishing touch.

Ordinary lawn moss makes a soft, green topping, but, if you want a more vibrant colour, choose some dyed reindeer moss, which is obtainable from florists. Gravel or horticultural grit give a natural finish, but for a more colourful display that perhaps tones in with your indoor decorations use coloured stones, such as those sold for fish tanks, as a more exciting alternative. A thin layer scattered on the surface of the compost (soil mix) will make a neat addition, especially while you wait for the bulbs to flower.

To give bulbs that are being brought into flower for Christmas or the New Year festivities a seasonal look, you might like to add nuts or fir cones or even decorate pots with silver-painted walnuts or glittery fleece. Starry wire decorations, glass

An alternative approach is to use crushed horticultural grit with some of your favourite shells arranged on top.

Plain beech twigs provide useful supports for floppy freesia foliage. Put them round the edge of the pot.

droplets and gift wrapping tape are all possible extras. Look around your cupboards, there's sure to be something you can use!

Another possible decorative addition are candles, which will add atmosphere to any dark winter's night and can even make the container pretty long before all the flowers open. Fit them into a simple candle holder with a plastic spike on the end – these are readily available from florists – and gently push them into the compost. Never leave lit candles unattended.

Providing support

Although it is not always necessary, some bulbs and corms – freesias, for example – will benefit from the support of canes or twigs to prevent the foliage and flowers from flopping over. Act at the first sign of any waywardness.

Many taller subjects, including *Narcissus papyraceus* and its relatives, will benefit from the support of small beech clippings, which are sturdy and offer many smaller twigs for support, low down as well as

higher up. They can be left uncoloured or sprayed with paint to match the container. Whichever finish you prefer, they will do the job well and look attractive.

Another good support is *Ribes sanguineum* (flowering currant), which has strong, sturdy stems and can be sprayed silver or any other colour. Use it where the narcissi are flowering after, rather than before,

Crushed horticultural grit on top of compost gives a neat finish, while the additional green slates provide extra interest.

Starry decorations on thin wire stems add seasonal appeal. They also offer interest to the arrangement even before flowering begins.

early winter. *R. sanguineum* has fewer sideshoots than beech, but it has the advantage that when it is brought indoors and stuck into moist compost, it continues to live and will produce pretty white flowers. By the time the narcissi have finished blooming, the twigs may well have rooted and be producing buds.

Hyacinths can be supported by pieces of cane or long chopsticks tied with string or raffia. You may even find that a long cocktail stick (toothpick) is all that's required.

The beautiful *Gloriosa superba* 'Rothschildiana' is a scrambling herbaceous plant, climbing to 1.8m (6ft) in just one summer. Give it the support of a wall frame or a free-standing willow frame to which the tendrils can cling. The flamboyant flowers will be seen to good effect against the background of stems.

Bulbs that need support

Freesia	Hyacinthus
Gloriosa superba	Narcissus
'Rothschildiana'	papyraceus

Reindeer moss dyed bright green or red is available from florists and garden centres.

Hyacinths put on lots of root growth before flowering and this is shown off well when they are grown in water. Red glass beads add a touch of warmth as well as seasonal drama.

White marble chippings make an attractive finish to any display, including these forced crocus corms, which are just beginning to emerge. Soon they will reveal glorious papery purple flowers.

Cyclamen

With their swept-back petals and pouting mouths, cyclamen would appear to have a flare for drama. Like garden cyclamen, the cyclamen sold as indoor houseplants in autumn grow from tubers, which root both from the base and the sides.

They are all derived from *Cyclamen persicum*, which is a spring-flowering plant native to the countries of the eastern Mediterranean and Rhodes, Crete and Libya. In the wild the flowers are white, pale mauve, pale pink or deep pink. The leaves are variable but often have intricate silver zoning, spotting or margins.

Many cultivars have been bred from these beautiful plants, which means that forms are now available with blooms in white and many shades of salmon-pink, scarlet and purple as well as pink, and they often have a distinctive darker central spot. In addition, the flowers vary in shape and may be ruffled, double, single or twisted. They are often scented. In recent decades, attention has been given to breeding miniature flowers, more akin to the

Ruffled cyclamen flowers have a distinctive flair, and they are often combined with intricate leaf markings. Always choose a healthy plant. Look for one with stiff foliage, avoiding plants with any limp-looking leaves, and check that there are plenty of flower buds emerging from the base.

Remove any damaged leaves or fading flowers with a simple sharp tug close to the base of the stem.

The miniature cyclamen are floriferous, producing a mass of flowers with the fly-away petals that make them so endearing.

species found in the wild, which is a welcome move. Hybridizers have also emphasized foliage colour and form, with pride of place being given to intricate markings and contrasting patches of silver and green.

In the past few years, there has also been a move to breed plants that will thrive at lower temperatures and serve the dual purpose of flowering in outdoor containers in autumn as well as in indoor containers in winter. The resulting Miracle Series is a great bonus to all gardeners, both outdoor and indoor.

Another positive development has been the increased attention paid to producing highly fragrant flowers.

A plant in full flower will quickly fill an entire room with its sweet perfume.

Cyclamen will thrive in light, airy conditions, but they should be kept away from draughts and too much direct sunlight. They abhor both drought and high humidity. Too much or too little water will cause serious damage. Never water over the flowers and foliage, because this will encourage rot. It is far better to water around the plants at soil level, especially where several cyclamen are planted in a single container, or to water into a saucer below the plant if the container has drainage holes. Use soft water or clean rainwater.

Do not place pots of cyclamen close to a radiator or behind a closed curtain in the evening. A temperature of 18–21°C (64–70°F) is ideal, with a night-time temperature kept above 10°C (50°F). The plants will stay in flower for longer if they are fed once a fortnight with a weak liquid fertilizer.

Keep the plants clean and tidy by removing any fading flowers and yellowing leaves. You need to remove the entire stem, along with the dying flower or leaf, because a cut or a broken stem will encourage rot. Take firm hold of the stem near the base of the plant and give a quick, sharp tug.

After flowering has finished the plants should be allowed to go into a state of natural dormancy. Gradually reduce the amount of water you give until all the growth has died down. Then keep the plant completely dry for two or three months. Modest watering can start again. The tubers will not need repotting for a couple of years because they flower best with a restricted root run. When repotting is necessary, do it during the period of dormancy and use a soil-based planting medium.

Displaying cyclamen

Cyclamen look charming when they are shown off as a single specimen, and they will suit nearly every room in the house, adding scent and delicacy. The miniature hybrids are often sold in small plastic pots, which can be quickly disguised or easily made to fit into more attractive containers, including coloured flower vases and small china bowls.

A WIRE TABLE CENTREPIECE

1 Choose a medium-sized container, such as this wire basket, which is 23cm (9in) across and 13cm (5in) deep. Line it with moss.

3 Plant the cyclamen around the edge of the container, taking care to add compost right around the root ball of each plant. Leave a distinct gap in the centre for watering.

For greater impact make a massed display by planting three or four plants together in a medium-sized bowl or terrine or even a wire table centrepiece. Lighted candles will provide the final touch. Once planted, water only at soil level, remembering never to water directly over the tops of the tubers. It is, in fact, better to wait until the leaves go slightly limp and then to water only moderately.

2 Cover the moss with a circle of black plastic cut from a bin liner (trash bag), and fill two-thirds full with potting compost (soil mix).

4 Add some matching candles as a finishing touch, but take care never to leave the lit candles unattended.

Hippeastrum

The massive bulbs of hippeastrums can be bought in late summer and forced into flower before midwinter. However, most are available from early autumn until early winter, and these will flower after midwinter until spring, depending on the planting time.

Commonly available at this stage are the deep red 'Red Velvet' and 'Red Lion', the brilliant red and white 'Christmas Star', the orange 'Florida' and the pink and white 'Flamingo'. Rather more unusual is 'Yellow Goddess', which has creamy yellow flowers with a lime-green throat. Doubles are sometimes to be found as well, including the white, pink-edged 'Mary Lou'. A more recent introduction has been the Cybister types with their wispy petals such as 'Merenque' and 'Tango'.

It might still be possible to buy bulbs in mid-spring, when they will probably be cheaper. If the bulbs are firm, they will still flower. Indeed, the later they are planted, the more quickly they will spring into growth.

When planted in autumn or winter, the bulbs need warmth to come to life again after their dormant period. Choose a pot that is only about 2.5cm (1in) wider than the bulb itself. Use a soil-based potting compost (soil mix) if the pot has drainage holes, or an indoor bulb fibre if the pot has no holes. Some heavy grit at the base of the pot will help to stabilize the bulb when it is in flower and also assist with drainage.

Place the potted bulb in a warm spot – an airing cupboard, for example – where the temperature is 20–25°C (68–77°F). When the shoot has begun to emerge, expose it to moderate warmth and good light. Keep the compost moist during the growing period and apply a liquid feed, such as tomato fertilizer, every week or ten days once the bud has begun to open.

If you remove the first flowering stem you may find that another one soon emerges. The leaves will begin to grow at this stage. It is important to keep the bulb watered and regularly fed so that it can complete its cycle

'Yellow Goddess' is a sumptuous choice for any container whether grown on water or in compost (soil mix). Mature bulbs will each produce two or three flower spikes.

of growth. Some months later, when the leaves begin to yellow and wither, gradually withhold water and allow the bulb to go into a dormant period. Do not attempt to repot in

GROWING *HIPPEASTRUM* IN CONTAINERS

1 Plant two bulbs for a dramatic display. Add 5cm (2in) grit to the base of a container that is about 2.5cm (1in) wider than the bulb.

2 Add indoor bulb fibre and then plant the bulb so that the neck and shoulders sit just above the rim of the container.

3 Add a little more indoor bulb fibre around the neck, still leaving the shoulders exposed. Firm down the compost.

The bulbs of the *Hippeastrum* (amaryllis) are exceptionally large.

marbles or small stones to cover the small jar. Include a small piece of charcoal with the marbles to keep the water "sweet". Add a few more marbles and carefully place the bulb so that it rests inside the neck of the container with its roots barely touching the marbles. Add enough water to bring the level just below the base of the bulb. You might like to dress the container with pretty red beads or brightly coloured curly canes, which are available from florists. A single bulb will flower beautifully for weeks and may even produce two dramatic flowering spikes, by which time the bulb will have shrunk because it has used up all its food reserves. Bulbs planted in compost can be kept and encouraged to flower again another year, but it is best to discard those grown on water.

the first years, because hippeastrums resent root disturbance. After three or four years it will be necessary to repot, and this should be done in late summer. Leave the bulb outside in a dry, sheltered spot until autumn when it can be brought indoors again and given moisture and warmth to start the flowering cycle again. It might not flower at exactly the same time as it did the first year, but the results will still be good.

Growing on water

Hippeastrum bulbs can be grown on water in a similar way to prepared hyacinths and *Narcissus papyraceus*. Start the bulb into growth as already described, planted on moist compost, and keep it in a warm place for a short period. As soon as the bud begins to emerge, carefully wash off the compost. Plant the bulb on top of coloured stones, pebbles, marbles or glass beads, with the water level kept below the base of the bulb.

Hippeastrum bulbs are huge, so use a wide-necked glass container within which it can sit. Find a small, clean, empty glass jar with a light-coloured screw lid to fit inside the container. This allows more light to be reflected and cuts down on the number of marbles or beads that will be needed. Place the jar inside the larger container and add enough

These *Hippeastrum* 'Red Velvet' are blooming for a second time in the same container. It is important to feed them after flowering and to continue to water until the leaves show signs of yellowing. Then gradually withhold moisture and allow the leaves to die down, thus allowing the bulbs to complete their life-cycle. Do not disturb the roots; simply begin to water again when the first signs of new growth are seen. The bulbs can be allowed to flower in the same compost (soil mix) for three seasons.

Indoor winter-flowering narcissi

The species _Narcissus papyraceus_ is native to south-eastern France, south-western Spain and Portugal, where it flowers outdoors in winter, although many of the commercially available bulbs actually come from Israel. It is not surprising that when given warmth and moisture, the bulbs burst into growth after being planted indoors in autumn.

Closely related and behaving in the same way are the cultivars 'Ziva', 'Omri' and 'Galilee'. Grow these narcissi in a warm, well-lit place where a temperature of 16°C (60°F) can be maintained. Other narcissi that are suitable for forcing indoors are the cultivars 'Cragford' and 'Bridal Crown', both of which are easily available but later flowering. As a rule, the later they flower, the more important it is to give the bulbs a cool period of several weeks after planting. So if you are growing bulbs of either 'Cragford' or 'Bridal Crown' indoors, place them in a cool, dark place for about ten weeks, when the shoots should be around 5cm (2in) high.

Once flowering has begun, then the cooler the room temperature the longer the flowers will last, but do not allow the temperature to fall below freezing. If you have a balcony or veranda, you may even wish to place them outside in mild weather. This is also useful if you find the perfume too strong.

Narcissus papyraceus (syn. _N._ 'Paper White') and its forms produce stems with eight or ten flowers each, which means that just two or three bulbs will produce a really worthwhile display. They look equally attractive grown on compost (soil mix) or on water.

Narcissus papyraceus (syn. _N._ 'Paper White') looks festive surrounded by seasonal stars, which highlight the shape of its flowers.

You may choose to grow several different types of cultivar, keeping to a single type in each bowl, and by doing this you will be able to have blooms from early winter through to midwinter, and beyond.

If you use a container without drainage holes – a painted, metal or glazed pot, for instance – use specially formulated free-draining bulb fibre. This will give the bulbs a good growing medium and will help prevent the compost (soil mix) from becoming sour over the ensuing months. If you use a traditional plant pot with drainage holes, you can use a soil-based potting compost (soil mix), but place a saucer beneath it to protect your furniture or the windowsill.

Forcing narcissi

Narcissus papyraceus (syn. *N.* 'Paper White') is the easiest of all the narcissi to bring into flower in late autumn or winter. It usually flowers only six weeks after planting and, unlike the later flowering and other related daffodils, it requires no special period of cool or darkness to persuade it to grow and flower indoors. Decide when you want the bulbs to bloom and then work backwards. You may wish to try a succession of flowers by planting a number of pots over several weeks in order to have a supply of fragrant blooms. Each stem produces many flowers, so a display can quite easily include as many as five or six bulbs or as few as two or three. Whatever you choose, the results will be excellent. These bulbs do not tolerate frosty conditions outside, so unless you live in a mild climate, they are best discarded after flowering and new ones purchased for the following season, when the whole cycle can begin again.

Growing on water

Narcissus papyraceus and its cultivars also grow well on top of water because they are so quick to start into growth and then flower. Use a pretty bowl filled with gravel to stabilize the roots, or choose a glass container and fill it with coloured stones or glass nuggets. Gravel and chippings are available in a range of colours and grades for garden landscaping and for indoor fish tanks. A pattern of red and white stones or some seashore stones and shells would look interesting.

Add a small piece of charcoal among the stones to help keep the water fresh. The bulbs will use all their food reserves by growing on water and should be discarded after flowering. They will not produce flowers again.

FORCING NARCISSI

1 Choose firm, plump bulbs, and plant in compost (soil mix), allowing for about six weeks before flowering. Do not worry if the bulbs already have existing shoots, but take care that they are not damaged. Grit at the base of the container is not essential, but it is useful to aid drainage.

2 Fill the container with moistened bulb fibre, bringing the level to within 5cm (2in) of the rim. Plant the bulbs so that they are close together, but away from the sides of the container. A distance apart of about half their width is ideal. Approximately half the top of each bulb should be left exposed.

3 Mulch with moss to retain the moisture as well as to add an attractive finish. Natural moss available from a florist (or maybe the garden) has been used here, but coloured reindeer moss would make an attractive and more vibrant alternative.

4 You may need to support the leaves and stems with twigs. Only do so if you notice that the stems are beginning to flop, but then act immediately. Beech twigs are ideal, as they branch well all the way up the stem and offer support from top to bottom.

Spring bulbs indoors

Several bulbs are suitable for planting in small pots before being kept in cool but sheltered conditions outside – such as next to a house wall or in an open porch – and then being brought indoors once the flower buds first show, to flower a week or two earlier than they would otherwise.

Crocuses, *Eranthis hyemalis* (winter aconite), *Muscari* (grape hyacinths), dwarf daffodils, dwarf tulips and hyacinths will all bring pleasure if they are treated in this way.

The large *Crocus vernus* (Dutch crocus) are excellent candidates for growing in this way. If the corms are to be planted in containers with no drainage holes, add a layer of grit to the base of each pot and use specially formulated indoor bulb fibre to fill the pot. For a maximum show, five crocus corms can be planted in a circle near the bottom of each pot, with another layer of five corms planted above them. Make sure that the corms are not directly on top of each other. The pots should be kept in a light place, such as a potting shed or unheated

greenhouse, in winter and watered occasionally to keep the compost (soil mix) just moist. When the shoots just begin to show colour, they can be brought indoors. The display can then be appreciated at close range, with no danger of wind or rain spoiling the delicate petals.

Prepared hyacinths for midwinter flowering are available in a limited range of colours, but bedding hyacinths, which are grown in the garden or in outdoor pots, are available in an enormous number of delicate shades, including apricot as in *Hyacinthus orientalis* 'Gipsy Queen'; violet, lilac, mulberry and burgundy as in 'Violet Pearl', 'Amethyst', 'Mulberry Rose' and 'Woodstock'; blue and white as in 'Blue Jacket'; deep blue as in 'Blue Magic'; and many others. There are also some double-flowering forms, including white 'Ben Nevis', red 'Hollyhock', violet 'King Codro' and pink 'Rosette'. Any of these hyacinths can be grown in groups of three or more or as a single specimen in a simple terracotta pot. Hyacinths like good drainage so where they are grown outdoors, open to the winter rain, it

is advisable to choose a pot with drainage holes and to use a soil-based potting compost (soil mix).

Using spring bulbs already in growth

One of the easiest ways to enjoy bulbs indoors in late winter is to buy small pots of growing bulbs. Use a pretty coloured pot or a plain terracotta pot for display purposes and place it in a light but cool position to prolong the flowering period as much as possible. Too much heat or too much direct sunlight will mean that you will enjoy only the briefest of blooms.

Dwarf irises, scillas, *Fritillaria meleagris* (snake's head fritillary), hyacinths and dwarf tulips are among the many plants that are readily available, but of them all, the miniature *Narcissus* 'Tête-à-tête' is probably the most often grown. This is a dwarf, sturdy, multiheaded, hybrid daffodil with rich yellow flowers. After flowering, deadhead each flower and plant them out in the garden in spring so that the bulbs can complete their lifecycle and flower again year after year.

Some cultivars of *Crocus vernus* (Dutch crocus) have wonderfully bold purple flowers with strongly contrasting orange stamens.

A small, metal window box planted with narcissi is perfect for a kitchen windowsill or for the conservatory.

You will need secateurs (pruners), a florist's foam ring, a large plate or dish to display the arrangement, three or four pots of dwarf *Narcissus* 'Tête-à-tête', some foliage, such as *Euonymus japonicus* 'Aureus', long stems of *Corylus avellana* 'Contorta' (corkscrew hazel) and a few sprigs of flowering forsythia and viburnums, including white *Viburnum tinus* and pink *V.* x *bodnantense* 'Dawn'.

Growing *Narcissus* 'Tête-à-tête'

An effective method of displaying these little daffodils is to find a simple coloured container that is slightly larger than the pot in which they are already growing. Use grit or stones as necessary in the outer pot to get the level right, insert the pot of daffodils and add a covering of moss to disguise the inner pot and the surface of the compost (soil mix). Keep the bulbs moist and deadhead the flowers to keep them neat.

Another way of using them is to place the pot-grown plants in a small metal window box, again raising the levels with grit or stones and topping up with moss between each pot. Reindeer moss provides a lime-green finish or you could use a coloured moss from a florist. Keep the compost (soil mix) moist and deadhead the daffodils to keep them neat.

Wet the foam ring thoroughly and give the cut foliage a good long drink in water. Place the ring on a large plate or dish and arrange the pots of bulbs to sit inside. Cut small sprigs of foliage and arrange them in groups, pushing the stems into the foam. Add some flowering forsythia and viburnum in groups and a few single stems of the hazel to give extra height. Bear in mind that within a few days the narcissi will probably grow to about 20cm (8in) or more. If you keep the foam and bulbs moist, the arrangement should stay fresh for ten days or more.

Alternatively, incorporate these daffodils into a flower and foliage arrangement. Potted bulbs will last much longer than a bunch of cut flowers, so mix them with other late-winter foliage and flowers to create a vibrant indoor display. The choice of cut foliage in autumn and winter will depend on what is available. The variegated foliage of *Euonymus japonicus* 'Aureus' would be a good choice, as would the white flowers of *Viburnum tinus* or the long, twisted stems of *Corylus avellana* 'Contorta' (corkscrew hazel). Simple ivy leaves and berries are equally attractive.

Achimenes

These plants produce long, tubular flowers, ranging in colour from rose, scarlet and blue to violet, and the flowers, which have contrasting throats of gold or white, are sometimes blotched or spotted.

The rhizomes, which resemble miniature pine cones, are small and easily broken, so they are often sold, four or five at a time, in little plastic tubs surrounded by peat. For all their fragility, however, they are easily grown in shallow containers, and the cascading types are delightful in hanging baskets, where they will tumble over the sides. Successive plantings in winter and spring will produce flowers throughout summer and autumn.

Plant the rhizomes about 2.5cm (1in) deep and 5cm (2in) apart. Water sparingly at first, but as shoots appear keep the compost (soil mix) moist at all times. It is important to water regularly because a dry period will initiate dormancy, and there will be no flowers. Apply a liquid feed every two weeks when

Achimenes 'Prima Donna' has rich salmon-pink flowers that look beautiful planted on their own or mixed with a trailing form.

Achimenes 'Cascade Fairy Pink' has pretty light pink flowers. The dark green foliage has bronze-red undertones.

plants are in full growth. Pinch out shoots to encourage bushiness and provide supports if necessary. Provide bright light, but keep the plants shaded from strong, direct sunlight. In hot weather, spray the foliage with a mister to maintain humidity. You can improve humidity around plants by standing pot-grown specimens on a gravel-covered tray and keeping the gravel damp.

As the flowering period comes to an end, gradually withhold water until the soil has dried out. Remove the dead foliage and store the rhizomes in dry peat at a minimum temperature of 10°C (50°F). The rhizomes can be propagated when next planted. Do not worry too much if they break: every single scale will produce a new plant which can be used to propagate new plants.

PLANTING ACHIMENES IN A BASKET

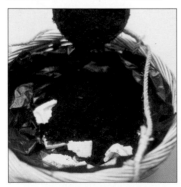

1 Line a wicker basket with black plastic (unless it is already pre-lined), add drainage material, such as polystyrene (styrofoam), broken pots or grit, and cover with a multi-purpose compost (soil mix), to within 2.5cm (1in) of the rim.

2 This basket has a 30cm (12in) diameter and contains eight rhizomes, planted about 5cm (2in) apart and 2.5cm (1in) deep. Two different types of achimenes can be alternated, such as *Achimenes* 'Cascade Violet Night' and *A.* 'Violet Charm'.

3 Mist to maintain humidity. Warmth, semi-shade and a damp atmosphere are ideal. The plants will flower for months on end and give endless pleasure.

Freesia

Freesias grow from corms, which may be planted indoors to flower in succession from late spring through to early summer, so that their perfume can be enjoyed over many weeks. They can also be purchased as "conditioned" bulbs and planted in pots indoors, before being moved outdoors, where they will flower in mid- to late summer.

Indoor freesias should be planted in early spring in moist, soil-based potting compost (soil mix), about 7.5cm (3in) apart and deep. Keep the compost moist throughout the growing period and apply a liquid feed every two weeks as soon as the buds show. Keep in cool to warm conditions but avoid too high a temperature, or the flowering period will be short.

There are both single- and double-flowered forms of freesia, and the plants vary in height from 10 to 30cm (4–12in). Many, though not all, freesias are exquisitely fragrant. But one of the drawbacks is their rather untidy foliage, especially at the time of flowering, so a wire ring support can be useful. For larger, more mature plants, beech twigs are ideal supports.

Freesias are sometimes unpredictable in their willingness to flower – you might be fortunate and have a wonderful pot filled with blooms, or you might have only one or two flowers. Regular moderate watering and regular fertilizer should ensure good results.

It is worth taking trouble with these plants because the scent is heavenly, with the yellow forms being best of all. Recent hybridization programmes have produced cultivars that are more reliable in terms of flowering and with even better scent.

Freesia flowers are a firm favourite in the florist shops both for their scent and delicate colours. Grow your own at home and you will be rewarded, year after year.

Conditioned freesia corms can be planted in pots indoors to flower in succession from late spring through to early summer.

Pure white *Freesia* 'Miranda' and light yellow *F.* 'Beethoven' in pots decorated with African animal-skin patterns.

Eucomis

Eucomis is commonly called the pineapple lily or pineapple flower because it produces a tuft of leafy bracts above the flower spike. It is native to southern Africa, where it grows in grassy, often damp, areas.

This is an easy bulb to grow indoors. In spring plant individual bulbs in a small pot, 10cm (4in) deep, in a well-drained, soil-based potting compost (soil mix), or mass the bulbs in groups of three or more in a larger pot. Water sparingly until shoots emerge and, as growth progresses, keep the compost moist at all times. After flowering, allow the plant to complete its lifecycle and gradually withhold water so that

it can rest during the dormant period before bringing it into growth again the following spring. In mild areas the bulb can be grown outside.

Eucomis autumnalis 'White Dwarf' is a particularly attractive plant with distinctive wavy foliage. It has a column of white flowers with yellow stamens, which open in succession, starting at the base; at the top the leafy hat brings the height to just over 30cm (12in). For a taller plant try *E. comosa* 'Sparkling Burgundy', which is memorable for the intense deep colour of its emerging leaves and later flower spike. This eventually reaches about 70cm (28in) with a generous number of dark pinkish-purple flowers.

Eucomis autumnalis 'White Dwarf' has a wonderful silhouette with its wavy foliage, its narrow column of scented flowers and its leafy top. This is an easy bulb to grow indoors.

Eucomis comosa 'Sparkling Burgundy' is an exciting plant to watch from the moment it first sends up its new leaves to the time its flower spike emerges, and, later, as the flowers open.

Eucomis flowers last for several weeks, opening at the bottom of the flower spike first and progressively higher up as the weeks pass by. This undemanding plant is rewarding both in its longevity and its simplicity.

Sinningia

Although the botanical name for this group of plants is *Sinningia*, the term gloxinia is better known among florists and flower arrangers. The plants are originally native to tropical areas of Brazil, Argentina and Mexico, where they have adapted to seasonal rainfall and periods of intervening drought, during which the tubers become dormant for a time.

The large, velvety flowers grow from tubers, which are shaped rather like those of begonias. They should be planted in late winter or early spring on top of moist, multipurpose compost (soil mix). Given gentle warmth and only moderate moisture at first, they soon start into growth and produce colourful plants, about 20cm (8in) in height and spread.

Flowers may be self-coloured or speckled, such as the lovely pink-spotted white 'Blanche de Méru', crimson 'Etoile de Feu', violet 'Hollywood', ivory and red Tigrina Group and purple and white 'Kaiser Wilhelm'.

Pot individual tubers into small containers with drainage holes in the base and use a multipurpose compost (soil mix). It is important to use containers with drainage holes because the leaves dislike being splashed with water and will quickly mark, so the plants should be watered from below. Keep the temperature at 21–23°C (70–73°F) until flowering and move to cooler conditions when flowering begins. The plants will have become quite leafy and take up a surprisingly large amount of space.

Alternatively, plant several tubers in one container mixing the colours to make a really colourful display. Provide the plants with well-lit conditions but do not stand in direct sunlight. Deadhead flowers to prolong flowering and apply a dilute liquid feed every two weeks. After

Sinningia 'Hollywood', with its gorgeous violet blooms, is a real show-stopper, and S. 'Etoile de Feu' is a glorious velvety crimson. The two together make a sumptuous display in a simple wicker window box.

flowering is over gradually withhold water and allow the rootball to go quite dry. Store in a cool, dry place at about 7°C (45°F) until the following season.

A DISPLAY OF SINNINGIAS

1 Choose a small plastic pot with drainage holes and find a slightly larger, ornamental pot for display purposes. Grit is useful in the base of the outer pot for raising the inner pot to the right height. It also provides a damp reservoir beneath the base of the plant, enabling the plant to be kept damp, which is particularly important in hot weather.

2 Use a moist, multipurpose compost (soil mix) to fill the pot to within 3cm (1¼in) of the rim. Create a small hollow, and plant the tuber so that it rests on top of the compost. Keep the temperature at 21–23°C (70–73°F) until flowering, and move to cooler conditions when flowering begins. Keep in well-lit conditions but avoid direct sunlight.

3 Avoid watering directly on top of the leaves. It is much better to water from below, occasionally removing the plant and sitting it in a saucer of water. Alternatively, remove the plant and add water to the base of the outer pot but take care not to leave the roots sitting in a pool of water. They will quickly fail if the compost is kept too sodden.

Summer bulbs indoors

Many summer-flowering bulbs, tubers and rhizomes are offered for sale as growing plants, often much earlier in the year than would be possible if they were grown on, at home, from their dry state.

Begonias and lilies, therefore, are available from spring onwards, with dahlias following on soon afterwards. They are happy kept inside, in warm, light conditions, but do not put them in a position where they will be in full, direct sun, or the flowers will last for only a few days, not weeks.

Terracotta containers always look warm and attractive, but there are many other ways of displaying plants. Silver or silver-coloured containers will give a more modern appearance indoors, and can look extremely elegant, especially if the plant is tall and beautifully shaped, such as a *Zantedeschia* (arum lily).

Do not forget to feed the plants every week to ten days with a liquid feed and keep them well watered. Frequent deadheading will help to prolong the flowering time of arum lilies, dahlias and begonias. After they have finished flowering, the

Here, dahlias are displayed individually in highly coloured containers. Just make sure there are drainage holes in the base of each inner pot.

Two or three Non-Stop begonias look marvellous in a pure white window box. There are so many delightful colours to choose from, including these soft pink shades or much stronger reds and oranges. Remember to deadhead regularly and apply a liquid feed every week.

Non-Stop begonias are so called because they continue to flower over a long period. They make excellent indoor plants.

lilies can be planted out in a sheltered part of the garden, where they will overwinter and come into flower again the following year. Begonia and dahlia tubers can be allowed to go into a dormant state, and then should be kept cool and dry until they can be brought into growth again the following spring.

Short-stemmed lilies are ideal for displaying indoors or on a balcony or veranda. 'Orange Pixie' grows to only 30cm (12in), while 'Peach Pixie' reaches 45cm (16in). Often lilies have a heady fragrance. For those suffering from pollen allergies, look out for the 'Kiss' lily types, which are double and pollen-free.

Zantedeschia 'Dusky Pink' is one of the many modern cultivars of the arum lily that have these beautifully shaped tubular flowers.

Zantedeschia (arum lily), with their boldly shaped flowers, look elegant displayed in a series of tall, modern silver containers.

Lilies make a wonderful statement with their brilliantly coloured flowers and attractive leaves. Find an old fruit or vegetable box and lightly colour-wash or spray it with paint to give a warm and interesting texture. Place the pots inside and use a little green or coloured moss to disguise the rims. After flowering, the lilies can be planted out in the garden, where they will overwinter and come into bloom again the following year.

Autumn bulbs indoors

Autumn-flowering nerines and hedychiums bring welcome colour into our lives when chilly days make life outdoors rather less enticing.

Nerine

The frilly pink flowers are one of the main characteristics of nerines, making them a favourite for the garden as well as the conservatory and indeed an important part of the cut-flower industry.

Although they are often known as the Guernsey lily, an island where they now grow in abundance, nerines actually originate from southern Africa. They are thought of as borderline hardy and some species, including the well-known *Nerine bowdenii* and its cultivars, are often grown in sheltered, sunny borders or in pots outdoors where they flower in early autumn. However, some species, such as *N. masoniorum*, are tender, and some forms are later to flower, including the purple-red cultivar 'Ancilla', white and purple 'Konak', fuchsia-pink *N. bowdenii* 'Pink Triumph', and *N. flexuosa* 'Alba', which has delightful, white, crinkly-edged petals. It is safer to enjoy all these nerines indoors.

Nerine bulbs have long necks. Purchase bulbs when they are

Nerines like to be planted with the neck above soil level. The leaves follow in late winter.

available, usually in late summer, and plant three bulbs to a pot, making sure that the top of the neck is just above soil level. Water freely when the flower buds appear but allow to become dry during the summer dormancy. The flowers will appear in autumn, with the leaves following in late winter. Remove any seedheads, unless wanted for propagation. Apply a low-nitrogen liquid feed in late winter, although not all growers recommend this treatment.

Do not divide the bulbs until it is absolutely necessary because they prefer to be congested. Eventually, however, flowering will decrease and you will need to separate the bulbs and replant them. Be aware that recently divided bulbs may not flower for the first year, because they resent being disturbed. The modern treatment of new bulbs, which are produced on a commercial scale, means that these will mostly likely bear flowers.

Planting several pots with different cultivars or species will give you colour in the conservatory for many weeks, varying from the palest pink to deep pink to purple red.

Nerine bowdenii 'Pink Triumph' has spectacular fuchsia pink flowers. Flowering in late autumn, it is one of the last nerines to flower and so is best treated as a conservatory plant where it can be protected from frosty weather.

Hybridization means that many more shades are becoming available, so the future should bring even more choice.

Hedychium

More commonly known as ginger lilies or garland lilies, hedychiums originate in lightly wooded areas of Asia, where they revel in the summer warmth and moisture. They may be grown outdoors as late summer- to autumn-flowering container plants or as cool conservatory specimens, when their ebullient foliage and scented flowers can be fully appreciated. They are rhizomatous plants, related to the edible ginger root from the genus *Zingiber* which is so highly prized in cooking, but species in the *Hedychium* genus are more showy with their flowers.

The best known of all the gingers is probably *Hedychium coronarium* (garland flower, white ginger lily), which is native to India. It can reach 3m (10ft) in height. The pointed buds eventually open to reveal long, terminal racemes, to 20cm (8in) long, of butterfly-like, white flowers with amber-yellow basal marks. *H. flavescens* (yellow ginger) is similar to *H. coronarium* but its flowers are yellow not white. The flowers of *H. densiflorum*, native to the Himalayas, have a more bottlebrush appearance, reaching 20cm (10in) long. It can grow 5m (15ft) high in ideal conditions, but is more likely to grow to 1.8m (6ft) in a conservatory. The cultivar *H. densiflorum* 'Assam Orange' has deep orange, fragrant flowers. *H. ellipticum*, a species native to northern India, has pointed leaves and a flower that appears as a 10cm (4in) spike with white and yellow-lobed flowers and purple filaments. It grows to about 1.8m (6ft) high.

Plant hedychiums in soil-based compost (soil mix) with the rhizomes just on the surface. They will cope well with confined conditions but growth is rapid, and as with many rhizomatous plants they are best divided in spring or potted on into a larger container. Remember that

Hedychium gardnerianum is one of the best known of all the ornamental ginger family, producing long racemes of butterfly-like creamy yellow blooms. These flowers are used in garlands in Nepal and Hawaii.

hedychiums will grow to 1.8m (6ft) tall or more, so choose a heavy pot that will not fall over. They enjoy warm, moist conditions, so place a gravel-filled tray beneath the pot which can be used as a water reservoir on sunny days when the temperature in the conservatory is likely to be high.

The rhizomes of hedychiums are stout and fleshy and leaf spikes are usually prominent, soon emerging into a leafy shoot. Growth is rapid and soon the shoot will be 2–3m (6–10ft) tall. Repot or divide in early spring so that the plant is poised ready to mature well.

Fleshy berries are characteristic of *Hedychium spicatum*. Although its flowers are not the most highly scented of the genus, the dried rhizomes are burned as incense, a derivative oil is used in perfumery and a powdered form is used for scenting tobacco.

Most hedychiums will grow to 1–3m (3–10ft) high, although the average is around 1.8m (6ft). Not all spiky shoots produce flowers, but the foliage is handsome in its own right. *Hedychium coronarium* is particularly attractive with its elliptical glaucous leaves.

A directory of bulbs

The bulb garden list is extensive, with plenty of choice for many different situations, whether your garden is in sun or shade, whether your soil is moist or well drained, whether you need dwarf or tall plants, whether you like fine foliage as well as flowers, whether you seek special colours such as vibrant oranges and reds, or soft salmons, creams and pale yellows, for example, not to mention a whole range of blues and deep dark purples. Here you will find details of the origins and correct growing conditions, propagation, pests and diseases, the flowering time, size of plant, colour, whether a flower is scented, hardiness rating and much more besides – all displayed in an easy-to-follow alphabetical list with scores of beautiful illustrations.

Advice is also given as to whether a plant is best suited to the garden beds and borders, or if it can be grown in grass, if it is suitable for containers on the terrace or patio, or if it is best grown indoors where temperatures are consistently warm. Some genera such as *Narcissus* will thrive in all these situations, whilst others are more selective and will only cope with a limited range of habitats. This bulb directory will enable you to select those plants you require for your own garden and home. Many of them are really easy to grow and you may be assured that in this list will be some of the most dramatic plants available to any gardener.

Agapanthus 'Loch Hope' is an evergreen perennial that flowers from July to September. It has extra-large beautiful blue flower-heads.

Bulb planner

Type of bulb	planting time	depth	spacing	flowering time
Achimenes	spring	2.5cm (1in)	2.5cm (1in)	summer and autumn
Agapanthus	spring	10cm (4in)	45–60cm (18–24in)	midsummer to early autumn
Allium	autumn	5–15cm (2–6in)	15–30cm (6–12in)	late spring to early autumn
Amaryllis	late summer	15cm (6in)	10cm (4in)	autumn
Anemone blanda	autumn	5cm (2in)	10cm (4in)	late winter to spring
Anemone coronaria	early spring	8cm (3in)	10cm (4in)	midsummer
Arum	autumn or spring	5cm (2in)	15cm (6in)	early summer
Asphodeline	autumn	8cm (3in)	30cm (12in)	late spring to summer
Begonia	spring	at soil level	20cm (8in)	summer to early autumn
Brimeura	autumn	5–8cm (2–3in)	2.5cm (1in)	spring
Calochortus	autumn	8cm (3in)	8cm (3in)	late spring to early summer
Camassia	autumn	10cm (4in)	10cm (4in)	late spring
Canna	spring	5cm (2in)	60cm (24in)	midsummer to autumn
Cardiocrinum	autumn	at soil level	60–90cm (24–36in)	late summer
Chionodoxa	autumn	5cm (2in)	5cm (2in)	late winter to mid-spring
Colchicum	late summer	10cm (4in)	10–15cm (4–6in)	autumn
Corydalis	autumn	8cm (3in)	10cm (4in)	spring
Crocosmia	spring	8–10cm (3–4in)	8cm (3in)	mid to late summer
Crocus, spring	autumn	8cm (3in)	5cm (2in)	autumn
Crocus, autumn	late summer	8cm (3in)	5cm (2in)	autumn
Cyclamen	autumn	2.5–5cm (1–2in)	10cm (4in)	autumn to early spring
Dactylorhiza	autumn	8cm (3in)	15cm (6in)	spring to late summer
Dahlia	early spring	15cm (6in)	30–90cm (12–36in)	summer to autumn
Dierama	autumn	5–8cm (2–3in)	30cm (12in)	summer
Eranthis	early autumn	5cm (2in)	8cm (3in)	mid- to late winter
Eremurus	autumn	just below soil	60cm (24in)	early to midsummer
Erythronium	autumn	10cm (4in)	10cm (4in)	spring
Eucomis	spring	15cm (6in)	20cm (8in)	late summer
Freesia	early spring	8cm (3in)	5–8cm (2–3in)	midsummer
Fritillaria	autumn	10–20cm (4–8in)	8–45cm (3–18in)	mid-spring to early summer
Galanthus	early autumn	8cm (3in)	10cm (4in)	mid- to late winter
Galtonia	spring	13cm (5in)	10cm (4in)	late summer

Allium oreophilium

Dahlia 'Kidd's Climax'

Begonia 'Picotee'

Lilium 'Her Grace'

Cyclamen coum

Type of bulb	planting time	depth	spacing	flowering time
Gladiolus	spring	8–10cm (3–4in)	10–15cm (4–6in)	midsummer
Gloriosa	spring	2.5cm (1in)	30cm (12in)	summer to autumn
Hedychium	spring	2.5cm (1in)	90–200cm (3–7ft)	late summer to early autumn
Hippeastrum	autumn onwards	neck above soil	20cm (8in)	winter onwards
Hyacinthoides	autumn	8cm (3in)	10cm (4in)	spring
Hyacinthus	autumn	10cm (4in)	20cm (8in)	spring
Iris reticulata	autumn	5cm (2in)	10cm (4in)	late winter
Kniphofia	spring	crown at soil level	60cm (24in)	summer to early autumn
Leucojum	autumn	8cm (3in)	8cm (3in)	late winter to autumn
Lilium	autumn	10–15cm (4–6in)	15–45cm (6–18in)	late spring to late summer
Muscari	autumn	5cm (2in)	5cm (2in)	spring
Narcissus	autumn	10–15cm (4–6in)	15cm (6in)	late winter to late spring
Nectaroscordum	autumn	5cm (2in)	10cm (4in)	late spring to early summer
Nerine	spring	2.5–8cm (1–3in)	8cm (3in)	early to late-autumn
Ornithogalum	autumn or spring	10–15cm (4–6in)	10–15cm (4–6in)	spring or mid- to late summer
Oxalis	autumn	5cm (2in)	10–15cm (4–6in)	early to late summer
Pelargonium	spring	2.5cm (1in)	30cm (12in)	summer to early autumn
Pleione	late winter	5cm (2in)	5cm (2in)	spring
Puschkinia	autumn	5cm (2in)	5cm (2in)	spring
Ranunculus	late winter to spring	5cm (2in)	8cm (3in)	late spring or summer
Schizostylis	spring	8cm (3in)	15–20cm (6–8in)	autumn
Scilla	early autumn	8–10cm (3–4in)	15–20cm (6–8in)	spring to early summer
Sinningia	spring	at soil level	13cm (5in)	summer
Sternbergia	late summer	15cm (6in)	8cm (3in)	autumn
Tigridia	spring	10cm (4in)	10cm (4in)	summer
Trillium	autumn or spring	10cm (4in)	30cm (12in)	mid-spring to early summer
Triteleia	autumn	8cm (3in)	10cm (4in)	early to midsummer
Tritonia	autumn	8cm (3in)	20cm (8in)	summer
Tulbaghia	spring	8cm (3in)	8cm (3in)	summer to early autumn
Tulipa	late autumn	8–15cm (3–6in)	8–20cm (3–8in)	spring
Veltheimia	autumn	top above soil	30cm (12in)	spring
Veratrum	spring	nose at soil level	60cm (24in)	early to midsummer
Watsonia	spring	15cm (6in)	10cm (4in)	late spring to late summer
Zantedeschia	spring	15cm (6in)	30–45cm (12–18in)	midsummer

Hippeastrum 'Mary Lou'

Narcissus cyclamineus

Tulipa 'Angelique'

Colchicum 'Violet Queen'

Erythronium 'Pagoda'

ACHIMENES
Hot-water plant, cupid's bower

This small but showy plant is often known as the hot-water plant because it used to be grown on top of the hot-water pipes in Victorian greenhouses, where it would thrive in the warmth and shade before being brought into the house. It is a genus of about 25 species of winter-dormant perennials from the subtropical forests of Central America. The many cultivars bear trumpet-shaped flowers in a wide range of colours, including dark and light pink, blue and primrose yellow. They may be vigorous upright or trailing perennials. The tiny rhizomes are quite fragile.
Cultivation In frost-prone areas grow indoors in a conservatory or as houseplants; in frost-free gardens they may be grown in a border. The plants enjoy light shade but not direct sunshine. The trailing forms are well suited to hanging baskets; the others may be grown in containers. Bring into growth in the spring at 16–18°C (61–64°F) and water sparingly at first. Plant rhizomes 2.5cm (1in) deep, allowing about one rhizome to 2.5cm (1in) of container – i.e. 10 rhizomes to a 25cm (10in) pot – in a soil-based compost (soil mix) or a proprietary loamless compost (soil-less mix). Water freely in summer. Apply a weekly liquid fertilizer. In autumn remove dead topgrowth and store in containers at 10°C (50°F) in completely

Achimenes 'Friendship'

dry conditions until spring.
Propagation Divide rhizomes or take stem cuttings in spring.
Pests and disease Aphids, thrips and red spider mites.

Achimenes 'Cascade Fairy Pink'
This trailing cultivar has solitary light pink flowers, 5cm (2in) across borne in generous numbers throughout summer and autumn. It makes an ideal partner for *A.* 'English Waltz'. H 20cm (8in) but will trail to 40cm (16in) S 20cm (8in). Tender/Z10.

Achimenes 'Cascade Violet Night'
This trailing cultivar has striking purple-blue flowers, 5cm (2in) across, which are borne in generous numbers throughout summer and autumn. It makes an ideal partner for *A.* 'English Waltz', 'Prima Donna' or 'Violet Charm'. H 20cm (8in) but will trail to 40cm (16in) S 20cm (8in). Tender/Z10.

Achimenes 'English Waltz'
The large, funnel-shaped, pink flowers look stunning against the dark green foliage with its bronze-red undertones. H 20cm (8in), S 20cm (8in). Tender/Z10.

Achimenes 'Friendship'
The rich lilac-pink flowers look wonderful in an indoor hanging basket or as a table houseplant. H 20cm (8in) S 20cm (8in). Tender/Z10.

Achimenes 'Prima Donna'
The rich salmon-pink flowers look beautiful planted on their own or mixed with a trailing form. H 20cm (8in) S 20cm (8in). Tender/Z10.

Achimenes 'Violet Charm'
The deep violet-blue flowers create a sumptuous picture whether planted on their own or mixed with a trailing form. H 20cm (8in) S 20cm (8in). Tender/Z10.

Flowers with salmon or apricot pink flowers	
Achimenes 'Prima Donna'	*Hyacinthus orientalis* 'Gipsy
Begonia 'Picotee Lace	Queen'
Apricot'	*Narcissus* 'Bell Song'
Crocosmia 'Lady Hamilton'	*Narcissus* 'Romance'
Crocosmia 'Solfatare'	*Narcissus* 'Roseworthy'
Dahlia 'Gerrie Hoek'	*Narcissus* 'Salome'
Dahlia 'Zingaro'	*Schizostylis coccinea* 'Sunrise'
Eremurus 'Oase'	*Tulipa* 'Apricot Beauty'
Eremurus 'Sahara'	*Tulipa* 'Apricot Parrot'
Gladiolus (several)	*Zantedeschia* 'Cameo'

AGAPANTHUS
African blue lily, lily of the Nile

The genus, which contains about 10 species of vigorous, clump-forming perennials with thick, fleshy roots, originates in southern Africa. The plants produce strap-shaped, arching leaves and rounded umbels of blue or white flowers, followed by decorative seedheads.
Cultivation Grow in full sun in moist but well-drained soil in borders or in containers. Plant so that the green portion of the stem appears just above soil level. Where grown in borders mulch in winter as added protection against frost. If grown in containers, use a large, deep pot and a soil-based potting compost (soil mix), with plenty of drainage at the base, and overwinter in a frost-free greenhouse. Overcrowding seems to encourage more generous flower production, so only divide when absolutely necessary. Newly planted specimens will appreciate additional moisture while they are in full growth. Apply a liquid feed monthly from spring until flowering.
Propagation Sow seed at 13–15°C (55–59°F) when ripe, or in spring. Seedlings take 2 to 3 years to flower. Divide in spring.
Pests and diseases Slugs, snails and viruses.

Agapanthus 'Ben Hope'
This cultivar has rounded umbels of open, trumpet-shaped, rich blue flowers, which make a magnificent display from mid- to late summer. H 1.2m (4ft) S 60cm (24in). Hardy/Z7–10.

Achimenes 'Cascade Fairy Pink'

Achimenes 'Prima Donna'

Agapanthus 'Ben Hope'

Agapanthus 'Castle of Mey'

Agapanthus 'Blue Giant'
This cultivar has rounded umbels of open, bell-shaped, rich blue flowers from mid- to late summer. H 1.2m (4ft) S 60cm (24in). Hardy/Z7–10.

Agapanthus 'Blue Moon'
This cultivar has rounded umbels of open, bell-shaped, pale blue flowers, which make a magnificent display in late summer and early autumn. H 60cm (24in) S 45cm (18in). Hardy/Z7–10.

Agapanthus 'Castle of Mey'
This is one of the daintier hybrids, producing rich dark blue flowers from mid- to late summer. H 60cm (24in) S 30cm (12in). Hardy/Z7–10.

Agapanthus 'Headbourne White'
Variable in colour, these summer to late-summer-flowering hybrids are amongst the hardiest grown. They are named after a garden at Headbourne Worthy near Winchester, England. It is a form of *Agapanthus campanulatus*, which originated from a packet of mixed agapanthus seed from the Kirstenbosch Gardens in South Africa. H 90cm (36in) S 50cm (20in). Hardy/Z7–10.

Agapanthus 'Loch Hope'
The deep blue flowers of this agapanthus, which is one of the tallest in the group, appear in late summer and early autumn above grey-green leaves. H 1.5m (5ft) S 60cm (24in). Hardy/Z7–10.

Agapanthus praecox subsp. maximus 'Albus'
This is a beautiful white form of the evergreen species from South Africa, flowering from late summer to early autumn. Best grown in containers in frost-prone sites. H 1.50m (5ft) S 60cm (24in). Borderline hardy/Z9.

Agapanthus praecox subsp. orientalis
(syn. *A. orientalis*)
This subspecies, native to South Africa, has bright blue flowers that in late summer make a striking contrast with the dark green leaves. In frost-prone areas it should be grown in containers. H 60–90cm (24–36in) S 60cm (24in). Half-hardy/Z9–10.

Agapanthus 'Snowball'
A shorter cultivar, with a strong stem and large, rounded umbels of white flowers, which appear in late summer and make a striking contrast with the dark green leaves. It is good beside border paths or in containers. H 40cm (16in) S 40cm (16in). Hardy/Z7–10.

Agapanthus 'Snowy Owl'
The rounded umbels of white flowers are decidedly different in appearance, with each flower being narrow and flared. The flowers open in late summer and are set off beautifully by the dark green leaves. Good for borders or containers. H 1.2m (4ft) S 60cm (24in). Hardy/Z7–10.

Agapanthus 'Headbourne White'

Agapanthus praecox subsp. maximus 'Albus'

ALLIUM
Ornamental onion
This is a large genus of about 700 species of perennial spring-, summer- and autumn-flowering bulbs, and some rhizomes, which originate in dry and mountainous areas of the northern hemisphere. Those described here are mainly late-spring- or early-summer-flowering bulbs. Alliums are commonly referred to as ornamental onions because of their distinctive smell. In fact, all parts generally smell of onions, including the leaves, which often wither by flowering time. They can look untidy so plant the taller varieties behind herbaceous plants, such as geraniums, hostas and hesperis so that they are hidden. Alliums produce short to tall, globe-like umbels of blue, white or yellow flowers, which are usually followed by decorative seedheads. Both the flowers and seedheads are often used for indoor flower arrangements. It is best to remove only the top part of the stem. The flowers are a rich source of nectar for bees. Contact with bulbs may irritate the skin in some people or aggravate some skin allergies.

Cultivation Best grown in full sun, in moist but well-drained soil in garden borders, although they will tolerate partial shade. Borderline hardy species, such as *A. caeruleum, A. cristophii, A. nigrum, A. schubertii, A. tuberosum* and *A. unifolium,* should be mulched in winter to provide extra protection, especially where soils are not so free-draining. Plant bulbs in autumn. As a general guide, aim to plant at a depth which is four times the diameter of the bulb: for *A.* 'Purple Sensation' this would be around 15cm (6in) deep, and for *A. sphaerocephalon* around 8cm (3in). Remove the old stems and leaves once they have withered.

Propagation Sow seed at 13–15°C (55–59°F) when ripe or in spring. Many alliums will self-seed, including *A. hollandicum* and *A. karataviense*; to avoid this, deadhead after flowering. Divide clumps in autumn.

Pests and diseases White rot, downy mildew and onion fly.

Allium caeruleum (syn. *A. azureum*)
Blue garlic
This species from north and Central Asia flowers in summer.

The dense umbels, 2.5cm (1in) across, are composed of 30–50 bright blue, star-shaped flowers, which sway on slender stems. The leaves die back before the flowers appear. Best in a dry situation. H 20–80cm (8–32in) S 2.5cm (1in). Borderline hardy/Z7–10.

Allium carinatum subsp. *pulchellum* (syn. *A. pulchellum*)
This allium originated in central and southern Europe, Russia and Turkey. It flowers in summer, but unlike *A. carinatum,* it does not produce bulbils, so that although it rapidly forms clumps, it is not invasive. It is almost evergreen. The loose umbels, 5cm (2in)

across, have up to 30 rich purple, bell-shaped flowers. The outer ones are pendent. *A. carinatum* subsp. *pulchellum* f. *album* is the white form. H 30–45cm (12–18in) S 5cm (2in). Hardy/Z7–10.

Allium cernuum
Nodding onion, wild onion
This dainty species is native to North America. In summer the stiff stem bends over sharply at the tip and bears pendent umbels, 6cm (2¹/2in) across, consisting of 25–40 nodding, bell-shaped, pink flowers. H 30–60cm (12–24in) S 5cm (2in). Hardy/Z4–10.

Allium cristophii
(syn. *A. albopilosum, A. christophii*)
This extremely popular allium species is native to Iran, Turkey and Central Asia. Flowering in early summer, the umbels are up to 20cm (8in) across and consist of about 50 star-shaped, lilac-purple flowers, which have a lovely rich, metallic sheen in sunlight. Foiled by hardy geraniums, it is perfect for planting beneath a wisteria arch or among early-flowering roses. H 30–60cm (12–24in) S 25cm (10in). Borderline hardy/Z7–10.

Allium 'Firmament'
This recently introduced cultivar, which is a hybrid between *A. atropurpureum* and *A. cristophii,* has dark purple flowers, borne in early summer. The umbels, to 20cm (8in) across, consist of about 50 star-shaped flowers. This is showy but expensive! H 80m (32in) S 25cm (10in). Hardy/Z4–10.

Bulbs that tolerate light or full shade

Allium moly	*Eranthis hyemalis*
Allium triquetrum	*Erythronium*
Allium ursinum	*Galanthus nivalis*
Anemone nemorosa	*Iris siberica*
Arum italicum	*Hyacinthoides non-scripta*
'Marmoratum'	*Hedychium*
Begonia	*Lilium martagon*
Cardiocrinum giganteum	*Ornithogalum nutans*
Cyclamen	*Trillium*

Allium cristophii

Allium x hollandicum

Allium neapolitanum

Allium flavum

This smaller but quite showy species is native to Europe and western Asia. In summer it bears loose umbels, only about 1cm ('/2in) across, of up to 60 bell-shaped, bright yellow flowers. The flowers bend downwards as they open. It self-seeds readily in a sunny spot. H 10–35cm (4–14in) S 5cm (2in). Hardy/Z4–10.

Allium giganteum

This tall species, which is native to Central Asia, flowers in late spring and early summer. The umbels are to 12cm (5in) across and consist of about 50 star-shaped, lilac-pink flowers. It makes a lovely feature on its own or mixed with A. x hollandicum and A. 'Purple Sensation' in a border with wisterias close by. H 1.2m (4ft) S 25cm (10in). Hardy/Z4–10.

Allium 'Globemaster'

This stately allium flowers in late spring and early summer, a second flush following the first and thus extending the season. For this reason, the leaves persist longer than on most alliums. It certainly

lives up to its name with flower globes 15–20cm (6–8in) across. They consist of about 50 showy star-shaped, deep purple flowers. H 80cm (32in) S 25cm (10in). Hardy/Z4–10.

Allium x hollandicum
(syn. A. aflatunense of gardens)
This species is native to Central Asia and flowers in late spring and early summer. The globes, which are to 10cm (4in) across, consist of about 50 star-shaped, purplish-pink flowers held in dense umbels. Bees love them. It is perfect for planting beneath laburnums and wisterias. H 70–90cm (28–36in) S 25cm (10in). Hardy/Z4–10.

Allium karataviense

Also native to Central Asia, this species flowers in late spring. The globes are 5–8cm (2–3in) across and consist of 50 or more small, star-shaped, pale pink flowers with purple midribs, borne on stiff stems. The pair of broad, grey, elliptical, almost horizontal leaves, 15–23cm (6–9in) long, are a special feature, so do not plant medium to large perennials

nearby and obscure them. This allium will self-seed, producing a pleasing massed effect. H 20cm (8in) S 10cm (4in). Hardy/Z4–10.

Allium karataviense 'Ivory Queen'

This cultivar is closely related to the species that grows in Central Asia, but it differs in having ivory white flowers with protruding yellow anthers. Flowering in late spring, the globes are 5–8cm (2–3in) across. As with the parent, the leaves are a special feature. H 20cm (8in) S 10cm (4in). Hardy/Z4–10.

Allium moly
Golden garlic
This small but showy species is native to southwestern and southern Europe. In summer it bears loose umbels, only 5cm (2in) across, of up to 30 bright

yellow, star-shaped flowers. H 15–25cm (6–10in) S 5cm (2in). Hardy/Z4–10.

Allium moly 'Jeannine'

This is slightly taller than the species and is regarded as an improved form. It flowers in summer, bearing loose umbels, only 5cm (2in) across, of up to 30 bright yellow, star-shaped flowers. H 30cm (12in) S 5cm (2in). Hardy/Z4–10.

Allium neapolitanum
(syn. A. cowanii)
This species is native to southern Europe and North Africa. It flowers in summer, bearing globes 5cm (2in) across of up to 30 small, star-shaped, pure white flowers. It is an attractive plant and is excellent in raised troughs. H 20–40cm (8–16in) S 5cm (2in). Borderline hardy/Z7–10.

Allium karataviense

Allium 'Purple Sensation'

Allium oreophilium

Allium schubertii

Allium nigrum
(syn. *A. multibulbosum*)
This species is native to the
Mediterranean. The umbels, 8cm
(3in) across, consist of about 30
creamy white, cup-shaped flowers,
each with a dark green ovary. The
flowers are borne in late spring to
early summer, and it is excellent
under laburnum or white wisterias.
H 70cm (28in) S 25cm (10in).
Borderline hardy/Z7–10.

Allium oreophilum
(syn. *A. ostrowskianum*)
This species is native to the
Caucasus and Central Asia. It
flowers in early summer, bearing

small, loose umbels, just 4cm
(1¹/2in) across, which consist of
up to 15 long-lasting, bell-shaped,
bright carmine-pink flowers. It
makes an easy and effective plant
for a sunny spot at the front of
a well-drained border. H 20cm
(8in) S 5cm (2in). Hardy/Z4–10.

Allium paniculatum
This species is native to Europe
and Central Asia. Flowering in
summer, the ovoid umbels are just
5cm (2in) across and consist of
up to 40 bell-shaped, pink, white
or yellowish-brown flowers with
prominent stamens. The flowers
become pendent as they open. It

provides a long-lasting display
and is best in a sunny, open
site that is not too damp.
H 30–70cm (12–28in) S 5cm
(2in). Hardy/Z4–10.

Allium 'Purple Sensation'
This popular cultivar flowers in
late spring and early summer.
The umbels are up to 10cm (4in)
across and consist of about 50
star-shaped, deep violet flowers.
It is a spectacular species either
planted on its own or mixed with
A. x hollandicum and *A. giganteum*,
where it will create a lovely
mixture of lighter and darker
shades and a variety of heights. It
is one of the best of all alliums.
H 60–90cm (24–36in) S 25cm
(10in). Hardy/Z4–10.

Allium rosenbachianum
This species is native to Central
Asia. It flowers in summer,
bearing globes that are 10cm
(4in) across and consist of 50 or
more star-shaped, deep purple
flowers with protruding violet
stamens. H 90cm (36in) S 15cm
(6in). Borderline hardy/Z7–10.

Allium roseum
Rosy garlic
This species is native to southern
Europe, North Africa and Turkey
and flowers in summer. The tiny
umbels are just 1cm (¹/2in) across
and consist of cup-shaped, pale
pink flowers, often with bulbils
present. These bulbils may be
invasive and are best removed.
H 10–65cm (4–26in) S 5cm
(2in). Hardy/Z4–10.

Allium sativum
Garlic
This species is thought to have
originated in Central Asia, but
its use in cooking has meant that
it is now so commonly grown
that its origins are obscure. It
is made up of ovoid bulbs, each
of 5–18 bulblets enclosed in a
papery tunic. Flowering in
summer, the umbels are just
2.5–5cm (1–2in) across and
consist of white, bell-shaped
flowers, often with bulbils
present. H 90cm (36in) S 25cm
(10in). Hardy/Z4–10.

Allium schoenoprasum
Chives
This species is native to a wide
area in Europe, Asia and North
America. Flowering in late spring
and early summer, it bears small
but showy globes, 2.5cm (1in)

Allium nigrum

Allium schoenoprasum

Allium sphaerocephalon

across, consisting of 30 or more small, bell-shaped, pale purple (sometimes white) flowers borne on stiff stems. The dark green leaves are cylindrical and hollow and are commonly used in cooking, as are the flowers. H 30–60cm (12–24in) S 30cm (12in). Hardy/Z4–10.

Allium schoenoprasum 'Forescate'

More vigorous than the common chive, this cultivar is taller and produces a brighter purplish-pink flowerhead. As with the species, both the leaves and flowers can be used in cooking. H 60cm (24in) S 40cm (16in). Hardy/Z4–10.

Allium schubertii

This species is native to the eastern Mediterranean and Central Asia. The large, rounded umbels, borne on stiff stems, are about 20cm (8in) across.

They have inner and outer zones of small, star-shaped, mauve-blue flowers, just like fireworks. The flowers appear in early summer. Plants need full sun to flower well but are definitely a talking point! H 40cm (16in) S 25cm (10in). Borderline hardy/Z7–10.

Allium sphaerocephalon Round-headed leek

This species, which is known for its drumsticks, is native to Europe, northern Africa and western Asia. Unlike many other alliums, it has ovoid umbels, 2.5cm (1in) across, which are formed from densely packed, pink to reddish-purple flowers and are borne in early to midsummer. It looks attractive with bronze foliage and is good as a cut flower for indoor arrangements. H 60cm (24in) S 8cm (3in). Hardy/Z5–10.

Allium triquetrum Three-cornered leek

This species is native to southern Europe but is now naturalized in Britain, making its home in milder areas in damp, shady conditions. It can be invasive, so keep it for wilder areas of the garden. Its Latin and common names reflect its characteristic triangular stems, which carry clusters of pendent white flowers, each with a green midrib. It flowers from mid- to late spring. H 35cm (14in) S 8cm (3in). Borderline hardy/Z7–10.

Allium tuberosum Chinese chives

The species is native to Southeast Asia. It flowers in late summer to autumn, bearing globes 5cm (2in) across which consist of many small, star-shaped, fragrant white flowers. The leaves, which are up to 35cm (14in) long, are edible, as are the flowers. H 25–50cm (10–20in) S 8cm (3in). Borderline hardy/Z7–10.

Allium unifolium

This species is native to Oregon and California, USA. The globes, which are borne in spring, are 6cm (2¹/₂in) across and consist

of up to 20 small, open bell-shaped, purple-pink flowers, making a lovely border display in the garden. H 30cm (24in) S 10cm (4in). Borderline hardy/Z7–10.

Allium ursinum Ramsons, wild garlic, wood garlic

A common woodland plant, this species is native to Europe and Russia, where it thrives in damp shady places. It may be easily recognized by its distinctive garlicky smell. Flowering in late spring, the globes are to 6cm (2¹/₂in) across and consist of 6–20 small, starry white flowers. H 30cm (24in) S 10cm (4in). Hardy/Z4–10.

Allium vineale 'Hair' False garlic, stag's garlic

This is closely related to the species, which is native to Europe, North Africa and western Asia. It is a distinctive form of allium, with hair-like protuberances giving a twisted appearance. Flowering in summer, it produces long stems with just a few flowers and many green bulbils. Beware: it self-seeds readily, so you may want to avoid it altogether. H 70cm (28in) S 8cm (3in). Hardy/Z4–10.

Allium unifolium

Amaryllis belladonna

AMARYLLIS

This is a genus of just one species of autumn-flowering, deciduous, perennial bulbs. They originally came from coastal hills and besides streams in the Western Cape, South Africa. The true amaryllis is often confused with the tender hippeastrum, which is commonly known and sold as amaryllis and to which it is distantly related. However, the true amaryllis has a solid stem, whereas the hippeastrum (from South America) has a hollow stem. The amaryllis is one of the stars of the autumn border, its wonderful pink, trumpet-shaped flowers creating a focal point when other plants may be over. The strappy leaves appear after flowering.

Cultivation The amaryllis is only borderline hardy so choose a warm, sunny site beneath a sheltered wall and make sure that the soil is well drained. Plant in late summer, when the large, round bulbs are dormant. Plant them so that their necks are just at soil level. Protect the foliage from frost with bracken or straw when temperatures fall below freezing. Alternatively, plant in

deep containers, using soil-based compost (soil mix) with additional leafmould and sand. Enjoy them outside or in a porch or conservatory, where you will be rewarded with the rich fragrance.

Propagation Sow seed at 16°C (61°F) when ripe. Grow on under glass for 1 or 2 seasons before planting in their final position outdoors. Remove offsets in spring after leaves die down or in late summer before growth begins.

Pests and diseases Slugs, narcissus bulb fly; under glass, aphids and red spider mite can be a problem.

Amaryllis belladonna
Belladonna lily, Jersey lily

The species is native to the Western Cape, South Africa. In autumn it produces umbels of 6 or more scented, pink, funnel-shaped flowers, 6–10cm (2¹/2–4in) long. The strappy, fleshy leaves appear after flowering. It looks especially effective planted among low-growing shrubs. In cooler areas it should be grown against a warm wall. This is a truly glorious bulb, which will add drama to any border scheme. H 60cm (24in) S 10cm (4in). Borderline hardy/Z7–10.

ANEMONE
Windflower

This is a genus of about 120 species, some of which have perennial rhizomatous or tuberous rootstocks, mainly flowering in spring and summer. The Greek word *anemos* means wind, which helps to explain why the anemone is commonly known as the windflower, for the delicate petals quiver in the breeze.

Cultivation Grow in sun or partial

shade in well-drained soil; plant in garden borders, in the eye of a tree or in outdoor containers. *A. nemorosa* prefers light shade. Plant the tubers of *A. blanda* 5cm (2in) deep as soon as they are available in autumn. Because they should not be allowed to dry out too much, soak them overnight before planting. As the tubers mature, they will grow to about 10cm (4in) across, producing many flowers. These will self-seed to create large colonies. The knobbly, misshapen tubers of *A. coronaria* De Caen Group and St Bridgid Group are also best soaked overnight before planting and then planted with the buds pointing upwards, 8cm (3in) deep, in autumn (with a mulch) or in spring. Allow to dry off after flowering. Plant the rhizomes of *A. nemorosa* 5cm (2in) deep in autumn.

Propagation Separate the tubers when dormant; plants will self-seed readily.

Pests and diseases Caterpillars, slugs, leaf spot and powdery mildew.

Anemone apennina

Originating from southern Europe, this is a particularly worthy garden plant for dry areas beneath deciduous trees in fine grass. It flowers in early to mid-spring. The pale blue flowers, 2.5cm (1in) or more across, are occasionally white or pink flushed. H 12cm (4¹/2in) S 30cm (12in). Hardy/Z6–9.

Anemone blanda

Anemone coronaria St Bridgid Group

Anemone nemorosa

Anemone blanda

Originating from the eastern Mediterranean, this is a very worthy garden plant, flowering for 6–8 weeks from late winter to mid-spring. The starry flowers, 2.5cm (1in) or more across, have 10–15 white, pale blue or dark blue, occasionally mauve and pink, petals. The attractive leaves are fern-like. They associate beautifully with primroses and all early dwarf daffodils and are excellent in garden borders or beneath the eye of a tree, where they will self-seed. They are also good for containers. H 10–15cm (4–6in) S 15cm (6in). Hardy/Z6–9.

Anemone blanda 'Radar'

This is a brightly coloured form, with magenta flowers and contrasting white centres. Like the species, it flowers for 6–8 weeks from late winter to mid-spring. The leaves are darker green than those of its parent. H 10–15cm (4–6in) S 15cm (6in). Hardy/Z6–9.

Anemone blanda 'White Splendour'

This is a particularly robust and welcome A. blanda, with its large, starry, bright white flowers that create a wonderfully welcome sight in early spring and last well into mid-spring. The attractive leaves are fern-like. The flowers show off well in front of dark foliage plants, and they associate beautifully with white-barked birches. H 15–20cm (6–8in) S 15cm (6in). Hardy/Z6–9.

Anemone coronaria De Caen Group and St Bridgid Group

Both groups derive from the original species, A. coronaria, which is found in the Mediterranean area. Plants in the De Caen Group bear single white, red, pink, mauve or blue flowers. These are 2.5–8cm (1–3in) across and have 6–8 petals. A. 'The Bride' is a stunning white. The St Bridgid Group includes plants with semi-double flowers with a mass of petals. Colours vary from red, pink, violet, blue to white. A. 'Lord Lieutenant' is a splendid blue. All these anemones should be grown in a sheltered spot near the front of a border or in containers. The flowers appear from late spring to early summer, depending on planting time. Generally allow 3 months between planting and early or midsummer flowering, but longer for a late-spring show. They make ideal cut flowers but should be picked while in bud. H 25cm (10in) S 15cm (6in). Hardy/Z8–10.

Anemone nemorosa
Wood anemone

Originating in the woodlands of Europe, this is a vigorous, carpeting plant, which flowers from spring to early summer. It bears dainty, demure white flowers, sometimes with a pink flush, about 2.5cm (1in) across and with 6–8 petals. It is useful for naturalizing in light shade beneath deciduous shrubs or in woodland areas. H 8–15cm (3–6in) S 30cm (12in). Hardy/Z4–8.

Anemone nemorosa 'Robinsoniana'

This is a lovely wood anemone with large, pale blue petals, named in 1870 at the Oxford Botanic Gardens. H 15cm (6in) S 30cm (12in). Hardy/Z4–8.

Anemone nemorosa 'Rosea'

This pale pink form of the wood anemone is very pretty and much sought after. Plant in a small colony where it can be treasured on its own. H 8–15cm (3–6in) S 30cm (12in). Hardy/Z4–8.

Anemone coronaria De Caen Group

Arum italicum 'Marmoratum'

ARUM
Cuckoo pint, lords and ladies

The genus contains 26 species of mainly spring-flowering, tuberous perennials found in partially shady locations as far afield as southern Europe, North Africa and western Asia to the Himalayas. All parts if eaten can cause severe discomfort, and contact with the sap may irritate the skin.

Cultivation Plant tubers 10–15cm (4–6in) deep in autumn or spring. Choose a well-drained site in sun or partial shade.

Propagation Sow seed in a cold frame in the autumn, first removing the outer pulp from the berries. Divide clumps of tubers after flowering.

Pests and diseases Trouble free.

Arum italicum 'Marmoratum'
(syn. *A. italicum pictum*)

This cultivar is related to a species that originates in southern Europe, Turkey and North Africa. The species is renowned for its glossy, arrow- or spear-shaped leaves, which have distinctive cream veins, and the leaves of this cultivar are veined with pale green or cream. It flowers in early summer and needs an open, sunny site to do best, when it will produce white spathes, 15–40cm (6–16in) long, each enclosing a spike of rich red berries in late summer. However, it is the foliage that is the main attraction, and grown in partial shade it will produce bigger leaves. These emerge in late autumn or winter, and their striking distinctive shape and markings make them particularly sought-after for flower arrangements. This is a useful plant for the winter garden, where it creates a fine backdrop for snowdrops and winter aconites. H 30cm (12in) S 15cm (6in). Hardy/Z7–9.

ASPHODELINE
Jacob's rod

This genus of up to 20 species of biennials and perennials originated in sunny, rocky meadows from the Mediterranean to the Caucasus. They grow from rhizomes and produce tall racemes of yellow or white flowers, with grass-like, basal and stem leaves.

Cultivation Grow in moderately fertile, well-drained soil in full sun. Mulch in autumn in cold areas.

Propagation Sow in a cold frame in spring. Divide in late summer or early autumn by teasing apart the fleshy rhizomes and replanting.

Pests and diseases Slugs, snails and aphids.

Asphodeline liburnica

This species is native to Austria, Greece, Italy and the Balkans. It forms neat clumps with slender stems and fine, linear, grey-green foliage. The bright yellow flowers appear in summer and are fragrant. H 25–60cm (10–24in) S 30cm (12in). Hardy/Z6–9.

Asphodeline lutea
King's spear, yellow asphodel

This perennial, native to central and eastern Mediterranean and western Turkey, is clump-forming and larger than *A. liburnica*. In late spring and summer it produces tall, dense racemes to 20cm (8in) long. The bright yellow flowers associate well with a foreground of lime-green foliage such as that of golden marjoram *Origanum vulgare* 'Aureum' and a background of bronze foliage such as *Cotinus* 'Grace'. H 1.2m (4ft) S 30cm (12in). Hardy/Z6–9.

Asphodeline lutea

Begonia 'Can-can'

BEGONIA

The genus was named in honour of Michel Bégon (1638–1710), a French botanist and governor of French Canada. It is a huge genus, containing about 900 species, some of which are tuberous-rooted. The tuberous begonias, whose tubers are dormant in winter, include the Tuberhybrida, Multiflora and Pendula types, which derive from species growing in the Andes. They may be found under the headings Fimbriata begonias, which bear carnation-type petals, Exotic begonias, whose flowers are two-toned, the Non-Stop flowering kinds, which are generally compact and good for bedding, and the Pendulous or Cascading types, which are useful in hanging baskets or raised beds.
Cultivation Grow in sun or partial shade in garden borders or containers. Start the tubers into growth in spring indoors, placing them on the surface of the compost (soil mix), the hollow side upwards, at 16–18°C (61–64°F). Move outside into summer flowering positions after all risk of frost has passed. Allow to dry after flowering. Lift tubers in autumn, dry off, dust with fungicide and store in cool, dry conditions at 5–7°C (41–45°F).
Propagation Sow seed and root basal cuttings in spring.
Pests and diseases Vine weevil is a major problem in late summer.

Begonia 'Billie Langdon'
Flowering from midsummer until early autumn, this *B. x tuberhybrida* cultivar is a large, upright begonia with pure white flowers, each to 18cm (7in) in diameter. The mid-green leaves can reach 20cm (8in) in length. It is best planted on its own in a heavy container. H 60cm (24in) S 45cm (18in). Tender/Z10.

Begonia 'Can-can'
Flowering from midsummer until early autumn, this is a *B. x tuberhybrida* cultivar with an upright habit. It has rich yellow flowers, to 17cm (6¹/₂in) across. The petals have a ruffled red edge, which makes a beautiful combination. Ideal for a single-specimen container. H 90cm (36in) S 45cm (18in). Tender/Z10.

Begonia 'Champagne'
Flowering from midsummer until early autumn, this is a *B. x tuberhybrida* cultivar. The double flowers, 5–8cm (2–3in) across, have creamy white petals and form generous clusters of cascading colour around the plant, trailing to 20cm (8in). This begonia is ideal for planting in wall pots, window boxes or hanging baskets, either on its own or combined with other summer-flowering bedding plants such as *Lobelia* and *Impatiens*. H 20cm (8in) S 20cm (8in). Tender/Z10.

Begonia 'Giant Flowered Pendula Yellow'

Begonia 'Flamboyant'
Flowering from midsummer until early autumn, this is a *B. x tuberhybrida* cultivar with an upright habit. It was first grown in 1911. It has single, dark scarlet-red flowers and is ideal for a container. H 30cm (12in) S 15cm (6in). Tender/Z10.

Begonia 'Giant Flowered Pendula Yellow'
Flowering from midsummer until early autumn, the double and single yellow flowers are 5cm (2in) across. This pendulous begonia, a *B. x tuberhybrida* cultivar, trails to 20cm (8in); it is ideal for hanging baskets and window boxes. There is also an attractive 'Giant Flowered Pendula Orange' as well as pink, white and red forms. H 20cm (8in) S 20cm (8in). Tender/Z10.

Begonia grandis subsp. *evansiana*
Flowering from midsummer until early autumn, this species is native to China, Malaysia and Japan. It has notched, olive-green leaves, 10cm (4in) long, which are pale green, sometimes red, on the underside. The pink or white flowers are fragrant. H 50cm (20in) S 30cm (12in). Half-hardy/Z10.

Bulbs with creamy flowers

Begonia 'Champagne'	Hippeastrum 'Yellow Goddess'
Camassia leichtlinii subsp. leichtlinii	Lilium 'Roma'
	Lilium 'Belle Epoque'
Crocus 'Cream Beauty'	Narcissus 'Topolino'
Crocus 'E.A. Bowles'	Narcissus 'Silver Chimes'
Galtonia candicans	Tulipa 'Peaches and Cream'
Gladiolus 'Charming Beauty'	Tulipa 'Spring Green'

Begonia 'Non-stop Orange'

Begonia 'Picotee Lace Apricot'

Begonia 'Helene Harms'

Flowering from midsummer until early autumn, this old cultivar, dating back to 1902, is an upright begonia with many semi-double, yellow flowers, 5–8cm (2–3in) across. The mid-green leaves are 20cm (8in) long. H 13cm (5in) S 15cm (6in). Tender/Z10.

Begonia 'Marginata Crispa'

Flowering from midsummer until early autumn, this B. x tuberhybrida cultivar has an upright habit. The yellow petals have ruffled red edges, which makes a delightful combination. Ideal for window boxes or containers. H 20cm (8in) S 20cm (8in). Tender/Z10.

Begonia 'Non-stop Orange'

Flowering from midsummer until early autumn, this is a B. x tuberhybrida cultivar. It is an upright begonia, with double orange flowers to 10cm (4in) across, and it looks wonderful in a container or window box. There are also double yellow, pink, red and white Non-stop begonias. H 18cm (7in) S 20cm (8in). Tender/Z10.

Begonia 'Pendula Cascade White'

Flowering from midsummer until early autumn, the flowers of this trailing begonia are finer than those of the Giant Flowered cultivars. They reach 5cm (2in) in diameter, but are held on slender stems. The plant will trail to 18cm (7in), making it ideal for hanging baskets and window boxes. There is also an attractive 'Pendula Cascade Orange' as well as yellow, pink and red forms. H 18cm (7in) S 20cm (8in). Tender/Z10.

Begonia 'Picotee'

Flowering from midsummer until early autumn, this cultivar is upright in habit, but its large, heavy flowers create a natural fountain effect, which provides colour all around the margins of the plant as well as in the centre. The rich yellow-orange flowers show patches of yellow, giving a two-toned effect, but the edges are deep orange, making a strong contrast. The colour will vary according to summer temperatures at both day and night. It is an excellent choice for large hanging baskets, window boxes, pots or troughs. H 20cm (8in) S 20cm (8in). Tender/Z10.

Begonia 'Picotee Lace Apricot'

Flowering from midsummer until early autumn, this cultivar is upright in habit. The rich apricot flowers are ruffled and edged in white. They make an excellent underplanting to orange fuchsias, such as 'Thalia'. H 20cm (8in) S 20cm (8in). Tender/Z10.

Begonia 'Roy Hartley'

Flowering from midsummer until early autumn, this cultivar has double pink flowers, to 10cm (4in) across, tinged with salmon-pink. It flowers from mid- to late summer. H 60cm (24in) S 40cm (16in). Tender/Z10.

Begonia sutherlandii

This elegant spreading species, which originates in South Africa and Tanzania, is an ideal subject for a hanging basket or window box and is perhaps best grown on its own where it can be shown to greatest advantage. The pendent, clear orange flowers are produced in succession throughout summer, providing a really colourful display. H 15–30cm (6–12in) S 45cm (18in). Half-hardy/Z10.

Begonia 'Picotee'

Brimeura amethystina

flowers, 4–6cm (1¹/₂–2¹/₂in) across, each with reddish-brown marks towards the base of the petals. The flowers appear in late spring to early summer. H 50–60cm (20–24in) S 5–10cm (2–4in). Borderline hardy/Z5–10.

CAMASSIA
Quamash
This is a genus of about 5 species of bulbs which thrive in damp meadowland. The common name was given by the Native Americans of the Pacific Northwest, where the plants originate. They are also sometimes known as wild hyacinths, which they resemble. They make an excellent choice for a natural garden where they will flower at the same time as buttercups and cow parsley.
Cultivation In autumn plant the bulbs in borders or grassland at a depth of 10cm (4in) and 10cm (4in) apart and allow to naturalize. They will form good groups. Grow in sun or partial shade.
Propagation Sow seed in pots in a cold frame as soon as ripe, or remove offsets in late summer.
Pests and diseases Trouble free.

Camassia cusickii
This species comes from northeastern Oregon. It flowers in late spring to early summer, bearing long racemes of cup-shaped, pale to deep blue flowers. It will cope with a fairly shady position. H 60–80cm (24–32in) S 10cm (4in). Borderline hardy/Z3–8.

BRIMEURA
This is a genus of only 2 species of bulbs coming from the mountain meadows and garigue of south-east Europe and the Pyrenees.
Cultivation Grow in sun or partial shade but choose a well-drained, humus-rich soil. Where temperatures fall below −10°C (14°F) provide a winter protection of bracken or leafmould. Plant the bulbs 5–8cm (2–3in) deep and 2.5cm (1in) apart.
Propagation Sow seed in pots in a cold frame as soon as it is ripe. Plant out after 2 years. Divide clumps when dormant in summer.
Pests and diseases None.

Brimeura amethystina
(syn. *Hyacinthus amethystinus*)
This late-spring- to early-summer-flowering bulb has narrow, semi-erect leaves. Each flowering stem bears up to 15 pendent, tubular, blue flowers, at first sight similar to those of a diminutive bluebell. H 10–25cm (4–10in) S 2.5–5cm (1–2in). Hardy/Z5–9.

CALOCHORTUS
Butterfly tulip, cat's ears, fairy lanterns, globe lily
This is a genus of about 60 species of bulbs from grasslands and open woodland of western North America and Mexico. The botanical name originates from the Greek words *kalós* (beautiful) and *chortos* (grass). The flowers are, indeed, beautiful, and the leaves are grass-like. The many common names also reflect the shape and habit of the flowers.
Cultivation Plant the bulbs 8cm (3in) deep and 8cm (3in) apart in pots containing soil-based compost (potting mix). Then they are best overwintered under cover to guard against rain. In late spring the pots can be buried in garden soil, where they can be allowed to flower. In mild, sunny areas plant direct into well-drained soil in sheltered borders in autumn. Whether the bulbs are in containers or garden soil, choose a site that is in full sun. After flowering, the bulbs divide and do not flower again the following year but miss 1–2 seasons.

Propagation Sow seed in pots in a cold frame as soon as ripe, or remove offsets in late summer.
Pests and diseases None.

Calochortus luteus 'Golden Orb'
This cultivar is derived from the species *C. luteus*, which grows in California, where it is known as the yellow mariposa. Tall, thin but sturdy, branched stems bear 1–7 deep yellow, open bell-shaped

Calochortus luteus 'Golden Orb'

Camassia cusickii

Camassia leichtlinii subsp. *suksdorfii*

CANNA
Indian shot plant

This is a genus of 50 species of rhizomatous herbaceous perennials from moist open areas of forests in Asia and the tropical parts of North and South America. The genus name comes from the Greek word *kanna* (reed).

Cultivation In spring plant the rhizomes under glass in large containers, 5cm (2in) deep and 60cm (2ft) apart. If required, move outside from early to midsummer. Choose a sunny, sheltered spot on the patio or if you wish, transplant from containers into sunny, sheltered borders. Alternatively, grow them in or near water. Deadhead to promote continuity of flowering. Apply a liquid feed every month. Before the foliage turns black with frost in autumn, remove the stems, dig up the roots and store in barely moist peat or leafmould in frost-free conditions. In just one season a single rhizome will produce a root system to 50cm (20in) across.

Propagation Sow seed at 21°C (70°F) in spring or autumn. Chip seed or soak for 24 hours in warm water before sowing. In early spring divide rhizomes into short sections, each with a prominent eye. Pot on and start into growth at 16°C (61°F), watering sparingly at first.

Pests and diseases Outdoors, slugs and caterpillars; indoors, red spider mite.

Canna 'Black Knight'
Flowering from midsummer to early autumn, this cultivar has attractive bronze foliage and luscious dark red flowers. H 1.8m (6ft) S 50cm (20in). Half-hardy/Z7–10.

Canna 'King Midas'
Flowering from midsummer to early autumn, this canna has dark green leaves and golden-yellow flowers with orange markings. H 1.5m (5ft) S 50cm (20in). Half-hardy/Z7–10.

Canna 'Louis Cottin'
Flowering from midsummer to early autumn, this is a cultivar with bronze foliage and yellow flowers spotted with red. Both the leaves and the flowers are apt to bleach so avoid planting it in full sun. H 1.2m (4ft) S 50cm (20in). Half-hardy/Z7–10.

Canna 'Lucifer'
Flowering from midsummer to early autumn, this is a short but free-flowering cultivar. It has racemes of bright red flowers, each edged with yellow, and attractive mid-green foliage. H 60cm (24in) S 50cm (20in). Half-hardy/Z7–10.

Camassia leichtlinii subsp. *leichtlinii*
(syn. *C. leichtlinii* 'Alba')
Indian lily
This subspecies comes from western North America, from California to British Columbia. It flowers in late spring, bearing tall racemes of star-shaped, creamy white flowers, each 5–8cm (2–3in) across. H 60–130cm (30–54in) S 10cm (4in). Borderline hardy/Z5–9.

Camassia leichtlinii subsp. *suksdorfii*
Indian lily
The species, which also comes from western North America, from California to British Columbia, bears tall racemes of star-shaped, blue to violet flowers, each 5–8cm (2–3in) across. Flowering in late spring, it associates well with *Narcissus poeticus* var. *recurvus* (pheasant's eye narcissus). H 60–130 (30–54in) S 10cm (4in). Borderline hardy/Z5–9.

Camassia quamash
Common camassia
This late-spring-flowering bulb bears a spike of star-shaped white, violet or blue flowers, each measuring 7cm (3in) across. It originates in North America, from Canada to Montana, and the bulbs were once an important source of food for Native Americans, who used to pit-roast or boil them. H 20–80cm (8–32in) S 10cm (4in). Borderline hardy, Z4–10.

Canna 'Durban'

Canna 'Roi Humbert'

Canna 'Lucifer'

Canna 'Monet'
Flowering from midsummer to early autumn, this canna has blue-green leaves and soft salmon-pink flowers. H 90cm (36in) S 50cm (20in). Half-hardy/Z7–10.

Canna 'Orange Perfection'
Flowering from midsummer to early autumn, this is another short cultivar. The flowers are a beautiful soft orange. H 60cm (24in) S 50cm (20in). Half-hardy/Z7–10.

Canna 'Picasso'
Flowering from midsummer to early autumn, this cultivar has blue-green leaves and yellow flowers spotted with red. Both flowers and leaves are apt to bleach so avoid a position in full sun. H 90cm (36in) S 50cm (20in). Half-hardy/Z7–10.

Canna 'President'
Flowering from midsummer to early autumn, this canna has long racemes of red flowers, 5cm (2in) wide, to accompany the mid-green foliage. This is a taller cultivar. H 90cm (36in) S 50cm (20in). Half-hardy/Z7–10.

Canna 'Roi Humbert'
Formerly known as *Canna* 'Red King Humbert', this canna flowers from midsummer to early autumn. It is a tall cultivar, with large racemes, 20–30cm (8–12in) long, of orange-scarlet flowers, which show up well against the leaves. The colour associates well with other bronze-foliage plants, such as grasses or *Foeniculum vulgare* 'Purpureum' (bronze fennel). H 2.1m (7ft) S 50cm (20in). Half-hardy/Z7–10.

Canna 'Rosemond Coles'
Flowering from midsummer to early autumn, this cultivar has long racemes of large red flowers, 8cm (3in) across, each edged with yellow and with yellow-spotted throats. The undersides of the petals are golden-yellow. H 1.5m (5ft) S 50cm (20in). Half-hardy/Z7–10.

Canna 'Striata'
Flowering from midsummer to early autumn, this cultivar has long racemes of orange flowers 8cm (3in) wide, and light green foliage striped with yellow veins. H 1.5m (5ft) S 50cm (20in). Half-hardy/Z7–10.

Canna 'Striped Beauty'
Flowering from midsummer to early autumn, this cultivar is shorter than most. It has creamy white veining in its foliage, and the flower buds open to reveal red flowers. H 80cm (32in) S 50cm (20in). Half-hardy/Z7–10.

Canna 'Tropicanna'
(syn. *C.* 'Phaison', *C.* Durban)
Flowering from midsummer to early autumn, this canna has tall spikes of orange flowers 5cm (2in) wide. They are set off by the wonderfully deep bronze foliage, which has striking pink veins. H 90cm (3ft) S 60cm (2ft). Half-hardy/Z7–10.

Canna 'Wyoming'
Flowering from midsummer to early autumn, this cultivar has pretty frilled orange flowers showing up well against the dark brown-purple leaves. H 1.8m (6ft) S 50cm (20in). Half-hardy/Z7–10.

Canna 'Picasso'

Canna 'Rosemond Coles'

Canna 'Wyoming'

Cardiocrinum giganteum

Chionodoxa sardensis

CARDIOCRINUM

This is a genus of 3 species of summer-flowering bulbous perennials, the most commonly grown of which is *Cardiocrinum giganteum*. The bulbs are grown for their lily-like flowers and attractive, heart-shaped leaves.
Cultivation Requires partial shade and moist, humus-rich soil. Avoid excessive dryness. They are ideal for growing in a woodland garden. In autumn plant bulbs just below the soil surface. Protect emerging growth in spring with a dry mulch. Water well in summer and provide a mulch of organic matter to prevent water evaporation.
Propagation The bulbs die after flowering, but offsets or daughter bulbs are produced and will flower in 3–5 years. Ripe seed may take seven years to flower.
Pests and diseases Lily viruses and slug damage.

Cardiocrinum giganteum
Giant lily
This species originates in the Himalayas, northwest Burma, southwest China and Japan. The leaves are broad and strongly veined. In late summer the magnificent tall racemes bear up to 20 fragrant, trumpet-shaped, cream flowers, streaked with purplish-red inside, which grow to 15cm (6in) long and are followed by decorative seedheads. Do not allow the soil to dry out. H 1.5–4m (5–13ft) S 45cm (18in). Hardy/Z7–9.

CHIONODOXA
Glory of the snow
This is a genus of 6 species of bulbs found on open mountain sides and forests in Crete, western Turkey and Cyprus. They are closely related to scillas.

Cultivation Choose a site in full sun and in autumn plant 5cm (2in) deep and 5cm (2in) apart.
Propagation Sow seed in pots in a cold frame as soon as they are ripe. Remove offsets in summer. They will naturalize easily.
Pests and diseases Largely trouble free.

Chionodoxa forbesii
Native to western Turkey, this species flowers in early spring, the racemes bearing up to 12 star-shaped, blue flowers, each with a white centre. H 10cm (4in) S 3cm (1¼in). Hardy/Z3–9.

Chionodoxa forbesii '**Pink Giant**'
Derived from a species growing in western Turkey, 'Pink Giant' is a most garden-worthy cultivar, producing long racemes of 4–12 star-shaped, pale pink flowers, 1–2cm (½–¼in) wide, with white centres. The flowers are borne from early to mid-spring, so plant in the border or put several in a container in association with violas and dwarf daffodils. H 15cm (6in) S 4cm (1½in). Hardy/Z3–9.

Chionodoxa sardensis
Also from western Turkey, this species is slightly smaller than *C. luciliae*. In early spring racemes bear 4–12 star-shaped, deep clear blue flowers with blue centres, perfect for associating with blue *Anemone blanda*. H 10cm (4in) S 3cm (1¼in). Hardy/Z3–9.

Chionodoxa forbesii 'Pink Giant'

Colchicum speciosum 'Album'

Colchicum 'The Giant'

COLCHICUM

Autumn crocus, naked ladies

Colchicums are commonly known as autumn crocus because of their resemblance to the better known spring-flowering crocus and as naked ladies because they flower before the leaves emerge. In the United States they are known as naked boys. The genus contains about 45 species, which are native to alpine and sub-alpine meadows and stony slopes of Europe, north Africa, western and central Asia, northern India and western China.

Cultivation Grow in well-drained soil in full sun. In summer or early autumn plant corms 10cm (4in) deep in open ground in borders or grassland.

Propagation Sow seed in pots in a cold frame as soon as ripe or separate corms when dormant in summer. Increases freely.

Pests and diseases Grey mould and slugs.

Colchicum autumnale
Meadow saffron

This species grows in the sub-alpine meadows of Europe. In autumn each corm produces 1–6 goblet-shaped, lavender-pink flowers, with petals 3–5cm (1–2in) long. The flowers soon flop over. The broad leaves, 25cm (10in) long, appear after flowering, growing most in spring. The leaves might dwarf other spring-flowering bulbs, so take care with the position. This is a good choice for naturalizing in grass. H 10–15cm (4–6in) S 10–15cm (4–6in). Hardy/Z4–9.

Colchicum bivonae

This species grows in the sub-alpine meadows of southern Europe, from Corsica and Sardinia to western Turkey. Large, funnel-shaped, pinkish-purple flowers, chequered with dark purple, appear in late summer and autumn. The leaves are produced in spring. H 10–15cm (4–6in) S 10–15cm (4–6in). Hardy/Z4–9.

Colchicum speciosum 'Album'

The species originated in Caucasus, northeastern Turkey and Iran, and this is the most widely grown cultivar. In autumn 1–3 goblet-shaped, weather-resistant, white flowers, with petals 5–8cm (2–3in) long, appear long before the glossy leaves, which emerge in late winter or early spring. This is an excellent plant in open ground in borders or grassland. Left undisturbed, the corms will eventually produce large clumps. H 20cm (8in) S 20cm (8in). Hardy/Z4–9.

Colchicum 'The Giant'

This hybrid is one of many cultivars, and in autumn it produces a succession of up to 5 large purplish-violet flowers, each with the typical goblet shape. H 20cm (8in) S 20cm (8in). Hardy/Z4–9.

Colchicum 'Pink Goblet'

The pretty pink goblet-shaped flowers are produced in early autumn. They are perfect for planting in open spaces between shrubs where they can be left to naturalize. H 20cm (8in) S 10cm (4in). Hardy/Zone 4–9.

Colchicum 'Violet Queen'

One to five pretty pinkish-violet flowers with pointed tepals are produced in early autumn. They are funnel-shaped and fragrant. H 15cm (6in) S 10cm (4in). Hardy/Zone 4–9.

Colchicum 'Waterlily'

This hybrid is unusual in that it has tightly double flowers, with pinkish-lilac petals. In autumn it produces a succession of up to 5 blooms. The heads are heavy, so it is best grown where it will be supported by surrounding plants such as violas and lamiums. H 10–15cm (4–6in) S 15–20cm (6–8in). Hardy/Z4–9.

Colchicum 'Violet Queen'

CORYDALIS

The flowers of corydalis are an unusual shape. Each bears a long spur on the upper petal, and this gave rise to the name of the genus, for the Greek word *korydalis* means lark, and the spur on the flowers was thought to resemble the spur of the lark. This is a genus of about 300 species of fleshy- or fibrous-rooted annuals and biennials and tuberous or rhizomatous perennials. Most are herbaceous, although a few are evergreen. Many are from wooded or rocky mountain sites in northern temperate regions.
Cultivation Grow *C. solida* in full sun (although it will tolerate partial shade) and *C. cava* and *C. fumariifolia* in partial shade. In autumn plant tubers 8cm (3in) deep in borders or beneath trees and shrubs, where they will quickly colonize.
Propagation Sow seed in pots in a cold frame as soon as ripe. Divide spring-flowering species in autumn. Plants increase freely.
Pests and diseases Snails and slugs.

Corydalis cava
(syn. *C. bulbosa* of gardens)
Native to Europe, this corydalis has dense spikes of dark purple or white flowers, each up 2.5cm (1in) long, with downward-curving spurs. It flowers in spring and dies down in summer. H 10–20cm (4–8in) S 10cm (4in). Hardy/Z6–8.

Corydalis fumariifolia
(syn. *C. ambigua* of gardens)
This species originates in Russia, China and Japan. The bright blue or purplish-blue flowers, about 2.5cm (1in) long, have flattened, triangular spurs. It flowers in spring and dies down in summer. H 10–15cm (4–6in) S 10cm (4in). Hardy/Z7–8.

Corydalis solida
Fumewort
This spring-flowering species, native to northern Europe and Asia, bears dense racemes of pale mauve-pink to red-purple or white flowers, each to 2cm (¼in) long, with downward-curving spurs, held above grey foliage. *C.* 'George Baker' AGM has deep reddish-pink flowers. Fumewort looks pretty with daffodils and other spring bulbs, all of which make ideal bedfellows. For those planted in partial shade, taller *Lilium martagon* (martagon lilies) can be planted to follow on later. H 18cm (7in) S 10cm (4in). Hardy/Z7–8.

Crinum x powellii 'Album'

CRINUM

The botanical name for the genus comes from the Greek word *krinon* (lily). It includes about 130 species of deciduous or evergreen bulbs, found near streams and lakes throughout tropical regions and South Africa. Contact with the sap may irritate the skin.
Cultivation Best grown in full sun outdoors in a sheltered border or in pots under glass. The bulbs are extremely large with long necks and can measure to 20cm (8in) in length. In spring plant so that the neck of the bulb is just above soil level. In a conservatory plant in soil-based compost (soil mix) with added sand and fertilizer, and grow in full or bright but filtered light. Water freely when in growth and keep moist after flowering. Provide a deep mulch in winter for plants in the garden.
Propagation Sow seed at 21°C (70°F) as soon as ripe. Remove offsets in spring.
Pests and diseases None.

Crinum x powellii 'Album'
This hybrid of two South African species has umbels of up to 10 widely flared, fragrant white flowers, to 10cm (4in) long. These are borne in late summer or early autumn above broad leaves, which may reach to 1.5m (5ft). It is an impressive plant, and grown well in moist but well-drained soil, it makes a beautiful garden specimen. *C. x powellii* AGM is pink. H 1.5m (5ft) S 30cm (12in). Borderline hardy/Z6–10.

Corydalis solida

Crocosmia 'Emberglow'

Crocosmia 'Solfatare'

CROCOSMIA

The name of the genus derives from *krokos*, the Greek word for saffron, and *osme* (smell), because the dried flowers smell of saffron when they are immersed in warm water. This is a small genus of only 9 species of clump-forming corms from grasslands in South Africa. The name montbretia is generally applied to all crocosmias, but strictly speaking montbretia is the hybrid *C. x crocosmiiflora*.

Cultivation Grow in sun or partial shade. In spring plant corms 8–10cm (3–4in) deep among shrubs or in a herbaceous border, but mulch during the first winter and in subsequent severe or prolonged frosty spells. In marginal areas plant beneath a sheltered, south-facing wall. Tall growth will benefit from support in early summer. Lift and divide clumps in spring to retain vigour.

Propagation Sow seeds in pots as soon as ripe. Divide in spring just before growth begins.

Pests and diseases Red spider mites may be a problem.

Crocosmia **'Bressingham Blaze'**
Appearing in late summer, the brilliant orange-red flowers contrast with the yellow throats to make colourful, arching sprays. The leaves are strappy, pleated and mid-green. H 75–90m (30–36in) S 8cm (3in). Borderline hardy/Z5–9.

Crocosmia **'Emberglow'**
The dark red flowers, which are borne in summer, make an impressive array on their arching stems. The leaves are strappy, pleated and mid-green. H 60–75m (24–30in) S 8cm (3in). Borderline hardy/Z5–9.

Crocosmia **'Emily McKenzie'**
In summer this smaller cultivar produces downward-facing, bright orange flowers, with attractive mahogany throat markings. The leaves are strappy and mid-green. H 60cm (24in) S 8cm (3in). Borderline hardy/Z5–9.

Crocosmia **'Firebird'**
Flowering in summer, this cultivar has upward-facing, bright orange-red flowers. The leaves are strappy and mid-green. H 80cm (32in) S 8cm (3in). Borderline hardy/Z5–9.

Crocosmia **'George Davison'**
Appearing in late summer, the lemon-yellow flowers of this cultivar make a lovely display on their slightly arching stems. The leaves are strappy and mid-green. H 60–75cm (24–30in) S 8cm (3in). Borderline hardy/Z5–9.

Crocosmia **'Lady Hamilton'**
Flowering in late summer, this attractive cultivar has golden-yellow flowers with apricot centres. The leaves are strappy and mid-green. H 60–75cm (24–30in) S 8cm (3in). Borderline hardy/Z5–9.

Crocosmia **'Lucifer'**
Flowering in midsummer, this cultivar has upward-facing, bright red flowers, 5cm (2in) long, on tall, slightly arching stems. The leaves are strappy, pleated and mid-green. H 1.2m (4ft) S 8cm (3in). Borderline hardy/Z5–9.

Crocosmia masoniorum
Flowering in midsummer, the upward-facing orange flowers are borne okn tall arching stems. H 1.2cm (4ft) S 8cm (3in). Borderline hardy/Z5–9.

Crocosmia **'Solfatare'**
Flowering in midsummer, this cultivar has bronze foliage with apricot yellow flowers borne on arching stems. H 60cm (24in) S 8cm (3in). Borderline hardy/Z5–9.

Crocosmia 'Lucifer'

Tall flowering bulbs over 70cm (28in)

Agapanthus 'Loch Hope'	Dahlia (many)
Allium giganteum	Eremurus 'Oase'
Allium 'Purple Sensation'	Eremurus x isabellinus
Asphodeline lutea	Galtonia candicans
Canna (most)	Lilium (most)
Crinum x powellii	Nectaroscordum siculum
Crocosmia 'Lucifer'	Tulipa 'Blue Heron'

CROCUS

The name is derived from the Greek *krokos* (saffron), and the genus includes the species *Crocus sativus*, cultivated for the spice saffron, which is obtained from its stigmas. The genus embraces more than 80 species of dwarf corms, found in a wide range of locations, from central and southern Europe, northern Africa, the Middle East, Central Asia and western China. Hundreds of cultivars have been produced from the original species. The crocus is one of our best-known late-winter and early-spring flowers, but there are several species that flower in autumn, as well as the true autumn crocus, which is quite distinct from, and not to be confused with, colchicums, which are sometimes referred to as autumn crocus.

Cultivation Grow in full sun. Plant corms 8cm (3in) deep in borders or containers in autumn for late winter- to spring-flowering crocuses and in late summer for autumn-flowering ones.

Propagation Many crocuses self-seed naturally. Remove baby corms during dormancy.

Pests and diseases Squirrels, mice and voles eat the corms; birds will pick off the flowers.

Crocus 'Blue Pearl'

Flowering in late winter to early spring, this hybrid is derived from a species that grows in southeastern Europe. The flowers have a soft blue outer colour, with white inner petals with yellow throats. The delicate colouring is superb. H 8cm (3in) S 5cm (2in). Hardy/Z3–8.

Crocus 'Cream Beauty'

Appearing in late winter to early spring, the flowers have a soft blue outer colour, with white inner petals with yellow throats. H 8cm (3in) S 5cm (2in). Hardy/Z3–8.

Crocus 'E. A. Bowles'

This spring-flowering crocus has beautiful pale cream flowers, brushed with a hint of darker grey on the reverse side of the petals. H 8cm (3in) S 5cm (2in). Hardy/Z3–8.

Crocus 'Snow Bunting'

This is a late-winter- and early-spring-flowering crocus with ivory-white flowers with a yellow base and purple feathering on the outside of the petals. It looks wonderful planted with *Anemone blanda*. H 8cm (3in) S 5cm (2in). Hardy/Z3–8.

Crocus 'Blue Pearl'

Crocus 'Zwanenburg Bronze'

Appearing in early spring, the pale yellow flowers are bronze on the outside. Plant them near purple violets or show them off by surrounding them with a gravel mulch. H 8cm (3in) S 5cm (2in). Hardy/Z3–8.

Crocus x *luteus* 'Dutch Yellow' (syn. *C.* 'Dutch Yellow')

The sterile flowers, which appear in winter to early spring, are a rich golden-yellow and associate well with other early-spring

Crocus niveus

flowers, such as dwarf daffodils, *Anemone blanda* and violas. This cultivar also looks effective planted in grass. Increase by dividing the clumps. H 8cm (3in) S 5cm (2in). Hardy/Z3–8.

Crocus niveus

This is an autumn-flowering crocus from southern Greece which produces one or sometimes two flowers when the leaves are just emerging. The flowers vary from white to lilac, with yellow throats and prominent orange styles. It thrives best in full sun with a gritty, poor to moderately fertile soil as it needs summer dormancy to flower well. H 10–15cm (4–6in) S 10cm (4in). Hardy/Zone 4–9.

Crocus nudiflorus

This autumn-flowering crocus from south-west France, north and eastern Spain produces just one rich purple flower before the leaves emerge. H 15–25cm (6–10in) S 10cm (4in). Hardy/Zone 4–9.

Crocus speciosus

Flowering in autumn, this species is found across a wide area from Turkey, the Crimea, the Caucasus and into Central Asia. The scented, violet-blue flowers are veined with darker blue and have prominent orange styles. The leaves follow in spring. H 10–12cm (4–4¹/₂in) S 5cm (2in). Hardy/Z3–8.

Crocus nudiflorus

Crocus tommasinianus

Crocus tournefortii

Bulbs for naturalizing

Anemone blanda
Anemone nemorosa
Camassia
Colchicum
Crocus tommasinianus
Cyclamen hederifolium
Eranthis hyemalis
Erythronium
Galanthus nivalis
Hyacinthoides non-scripta
Narcissus poeticus var.
 recurvus
Trillium

Crocus sieberi subsp. *sublimis* f.
tricolor
The species from which this hybrid has been developed originates in Greece. Flowers appear in late winter to early spring. Each petal has 3 bands of colour: yellow at the centre, then white, then blue-purple. The colouring is exquisite. H 5–8cm (2–3in) S 5–8cm (2–3in). Hardy/Z3–8.

Crocus sieberi 'Violet Queen'
The flowers appear in late winter to early spring. The petals are pale lilac-pink, which contrasts with the yellow at the centre. This is easy to grow and increases well. H 5–8cm (2–3in) S 5–8cm (2–3in). Hardy/Z3–8.

Crocus tommasinianus
Flowering in late winter to early spring, the species originates from woods and shady hillsides in southern Hungary, the former Yugoslavia and north-western Bulgaria. The flowers vary from pale silvery lilac to reddish-purple. On dull days the slender flowers are rather modest, but in sun they open to create a wonderful display. They are suitable for naturalizing in grass. H 8–10cm (3–4in) S 5–8cm (2–3in). Hardy/Z3–8.

Crocus tommasinianus 'Ruby Giant'
Appearing in late winter to early spring, the slightly rounded, deep violet-blue flowers, which are

sterile, associate well with white *Anemone blanda* and early primroses. H 8–10cm (3–4in) S 5–8cm (2–3in). Hardy/Z3–8.

Crocus tommasinianus 'Whitewell Purple'
The slightly rounded purple-red flowers, which appear in late winter to early spring, are paler towards their base and contrast wonderfully with the orange anthers. H 8–10cm (3–4in) S 5–8cm (2–3in). Hardy/Z3–8.

Crocus tournefortii
The leaves appear from late autumn to winter, at the same time as the flowers, which are pale lilac-blue, with orange stigmas and white anthers. The species is

native to southern Greece and Crete, and it requires a warm, sunny site. H 5–8cm (2–3in) S 5–8cm (2–3in). Borderline hardy/Z5–8.

Crocus vernus 'Jeanne d'Arc'
Flowering in early spring, this is a Dutch hybrid with large white flowers. It associates beautifully with early dwarf daffodils and early species tulips. H 10cm (4in) S 5–8cm (2–3in). Hardy/Z3–8.

Crocus vernus 'Pickwick'
Flowering in early spring, this Dutch hybrid has large white flowers streaked with lilac and dark purple. It is an eye-catching crocus, which associates well with early dwarf daffodils and early species tulips. H 10cm (4in) S 5–8cm (2–3in). Hardy/Z3–8.

Crocus vernus 'Remembrance'
Flowering in early spring, this Dutch hybrid has large, glossy violet flowers. It makes a perfect partner for early-flowering, dwarf, golden-yellow daffodils in borders, naturalized in grass or in containers. H 10cm (4in) S 5–8cm (2–3in). Hardy/Z3–8.

Crocus 'Zephyr'
Appearing in autumn, the pale silver-blue flowers, veined with dark blue, have yellow throats and white anthers. Leaves follow in spring. H 10–12cm (4–4¹/₂in) S 5cm (2in). Hardy/Z3–8.

Crocus sieberi subsp. sublimis f. tricolor

Crocus vernus 'Remembrance'

Cyclamen coum

Cyclamen cilicium

CYCLAMEN
Sowbread

The name of the genus derives from the Greek word *kyklos* (circle), probably in reference to the fact that the seed stalks of some species twist after flowering. The fruiting capsule is drawn down to soil level. The genus includes 19 species of tuberous perennials, found in a wide range of habitats from the eastern Mediterranean to Iran and south to Somalia, where there is winter rainfall and a dryish summer dormancy period. The rounded to heart-shaped leaves often have attractive silver markings.

Cultivation In autumn plant tubers 3–5cm (1¼–2in) deep in border soil. They do best in sheltered conditions and in partial shade beneath trees and shrubs.

Propagation Sow seed as soon as ripe, in darkness, at 6–12°C (43–54°F) or, for *C. persicum*, at 12–15°C (54–59°F). Soak seed for 10 hours before sowing and then rinse. *C. hederifolium* will self-seed naturally.

Pests and diseases Squirrels, mice and voles eat the tubers. Cyclamen are also prone to vine weevils, red spider mites, cyclamen mite and, under glass, grey mould.

Cyclamen cilicium

This species comes from southern Turkey and flowers in autumn. The pink or white flowers, with a darker maroon stain towards the mouth, appear at the same time as the leaves, which are rounded or heart-shaped and often patterned. It is perfect for under a spreading evergreen tree or shrub, where it will be protected from excess moisture and colder temperatures. H 12cm (4½in) S 5–8cm (2–3in). Borderline hardy/Z5–9.

Cyclamen coum

This species comes from Bulgaria, the Caucasus, Turkey and Lebanon. Appearing in late winter and early spring, the nodding, white to pale pink or pale purple flowers have darker staining towards the mouth. The rounded leaves often have silver markings. This cyclamen associates well with snowdrops. H 5–8cm (2–3in) S 10cm (4in). Hardy/Z5–9.

Cyclamen coum subsp. *caucasicum* 'Album'

This is the white form of the species, flowering in late winter and early spring. Its only colouring is the pink nose or staining towards the mouth of the flower. H 5–8cm (2–3in) S 10cm (4in). Hardy/Z5–9.

Cyclamen coum subsp. *caucasicum* Pewter Group 'Maurice Dryden'

The foliage is most distinctive: the pewter-silver leaves have a dark green midrib and edge. The large flowers are white tinged with pink, appearing first in late winter and lasting to early spring. H 5–8cm (2–3in) S 10cm (4in). Hardy/Z5–9.

Cyclamen hederifolium (syn. *C. neapolitanum*)

This species is native to Europe from Italy to Turkey. Appearing in autumn, the pink fly-away flowers have a maroon stain towards the mouth. The flowers are sometimes scented. The ivy- or heart-shaped leaves are often patterned and normally appear after the flowers. These leaves make an excellent display throughout the winter months, making it a very valuable, though diminutive, garden plant. *C. hederifolium* var. *hederifolium* f. *albiflorum* has pure white flowers without basal markings. H 10cm (4in) S 5–8cm (2–3in). Hardy/Z5–9.

Cyclamen hederifolium

Cyclamen persicum

Dactylorhiza praetermissa

Cyclamen mirabile
This species comes from southwestern Turkey. Appearing in autumn, the attractive pale pink flowers have delicately serrated petals, with purple-stained mouths. The leaves are heart-shaped and patterned with silver blotches. H 10cm (4in) S 5–8cm (2–3in). Borderline hardy/Z5–9.

Cyclamen persicum
This species comes from the southeastern Mediterranean to northern Africa. The pink, red or white flowers have darker staining towards the mouth, and the heart-shaped leaves are often attractively patterned. Many

cultivars have been bred, and there are forms in various shades and sizes to choose from. Among the many florist's cyclamens are the ruffled-petalled, white-flowered 'Victoria', which is 30cm (1ft) high. They are normally grown as pot plants and are ideal for cool conservatory planting schemes or a north-facing windowsill indoors, when they flower from midwinter to early spring. The scented, miniature Miracle Series, which are only about 15cm (6in) high, are suitable for planting out in a sheltered spot in the garden, where they will flower from autumn right through to spring. H 10–30cm (4–12in) S 15cm (6in). Borderline hardy, Z5–9.

DACTYLORHIZA
Marsh orchid, spotted orchid
This is a genus of about 30 species of tuberous orchids, which are not widely grown but deserve a place in woodland gardens, where they will flower from late spring to midsummer.
Cultivation Plant the long, narrow tubers 8cm (3in) deep in moisture-retentive but well-drained soil in partial shade. They will appreciate being in a sheltered corner and will benefit from an annual mulch of leafmould.
Propagation In autumn lift and divide tubers, making sure each piece has a shoot.
Pests and diseases Slugs and snails.

Dactylorhiza maculata
Heath spotted orchid
The variable species, in both size and colour, is native to Europe and North Africa. From mid-spring to late summer it bears spikes of flowers, which may be shades of pink, red or purple or even white. The leaves may be plain green or have red-brown markings. They prefer less fertile, slightly acidic soil. H 15–60cm (6–24in) S 15cm (6in). Hardy/Z6.

Dactylorhiza praetermissa
(syn. *D. majalis* subsp. *praetermissa*)
Southern marsh orchid
In late spring to early summer this plant, which is native to northwestern Europe, produces a dense spike of purple-red flowers, which are often streaked and spotted with black. Plant in moisture retentive but not boggy soil. Additional grit is helpful in heavy clay. H 30–70cm (12–28in) S 15cm (6in). Hardy/Z6.

Dactylorhiza maculata

Bulbs with distinctive leaves

Allium karataviense	Dahlia 'Yellow Hammer'
Arum italicum 'Marmoratum'	Erythronium californicum
Canna 'Striata'	'White Beauty'
Canna 'Tropicanna'	Tulbaghia violacea 'Silver
Cardiocrinum giganteum	Lace'
Cyclamen coum 'Maurice	Tulipa 'New Design'
Dryden'	Tulipa 'Red Riding Hood'
Dahlia 'Bishop of Llandaff'	Zantedeschia 'Cameo'

DAHLIA

The genus was named in honour of the Swedish botanist Dr Anders Dahl (1751–89), who was a pupil of Linnaeus. It includes about 30 species and some 2,000 cultivars of bushy, tuberous-rooted perennials from mountainous areas of Mexico and Central America to Colombia. The dahlia is one of the showiest flowers in the summer border. There is a wide range of colours, including both strident and pastel shades of yellow, orange, red, lavender, deep purple and pink as well as white, and some forms combine more than one colour. They vary in flower size from 5cm (2in) across, as with the Pompon dahlias, to enormous, dinner-plate-sized flowers, almost 30cm (12in) across. They are also available as dwarf patio cultivars and large exhibition dahlias.

Cultivation Start tubers into growth under glass in early spring but do not plant out until all risk of frost has passed in early summer. Choose a sunny site with rich, well-drained soil. Most medium to tall dahlias will need staking or a sturdy support. In autumn cut off the topgrowth, lift the tubers and store them in dry, frost-free conditions. In warmer, sheltered areas dahlias may be left in the ground over the winter, particularly if a dry mulch is applied before temperatures drop below freezing.

Dahlia 'Omo'

Propagation Start tubers into growth in early spring and either take basal shoot cuttings or divide tubers into smaller sections, making sure each has a shoot.

Pests and diseases Caterpillars, slugs and earwigs may cause problems outdoors; stored tubers may rot.

All the following dahlias will flower from midsummer to autumn. They are all half-hardy.

Single-flowered dahlias (Division 1)

A central disc is surrounded by 1 or 2 rows of petals. Mostly dwarf, these dahlias are suitable for bedding and container use. No staking is required.

Dahlia 'Dark Desire'

An attractive but unusual cultivar, this has rich, dark chocolate-purple petals, set off by a central yellow disc. The wiry stems are dark and slim, making this a good choice for a border or raised bed where the plant as a whole can be fully appreciated. H 90cm (36in) S 30cm (12in). Half-hardy/Z8–10.

Dahlia 'Ellen Houston'

The orange-red flowers contrast beautifully with the purple-tinged foliage of this plant. H 30cm (12in) S 30cm (12in). Half-hardy/Z8–10.

Dahlia 'Omo'

This pretty dahlia is white with a yellow disc. H 45cm (18in) S 45cm (18in). Half-hardy/Z8–10.

Dahlia 'Yellow Hammer'

This is a distinctive, bushy dwarf bedding dahlia with yellow blooms held above dark bronze foliage. H 60cm (24in) S 45cm (18in). Half-hardy/Z8–10.

Dahlia 'Ellen Houston'

Dahlia 'Yellow Hammer'

Dahlia 'Hillcrest Regal'

Dahlia 'Clair de Lune'

Anemone-flowered dahlias (Division 2)
The flowers are double, with one or more rings of petals around a central group of tubular florets.

Dahlia 'Freya's Paso Doble'
This well-known dahlia has white outer petals and a raised central yellow cushion of much shorter petals. H 90cm (36in) S 60cm (24in). Half-hardy/Z8–10.

Dahlia 'Scarlet Comet'
The vivid red flowers have upright central petals. H 1.2m (4ft) S 60cm (24in). Half-hardy/Z8–10.

Collerette dahlias (Division 3)
These dahlias have an outer ring of ray-florets which may overlap, surrounding an inner ring of shorter florets forming a collar around a central disc. Flowerheads are 10–15cm (4–6in) across.

Dahlia 'Clair de Lune'
The inner collar of cream petals is surrounded by an outer ring of lemon-yellow petals. This dahlia can be grown in borders or containers, and it looks lovely against bronze or pale green foliage. H 1.1m (3ft 6in) S 90cm (36in). Half-hardy/Z8–10.

Dahlia 'Hillcrest Regal'
This dahlia has maroon flowers with a white-tipped collar, which contrast well with the central yellow disc. H 1.1m (3ft 6in) S 60cm (24in). Half-hardy/Z8–10.

Waterlily-flowered dahlias (Division 4)
The flowers are classified as large, medium, small or miniature, and are fully double and flattened.

Dahlia 'Figurine'
The small flowers have petals that are a blend of pink and white, fading towards the centre. H 1.2m (4ft) S 60cm (24in). Half-hardy/Z8–10.

Dahlia 'Gerrie Hoek'
This charming dahlia has small flowers with pale pink outer petals and darker pink inner petals. H 1.2m (4ft) S 60cm (24in). Half-hardy/Z8–10.

Dahlia 'Zingaro'
This pretty compact dahlia has petals blending from pink through warm orange-pink to yellow. It is suitable for a medium to large container. H 60–75cm (24–30in) S 35cm (14in). Half-hardy/Z8–10.

Dahlia 'Figurine'

Bulbs with pink flowers

Allium cernuum
Allium roseum
Amaryllis belladonna
Begonia (many)
Chionodoxa forbesii 'Pink Giant'
Colchicum autumnale 'September'
Dahlia 'Figurine'
Dahlia 'Kidd's Climax'

Hyacinthus orientalis 'Pink Pearl'
Lilium 'Pink Perfection'
Nerine bowdenii 'Pink Triumph'
Nerine undulata
Nerine 'Zeal Giant'
Schizostylis coccinea 'Jennifer'
Tulipa 'Angélique'
Tulipa 'Ester'

Dahlia 'Alva's Supreme'

Dahlia 'Kidd's Climax'

Decorative dahlias (Division 5)
The flowers are classified as giant, large, medium, small or miniature. They are double and the tips of the petals are bluntly pointed.

Dahlia **'Alva's Supreme'**
The giant flowers, 25–30cm (10–12in) across, are pale yellow. H 1.1m (3ft 6in) S 60cm (24in). Half-hardy/Z8–10.

Dahlia **'Arabian Night'**
The small flowers have velvety red petals that are long, broad and gently rounded, and they look attractive against its dark green foliage. It is a popular dahlia, which can be grown in borders but also looks effective in large half-barrels. H 1m (3ft 3in) S 1m (3ft 3in). Half-hardy/Z8–10.

Dahlia **'David Howard'**
The miniature flowers are golden-orange and look delightful against the lovely bronze foliage. H 75cm (30in) S 75cm (30in). Half-hardy/Z8–10.

Dahlia **'Kidd's Climax'**
This is one of the most beautiful dahlias of all time. It is a delicate blend of pink suffused with golden yellow, making it an old favourite that has been winning prizes for over 50 years. H 1.1m (3ft 6in) S 60cm (24in). Half-hardy/Z8–10.

Dahlia **'Smokey'**
The small flowers are a wonderful mixture of purple and white. H 1.1m (3ft 6in) S 90cm (3ft). Half-hardy/Z8–10.

Ball dahlias (Division 6)
The globe-shaped flowers are small or miniature and all are fully double.

Dahlia **'Barberry Carousel'**
The small globe-shaped flowers are lavender blended with white, making a delightful combination. H 90cm (36in) S 60cm (24in). Half-hardy/Z8–10.

Dahlia **'Cherida'**
The small globe-shaped flowers are bronze-tinged lilac. H 1m (3ft 3in) S 60cm (24in). Half-hardy/Z8–10.

Dahlia **'Cryfield Rosie'**
The small yellow flowers are tinged with red. H 1m (3ft 3in) S 60cm (24in). Half-hardy/Z8–10.

Dahlia **'Jomanda'**
The small globe-shaped flowers are terracotta red. H 1m (3ft 3in) S 60cm (24in). Half-hardy/Z8–10.

Dahlia **'Regal Boy'**
The small ball-shaped flowers are an exciting rich royal purple. H 1m (3ft 3in) S 60cm (24in). Half-hardy/Z8–10.

Dahlia **'Robin Hood'**
Small globe-shaped flowers with warm orange-bronze blends. H 90cm (36in) S 60cm (24in). Half-hardy/Z8–10.

Dahlia **'Sunny Boy'**
Orange perfectly formed petals create a small ball-shaped dahlia. H 90cm (36in) S 60cm (24in). Half-hardy/Z8–10.

Dahlia 'David Howard'

Dahlia 'Jomanda'

Dahlia 'Brilliant Eye'

Dahlia 'Noreen'

Pompon dahlias (Division 7)
The flowers are fully double and
more globose than ball dahlias
(Division 6). The petals are
round or blunt at the tips.
Although the plants are to 90cm
(36in) high, the flowers are only
5cm (2in) across.

Dahlia **'Brilliant Eye'**
The bright red, rolled petals make
neat flowers. This dahlia looks
lovely in association with blue
caryopteris or asters (Michaelmas
daisies). H 90cm (36in) S 60cm
(24in). Half-hardy/Z8–10.

Dahlia **'Moor Place'**
A good exhibition cultivar, its
flowers are maroon purple, and
the leaves are glossy and dark
green. H 90cm (36in) S 60cm
(24in). Half-hardy/Z8–10.

Dahlia **'Noreen'**
A good exhibition cultivar, this
dahlia has pinkish-purple flowers.
H 90cm (36in) S 60cm (24in).
Half-hardy/Z8–10.

Dahlia **'Rhonda'**
A good exhibition cultivar, this
has perfect pale lilac-pink flowers.
The leaves are glossy and dark
green. H 90cm (36in) S 60cm
(24in). Half-hardy/Z8–10.

Dahlia **'Small World'**
This is regarded as one of the
best white dahlias. The flowers are
sometimes flecked with purple. It
associates well with plants with
silver foliage. H 90cm (36in) S
60cm (24in). Half-hardy/Z8–10.

**Cactus-flowered dahlias
(Division 8)**
The flowers are classified as giant,
large, medium, small or miniature.
They are fully double and have
rolled, pointed petals.

Dahlia **'Doris Day'**
This small cactus-flowered dahlia
has long, dark red petals and
makes a compact bush. The
flowers are ideal for cutting.
H 90cm (36in) S 60cm (24in).
Half-hardy/Z8–10.

Dahlia **'Kiwi Gloria'**
This is a small cactus-flowered
dahlia with delicate lilac and white
blooms. It is a top exhibition
dahlia but needs "stopping" (the
removal of the growth centre) to
perform well, and it is not
regarded as easy for the average
gardener. H 1m (3ft 3in) S 60cm
(24in). Half-hardy/Z8–10.

Dahlia **'Summer Night'**
The flowers of this attractive
dahlia have deep red, long, narrow,
pointed petals and almost black
centres, making a memorable
combination. It makes an excellent
choice for the border as well as
being a favourite cut flower for
the house. H 1m (3ft 3in) S
60cm (24in). Half-hardy/Z8–10.

Dahlia 'Doris Day'

Fritillaria imperialis 'Maxima Lutea'

Fritillaria imperialis 'The Premier'

FRITILLARIA
Fritillary

This is a genus of about 100 species of bulbs offering a wide range of flowering types, from giant, showy crown imperials to the small but much-loved snake's head fritillaries. They are found throughout the temperate regions of the northern hemisphere, from the Mediterranean through southwestern Asia and also western areas of North America.
Cultivation In autumn plant the large bulbs of *F. imperialis* and *F. persica* 20cm (8in) deep in garden soil where they will not be disturbed, or in large containers in compost (soil mix). *F. meleagris* has much smaller bulbs and should be planted 10cm (4in) deep. Fritillaries benefit from a layer of grit beneath the bulb at the time of planting and extra

lime, unless the soil is alkaline. Bulbs of *F. imperialis* are large and prone to rotting, so plant them tilted to one side to prevent water accumulating in their centres. They like a hot, dry summer after flowering. The smaller fritillaries may be grown in clumps, and the larger ones can be grouped or spaced 90cm (36in) apart so that each plant can be fully appreciated.
Propagation Divide the offsets in late summer.
Pests and diseases Prone to damage from slugs and lily beetle.

Fritillaria imperialis
Crown imperial

The species is native to areas from southern Turkey to Kashmir. It is a large bulb, which in late spring produces a stout stem topped by impressive umbels of

3–6 pendent bells, which may be orange ('The Premier'), yellow ('Maxima Lutea' AGM) or, more often, red ('Rubra'), out of which a crown of glossy, leaf-like bracts emerges. Both the bulbs and the flowers have a distinctive foxy smell. Introduced into Europe before 1592, this has long been a favourite plant, both in the grand, formal garden and in the cottage garden. H 70cm (28in) S 25cm (10in). Hardy/Z5–9.

Fritillaria meleagris
Snake's head fritillary

Originally native to an area extending from Britain to western Russia, in mid-spring the small bulb produces a wiry stem with 1 or 2 broadly bell-shaped flowers in pink, purple or white, each with strong chequerboard markings. The patterning may have given

rise to the common name; alternatively, the name may derive from the snake's head appearance of the seedhead, which appears soon after the petals have dropped. Grown in grassland, they are perfect companions for cowslips and ladysmock. In a container they look dramatic beneath white *Narcissus* 'Thalia'. H 20cm (8in) S 8cm (3in). Hardy/Z3–8.

Fritillaria michailovskyi

This fritillary is native to northeastern Turkey. The bulb produces a short stem with 1–4, sometimes even 7, broadly bell-shaped flowers, which are brown-purple on the outside but are tinged with green. The tips have an attractive yellow rim. They appear in late spring. Plant them at the front of a sunny border, where they will not be crowded out by taller plants. H 10–20cm (4–8in) S 5cm (2in). Hardy/Z5–8.

Fritillaria persica 'Adiyaman'
Persian lily

The species from which this cultivar has been developed originated from southern Turkey to Iran. The cultivar is rather taller than the species, and it flowers more generously. In late spring the bulb produces a stout stem with more than 30 dark purple, bell-shaped flowers, each covered with a waxy bloom. They look exquisite beside bright red *Tulipa* 'Apeldoorn' and the later dark purple *T.* 'Queen of Night'. H 1.5m (5ft) S 15cm (6in). Hardy/Z7–8.

Fritillaria uva-vulpis

This species is native to southeastern Turkey, north Iraq and west Iran. The bulb produces a short stem with a single, sometimes 2, narrowly bell-shaped flowers, 5cm (2in) long, which are brownish-purple, yellow within and yellow at the recurving tips. They appear in late spring and early summer. Plant them near the front of a sunny border, where they will not be overcrowded by taller plants. H 20cm (8in) S 5cm (2in). Hardy/Z7–8.

Fritillaria michailovskyi

Fritillaria persica 'Adiyaman'

GALANTHUS
Snowdrop

The genus name is derived from the Greek words *gala* (milk) and *anthos* (flower), a description for one of our most familiar bulbs, which is better known as the snowdrop. This is one of the first bulbs to flower after midwinter, growing taller as the days lengthen. The genus includes 19 species of bulbs from Europe to western Asia, mostly in upland wooded sites. They associate well with *Eranthis hyemalis* (winter aconite), winter-flowering heathers and dwarf Reticulata irises.

Cultivation Grow in sun or partial shade in moist soil that does not dry out in summer. Plant the bulbs 5cm (2in) deep in garden soil or short grass as soon as they are available in early autumn. They can be difficult to establish, although once they have settled down they will form good clumps and may self-seed. Alternatively, buy snowdrops 'in the green' – that is, those that have already flowered but still have their leaves. Plant them immediately after purchasing, and they should establish well. Plant groups of single and double snowdrops near each other in a border or in grassland. They will establish more quickly in border soil than in grassland, but even here, given time, they will form large groups.

Propagation Lift and divide clumps of bulbs after flowering. They will self-seed.

Pests and diseases Narcissus bulb fly and grey mould.

Galanthus 'Atkinsii'

This is a vigorous, comparatively tall snowdrop, which comes into flower in the late winter. It has elongated white flowers 3cm (1¼in) long. The three outer petals open to reveal three shorter inner petals, with a heart-shaped green tip to each inner petal. The flowers have a strong honey scent. H 20cm (8in) S 8cm (3in). Hardy/Z3–9.

Galanthus elwesii

This species is native to the Balkans and Turkey, and although it is less well known than the common snowdrop *G. nivalis*, some people think it is the superior species. It is a larger plant, with broad, rather glaucous leaves. The honey-scented flowers, which have large green spots on the inner petals, appear in late winter. H 12–23cm (4½–9in) S 8cm (3in). Hardy/Z3–9.

Galanthus nivalis
Common snowdrop

Originally from Europe in an area stretching from the Pyrenees to Ukraine, the species may also be native to Britain. In late winter it bears small, pure white, single flowers, 1–2cm (½–¾in) long, which fall like little drops of snow. The three outer petals open to reveal three shorter inner petals, each with an inverted, V-shaped, green mark at the tip. They have a delicious honey scent which is worth investigating. H 10cm (4in) S 10cm (4in). Hardy/Z3–9.

Galanthus 'S. Arnott'

Galanthus nivalis 'Flore Pleno'

The double form of the common snowdrop bears small, double, pure white flowers, 1–2cm (½–¾in) long, which hang from the stems, showing irregular outer petals and heavily marked, green and white smaller petals inside. They are sterile but will multiply from offsets. They look beautiful with a curtain of dark green ivy to set them off. H 10cm (4in) S 10cm (4in). Hardy/Z3–9.

Galanthus 'S. Arnott'

Named after the nurseryman Sam Arnott, this comparatively tall snowdrop flowers in late winter and early spring. The large, rounded, pure white flowers, 2–4cm (¾–1½in) long, fall like rounded drops of snow from a slender stem. The 3 outer petals open to reveal 3 shorter inner petals, each with green markings at the base and apex. They have a strong honey scent. H 20cm (8in) S 8cm (3in). Hardy/Z3–9.

Dwarf flowers

Allium karataviense
Anemone blanda
Colchicum speciosum
Crocus
Cyclamen coum
Cyclamen hederifolium
Eranthis hyemalis
Galanthus nivalis
Iris danfordiae
Iris reticulata
Muscari 'Valerie Finnis'
Narcissus 'Topolino'
Narcissus 'Tête-à-tête'
Tulipa (various species)

Galanthus nivalis 'Flore Pleno'

Galanthus 'Atkinsii'

Galtonia candicans

GALTONIA

The genus is named after Sir Francis Galton (1822–1911), a British scientist who travelled widely in South Africa where the 3 species of bulbs in the genus originate. They grow mainly in moist grasslands in their native home, but only one species is commonly grown in gardens.
Cultivation Grow in full sun in moist soil that does not dry out in summer. Plant the bulbs in early spring, 13cm (5in) deep, in well-drained garden soil among shrubs or in a herbaceous border. Add grit to heavy soils. They are borderline hardy, and it is advisable to mulch ground where frost occurs, and in areas where the ground freezes solid it is best to lift the bulbs in winter and store them in a frost-free place.

Propagation Remove offsets in early spring or sow seeds in spring (keep seedlings frost-free for the first 3 years).
Pests and diseases None.

Galtonia candicans
Cape hyacinth, summer hyacinth
The species originates from the Orange Free State, Eastern Cape, Natal and Lesotho. It is a tall plant, bearing up to 30 pendent, creamy white flowers, each up to 5cm (2in) long, on tall, sturdy stems in succession over several weeks in late summer. They are best planted in the border in bold groups and they show up well against plants with dark green foliage or against a wall. They may need replacing in their fourth year. H 1.1m (3ft 6in) S 10cm (4in). Hardy/Z7–10.

GLADIOLUS

The name of the genus derives from the Latin word *gladius* (sword), a reference to the shape of the leaves. There are about 180 species of corms in the genus, with more than 10,000 hybrids and cultivars. The species are found principally in South Africa, but they also occur in Mediterranean countries, north-western and eastern Africa, Madagascar and western Asia.
Cultivation Grow in full sun in moist soil that does not dry out in summer. In spring plant the corms 8–10cm (3–4in) deep in garden soil. Lift and dry off in autumn. Divide the new corms from the old ones, discarding the latter, and replant the new ones the following spring.
Propagation Remove cormlets when dormant. Alternatively, sow seed of hardy species in a cold frame in spring; sow seeds of half-hardy to tender plants at 15°C (59°F) in spring.
Pests and diseases Grey mould, thrips, aphids and slugs.

Gladiolus communis subsp. byzantinus
(syn. *Gladiolus byzantinus*)
This gladiolus originates from Spain, northwestern Africa and Sicily. It produces up to 20 funnel-shaped, magenta-pink flowers, each to 5cm (2in) across. From late spring to early summer they are borne in succession on tall flower spikes, starting at the

base. It is borderline hardy, and it is best to mulch the ground where frost occurs, and in areas where the ground freezes solid it is best to lift the bulbs during winter. H 90cm (36in) S 8cm (3in). Hardy/Z6–10.

Gladiolus papilio
Originating from eastern South Africa, this species flowers from mid- to late summer. It produces hooded flowers, which range from yellow to yellow-green and are heavily flushed with purple. It spreads by means of stolons. It is borderline hardy, so it is advisable to mulch ground where frost occurs, and in areas where the ground freezes solid it is best to lift and store the bulbs in winter. H 90cm (36in) S 8cm (3in). Hardy/Z6–10.

Gladiolus hybrids
A vast number of hybrids have been bred over the last hundred years, but they fall into 3 main groups. Grandiflorus Group hybrids, which have one flower spike only, are mainly classified according to flower size: giant, large, medium, small and miniature. This group includes the Butterfly gladioli, which have ruffled petals and, often, a contrasting patch of colour on the lower petals. Nanus Group hybrids produce several slender spikes with loosely arranged flowers. Primulinus Group gladioli have a single thin, whip-

Gladiolus communis subsp. *byzantinus*

Gladiolus 'Seraphim'

Gladiolus 'Charming Beauty'

Gladiolus 'Nymph'

GLORIOSA

This genus of only one species is unusual because it is one of the few tuberous perennials to climb. It is native to tropical Africa and India. All parts of the plant are poisonous.

Cultivation Grow indoors in full sun. In early spring plant tubers 8–10cm (3–4in) deep in a large container, using a soil-based potting compost (soil mix) with added grit. Place in full light. Water well when growth begins and apply a liquid feed every 2 weeks. Offer support for the plant to climb up. Keep tubers dry in winter.

Propagation Separate the tubers in spring. Alternatively, sow seed at 19–24°C (66–75°F) in spring.

Pests and diseases Aphids.

Gloriosa superba **'Rothschildiana'**

The graceful flowers, 8–10cm (3–4in) across, have bright red petals edged with yellow. They are borne from the upper leaf axils from summer to autumn. The bright green leaves are glossy. This plant is excellent for growing in a conservatory. Handling the tubers may irritate the skin. H 1.8m (6ft) S 30cm (12in). Tender/Z10.

---

like flower spike and bear triangular flowers. All hybrids are half-hardy/Z7–10.

Gladiolus 'Charming Beauty'
This is a Nanus gladiolus with rose-coloured, funnel-shaped flowers, to 5cm (2in) across, which are blotched with creamy white. It flowers from mid- to late summer. It can survive relatively mild winters in a border, if well mulched. H 60cm (24in) S 8cm (3in). Half-hardy/Z7–10.

Gladiolus 'Green Woodpecker'
This medium-sized Grandiflorus hybrid has funnel-shaped, greenish-yellow, ruffled flowers, to 5cm (2in) across, with wine-red marks on the throats. They are borne on a tall, upright stem. The flowers appear from mid- to late summer. H 1–1.5m (3–5ft) S 8cm (3in). Half-hardy/Z7–10.

Gladiolus 'Leonore'
This is a Primulinus gladiolus, which bears buttercup yellow flowers on a single flower spike, to 55cm (22in) long. It flowers in midsummer. H 90cm (36in) S 8cm (3in). Half-hardy/Z7–10.

Gladiolus 'Nymph'
This is a Nanus gladiolus with dainty white flowers, to 5cm (2in) across, each with a red mark on the throat. They are borne in succession on 25cm (10in) flower spikes. It looks dainty in a border and is a good partner for grey foliage. H 70cm (28in) S 8cm (3in). Half-hardy/Z7–10.

Gladiolus 'Seraphim'
This is a medium-sized Grandiflorus hybrid with pretty, pink, ruffled flowers, to 5cm (2in) across, each with a white throat. The blooms are borne in

succession on tall flower spikes in midsummer. It should be grown in a border and looks lovely near lime-green foliage. H 70cm (28in) S 8cm (3in). Half-hardy/Z7–10.

Gladiolus 'Zephyr'
This is a large-flowered Grandiflorus hybrid with ruffled light lavender pink flowers and small ivory throats, produced in midsummer. H 1.7m (5ft 6 in) S 15cm (6in). Half-hardy/Z7–10.

Bulbs that require full sun

Agapanthus	*Gladiolus*
Allium schubertii	*Iris bucharica*
Alium karataviense	*Iris danfordiae*
Amarayllis belladonna	*Iris reticulata*
Canna	*Nerine*
Chionodoxa	*Ornitholgalum dubium*
Crinum x powellii 'Album'	*Schizostylis*
Dahlia	*Sternbergia lutea*
Eremurus	*Tigridia*
Galtonia candicans	*Tulipa*

Gloriosa superba 'Rothschildiana'

Hedychium coccineum

Hedychium spicatum

HEDYCHIUM
Ginger lily

This genus of about 40 species of perennial rhizomes is found at the edge of forests and in damp places in tropical Asia, the Himalayas and Madagascar. The flowers are often sweetly fragrant and can be used in cooking. The roots, sap and flowers are mostly scented of ginger.

Cultivation In warmer areas some hedychiums can be grown permanently in borders outdoors. Grow in moist but well-drained soil, in sun or partial shade, with shelter from cold winds. Mulch in winter. In frost-prone areas, they can be bedded out into borders or grown in containers and treated as conservatory plants or summer patio plants. Use a tall, heavy pot

and a soil-based compost (soil mix), with added grit. Keep in a warm spot until the first signs of a new bud appear at the top of the rhizome, water freely in the growing season and provide high humidity and indirect light. Apply a liquid fertilizer every 4 weeks through the flowering season. Cut down after the first autumn frosts and move to a frost-free place for the winter months. Keep barely moist until early spring. Plants given the early warmth of growth under glass will flower earlier.

Propagation Divide the rhizomes in spring. Alternatively, sow seeds at 21–24°C (70–75°F) as soon as they are ripe.

Pests and diseases Aphids and red spider mite may be a problem if the plants are grown indoors.

Hedychium coccineum
Red ginger lily, scarlet ginger lily
This is a species from the Himalayas. It produces sharply pointed mid-green leaves and, in late summer and early autumn, racemes of tubular red, pink, orange or white flowers with prominent red stamens. Despite its status as half-hardy, it has been known to survive cold winters with a mulch. In frosty areas, however, it is better to grow it in a container which can be moved into frost-free conditions for the winter. H 1.8m (6ft) S 1m (3ft 3in) or more. Half-hardy/Z9–10.

Hedychium coccineum 'Tara'
The flowers of this cultivar are orange with red stamens. H 1.8m (6ft) S 1m (3ft 3in) or more. Borderline hardy/Z8–10.

Hedychium coronarium
Garland flower, white ginger lily
This species is native to India. It has sharply pointed mid-green leaves and in late summer and early autumn bears clusters of fragrant, white, butterfly-like flowers. H 90–120cm (3–4ft) S 90cm (36in) or more. Half-hardy/Z9–10.

Hedychium densiflorum 'Assam Orange'
The species, which comes from the Himalayas, was collected by Frank Kingdon-Ward in 1938. Like the species, this cultivar has sharply pointed, glossy, mid-green leaves, but in late summer it produces clusters of fragrant, deep orange flowers in dense racemes like bottle brushes. H 1–1.8m (3–6ft) S 1.8m (6ft). Borderline hardy/Z8–10.

Hedychium gardnerianum
Kahili ginger
This species is native to Northern India and the Himalayas. It produces long stems with broad grey-green foliage, crowned in late summer with wonderful butterfly-like, creamy-yellow flowers with red stamens. It is superbly fragrant. It could be grown in a pot or, in warm areas, near a pond. H 2m (6ft) Borderline hardy/Z8–10.

Hedychium spicatum
This is a species from the Himalayas. It has sharply pointed, glossy, mid-green leaves and in late summer produces large white flowers with a prominent lip and red to orange blotches. They are delicately scented. H 1–1.5m (3–5ft) S 1.8m (6ft). Borderline hardy/Z9–10.

HIPPEASTRUM

This genus of about 80 species of bulbs, found in Central and South America, is associated with many colourful large-flowered hybrids, which are often – incorrectly and confusingly – known as amaryllis. Each bulb will produce consecutively, 1–3 flowerheads, each on a hollow stem. Each flowerhead will normally have 2–5 individual flowers. The flowerheads are frequently as large as 20cm (8in) in diameter, although those of the miniature cultivars will be around 12.5 (5in) across. There are many exciting new developments, including the introduction of the Cybister types, which have tapering spidery petals in combinations of several exotic colours. Note that all parts are mildly toxic if ingested.

Cultivation In warmer areas, including zones 9–10, the bulbs can be grown permanently outdoors in borders or containers. In frost-prone areas bulbs are usually available throughout autumn until the following spring, and it is possible to grow them outdoors as summer container plants as long as planting is left until spring. Place them outside, after all risk of frost has gone, in sun or light shade and they will flower in 4–6 weeks. In frost-prone areas hippeastrums are more usually grown indoors in pots as houseplants. From autumn to winter plant the bulbs so that the neck and shoulders are above the surface of the compost. Take care that you do not damage the long, fleshy roots. Use a tall, heavy pot and a soil-based compost (soil mix) with added grit. Keep in a warm spot until the first signs of a new bud appear at the top of

Hedychium gardnerianum

Hedychium densiflorum 'Assam Orange'

Hippeastrum 'Christmas Star'

Hippeastrum 'Mary Lou'

the bulb. Bring into full light and keep the soil moist, applying a liquid fertilizer every 2 weeks. After flowering, allow the leaves to complete their life-cycle and then keep the compost dry while the bulbs are dormant. Bring bulbs into growth again the following autumn. They resent root disturbance, so it is best to pot on every 3–5 years at the end of the dormancy period. Often, the later the bulbs are started into growth, the quicker they will come into flower. Try growing them on pebbles and water in late winter (but discard the bulbs after flowering).
Propagation Remove offsets in autumn. Alternatively, sow seeds at 16–18°C (61–64°F) as soon as ripe and keep seedlings growing without a dormant period until they eventually come into flower.
Pests and diseases Aphids.

Hippeastrum 'Apple Blossom'
This cultivar produces white flowers with pink tinges to the tips of the petals. The flowers reach 10–15cm (4–6in) across. It will flower in midwinter or later depending on time of planting. H 30–50cm (12–20in) S 30cm (12in). Tender/Z10.

Hippeastrum 'Christmas Star'
Grown as a houseplant, this cultivar is a great favourite for a cheerful midwinter show with its rich red petals and white centres. It produces 4–6 umbels of funnel-shaped flowers, about 25cm (10in) across. The flowers are borne on stout, leafless stems. Often 2 or 3 flowerheads are produced in succession on new stems. The leaves tend to follow later. H 50cm (20in) S 30cm (12in). Tender/Z10.

Hippeastrum 'Mary Lou'
This cultivar has glorious double, white flowers, but each petal is edged with pink, which produces an exquisite effect. The total width of all the flowers is about 25cm (10in). They are borne on stout, leafless stems. Often 2 or 3 flowerheads are produced in succession on new stems. As a houseplant, it will flower in midwinter or later depending on the time of planting. Buy two or three bulbs and plant in the same container for a sumptuous display. The leaves will follow later, although they might begin to emerge soon after the flowers have opened. H 50cm (20in) S 30cm (12in). Tender/Z10.

Hippeastrum 'Merengue'
This cultivar is a recent introduction of the Cybister type, with its spidery flowerheads and exotic combination of deep red and brown flowers. These are borne on stout, leafless stems. Often 2 or 3 flowerheads are

Hippeastrum 'Apple Blossom'

Hippeastrum 'Red Velvet'

Hippeastrum 'Tango'

Hippeastrum 'Yellow Goddess'

produced in succession on new stems. As a houseplant, it will flower in midwinter with the leaves following later. H 45cm (18in) S 30cm (12in). Tender/Z10.

Hippeastrum 'Red Lion'

This cultivar produces scarlet flowers, which can reach 15cm (6in) in diameter, with a total width of 25cm (10in). When it is grown as a houseplant, the flowers provide a welcome burst of colour in midwinter. H 30–50cm (12–20in) S 30cm (12in). Tender/Z10.

Hippeastrum 'Red Velvet'

This cultivar produces bright red flowers on tall stems. Individual flowers may reach 15cm (6in) in diameter, with a total width of 25cm (10in). As a houseplant, they give seasonal cheer in midwinter. H 60cm (24in) S 30cm (12in). Tender/Z10.

Hippeastrum 'Tango'

This cultivar is another recent introduction of the Cybister type, and it has wispy flowerheads of a striking combination of cherry red and green flowers. These are borne on stout, leafless stems. Often 2 or 3 flowerheads are produced in succession on new stems. Grown as a houseplant, it will flower in midwinter, with the leaves following later. Left until a late-spring planting, the flowers can be delayed until midsummer. H 45cm (18in) S 30cm (12in). Tender/Z10.

Hippeastrum 'Yellow Goddess'

The creamy yellow colouring is unusual among hippeastrum cultivars, and the flowers are made all the more attractive by their lime-green throats. The flowers are borne on stout, leafless stems. Often 2 or 3 flowerheads are produced in succession on new stems. Grown as a houseplant, it will flower in midwinter with the leaves following later. Left until a late-spring planting, the flowering can be delayed until midsummer. H 45cm (18in) S 30cm (12in). Tender/Z10.

Bulbs with green in the flowers

Eucomis bicolor
Galanthus nivalis 'Flore Pleno'
Gladiolus 'Green Woodpecker'
Hippeastrum 'Yellow Goddess'
Leucojum aestivum
Leucojum vernum
Nectaroscordum siculum
Ornithogalum nutans
Ornithogalum thyrsoides
Ornithogalum umbellatum
Tulipa 'Spring Green'
Tulipa urumiensis
Veratrum album
Zantedeschia aethiopica 'Green Goddess'

HYACINTHOIDES
Bluebell

This is a much-loved genus of 3 or 4 species of bulbs from deciduous woods and moist meadows of western Europe and northern Africa. There is nothing more enchanting in mid- to late spring than the sight of a mass of bluebells on a grassy bank or creating a sea of blue in the dappled shade of a wood. It is best to avoid planting them in a border because they are invasive and will eventually take over.

Cultivation Grow in partial shade under shrubs or trees in border soil or short grass. In autumn plant bulbs 8cm (3in) deep. Allow to self-seed, or deadhead flowers to prevent this from happening. Bluebells can also be successfully planted beneath hedgerows, in borders, grass or containers, although their favourite home will be beneath deciduous trees where the canopy of leaves is light.

Propagation Sow seed in containers in a cold frame as soon as ripe. Remove offsets from mature bulbs during the summer dormancy. They will self-seed. The English bluebell and the Spanish bluebell flower at the same time and will often hybridize naturally in the garden if planted close to each other. If you want to protect the English bluebell, avoid planting the Spanish bluebell altogether.

Pests and diseases None.

Hippeastrum 'Red Lion'

Hyacinthoides hispanica

Hyacinthus orientalis 'Amethyst'

Hyacinthoides hispanica
(syn. *Endymion hispanicus, Scilla campanulata, S. hispanica*)
Spanish bluebell
Found growing in woods and among shady rocks in Portugal, Spain and northern Africa, this spring-flowering bulb bears single blue, mauve or pink flowers on erect racemes of up to 15 bell-shaped, unscented flowers all the way around the stem. The leaves are broader than those of the English bluebell. Plant them among rhododendrons and azaleas for good colour associations or with small silver-foliage plants in a container. H 40cm (16in) S 10–15cm (4–6in). Hardy/Z4–9.

Hyacinthoides non-scripta
(syn. *Endymion non-scriptus, Scilla non-scripta, S. nutans*)
English bluebell
This species is found in woods and meadows of western Europe, beneath hedgerows or in oak and beech woods in spring. It bears single blue, sometimes pink or white, flowers in graceful racemes, which bend over at the tip. Up to 12 pendent, narrow, bell-shaped, scented flowers are borne on one side of the stem. To naturalize, plant 50–100 bulbs to 1 square metre (1 sq yd). The white-flowered form is *H. non-scripta* 'Alba'. H 20–40cm (8–16in) S 8–10cm (3–4in). Hardy/Z6–9.

HYACINTHUS
Hyacinth
This is one of the most fragrant of all spring-flowering bulbs. The genus contains only 3 species, found on limestone slopes and cliffs in western and Central Asia, but the many well-known cultivars have been bred from *H. orientalis*, which is native to central and southern Turkey, north-western Syria and Lebanon. It is an excellent bulb for indoor and outdoor use. Note that touching the bulbs can cause skin irritation, so wear gloves when handling.
Cultivation Outdoors grow in sun or partial shade in borders or in containers. Good drainage is important, so when planting in pots use a soil-based compost (soil mix) with extra grit. Flowers appear in early to mid-spring and combine beautifully with white or blue *Anemone blanda*, Double Early tulips, primroses, polyanthus and violas. Bedding hyacinths (ordinary hyacinths) should be planted in autumn, at a depth of 10cm (4in). Use soil-based compost in containers, with extra grit to ensure good drainage. For indoors choose specially treated (prepared) bulbs, which are available in late summer and early autumn. A wide range of colours is available, but not as wide as that available for bedding out.

Prepared bulbs should be planted in early autumn so that the flowers will appear in early winter. From planting to flowering normally takes about 12 weeks. Where the bowl or pot has no drainage holes, use a special bulb compost (planting medium). Alternatively, place the bulb on top of water in a special hyacinth glass (with a narrow neck to support the bulb). Keep the bulbs in a dark, cool place at 10°C (50°F) for about 8 weeks to allow the roots to develop. Bring into a light but not sunny spot until the flower bud is visible. Thereafter, take into a warm room and allow to flower. After flowering, discard bulbs that have been grown on water. All other container-grown hyacinths can be transferred to the garden, where they will flower for many years.
Propagation Remove offsets from mature bulbs while dormant in summer.
Pests and diseases None.

Hyacinthus orientalis 'Amethyst'
The distinctive lilac-amethyst flowers, which are borne in early to mid-spring, are richly scented and combine well with pink primroses and grey-foliage plants. H 20–30cm (8–12in) S 8cm (3in). Hardy/Z6–9.

Hyacinthoides non-scripta 'Alba'

Hyacinthus orientalis 'Blue Jacket'

Hyacinthus orientalis 'City of Haarlem'

Hyacinthus orientalis 'Ben Nevis'

This is a double hyacinth with white, delightfully scented flowers. Plant with white violas for a stunning all-white effect. The flowerheads are heavy and may need support. H 20–30cm (8–12in) S 8cm (3in). Hardy/Z6–9.

Hyacinthus orientalis 'Blue Jacket'

This is an excellent dark blue hyacinth, with fragrant flowers, which would combine well with rich blue *Muscari armeniacum* to make an all-blue effect. H 20–30cm (8–12in) S 8cm (3in). Hardy/Z6–9.

Hyacinthus orientalis 'Carnegie'

The racemes consist of up to 40 waxy, single, pure white, tubular, bell-shaped flowers, which are richly scented and borne on stout, leafless stems. They combine beautifully with Double Early tulips. H 20–30cm (8–12in) S 8cm (3in). Hardy/Z6–9.

Hyacinthus orientalis 'City of Haarlem'

This is one of the cultivars that is available as both prepared and ordinary bedding bulbs, so check before buying. The beautiful single, pale lemon-yellow flowers are wonderfully scented and look lovely grown indoors, where they flower in midwinter, or outdoors, where they flower from early to mid-spring, especially when they are partnered with blue *Muscari armeniacum* and violas. H 20–30cm (8–12in) S 8cm (3in). Hardy/Z6–9.

Hyacinthus orientalis 'Delft Blue'

This cultivar is available as both prepared and ordinary bedding bulbs. The soft blue flowers are wonderfully scented and look charming grown indoors, when they flower in midwinter, or outdoors, when they flower from early to mid-spring, with pale blue or white *Anemone blanda* or violas. H 20–30cm (8–12in) S 8cm (3in). Hardy/Z6–9.

Hyacinthus orientalis 'Gipsy Queen'

The delightful salmon-pink flowers of this hyacinth are richly scented and look striking planted in old terracotta pots, where they will flower from early to mid-spring. They combine wonderfully with pale yellow, blue or white primroses. H 20–30cm (8–12in) S 8cm (3in). Hardy/Z6–9.

Hyacinthus orientalis 'Hollyhock'

The double, crimson-red, tubular, bell-shaped flowers are borne on stout, leafless stems from early to mid-spring. It will combine beautifully with blue polyanthus or with *Tanacetum parthenium* 'Aureum' (golden feverfew). H 20–30cm (8–12in) S 8cm (3in). Hardy/Z6–9.

Hyacinthus orientalis 'Jan Bos'

This cultivar is available as both prepared and ordinary bedding bulbs. The single, richly-coloured cerise-red flowers are scented and look festive grown indoors, when they flower in midwinter, or outdoors, when they flower from early to mid-spring. They are an excellent partner for black violas. H 20–30cm (8–12in) S 8cm (3in). Hardy/Z6–9.

Hyacinthus orientalis 'L'Innocence'

This old favourite is available as both prepared and ordinary bedding bulbs. The single white flowers are scented and look wonderful indoors, when they flower in midwinter, or outdoors, when they flower in mid-spring. They are a good planting partner for pale yellow primroses and pastel-coloured violas. H 20–30cm (8–12in) S 8cm (3in). Hardy/Z6–9.

Hyacinthus orientalis 'Pink Pearl'

This cultivar is available as both prepared and ordinary bedding bulbs. The single rose-pink flowers are deservedly popular. They are scented and look great indoors, when they flower in midwinter, or outdoors, when they flower in mid-spring. Plant with blue primroses and violas. H 20–30cm (8–12in) S 8cm (3in). Hardy/Z6–9.

Hyacinthus orientalis 'Woodstock'

The unusual, single, deep burgundy flowers combine well with grey-foliage plants or pink primroses in early to mid-spring. H 20–30cm (8–12in) S 8cm (3in). Hardy/Z6–9.

Hyacinthus orientalis 'Jan Bos'

Hyacinthus orientalis 'Woodstock'

Hyacinthus orientalis 'Pink Pearl'

Iris 'Blue-eyed Brunette'

Iris 'Chantilly'

Iris 'Dancer's Veil'

IRIS

This is a large genus containing more than 300 species of winter-, spring- and summer-flowering bulbs, rhizomes and fleshy-rooted perennials, found in a wide range of habitats throughout the northern hemisphere. The name means "rainbow", an apt description given the many colours – from primrose-yellow to indigo – of the flowers.

Cultivation The bearded iris (growing from rhizomes) and the bulbous iris are best grown in full sun. The beardless iris (see *Iris sibirica* below) will grow in sun or partial shade. Most of the bearded and beardless iris prefer a neutral to acid soil, whereas the bulbous varieties thrive in a neutral to alkaline soil. Rhizomes of the bearded iris are best planted so that they rest on top of the soil, but those of the beardless irises are best planted below soil level. Bulbs of *Iris danfordiae* should be planted only 5cm (2in) deep; other bulbs should be planted 8cm (3in) deep in the border or containers in autumn, although the Xiphium Iris hybrids can also be planted in spring.

Propagation Separate rhizomes and bulb offsets from midsummer to early autumn.

Pests and diseases Slugs and snails are the main problems.

Bearded Irises

These are grown from fleshy rhizomes, which produce sword-like leaves and large flowers with higher erect petals, which are known as standards, and lower petals, referred to as the falls. There are conspicuous hairs on these lower petals, referred to as the beard.

Iris 'Annabel Jane'

This is a vigorous, rhizomatous, tall bearded iris, which has lilac-blue flowers from late spring to early summer. H 1.2m (4ft) S 60cm (24in). Hardy/Z4–9.

Iris 'Batik'

With fluted petals of royal purple, this bearded rhizomatous iris has eye-catching flowers that are wildly streaked with white on both standards and falls. They appear from late spring to early summer. H 60cm (24in) S 50cm (20in). Hardy/Z4–9.

Iris 'Blue-eyed Brunette'

This is a vigorous, rhizomatous, tall bearded iris, which has rich red-brown flowers with gold beards from late spring to early summer. H 1m (3ft 3in) S 50cm (20in). Hardy/Z4–9.

Iris 'Chantilly'

This is a vigorous, rhizomatous, tall bearded iris, which has pale lavender flowers from late spring to early summer. H 1m (3ft 3in) S 50cm (20in). Hardy/Z4–9.

Iris 'Dancer's Veil'

The lightly ruffled flowers are predominantly white with violet blue markings at the margins of the gently waving petals. They appear from late spring to early summer. H 90cm (36in) S 60cm (24in). Hardy/Z4–9.

Beardless Irises

Like bearded irises, these are also grown from fleshy rhizomes, which produce the characteristic iris flower but without any beard on the lower petals. The group includes *I. pseudacorus* as well as *I. sibirica* and its many hybrids.

Iris pseudacorus
Yellow flag

This species is found in a wide area, from Europe through to western Siberia, Turkey and Iran. It is a vigorous rhizomatous beardless iris, with ribbed grey-green leaves and yellow flowers, which appear from early to midsummer. It is suitable for damp places, such as boggy areas or the margins of ponds. H 90–150cm (3–5ft) S 1.8m (6ft) or more. Hardy/Z4–9.

Iris 'Batik'

Iris pseudacorus

Iris sibirica 'Tropic Night'

Iris danfordiae

Iris sibirica
Siberian iris
This species, which is native to central and eastern Europe, northeastern Turkey and Russia, is a rhizomatous beardless iris with narrow, grass-like leaves. In early summer it bears violet-blue petals with white splashes on the falls. H 60–90cm (24–36in) S 8cm (3in). Hardy/Z4–9.

Iris sibirica 'Tropic Night'
Like its parent, this cultivar is a rhizomatous beardless iris. It has rich blue flowers with white splashes on the falls. H 60cm (24in) S 8cm (3in). Hardy/Z4–9.

Bulbous Irises
Irises in this group are mainly grown from small bulbs, although those of I. bucharica are significantly larger. They flower in late winter through to summer, depending on the species.

Iris bucharica
This is a vigorous species, native to northeast Afghanistan and Central Asia, which produces long glossy leaves and in late spring to early summer masses of pretty yellow and white flowers. H 20–40cm (8–16in) S 10cm (4in). Hardy/Z4–9.

Iris danfordiae
This small species from Turkey has scented lemon-yellow flowers, 5cm (2in) across, with green markings. Flowering in late winter, they look effective with winter-flowering heathers and in small pots. H 10cm (4in) S 5cm (2in). Hardy/Z6–9.

Reticulata Irises
The species I. reticulata, from the Caucasus, is one of the first bulbs to flower in the New Year. A number of hybrids have been raised, and although excellent for rock gardens and small containers, including hanging baskets, they will not flower reliably a second year, so it is best to replant.

Iris 'George'
A Reticulata iris with fragrant, rich purple flowers, 4–6cm (1¹⁄₂–2¹⁄₂in) across, which have a yellow stripe down the centre of the fall petal. H 15cm (6in) S 5cm (2in). Hardy/Z6–9.

Iris 'Joyce'
A Reticulata iris with sky blue flowers, 5cm (2in) across, with orange on the falls. They look pretty on their own in a small pot. H 10–15cm (4–6in) S 5cm (2in). Hardy/Z6–9.

Iris 'Pauline'
A Reticulata iris with sweetly scented, dark purple flowers, 5cm (2in) across, with white crests on the falls. They look really wonderful in a container with Viburnum tinus (laurustinus) or Euphorbia myrsinites. H 10–15cm (4–6in) S 5cm (2in). Hardy/Z6–9.

Iris bucharica

Iris 'George'

Iris 'Joyce'

Iris 'Bronze Beauty'

Iris 'Silvery Beauty'

KNIPHOFIA
Red-hot poker, torch lily

The genus, which is native to southern Africa, contains about 70 species, from which many cultivars have been developed. They are mostly tall plants, bearing dense racemes of flowers on sturdy, erect stems, which rise from clumps of grassy leaves. Some species are evergreen.
Cultivation Grow in sun in fertile, well-drained soil. Plant rhizomes.
Propagation Sow seed in spring and keep the pots in a cold frame until ready to plant out. Divide clumps in late spring.
Pests and diseases Thrips and root rot.

Kniphofia **'Percy's Pride'**
This tall perennial produces racemes of green-tinged, yellow flowers in late summer and early autumn. H 1.2m (4ft) S 60cm (24in). Hardy/Z6–9.

Kniphofia rooperi
(syn. *K.* 'C.M. Prichard')
The flowers, which are borne from early to late autumn, are a mixture of autumnal shades of orange and yellow. In contrast to the tapering flower spikes of most red-hot poker plants, this one has flowers that form a wedge-shape. It is a robust, hardy, evergreen perennial with broad, strappy, dark green leaves. H 1.2m (4ft) S 60cm (24in). Hardy/Z6–9.

Xiphium Irises
This is a large group derived from the bulbous *I. xiphium* (known as the Spanish iris) hybridized with *I. tigitana* (from northwest Africa) by horticulturists in the Netherlands, hence the common name, Dutch irises. They are beautiful flowers, available in a wide range of colours. As well as being excellent cut flowers, they make wonderful plants for the herbaceous border, where they flower in late spring to early summer. The ones listed below are slightly shorter than most. They look sumptuous beneath wisteria arches and marvellous partnering herbaceous poppies and alliums, where they will bloom year after year. H 45cm (18in) S 8cm (3in). Hardy/Z5–8.

Iris **'Bronze Beauty'**
The flowers of this lovely iris combine deep bronze and gold. H 45cm (18in) S 8cm (3in). Hardy/Z5–8.

Iris **'Gypsy Beauty'**
The flowers are deep blue and bronze. H 45cm (18in) S 8cm (3in). Hardy/Z5–8.

Iris **'Oriental Beauty'**
The flowers are a wonderful combination of lilac and yellow. H 45cm (18in) S 8cm (3in). Hardy/Z5–8.

Iris **'Sapphire Beauty'**
The flowers are a rich blue with orange on the fall and look great besides alliums or poppies. H 45cm (18in) S 8cm (3in). Hardy/Z5–8.

Iris **'Silvery Beauty'**
The flowers combine pale blue and silver-grey. This delightful Xiphium iris flowers alongside white or purple alliums such as *A. nigrum*, *A.* 'Purple Sensation' and *A. cristophii*. H 45cm (18in) S 8cm (3in). Hardy/Z5–8.

Iris **'Symphony'**
This iris combines white standards with primrose-yellow and orange falls. H 50cm (20in) S 8cm (3in). Hardy/Z5–8.

Iris 'Oriental Beauty'

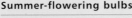

Summer-flowering bulbs

Agapanthus	Gladiolus
Allium caeruleum	Hedychium coronarium
Allium carinatum subsp. pulchellum	Iris bearded
	Iris sibirica
Allium cernum	Iris pseudacorus
Allium cristophii	Kniphofia 'Percy's Pride'
Allium flavum	Lilium 'Moneymaker'
Allium roseum	Lilium regale
Allium sphaerocephalon	Lilium candidum
Begonia	Ornithagalum thyrsoides
Canna	Pelargonium schottii
Cardiocrinum giganteum	Tigridia pavonia
Dahlia	Tritonia
Eucomis	Tulbaghia
Galtonia candicans	Zantedeschia

Kniphofia rooperi

Lilium 'Admiration'

Leucojum aestivum

LEUCOJUM
Snowflake

The name is derived from the Greek words *leukos* (white), a clue to the colour of the flowers, and *ion* (violet), a reference to their delicate fragrance. The genus includes about 10 species of bulbs found in a range of habitats from western Europe to the Middle East and northern Africa. The species grown most often in gardens are the spring and summer snowflakes. They look similar to snowdrops, but the petals are of equal length (the snowdrop has 3 long and 3 short petals).

Cultivation L. *aestivum* and *L. vernum* can be grown in full sun or partial shade but the soil must be reliably moist. Both species will naturalize well in damp grass and damp woodlands. *L. roseum* prefers a sunny, well-drained site and will need protection in winter from prolonged frost and dampness. In autumn plant the bulbs 8cm (3in) deep in the border where they can form a good-sized clump.
Propagation Separate bulb offsets from midsummer to early autumn.
Pests and diseases Slugs and narcissus bulb fly.

Leucojum aestivum 'Gravetye Giant'
Summer snowflake

The parent species is native to northwestern, central and eastern Europe and the Middle East. This cultivar, which is taller and more robust than the species, bears 2–8 white, bell-shaped flowers, with a distinctive green tip at the end of each petal, on each stem. They look lovely near water, where their reflection can be fully enjoyed. Despite the common name, the flowers appear in mid- to late spring. H 90cm (36in) S 8cm (3in). Hardy/Z4–9.

Leucojum roseum

The species originates in Corsica and Sardinia. The solitary, pale pink flowers, 1cm ($^{1}/_{2}$in) long, open in early autumn and look lovely with autumn crocuses or colchicums. The narrow leaves appear with, or a short while after, the flowers. H 10cm (4in) S 5cm (2in). Borderline hardy/Z6–9.

Leucojum vernum
Spring snowflake

This species comes from southern and eastern Europe. It has white, bell-shaped flowers with a distinctive green tip at the end of each petal, borne singly, or occasionally two on each stem. It flowers in midwinter and early spring. It will naturalize well in damp grass where left undisturbed and look wonderful as a large display beneath deciduous trees. H 20–30cm (8–12in) S 8cm (3in). Hardy/Z4–8.

LILIUM
Lily

The genus name *Lilium* is an old Latin name, akin to *leirion*, which was used by Theophrastus to refer to *Lilium candidum* (Madonna lily), one of the oldest established plants in gardens. The Greeks admired it for its beauty and food value, and it was used on many ceremonial occasions. The Romans took it with them as they conquered neighbouring lands. In the Christian era it became a symbol of Christ's mother and was grown in monastic gardens throughout Europe. Although historically this one species has been of major importance, there are more than 100 species of bulbs in the genus, which come mainly from scrub and wooded areas of Europe, Asia and North America. A large number of garden hybrids have been developed from the species, giving today's gardeners an enormous choice of colour and form.
Cultivation Most lilies prefer acid to neutral soil, but some, such as *L. candidum* and *L. henryi*, like alkaline soils, and the Asiatic hybrids, *L. pyrenaicum*, *L. regale* and *L. martagon* will certainly tolerate alkaline conditions. Lilies require shade at their base and sun at the top. Although a few tolerate light overhead shade, none thrives in full shade. In early autumn plant plump, firm bulbs on a bed of sand or grit to facilitate good drainage if the soil is heavy. Some bulbs are much bigger than others, and as a rule plant at a

Species for spring

Anemone blanda	Muscari armeniacum
Anemone nemorosa	Muscari azureum
Camassia leichtlinii	Leucojum aestivum
Chionodoxa forbesii	Narcissus bulbocodium
Chionodoxa luciliae	Narcissus poeticus var.
Chionodoxa sardensis	recurvens
Corydalis solida	Ornithogalum nutans
Fritallaria imperialis	Scilla peruviana
Fritillaria meleagris	Trillium undulatum
Hyacinthoides non-scripta	Tulipa tarda
Iris bucharica	Tulipa urumiensis

Lilium 'Concorde'

Lilium 'Enchantment'

Lilium 'Eros'

depth 2–3 times the height of the actual bulb. Stem-rooting lilies should be planted deeper, at around 3 times the height of the bulb. Exceptions are *L. candidum* and *L. x testaceum*, which need to be planted close to the soil surface. Grow in a border where they can be left undisturbed for many years and form a good-sized clump. Alternatively, plant in containers, for which dwarf lilies are ideally suited. Some bulbs, including all Division 4 lilies and most Division 7 lilies, require ericaceous compost. All will benefit from extra horticultural grit in the mix, at a ratio of 2 parts compost to 1 part grit, with an extra layer of grit just beneath the bulbs.

Propagation Sow seed as soon as it is ripe in containers in a cold frame. Remove scales and offsets or bulblets from dormant bulbs as soon as the foliage dies down.

Detach stem bulbils, where produced, in late summer.
Pests and diseases Lily beetle, slugs and aphids. Grey mould can be a problem in a cool, wet spring.

Asiatic Hybrids (Division 1)

Derived from Asiatic species and hybrids, these are sturdy, stem-rooting lilies. They produce dark purple bulbils in the axils from which new bulbs can be propagated. They will tolerate a range of soils, including alkaline. There are 3 subdivisions: 1a upward-facing flowers (the group includes the double, pollen-free lilies and several much shorter pot and border lilies); 1b outward-facing flowers; and 1c pendent flowers.

Lilium 'Admiration'
Division 1a. This lily produces large, upward-facing, scentless flowers; the tepals are creamy yellow. H 40cm (16in). Hardy/Z4–8.

Lilium 'Apollo'
Division 1a. This short lily has unscented, white flowers in midsummer. It is excellent for containers. H 60cm (24in). Hardy/Z4–8.

Lilium 'Aphrodite'
Division 1a. This is a double form with upward-facing pink flowers. It is sterile and has no pollen, so is the perfect choice for gardeners who suffer from pollen allergies. It is medium height and ideal for containers. H to 70cm (28in). Hardy/Z4–8.

Lilium 'Bronwen North'
Division 1c. This is a striking, easily grown lily for the mixed border. In early summer, medium, slightly scented, turkscap flowers hang from the stems; the tepals are pale mauve-pink, spotted and lined with purple. H to 90cm (36in). Hardy/Z4–8.

Lilium 'Concorde'
Division 1a. A wonderful border plant, this has unscented, lemon-yellow flowers, greenish at the base, from early to midsummer. It associates well with grey foliage. H to 90cm (36in). Hardy/Z4–8.

Lilium 'Enchantment'
Division 1a. In summer this lily has showy, vivid orange, cup-shaped, unscented flowers, 12cm (4¹/₂in) across, which are marked with dark purple spots. The dark spotting on the petals combines well with deep bronze foliage plants in the border. It is a good lily for containers, where it can stay for 2–3 years. H 60–90cm (24–36in). Hardy/Z4–8.

Lilium 'Eros'
Division 1c. 'Eros' is an easily grown lily that associates well with cottage garden plants. In midsummer it produces fragant turkscap flowers; the tepals are pinkish-orange, spotted maroon. H 1.2m (4ft). Hardy/Z4–8.

Lilium 'Fata Morgana'
Division 1a. This is a double form with upward-facing yellow flowers, which are slightly

speckled red. It is sterile and has no pollen, so is suitable for gardeners with pollen allergies. It is medium height and ideal for containers. H to 70cm (28in). Hardy/Z4–8.

Lilium 'Fire King'
Division 1b. This is a vigorous lily with orange-red, shallowly funnel-shaped, unscented flowers, marked with purple spots. They open in midsummer. It is excellent for containers, where it can stay for 2–3 years. H 1–1.2m (3–4ft). Hardy/Z4–8.

Lilium 'Gran Sasso'
Division 1a. This is an excellent variety for general garden use. In early and midsummer, it produces large, upward-facing, unscented flowers, up to six per stem. The tepals are rich orange, heavily spotted with maroon. H 1–1.2m (3–4ft). Hardy/Z4–8.

Lilium 'Bronwen North'

Lilium 'Gran Sasso'

Lilium 'Her Grace'

Lilium 'Maxwill'

Lilium 'Peggy North'

Lilium 'Silhouette'

Lilium 'Her Grace'

Division Ia. In midsummer, this lily produces large, upward-facing, unscented, bowl-shaped flowers; the tepals are rich clear yellow. It is excellent for general garden use, can be planted in a container and used in flower arrangements as a cut flower. H to 1.2m (4ft). Hardy/Z4–8.

Lilium 'Karen North'

Division Ic. This is an elegant, prolific lily. In midsummer, it produces medium, lightly scented turkscap flowers; the tepals are orange-pink, lightly spotted with darker pink. It is excellent for planting in containers and for general garden use. H to 1.2m (4ft). Hardy/Z4–8.

Lilium 'Maxwill'

Division Ic. This lily produces a tall, stout stem with racemes of unscented turkscap-shaped flowers which are a brilliant orange-red with black spots. It is ideal for growing in front of shrubs in well-drained soil in full sun or partial shade and looks lovely with other midsummer-flowering plants, such as *Crocosmia* 'Lucifer' and yellow achilleas. H 1.5–2.1m (5–7ft). Hardy/Z4–8.

Lilium 'Orange Pixie'

Division Ia. This short lily bears unscented bright orange flowers with darker spots in early to midsummer. It is excellent for containers. H 30cm (12in). Hardy/Z4–8.

Lilium 'Peach Pixie'

Division Ia. This short lily has unscented, orange to rose-pink flowers in early to midsummer. It is perfect for terracotta containers or raised beds around the patio or terrace. H 45cm (18in). Hardy/Z4–8.

Lilium 'Pink Tiger'

Division Ib. This is a vigorous lily with beautiful shallowly funnel-shaped, unscented, salmon-pink flowers, streaked with deeper apricot and marked with purple spots. They open in midsummer. It is excellent for containers. H 1.3m (4ft 6in). Hardy/Z4–8.

Lilium 'Peggy North'

Division Ic. In midsummer this lily produces medium-sized, lightly scented, turkscap flowers; the tepals are glowing orange, spotted with dark brown. It is an excellent lily for a mixed or herbaceous border. H to 1.5m (5ft). Hardy/Z4–8.

Lilium 'Red Carpet'

Division Ia. This short lily bears unscented cherry-red flowers in midsummer. It is excellent for containers. H 35cm (14in). Hardy/Z4–8.

Lilium 'Roma'

Division Ia. This lily produces fragrant, creamy white flowers, lightly spotted with maroon, on a tall stem from early to midsummer. It associates well with lime-green or grey foliage. H to 1.2m (4ft). Hardy/Z4–8.

Lilium 'Silhouette'

Division Ia. This lily produces large, upward-facing, scentless flowers; the tepals are white, flushed creamy yellow at the base, and spotted and edged maroon. Its unique markings are best appreciated in flower arrangments. H to 1m (3ft 3in). Hardy/Z4–8.

Lilium 'Sun Ray'

Division Ia. This short lily has unscented, bright yellow flowers with dark spots in early to midsummer. It is a good colour for terracotta containers. H 50cm (20in). Hardy/Z4–8.

Lilium 'Karen North'

Lilium 'Orange Pixie'

Lilium 'Roma'

Lilium 'Sweet Kiss'

Lilium 'Shuksan'

Lilium 'Sweet Kiss'

Division 1a. This double form has upward-facing yellow flowers. It is sterile and produces no pollen so is a perfect choice for gardeners with pollen allergies. It is medium height and ideal for containers, where it needs no support, and multiplies well to form large clumps in just a few years. H to 70cm (28in). Hardy/Z4–8.

Lilium 'White Kiss'

Division 1a. This double form has upward-facing white flowers, which are spotted brown. It is sterile and produces no pollen so is a good choice for gardeners who have pollen allergies. It is medium height and ideal for containers, where it needs no support and multiplies well. H to 70cm (28in). Hardy/Z4–8.

Martagon Hybrids (Division 2)

Derived mainly from *L. martagon*, a species that is native to a large area from Europe to Mongolia, and *L. hansonii*, which is native to Russia, Korea and Japan, these hybrids are mainly stem-rooting lilies with turkscap flowers (with highly recurved petals). They are suitable for dry shade or woodland and will tolerate a range of soils. All are hardy/Z4–8.

Lilium 'Mrs R.O. Backhouse'

This well-known lily is one of the oldest cultivars in cultivation, dating from the end of the 19th century. It has unscented, turkscap flowers, which hang from the stem in early to midsummer. The sepals are orange-yellow with maroon spotting and are flushed pink on the outside. H 1.3m (4ft 6in). Hardy/Z4–8.

Candidum Hybrids (Division 3)

Derived from *L. chalcedonicum, L. candidum* and other European species (but not *L. martagon*), this is a small group of lilies with turkscap flowers that are sometimes scented. They are usually not stem-rooting. They tolerate alkaline conditions.

Lilum x *testaceum* Nankeen lily

This lily bears fragrant turkscap flowers from early to midsummer. The petals are light apricot-pink, spotted with red. Grow in full sun or partial shade. H 1–1.5m (3–5ft). Hardy/Z4–8.

American Hybrids (Division 4)

Derived from American species, these are rhizomatous lilies, bearing sometimes scented, usually turkscap flowers. They are not stem-rooting. The group includes the Bellingham hybrids, which date from the 1920s; these have occasionally fragrant turkscap flowers, which vary from yellow to orange to orange-red, all spotted with deep brown, and all appearing in early to midsummer. They are excellent for naturalizing in light shade, and good for informal situations such as open woodland or the back of a border. They need acidic, preferably moist soil.

Lilium 'Shuksan'

This selected form has lightly scented tangerine-yellow flowers tipped with red and spotted with black or reddish-brown. H to 1.2m (4ft). Hardy/Z4–8.

Longiflorum Hybrids (Division 5)

Derived from *L. formosanum*, native to Taiwan, and *L. longiflorum*, from southern Japan and Taiwan, this is a small but growing group that includes fragrant, trumpet- or funnel-shaped flowers, which are usually grown for the cut-flower trade. They will tolerate a range of soils, including alkaline.

Lilium 'Centurion'

This lovely lily produces large, outward-facing, sweetly scented, funnel- to trumpet-shaped flowers, up to four per stem, that open flat; the tepals are creamy salmon, with heavy spotting towards the base. H to 90cm (36in). Hardy/Z4–8.

Trumpet and Aurelian Hybrids (Division 6)

Derived from Asiatic species (but not *L. auratum, L. japonicum, L. rubellum* or *L. speciosum*), these are mostly hardy, fragrant, stem-rooting lilies. They tolerate alkaline conditions. There are four subdivisions: 6a trumpet-shaped flowers; 6b (usually) outward-facing, bowl-shaped flowers; 6c shallowly bowl-shaped flowers, which often open flat; and 6d flowers which have distinctly recurved petals.

Lilium African Queen Group

Division 6a. This is a wonderful group of cultivars with large, fragrant, outward-facing to nodding, trumpet-shaped flowers, which are brownish-purple on the outside and yellow or orange-apricot on the inside. The flowers appear in mid- to late summer. Simply sumptuous, but plants might need support. H 1.5–1.8m (5–6ft). Borderline hardy/Z4–8.

Lilium Pink Perfection Group

Division 6a. This is another marvellous group of cultivars with large, scented, outward-facing to slightly nodding, trumpet-shaped flowers, which are borne at eye level. They are pink with a combination of purple and soft yellow, and are excellent in pots, flowering in midsummer. Plant with *L*. African Queen Group for sheer effect and continuity of colour. Plants might need support. H 1.5–1.8m (5–6ft). Hardy/Z4–8.

Lilium Golden Splendor Group

Division 6a. Cultivars in this group produce vigorous, slightly variable flowers on strong stems in midsummer. The blooms are large, scented, outward-facing and somewhere between trumpet-shaped and bowl-shaped. They are various shades of yellow, with dark burgundy-red colouring on the outside. They are good for pots or the border, where they might need support. H 1.2–1.8m (4–6ft). Hardy/Z4–8.

Lilium 'Centurion'

Lilium 'White Henryi'

Lilium 'Belle Epoque'

Lilium 'Royal Class'

Lilium 'Star Gazer'

Lilium 'White Henryi'

Division 6d. This has large, fragrant flowers, which open flat in late summer. They are white, flushed deep orange at the base. H to 1.5m (5ft). Borderline hardy/Z4–8.

Oriental Hybrids (Division 7)

Derived from species from the Far East, such as *L. auratum*, *L. japonicum* and *L. speciosum*, these lilies flower mostly in late summer and are often scented. Most are lime-hating and require acid soil. There are four subdivisions: 7a trumpet-shaped flowers; 7b bowl-shaped flowers; 7c flat flowers; and 7d flowers with distinctly recurved petals.

Lilium 'Acapulco'

Division 7d. This lily has fragrant, rich pink flowers with recurving petals. H to 1m (3ft 3in). Hardy/Z4–8.

Lilium 'Belle Epoque'

Division 7b. This lily produces large, outward-facing, bowl-shaped scented flowers, up to 8 per stem; the tepals vary in colour from white to soft pink, with a central cream band. H to 1m (3ft 3in). Hardy/Z4–8.

Lilium 'Casa Blanca'

Division 7b. The fragrant, pure white flowers have orange-red anthers. H 1.2m (4ft). Hardy/Z4–8.

Lilium 'Cosmopolitan'

Division 7b. This hybrid lily has fragrant, bowl-shaped flowers in midsummer; tepals are pink to red. H 1m (3ft 3in). Hardy/Z4–8.

Lilium 'Hotlips'

Division 7c. This is a sensational and popular lily. The fragrant white flowers, which are streaked and spotted with red, appear in late summer. H to 90cm (36in). Hardy/Z4–8.

Lilium 'Imperial Gold'

Division 7c. The large, fragrant, star-shaped, glistening yellow flowers have a yellow stripe in the centre. The flowers appear in late summer. H 1.8m (6ft). Hardy/Z4–8.

Lilium 'Journey's End'

Division 7d. This lily bears racemes of large, unscented, broad turkscap flowers. They are deep pink with maroon spots and white tips and appear in late summer. H 1–1.8m (3–6ft). Hardy/Z4–8.

Lilium 'Mona Lisa'

Division 7c. The white flowers are heavily spotted with red and have a broader stripe of red in the centre. They are borne from mid-to late summer. H to 90cm (36in). Hardy/Z4–8.

Lilium 'Omega'

Division 7d. This lily has short stems with racemes of large rose-pink flowers with yellow centres and sparse red spotting. It flowers in late summer. H 60–80cm (24–32in). Hardy/Z4–8.

Lilium 'Royal Class'

Division 7b. The fragrant flowers vary from white to soft pink and have a central yellow band and prominent papillae. H to 90cm (36in). Hardy/Z4–8.

Lilium 'Star Gazer'

Division 7c. This lily has deep rose-red flowers edged with white.

It is suitable for deep containers but needs ericaceous compost. This is not a fragrant lily, yet it is one of the most popular species. It flowers in midsummer. H 70–100cm (28–39in). Hardy/Z4–8.

Lilium 'White Mountain'

Division 7c. This lily has beautiful white flowers with a yellow band right down the centre of each petal. It flowers in late summer. H to 80cm (32in). Hardy/Z4–8.

Other Hybrids (Division 8)

This diverse division includes all the remaining hybrids that are not included in the other groups.

Lilium 'Moneymaker'

This bears up to 6 sweetly scented, clear pink flowers in midsummer. H 90cm (36in). Hardy/Z4–8.

Lilium 'Cosmopolitan'

Lilium 'Moneymaker'

Lilium auratum

Lilium davidii

Lilium formosanum

Lilium longiflorum

Species Lilies (Division 9)
This group includes all true species and their forms.

Lilium auratum
Golden-rayed lily
Native to Japan, this lily has the largest flowers of all. From late summer to autumn it bears up to 20, and sometimes as many as 30, sweetly scented, white and gold flowers with crimson spots, to 30cm (12in) across. It requires acid soil and full sun, with light shade provided by low-growing plants. H 1–1.8m (3–6ft) S 10cm (4in). Hardy/Z4–9.

Lilium candidum
Madonna lily
This lily is native to southeastern Europe and countries of the eastern Mediterranean. It bears 5 or more white, faintly scented, trumpet-shaped flowers, 5–8cm (2–3in) long, with bright yellow

anthers. They have a sweet scent and appear in midsummer. This is the only lily to produce overwintering basal leaves. It requires neutral to alkaline soil. H 1–1.8m (3–6ft), S 10cm (4in). Hardy/Z4–9.

Lilium davidii
This species is native to western China. In summer it produces up to 12 nodding turkscap flowers, borne on long stalks. The flowers are vermilion-orange, spotted black. It is a stem-rooting lily that tolerates a wide range of soils, including lime, but it does best in humus-rich soil. H 1–1.3m (3ft–4ft 6in) S 10cm (4in). Hardy/Z5–8.

Lilium duchartrei
Marble martagon lily
This species from western China produces up to 12 nodding turkscap flowers, borne on long

stalks in summer. The flowers are white, spotted with deep purple inside and with a purple flush, aging to red, on the outside. It grows from a rhizomatous bulb and spreads by stolons; it will form large colonies in good conditions. It tolerates lime but does best in well-drained soil in a cool, lightly shaded position. H 60–100cm (24–36in) S 10cm (4in). Hardy/Z4–8.

Lilium formosanum
This elegant, stem-rooting lily, originally from Taiwan, grows from rhizomatous bulbs. It has slender, fragrant, trumpet-shaped white flowers, 12–20cm (4½–8in) long, with a reddish-purple flush on the outside. The flowers are borne from late summer to early autumn. This lily requires a moist, acid soil. H 60–150cm (2–5ft) S 10cm (4in). Borderline hardy/Z5.

Lilium hansonii
This vigorous species, originally from eastern Russia, Korea and Japan, produces racemes of up to 12 nodding turkscap flowers, gloriously orange-yellow with brown-purple spots towards the base. It is a stem-rooting lily, which tolerates a wide range of soils, but likes good drainage and a position in partial shade. H 1–1.5m (3–5ft) S 10cm (4in). Hardy/Z5–8.

Lilium lancifolium
Tiger lily
This species is native to eastern China, Korea and Japan. It bears up to 40 (but more usually 5–10) orange-red, purple-speckled flowers. It is robust, clump-forming and stem-rooting and flowers from late summer to early autumn. It prefers moist acid soil but tolerates some lime. H 60–150cm (2–5ft) S 10cm (4in). Hardy/Z4–9.

Lilium longiflorum
Easter lily
This elegant lily, which is originally from south Japan and Taiwan, is a vigorous, stem-rooting plant, which is lime tolerant. It prefers partial shade. In midsummer it produces short racemes of 1–6 fragrant, trumpet-shaped, pure white flowers, to 18cm (7in) long, with yellow anthers. This is a flower that is often grown to decorate churches at Easter-time. H 40–100cm (16–39in) S 10cm (4in). Half-hardy/Z5.

Lilium candidum

Lilium duchartrei

Lilium martagon

Lilium martagon
Martagon lily, turkscap lily
This lily, which is native to a wide area stretching from Europe to Mongolia, has glossy, nodding, pink to purplish-red flowers with dark purple spots. The flowers, which appear in early and midsummer, are in the shape of a Turk's cap and are 5cm (2in) across. It is ideal among shrubs in well-drained soil in full sun or partial shade. It will tolerate a range of soils. *L. martagon* var. *album* AGM is white. H 1–1.8m (3–6ft) S 10cm (4in). Hardy/Z4–8.

Lilium pyrenaicum
Originally from the Pyrenees, this is a stem-rooting, clump-forming lily, which bears racemes of up to 12 unpleasantly scented yellow flowers with dark maroon spots. The flowers, which appear in early and midsummer, are turkscap type and are 5cm (2in) across. It is ideal growing among shrubs in well-drained soil in sun or partial shade. It needs neutral to alkaline soil. H 30–90cm (12–36in) S 10cm (4in). Hardy/Z4–8.

Lilium regale
Regal lily
This lily, which originated in western China, enjoys a position in full sun. In summer it bears large, trumpet-shaped, scented, white flowers, 13–15cm (5–6in) long, with purple streaking on the reverse. It can be grown in the border, although it may need support. It will tolerate a range of soils, although excessively alkaline soils should be avoided. It is excellent growing among deep red

Lilium regale

or white, late-flowering, old-fashioned roses. It is also suitable for large, deep containers. It is a wonderful, easy-to-grow lily. H 60–180cm (2–6ft) S 10cm (4in). Hardy/Z4–9.

Lilium speciosum var. *rubrum*
Originally from eastern China, Japan and Taiwan, this lily is admired for its carmine-red flowers, which appear in late summer. Each flower, to 18cm (7in) across, has darker crimson spots and is turkscap in shape. This lily needs moist, acid soil and a position in partial shade. It might need staking. It is excellent in deep containers. A number of selected forms have been developed, including *L. speciosum* var. *album*, which has white flowers, while var. *roseum* has deep pink flowers. H 90cm (36in) S 10cm (4in). Hardy/Z5–8.

Lilium speciosum 'Uchida'
This is a lily of garden origin, a selection of a species from eastern China, Japan and Taiwan. In late summer and autumn, erect stems carry large, fragrant, outward-facing or hanging turkscap flowers; the tepals are brilliant crimson, spotted with green or darker red, with white tips. H to 2m (6ft 6in). Hardy/Z5–8.

Lilium tsingtauense
This is a species from China and Korea. It is a distinctive lily, flowering in midsummer, when it produces elegant, upward-facing, unscented, bowl-shaped flowers that open flat. The flowers have orange or vermilion-orange petals spotted with purple. Planted in sun or partial shade, it thrives in moist, acid soil but will tolerate some lime. H 90cm (36in) S 10cm (4in). Hardy/Z5–8.

Lilium speciosum 'Uchida'

Lilium wallichianum
Originally from the Himalayas, this is a fragrant lily with white or cream trumpet-shaped flowers, which flare to 20cm (8in) across and are tinged with green on the exterior. The flowers are borne in late summer to autumn. It is stem-rooting and needs moist, acid soil. It is not hardy but will grow in deep containers. H 1–1.8m (3–6ft) S 10cm (4in). Half-hardy/Z5–8.

Lilium wilsonii
This lily originates in Japan. It flowers in summer, bearing large, upward-facing, unscented, bowl-shaped flowers. The blooms are orange-red, striped yellow at the base and spotted with dark brown. This lily needs well-drained soil in sun or partial shade. H 1.1m (3ft 6in) S 10cm (4in). Hardy/Z5–8.

Lilium speciosum

Lilium tsingtauense

Lilium wilsonii

MUSCARI
Grape hyacinth

The name of this genus derives from the Latin word *muscus* (musk scent), the fragrance carried by some of the species. The genus contains 30 species of bulbs from the Mediterranean to south-western Asia, the best known of which is *Muscari armeniacum*, whose cultivars are so useful in borders, grassland and all types and sizes of containers.

Cultivation Plant in full sun, although they will also tolerate partial shade in pots. In autumn plant bulbs 5cm (2in) deep in small to large groups. They will multiply rapidly.

Propagation Sow seed in containers in a cold frame in autumn. Remove offsets in summer.

Pests and diseases Viruses can be a problem.

Muscari armeniacum

The species comes originally from south-eastern Europe to Caucasus. For many weeks from early to mid-spring dense racemes, 2–8cm (¼–3in) long, of beautiful blue flowers are borne in grape-like bunches at the top of the stem. This is one of the prettiest of all the blue bulbs, and it looks sumptuous as a mass planting beneath roses or along a path. It makes an excellent association with all Double Early tulips and is especially delightful with pink *Tulipa* 'Peach Blossom'. The only drawback is that the foliage can grow long and untidy, but the exquisite colouring and long duration of flowering make up for any waywardness. H 20cm (8in) S 5cm (2in). Hardy/Z2–9.

Muscari armeniacum

Muscari armeniacum 'Valerie Finnis'

Muscari armeniacum 'Blue Spike'

This is one of several cultivars available derived from *Muscari armeniacum*. It has double, soft blue flowers on a spike that reaches 15cm (6in), making it a little shorter than the species. It also flowers slightly later in mid-spring. It is good in the border or in a small container. H 15cm (6in) S 5cm (2in) Hardy/Z2–9.

Muscari armeniacum 'Valerie Finnis'

This is a recent introduction, which was found in the Northamptonshire garden of plantswoman Valerie Finnis. Derived from *Muscari armeniacum*, it produces lovely pale blue flower spikes. It is so easy to grow that it promises to become a favourite for mid-spring gardens. It is perfect for a window box, hanging basket or small pot along with mid-spring-flowering miniature daffodils and violas. H 15cm (6in) S 5cm (2in). Hardy/Z2–9.

Muscari aucheri

The species is native to Turkey. In mid-spring dense racemes of beautiful bright blue flowers are borne. They have constricted white mouths and, usually, are crowned with paler blue sterile flowers. H 10–15cm (4–6in) S 5cm (2in) Hardy/Z2–9.

Muscari azureum

This is another species that originated in Turkey. In mid-spring it bears racemes of bright blue flowers with a darker stripe on each lobe. H 10cm (4in) S 5cm (2in). Hardy/Z2–9.

Muscari botryoides f. album
Pearls of Spain

The species is native to France, Germany and Poland southwards throughout central and south-eastern Europe. This muscari has slender racemes of scented, white flowers in mid-spring. They are borne in bunches at the top of the stem like tiny grapes. It is daintier than *M. armeniacum* and has much neater leaves. H 15–20cm (6–8in) S 5cm (2in). Hardy/Z3–9.

Muscari comosum
Tassel grape hyacinth

The species is native to southern Europe, Turkey and Iran. In late spring and early summer it bears racemes of creamy brown flowers with violet-blue, upper sterile flowers borne in tassels on top. *M. comosum* 'Plumosum' has feathery heads made up of entirely purple sterile threads. H 20–60cm (8–24in) S 5cm (2in). Borderline hardy/Z2–9.

Muscari latifolium

This species is originally from the open pine forests of northwestern Turkey. The slender racemes of dark violet flowers have a crown of paler sterile flowers on top. This bulb produces one broad leaf, hence its specific name *latifolium*. It is an excellent bulb for containers if they can be kept in a sheltered place in winter. H 20cm (8in) S 5cm (2in). Borderline hardy/Z2–10.

Muscari neglectum
(syn. M. racemosum)

This species is native to North Africa and southwest Asia. The slender racemes of blue-black flowers with constricted white mouths are borne in spring on dense racemes. It has many mid-green leaves, channelled to almost cylindrical. It is good in containers or for a special place at the front of a border. H 20cm (8in) S 5cm (2in). Hardy/Z2–10.

Muscari latifolium

NARCISSUS
Daffodil

This group of bulbs is sometimes known by its Latin name, *Narcissus*, and sometimes by its common name, daffodil. There are about 50 species, originally growing in a wide range of habitats in Europe and North Africa, where they are found in meadows and woodlands and even in rock crevices. As a harbinger of spring, this is one of the best-loved of all bulbs, and many thousands of cultivars have been grown over the years. The predominant colour is yellow but many are white. Sometimes the outer petals are one colour and the trumpet another, giving rise to bicolour plants; pink and orange are additional colour variations.

The length and shape of the trumpet can vary considerably. Sometimes it is long and narrow, as in the species *N. cyclamineus*; sometimes is shorter, when it becomes known as the eye, as in *N. poeticus* var. *recurvus*. Sometimes the trumpet is frilly around the edge, and it may even be split, as in the butterfly daffodils, such as 'Cassata'. Usually the flowers are held singly but occasionally they are multiheaded – 'Hawera', for example, can have as many as 3 or 4 blooms – and some, including 'Paper White Grandiflora', might have 8–10 or even more. Occasionally, the flowers are double, even in the species, but double flowers are more often seen in the cultivars, such as 'Ice King' or 'Tahiti'. Some daffodils have a strong scent, particularly those derived from *N. poeticus*, such as the cultivars 'Sir Winston Churchill' and 'Cheerfulness'. Fragrance is also common in indoor midwinter-flowering bulbs, such as 'Paper White Grandiflora'.

Most cultivars reach 40cm (16in) or more when in flower, but there is a group of dwarf daffodils, which have become increasingly popular. They are derived from species such as *N. bulbocodium*, *N. cyclamineus*, *N. jonquilla*, *N. minor* and *N. triandrus* and forms like *N. tazetta* subsp. *lacticolor* (syn. *N. canaliculatus*). Of these, the cultivars originating from *N. cyclamineus* and *N. triandus* are exceptionally useful and reliable. These are generally sturdy and will stand up well to wind. They are eminently suitable for borders and look pretty in small-scale gardens with confined space. They are also ideal for pots and windowboxes where the proportions are good, and the bulbs are quite small so they do not take up too much planting space. These bulbs will grow to great effect in open grassland too.

The early-spring flowerers are particularly suitable in this respect, their flowering time coinciding with a period when the grass is short early in the season.

All daffodils make good cut flowers. Cutting the flowers will not weaken the flowering ability in the following season, although removing the leaves will have a detrimental effect.

Cultivation All narcissi grow well in sun or partial shade, where the soil is moist in autumn and the spring growing season. Daffodils are tolerant bulbs that will grow in any reasonable garden soil as long as it is well drained, but the species and cultivars of *N. cyclamineus*, *N. triandrus* and *N. bulbocodium* prefer acidic to neutral conditions and *N. jonquilla* and *N. tazetta* prefer slightly alkaline soil. If they are in containers use an ericaceous mix. The cultivars of *N. cyclamineus* are not choosy and will grow well in any good garden soil. If they are in containers use an ordinary soil-based potting compost (soil mix). Those planted for midwinter flowering indoors will benefit from being in a proprietary indoor bulb compost.

For groups planting distance is usually about 15cm (6in) in each direction. Planting depths depend on the size of the bulbs, but as a rule plant the bulb so that its nose is twice the depth of the bulb below soil level. With larger bulbs this might be 15cm (6in) deep or more, whereas for the dwarf daffodils, of which the bulbs are often much smaller, the depth is usually about 10cm (4in). The only exception is in the treatment of indoor midwinter-flowering bulbs, which are planted so that the top of each bulb is level with the compost.

To promote healthy bulbs for the following year's flower production, deadhead after flowering so the plant does not waste energy on producing seedheads. If the daffodils are planted in grass, allow the leaves to die down naturally for at least 6 weeks after flowering before you mow. When they are planted in borders, simply remove

Narcissus 'Dutch Master'

yellowing leaves once the natural dying process is complete. On poor soils and in containers apply a high-phosphate feed in spring to allow the bulb to build up energy for the following season.
Propagation Seed can take up to seven years to produce a flowering bulb. Remove offsets as leaves fade in summer or early autumn.
Pests and diseases Narcissus bulb fly, narcissus eel worm, slugs, fungal infections and viruses may be a problem.

Trumpet Daffodils (Division 1)
The trumpet is the same length as, or longer than, the petals. All narcissi in this group are hardy/Z3–9.

Narcissus 'Arctic Gold'
This is a vigorous and free-flowering daffodil with mid-green foliage and smooth, waxy, rich golden-yellow flowers almost 10cm (4in) wide, which appear in mid-spring. The trumpets are widely flanged and deeply notched. H 40cm (16in).

Narcissus 'Dutch Master'
This is a uniform soft yellow daffodil with a large cup. Flowering in early spring, this is a typical daffodil for borders or grassland. H 35cm (14in).

Narcissus 'Golden Harvest'
This is one of the leading golden-trumpet daffodils. Early to flower in spring, it makes a welcome addition to any border or grassland. H 35cm (14in).

Narcissus 'Golden Harvest'

Narcissus **'King Alfred'**
This daffodil is golden-yellow. One of the best known of all daffodils, it flowers in mid-spring. Plant in borders or grassland, although its large cup makes it susceptible to flopping in rain. H 35cm (14in).

Narcissus **'Little Gem'**
This is a well proportioned, dwarf miniature trumpet daffodil. It flowers in early spring and is perfect for hanging baskets, small pots, raised troughs and windowboxes or for the front of a border. H 20cm (8in).

Narcissus **'Mount Hood'**
This lovely daffodil is ivory-white both in its trumpet and perianth. Flowering in late spring, it makes an attractive daffodil to extend the season. Plant in borders or grassland. H 35cm (14in).

Narcissus **'Rijnveld's Early Sensation'** (syn. *N.* 'January Gold')
This daffodil, which will stand up to cold weather, is one of the earliest to flower. It has a yellow trumpet and petals. It is strong and robust and a good choice for late-winter colour. Plant in borders or grassland. H 35cm (14in).

Narcissus **'Rose Caprice'**
This two-toned daffodil has white petals and salmon-pink cups. It flowers in mid-spring and is ideal for medium to large containers and borders. H 35cm (14in).

Narcissus 'Topolino'

Narcissus 'Carlton'

Narcissus 'Pinza'

Narcissus **'Spellbinder'**
This is a special daffodil with a reverse bicolour, aging to nearly white with a yellow rim to the trumpet. It makes an attractive mid-season daffodil. Plant in borders or in grassland. H 35cm (14in).

Narcissus **'Topolino'**
This little daffodil has white petals and a primrose-yellow trumpet, which looks down gently to the ground. Early to flower, it is quite excellent in containers with early primroses and violas and makes a natural grouping in grass. It is good for borders too. H 20cm (8in).

Narcissus **'W. P. Milner'**
This dainty daffodil, with milky white petals and bicolour white and cream trumpet, flowers in early spring. It is pretty in small baskets and troughs and makes a lovely grouping in borders partnering white or purple violets and *Anemone blanda.* H 23cm (9in).

Large-cupped Daffodils (Division 2)
The cup is longer than one-third of, but not as long as, the perianth segments. These daffodils usually flower in mid-spring. All are hardy/Z3–9.

Narcissus **'Carlton'**
This is a soft yellow daffodil with a large cup, which is frilly at the mouth. An excellent naturalizer, it is a delightful daffodil for borders or grassland, flowering in mid-spring. H 45cm (18in).

Narcissus **'Delibes'**
This is an unusual daffodil, with an apricot-yellow perianth and dark red cup. It is good for planting in borders or grassland. Flowering in early spring, it is a useful daffodil to start the season. H 35cm (14in).

Narcissus **'Flower Record'**
This white daffodil has a medium-sized yellow cup edged with orange. It is suitable for borders or grassland and flowers in mid-spring. H 40cm (16in).

Narcissus **'Ice Follies'**
This is a popular white daffodil with a widely flared, creamy white crown, which pales with maturity. Early to flower, it makes a welcome addition to any spring border and grows well in grass. It is free to flower and increases well. H 35cm (14in).

Narcissus **'Juanita'**
This is a yellow daffodil with a medium orange cup. Suitable for planting in borders or in grassland, it is a useful daffodil to start the season in early spring. H 35cm (14in).

Narcissus **'Pink Smiles'**
Flowering in mid-spring, this is a white daffodil with a lovely rose-pink cup. It is suitable for planting in grassland or borders where it will associate handsomely with either lime-green or bronze foliage, as well as other white flowers. H 35cm (14in).

Narcissus **'Pinza'**
This is a striking daffodil with rich yellow petals and a deep red cup. It will flower in mid-spring. It looks very attractive planted against a dark background or with rich blues. H 35cm (14in).

Bulbs with yellow flowers

Asphodeline lutea	*Erythronium* 'Pagoda'
Begonia (many)	*Freesia* 'Dijon'
Calochortus luteus 'Golden Orb'	*Freesia* 'Winter Gold'
Canna 'Louis Cottin'	*Fritillaria imperialis* 'Maxima Lutea'
Canna 'Picasso'	*Hyacinthus orientalis* 'City of Haarlem'
Crocosmia 'George Davison'	*Lilium* 'Golden Splendor'
Crocosmia 'Lady Hamilton'	*Narcissus* (most)
Crocosmia 'Solfatare'	*Sternbergia lutea*
Crocus x luteus 'Dutch Yellow'	*Tulipa* 'Golden Apeldoorn'
Dahlia (many)	*Tulipa* 'Honky Tonk'
Eranthis hyemalis	*Tulipa* 'Monte Carlo'

Narcissus 'Pipe Major'
This is a showy daffodil with yellow petals and a strong orange-red cup. It flowers in late spring and looks lovely in borders or grassland. H 35cm (14in).

Narcissus 'Rainbow'
This is a delicate white daffodil. It has a beautiful peach cup with a coppery pink rim. It looks stunning in borders, especially when planted near lime-green or bronze foliage. It is also excellent in grassland. Because it is later to flower, it is useful for extending the season from mid- to late spring. H 40cm (16in).

Narcissus 'Red Devon'
This daffodil has a yellow perianth and a red cup. It flowers in mid-spring, and is a striking addition in borders or grassland. H 40cm (16in).

Narcissus 'Roseworthy'
This beautifully proportioned white daffodil, with its rich pink trumpet, is lovely. It flowers in mid- to late spring and looks stunning in a medium to large container, and is even better when the container is raised and backlit with spring sunshine. This is also a good daffodil for borders. H 35cm (14in).

Narcissus 'Roseworthy'

Narcissus 'Segovia'

Narcissus 'Rip van Winkle'

Narcissus 'St Keverne'
This is a lovely golden-yellow daffodil, bred in Cornwall, with clear lemon-yellow perianth and a deeper gold cup. It is an ideal choice for the early-spring garden whether in borders or grassland. H 35cm (14in).

Narcissus 'St Patrick's Day'
This is a delicate, two-toned cultivar with creamy white perianth and lime-green trumpet. It flowers in mid-spring and looks good in borders, where its unusual colour combination can be seen to full effect. H 35cm (14in).

Narcissus 'Salome'
This beautiful white daffodil, with its delicate pink trumpet, is stunning for borders. It flowers in late spring. H 35cm (14in).

Small-cupped Daffodils (Division 3)
The cup is less than one-third the length of the petals. Hardy/Z3–9.

Narcissus 'Merlin'
This beautiful daffodil has white petals and a flattened, pale yellow cup trimmed with a band of red. It flowers from mid- to late spring. H 45cm (18in).

Narcissus 'Segovia'
This is an excellent dainty bicolour daffodil, with white petals and a pale yellow cup. Flowering from mid- to late spring, this is good for the front of the border and for small containers. H 25cm (10in).

Double Daffodils (Division 4)
The petals or the cup (or both) are double, which sometimes gives a muddled appearance. Nearly all are hardy/Z3–9.

Narcissus 'Bridal Crown'
Developed from *N. tazetta* (and sometimes classified as Division 8), this is a white, multiheaded daffodil. It is fragrant and makes a lovely indoor daffodil to flower in midwinter. H 35cm (14in). Half-hardy/Z8.

Narcissus x odorus 'Double Campernelle'
(syn. *N.* 'Double Campernelle')
This is a pretty double yellow daffodil and delightfully fragrant. It flowers in early spring and is ideal for pots and window boxes. H 25cm (10in).

Narcissus 'Rip van Winkle'
(syn. *N. minor* var. *pumilis* 'Plenus')
The parent species originated from the Pyrenees. Flowering in early spring, it has rather lax stems to support the weight of the spiky double yellow flowers, but it looks pretty in short grass or a border. H 20cm (8in).

Narcissus 'Salome'

Narcissus 'Thalia'

Narcissus 'Tahiti'

Narcissus 'Yellow Cheerfulness'

Narcissus 'Sir Winston Churchill'

This much-loved cultivar is derived from fragrant *N. x medioluteus* (syn. *N. x poetaz*). The daffodil is white and multiheaded. Sturdy in growth, it is excellent for borders or grassland and, being later to flower, is a useful daffodil to extend the season. It will follow on well from the earlier-flowering 'White Lion'. H 40cm (16in).

Narcissus 'Tahiti'

This is a double yellow cultivar with fine red segments. It is late to flower and is a useful and showy daffodil to extend the season. A prize daffodil for planting in borders rather than in grassland. H 40cm (16in).

Narcissus 'Unique'

This is a double white cultivar with yellow segments. Late to flower, it makes an attractive daffodil that is a good choice for extending the season. It is best planted in borders rather than in grassland. H 40cm (16in).

Narcissus 'White Lion'

This is a double white cultivar with pale lemon-yellow segments. It flowers in mid-season and makes an excellent contribution to borders or grassland where it associates well with the later-flowering 'Sir Winston Churchill'. H 40cm (16in).

Narcissus 'Yellow Cheerfulness'

A cultivar of *N. x medioluteus* (syn. *N. x poetaz*), this is a double primrose-yellow daffodil with a neat button cup. There are often several flowers on each stem. It is fragrant, sturdy and excellent for borders. It flowers in late spring, so is a useful daffodil to extend the season. H 40cm (16in).

Triandrus Daffodils (Division 5)

Derived from *N. triandrus*, which is native to Spain, Portugal and north-western France, these cultivars flower in mid-spring. Each stem usually produces 2–6 flowers. All are hardy/Z3–9.

Narcissus 'Hawera'

This is an excellent multiheaded daffodil, with dainty lemon-yellow flowers. The oval petals are reflexed. It is derived from *N. triandrus* and *N. jonquilla* and dates from the 1930s. Flowering from mid- to late spring, this daffodil is long-lasting, good for the front of a border and excellent for small containers. H 15cm (6in).

Narcissus 'Ice Wings'

Ice-white trumpets and white reflexed petals give this lovely multiheaded daffodil its name. Derived from *N. triandrus*, it flowers in mid-spring and looks lovely in borders or containers. H 30cm (12in).

Narcissus 'Thalia'

This is an excellent multiheaded daffodil, with white trumpets and white reflexed petals. It is derived from *N. triandrus* and flowers in mid-spring. It looks pretty at the front of borders and in containers. H 30cm (12in).

Narcissus 'Ice Wings'

Bulbs with double flowers

Anemone 'Lord Lieutenant'
Begonia (many)
Colchicum 'Waterlily'
Dahlia (many)
Galanthus nivalis 'Flore Pleno'
Hyacinthus orientalis 'Ben Nevis'
Hyacinthus orientalis 'Hollyhock'
Narcissus 'Rip van Winkle'
Narcissus 'Tahiti'
Narcissus 'White Lion'
Tulipa 'Angélique'
Tulipa 'Peach Blossom'

Narcissus 'February Gold'

Narcissus 'Foundling'

Cyclamineus Daffodils (Division 6)

Derived from *N. cyclamineus*, which is native to north-west Portugal and north-west Spain, these daffodils produce a single flower with swept-back petals. They usually have a long cup or trumpet, and flowers appear from early to mid-spring. The species will naturalize well in damp conditions, preferring acidic soils, where it will succeed in partial shade. The cultivars thrive in any garden soil. They are usually dwarf. All are hardy/Z3–9.

Narcissus 'Jetfire'

Narcissus 'February Gold'

This is one of the best of all the dwarf daffodils, with a pretty golden-yellow trumpet and fly-away petals. It flowers in early spring. Strong, sturdy and long in flower, it is ideal for grassland, borders and many containers. It will naturalize well. H 25cm (10in).

Narcissus 'Foundling'

This is a popular daffodil, with broad, white, fly-away petals surrounding a delicate deep pink cup. Flowering from early to mid-spring, it is ideal for pots and raised troughs or for a special place in the border. H 25–30cm (10–12in).

Narcissus 'Jack Snipe'

This is one of the best dwarf bicolour daffodils. It has white reflexed petals and a golden-yellow trumpet. Good for borders and grassland, where it will naturalize well, and for containers. It flowers in early spring. H 25cm (10in).

Narcissus 'Jenny'

The combination of creamy white trumpet and matching fly-away petals makes this a popular choice for the garden or small containers. It flowers in early spring. H 25–28cm (10–11in).

Narcissus 'Jetfire'

This is a striking dwarf daffodil, with a golden-orange trumpet and reflexed yellow petals. Strong, sturdy and long in flower, it is ideal for borders. It flowers in early spring and will naturalize well. H 25cm (10in).

Narcissus 'Peeping Tom'

Slightly taller than the others listed in this category, this daffodil has the reflexed petals reminiscent of its cyclamineus parent and a long golden-yellow trumpet. It flowers in early spring. It is good for borders, grassland, where it will naturalize well, and containers. H 30cm (12in).

Jonquilla and Apodanthus Daffodils (Division 7)

Derived from *N. jonquilla*, which originates in southern and central Spain and southern and eastern Portugal, these daffodils have 1–5 scented flowers on a single stem. All are hardy/Z3–9.

Narcissus 'Bell Song'

This pretty daffodil, which opens slightly lemon-yellow but then fades to ivory-white, has a neat, flat, pink crown. It flowers in mid-spring and is fragrant. It is ideal for pots, raised troughs and window boxes or for a special place in the border. H 25–30cm (10–12in).

Narcissus 'Peeping Tom'

Narcissus 'Bell Song'

Narcissus 'Pipit'

Narcissus 'Suzy'

Narcissus 'Ziva'

Narcissus 'Minnow'

Developed from *N. tazetta*, this is a multiheaded daffodil, with rounded flowers. The dainty creamy white blooms have pale yellow cups. It flowers in early spring and is good for pots, raised troughs and window boxes or for the front of the border. H 33cm (13in).

Narcissus 'Paper White Grandiflorus'

Developed from *N. papyraceus*, which is native to southern France, southern Spain and North Africa, this daffodil bears bunches of 5–10 fragrant, glistening white flowers, 1cm ('/2in) across. H 40cm (16in). 'Ziva' is similar but slightly shorter; 'Omri' is also shorter but has creamy white flowers. They are useful as indoor pot daffodils to flower in midwinter, and all are fragrant. Use a proprietary indoor bulb compost and, 6 weeks before the flowers are required, plant so that the top of the bulbs is level with the compost. Half-hardy/Z8.

Narcissus 'Pipit'

This is a delightful, multiheaded daffodil with gorgeous lemon-yellow flowers, often streaked with white. The petals are reflexed. The cups reverse to near white with age. It flowers for a long time, from mid- to late spring, and is an excellent choice for larger containers and for borders. It increases well. H 30cm (12in).

Narcissus 'Quail'

This is a rich golden-yellow daffodil. It is multiheaded and fragrant, flowering from mid- to late spring. It is a good choice for small to medium containers and for borders. H 30cm (12in).

Narcissus 'Sun Disc'

This tiny daffodil has unusual flowers, which are like miniature golden-yellow discs. The crowns

are almost flat. It increases rapidly, but is so small that it needs a position at the front of a border or in small containers, such as a wall pot or hanging basket. It flowers in mid-spring. H 15cm (6in).

Narcissus 'Suzy'

This is a highly distinctive yellow daffodil with wide but shallow orange crowns. It is heavily scented. Taller than most of the others in this category, it is suitable for planting in borders and for medium to large containers. It flowers in mid-spring. H 40cm (16in).

Tazetta Daffodils (Division 8)

These are either small-flowered cultivars, with up to 20 flowers on each stem, or large-flowered cultivars, with 3 or 4 flowers on each stem. They have broad petals

and small cups. They are usually scented and make good cut flowers. 'Minnow' and 'Silver Chimes' are hardy/Z3–9, but the others are half-hardy and should be grown indoors. They flower in late autumn to mid-spring.

Narcissus 'Geranium'

This has a pure white perianth and an orange cup. It is double, multiheaded and fragrant. Sturdy and excellent for borders, this is a late-spring-flowering daffodil that is useful for extending the season. H 35cm (14in).

Narcissus 'Martinette'

This bears several yellow flowers on each stem, each bloom having a neat but striking orange cup. Fragrant and early to flower, this is useful for small to medium containers or borders. H 30cm (12in).

Narcissus 'Silver Chimes'

This is a fragrant white daffodil with up to 6 nodding heads on each stem. The small crown has a touch of creamy yellow, which has a softening effect. Flowering in mid-spring, it needs a warm, dry spot at the front of a sunny border or beneath a sunny wall. It is excellent for small to medium containers in a sheltered site where it can be fully appreciated. H 30cm (12in).

Narcissus 'Minnow'

Narcissus 'Silver Chimes'

Narcissus cyclamineus

Poeticus Daffodils (Division 9)
Developed from *N. poeticus*, which
originally came from a wide area
extending from France to Greece,
this group have spreading, pure
white petals and shallow cups,
rimmed with red. They appear in
late spring. All are hardy/Z3–9.

Narcissus 'Actaea'
The pure white flowers, which
appear in mid-spring, have a
brilliant scarlet eye. This is a
delightful cultivar for borders or
grassland. H 40cm (16in).

Narcissus 'Actaea'

Wild Species (Division 10)
The plants in this group are
species and naturally occurring.
They prefer sandy or peaty soil
and do best when they are
planted on a sloping bank of fine
grasses, where the ground is damp
in spring and dry in summer,
where they will self-seed. All
are hardy/Z3–9.

Narcissus bulbocodium
Hoop-petticoat daffodil
This tiny species daffodil grows
in southern and western France,
Spain, Portugal and Northern
Africa, where it flowers in
mid-spring. It is a distinctive
daffodil, with a funnel-shaped
cup, which flares out like an
old-fashioned hoop-petticoat.
The leaves are like dark green
needles. *N. bulbocodium* var.
conspicuus has a rich golden-yellow
trumpet, 4cm (1¹/2) wide, and is
slightly larger than *N. bulbocodium*.
N. 'Golden Bells' is regarded
as an improved form of the
species, with flowers that are
almost twice the size of the
species. H 10cm (4in).

Narcissus tazetta **subsp.** *lacticolor*
(syn. *N. caniculatus*)
A pretty species daffodil,
flowering in mid-spring, this has
3 or 4 sweetly scented flowers on
each stem. The tiny yellow cup is
surrounded by reflexed white
petals. It is ideal for pots, raised
troughs and window boxes or
for a special place in the border.
H 15cm (6in).

Narcissus cyclamineus
This is a species daffodil whose
characteristic swept-back petals
give it a distinctive shape,
reminiscent of a cyclamen, hence
its name. It is native to north-
west Portugal and north-west
Spain, and it is a parent of many
dwarf hybrids. Flowering in early
spring, it will naturalize well in
damp conditions, preferring acidic

Narcissus **bulbocodium**

Narcissus 'Cassata'

Narcissus 'Quince'

soils, where it will succeed in partial shade. The cultivars thrive in most types of garden soil. H 15–20cm (6–8in).

Narcissus poeticus var. *recurvus*
Old pheasant's eye, pheasant's eye
Widely naturalized in the alpine meadows of southern Europe, this produces stunning flowers with tiny yellow, red-edged, flattened cups surrounded by glistening white recurved petals. This is an exceptionally good naturalizer and is one of the best-loved daffodils. It is also one of the last to flower in late spring. H 45cm (18in).

Split-corona Daffodils (Division 11)
The flowers are usually solitary with cups that are split for more than half their length. All are hardy/Z3–9.

Narcissus 'Cassata'
This is known as one of the butterfly daffodils with white perianth and lemon split corona. Flowers appear in mid-spring, and it is a showy plant for a prime spot in a spring border. It is not a good naturalizer in grass. It is a really choice plant for flower arrangers. H 35cm (14in).

Miscellaneous (Division 12)
These are daffodils that do not fit easily into any of the other categories. The following are hardy/Z3–9.

Narcissus 'Jumblie'
This is a memorable little golden-yellow daffodil, which is multi-headed and has little trumpets facing randomly in different directions, hence its name. It flowers in early spring. Short and sturdy, it is ideal for hanging baskets, small pots, raised troughs and window boxes or for the front of a border. H 20cm (8in).

Narcissus 'Quince'
This is a pretty little daffodil, with several flowers on each stem, each one with a deep golden-yellow trumpet surrounded by primrose-yellow petals. It flowers in mid-spring and is a good choice for small containers and borders. H 15cm (6in).

Narcissus 'Tête-à-tête'
This is an excellent multiheaded daffodil, with golden-yellow trumpet and petals. Early to flower, it is an excellent choice for the front of a border or for small containers. H 15cm (6in).

Narcissus poeticus var. recurvens

Narcissus 'Tête-à-tête'

NECTAROSCORDUM
Honey lily

This is a genus of just 3 species of bulbous, onion-scented, herbaceous perennials, similar to alliums, found in damp or shady woodlands and dry mountain slopes of southern Europe, west Asia and Iran. The flowers have large nectaries on the ovary, which gives rise to the name from the Greek word *nectar*; the Greek word *skorodon* refers to the plants' garlic scent, particularly of the leaves.
Cultivation Grow in any moderately fertile soil in full sun or partial shade. Plant bulbs 5cm (2in) deep in autumn. They may self-seed, particularly in light soils.
Propagation Sow seed in a cold frame in autumn. Remove offsets in summer.
Pests and diseases Trouble free.

Nectaroscordum siculum
(syn. *Allium siculum*)

Originally from France and Italy, this produces unusual but attractive flowerheads, which are recognizable by the loose umbels of bell-shaped flowers that appear in late spring and early summer. The flowers themselves are white or cream with a pink flush, tinted green at the bases. Although pendulous as flowers, they become erect as seedheads, which remain attractive for several weeks. The leaves die down soon after flowering. *N. siculum* subsp. *bulgaricum*, which comes from south-eastern Europe, north-eastern Turkey and Ukraine, is similar in height but has off-white flowers, flushed green and purple-red. H 1.2m (4ft) S 10cm (4in). Hardy/Z7–10.

NERINE

This is a genus of about 30 species of bulbs found on well-drained sites on cliffs, rocky ledges and mountain screes in southern Africa. Although all species in the genus are sometimes referred to as the Guernsey lily, this common name is properly applied only to *N. sarniensis* (see below). In 1659 a ship of the East India Company, bound for the Netherlands, was shipwrecked in the English Channel off the island of Guernsey. Boxes of bulbs, among them *N. sarniensis*, were washed ashore, and the islanders noted that the bulbs had taken root in the sand and began to cultivate them. Because the ship had come from the Far East, they thought the bulbs had originated from Japan. The real origin was not established for more than a hundred years, when they were recognized as those growing on Table Mountain in South Africa. All parts of the plant may cause mild stomach ache if ingested.
Cultivation Nerines require full sun and a well-drained site. Plant bulbs outdoors in early spring so that the noses are just above soil level and the shoulders well below.

Nerine bowdenii 'Blush Beauty'

Indoors bulbs should be planted in autumn or early spring in pots in soil-based compost (soil mix), again with the noses just above soil level. The flowers appear in autumn, the leaves follow in late winter, and the plant is dormant in summer, when it likes a dry, warm period. They flower best when congested. After flowering, apply a low-nitrogen liquid fertilizer.
Propagation Sow seed at 10–13°C (50–55°F) as soon as ripe. Divide clumps after flowering.
Pests and diseases Slugs.

Nerine bowdenii

Originally from Eastern Cape Province, Orange Free State and northern KwaZulu/Natal in South Africa, this nerine bears umbels of up to 7, sometimes more, funnel-shaped, slightly scented, pink flowers, each to 8cm (3in) across. The flowers, which are borne on stout stems, have wavy-edged, recurved petals. The flowers appear in autumn and are followed by the leaves in late winter. The plant goes dormant in summer, when it likes a dry, warm period. It soon forms large clumps. It must have a well-drained site and is a good choice for the foot of a sunny, south-facing wall where the pink flowers look striking. In cold areas provide a dry mulch in winter. *N. bowdenii* 'Alba' has white flowers occasionally tinged pink. H 45cm (18in) S 8cm (3in). Borderline hardy/Z8–10.

Nerine bowdenii 'Blush Beauty'

The flowers are borne on tall stems, bearing slender pale pink blooms. This is an unusual but attractive cultivar that is good for borders and for containers; pale blue glazed ones would be most attractive. For best results, allow the bulbs to become congested, then they will be more floriferous. H 1.2m (4ft) S 8cm (3in). Borderline hardy/Z8–10.

Nectaroscordum siculum

Species for autumn

Amaryllis belladonna	*Cyclamen hederifolium*
Colchicum autumnale	*Cyclamen mirabile*
Colchicum bivonae	*Nerine bowdenii*
Crocus niveus	*Nerine sarniensis*
Crocus sativus	*Sternbergia lutea*
Crocus speciosus	*Tulbaghia violacea*
Cyclamen cicilium	

Nerine bowdenii 'Pink Triumph'

Nerine bowdenii 'Mark Fenwick'

Nerine bowdenii 'Codora'

This cultivar of *N. bowdenii* flowers in early and mid-autumn. It bears vibrant red flowers on strong stems. Leave undisturbed in the container and allow it to become congested, when it will flower all the better. H 45cm (18in) S 8cm (3in). Borderline hardy/Z8–10.

Nerine bowdenii 'Mark Fenwick'

This is one of the taller cultivars of *N. bowdenii*, and it has longer, darker stems and broader pink flowers than the species. Leave undisturbed in the container and allow to become congested, when it will flower all the better. H 60cm (24in) S 8cm (3in). Borderline hardy/Z8–10.

Nerine bowdenii 'Pink Triumph'

Like other cultivars of *N. bowdenii*, this is borderline hardy, but because of its later flowering period – usually late rather than mid-autumn – it is safer to grow it in a container and enjoy it in a cool conservatory. It produces rich fuchsia-pink flowers with wavy margins, borne on strong stems. Leave undisturbed in the container and allow it to become congested, when it will flower all the better. H 45cm (18in) S 8cm (3in). Borderline hardy/Z8–10.

Nerine sarniensis
Guernsey lily

This nerine is native to South Africa's Northern Cape and Eastern Cape Province. It bears a distinctive spherical head of up to 20 deep orange-pink flowers with wavy margins to the petals. It flowers in early autumn. H 45–60cm (18–24in) S 12–15cm (4¹/₂–6in). Half-hardy/Z9–10.

Nerine 'Stephanie'

This cultivar flowers in early autumn. It produces pretty, creamy white flowers with a pale lilac-pink flush. Leave undisturbed in the container and allow it to become congested, when it will flower all the better, H 45cm (18in) S 8cm (3in). Borderline hardy/Z8–10.

Nerine undulata
(syn. *N. crispa*)

This nerine comes from low altitudes in South Africa's Eastern Cape Province and the Orange Free State. In autumn it produces umbels of 8–12 funnel-shaped, mid-pink flowers, to 5cm (2in) across, with characteristic narrow, crinkled petals. H 30–45cm (12–18in) S 10–12cm (4–4¹/₂in). Half-hardy/Z9–10.

Nerine 'Zeal Giant'

This is another of the taller cultivars of *N. bowdenii*. It has long stems and broad pink flowers. Leave undisturbed in the container. It takes a long time to form a good clump, but be patient. Allow it to become congested and eventually it will flower even better. H 60cm (24in) S 8cm (3in). Borderline hardy/Z8–10.

Nerine 'Zeal Giant'

Nerine undulata

Ornithogalum nutans

Ornithogalum dubium

ORNITHOGALUM
Star-of-Bethlehem

This genus contains 80 species of bulbs from a wide range of locations, from dry and rocky areas to meadows and woodlands in central and southern Europe, the Mediterranean, the former USSR, western and south-western Asia, tropical Africa and South Africa. Note that all parts may cause severe stomach ache if ingested and the sap may irritate the skin.

Cultivation Ornithogalums grow best in well-drained alkaline soil in full sun. In spring plant the bulbs of *O. arabicum* and *O. thyrsoides* 15cm (6in) and 10cm (4in) deep, respectively, in borders outdoors. After flowering lift them, and keep them dry and frost-free in winter. Alternatively, plant in pots in autumn in soil-based compost (soil mix). Keep in a cool, frost-free place and move outside in summer. In autumn plant the bulbs of *O. umbellatum* and *O. nutans* 8cm (3in) and 5cm (2in) deep, respectively, in borders outdoors

or in thin grassland where they should naturalize.

Propagation Sow seed in a cold frame in autumn or spring. Remove offsets during dormancy.

Pests and diseases None.

Ornithogalum arabicum

Originally from Mediterranean countries, in early summer this species has tall stems with a flattish head of usually 6–12 scented, cup-shaped, cream or white flowers, each with a distinctive black ovary. H 30–75cm (12–30in) S 8cm (3in). Half-hardy/Z7–10.

Ornithogalum dubium

The species is native to Cape Province in South Africa. It produces dense racemes packed with cup-shaped, orange, red, yellow or rarely white flowers, with yellow-green ovaries. They open in long succession from late spring or later depending on planting time. A late-spring planting will bring flowers in early autumn. H 30–45cm (12–18in) S 5cm (2in). Half-hardy/Z7–10.

Ornithogalum nutans

The species, which originated in Europe and southwestern Asia, flowers in late spring. Racemes of up to 20 semi-pendent, funnel-shaped, white flowers, with recurved tips to the petals, are produced. Each flower has a green stripe on the outside so that the whole effect is of a pretty grey-green rather than pure white. They will grow happily in borders or in grass, where they will naturalize well, but they prefer partial shade. H 20cm (8in) S 5cm (2in). Hardy/Z6–10.

Ornithogalum thyrsoides
Chincherinchee

This summer-flowering bulb, which is native to the Western Cape in South Africa, produces dense racemes packed with cup-

shaped white flowers, cream or green at the base, which open in long succession. H 30–40cm (12–16in) S 10cm (4in). Half-hardy/Z7–10.

Ornithogalum umbellatum
Star-of-Bethlehem

Native to Europe, Turkey, Syria, Lebanon, Israel and northern Africa, from mid- to late spring this bulb produces corymb-like racemes of 6–20 star-shaped white flowers on long stalks. Each flower has a green stripe down the outside. The long leaves wither as the flowers open. Although they like a sunny spot, they will tolerate partial shade, but the flowers need sunshine to open out. They will colonize well. H 15cm (6in) S 10cm (4in). Hardy/Z7–10.

Ornithogalum umbellatum 'Star-of-Bethlehem'

OXALIS

This is a large genus containing about 500 species of bulbs, tubers, rhizomes or fibrous-rooted annuals or perennials, widely distributed in woodlands or open areas from South America to southern Africa. The name *Oxalis* is derived from the Greek words *oxys* (sharp) and *als* (salt), which is a direct reference to the plants' sap, which is acidic. The plants have clover-shaped leaves, which often twist and close at night or on hot days.

Cultivation Most species like a position in sun, but some will tolerate shade. In autumn plant the fibre-covered bulbs 5cm (2in) deep in sunny borders outdoors, where they will soon form large, compact clumps. Bulbs of *O. tetraphylla* can also be planted in spring. *O. triangularis* can be grown in pots in the conservatory.

Propagation Sow seed at 13–18°C (55–64°F) in late winter or early spring. Divide in spring.

Pests and diseases Prone to rust, slugs and snails.

Oxalis adenophylla

This clump-forming perennial, which is native to the Andes, Chile and Argentina, grows from fibre-covered bulbs. The bulbs produce a plethora of heart-shaped, grey-green leaves. The foliage makes an attractive backdrop for the small, cup-shaped, purplish-pink flowers, which are distinctive for their darker veins and purple throats. They appear in spring. The colouring of *O. adenophylla* 'Silver Shamrock' is particularly pleasing. H 10cm (4in) S 15cm (6in). Hardy/Z7–10.

Oxalis tetraphylla
(syn. *O. deppei*)
Good-luck plant, lucky clover

The species comes from Mexico and in early summer produces loose, umbel-like cymes of reddish-purple flowers, 2.5cm (1in) across, which appear above the 4 deeply lobed, clover-like leaflets. These have purple bands at the bases. It needs a sheltered site. H 15cm (6in) S 10cm (4in). Borderline hardy/Z7–9.

Oxalis triangularis
Love clover

Native to Brazil and not hardy, in summer this bulb produces loose sprays of light pink flowers, 2.5cm (1in) across. They are borne above strongly contrasting triangular, rich burgundy red leaves. Plant outside in well-drained soil and use as summer groundcover, for edging rock gardens or at the base of steps, where it will naturalize quickly in a sunny spot. Alternatively, plant in spring in a small container and keep in dry, cool conditions until the leaves appear. Then increase the levels of moisture and light. It makes a good houseplant. H 15cm (6in) S 15cm (6in). Half-hardy/Z7–10.

Pelargonium 'Schottii' syn. P. x schottii

PELARGONIUM

This is a genus of about 250 species of mainly evergreen perennials (some from tuberous roots), succulents, subshrubs and shrubs, commonly but incorrectly known as geraniums. They occur in a range of habitats, from deserts to mountains, mainly in South Africa but also in Somalia, Australia and the Middle East.

Cultivation Pelargoniums require full sun and good drainage. Use a gritty compost (soil mix) and give plants a well-lit, well-ventilated position with a minimum temperature of 5°C (41°F). Water carefully, avoiding the central stem and tuberous roots, and keep nearly dry during periods of low temperatures and low light levels. Some tuberous species die back entirely while dormant; *P.* 'Schottii' does not. Gradually start watering again when growth appears more active, in early spring. These are tender plants and may be grown as houseplants or outside in the summer garden.

Propagation The species will come true from seed sown at 13–18°C (55–64°F) in late winter or early spring. Take softwood cuttings in summer.

Pests and diseases Prone to vine weevils, aphids and grey mould.

Pelargonium 'Schottii'
(syn. *P.* x *schottii*)

The species from which this form has developed originated in South Africa, and it is one of the more unusual pelargoniums to grow from a tuberous root. It produces velvety grey leaves, which are deeply incised and attractive. The flowers, which are borne on long stems, are in clusters of single, wine-coloured blooms with faint black stripes. It is a lovely plant for a container in a special place outdoors during the summer or in a conservatory. H 30cm (12in) S 30cm (12in). Tender/Z9–10.

Oxalis triangularis

Pleione formosana

Ranunculus asiaticus

PLEIONE

This genus has about 20 species of small, terrestrial, deciduous orchids from high wet forest or woodlands from northern India to southern China and Taiwan. Each pseudobulb will produce a solitary flower and one folded leaf.

Cultivation Grow indoors as a houseplant in a semi-shaded position or outdoors in a container in a sheltered, partially shaded site, only after all risk of frost has passed. In late winter or early spring plant the pseudobulbs 5cm (2in) deep so that the top one-third of the pseudobulb can still be seen. Plant singly or 5cm (2in) apart in small containers or window boxes, using a peat-based compost (soil mix). When in full growth, feed with a weak fertilizer. Flowers usually appear 4–6 weeks after planting. Deadhead after flowering and eventually bring outdoor containers inside to store in frost-free conditions until spring.

Propagation Divide annually, discarding old pseudobulbs.

Pests and diseases Aphids, red spider mites, slugs and mealybugs.

Pleione formosana

The species is native to eastern China and Taiwan. The elegant rose-lilac flowers have a central white lip, which has red or brown markings and a fringed edge. It is commonly known as the windowsill orchid and will flower in spring indoors. Plants in the *P. formosana* Alba Group have glorious white flowers with a central white lip, which has striking red or brown markings and a fringed edge. H 12cm (5in) S 30cm (12in). Half-hardy/Z10.

PUSCHKINIA

This little bulb was named after a Russian botanist, Count Apollos Mussin-Puschkin, who died in 1805. It is a genus of only one species and originates in the mountains of Turkey, Syria, Lebanon, Iraq and Iran, as well as the Caucasus. It flowers in damp meadows and scrub where the snows have just melted.

Cultivation It thrives in full sun or light shade. In autumn plant the bulbs 5cm (2in) deep at the front of a border or in a stone trough. It is dainty in growth and is good among other small plants. They form large groups in nature.

Puschkinia scilloides var. libanotica

Propagation Sow seed in containers in a cold frame in summer or autumn. Remove offsets in summer as leaves die down.

Pests and diseases Viruses can sometimes cause damage.

Puschkinia scilloides var. libanotica

This spring-flowering bulb produces compact racemes, which bear 4–10 tiny pale blue flowers, just 1cm (¹/₂in) across. Each petal has a darker blue stripe down the centre and a central white cup. *P. scilloides* var. *libanotica* has slightly smaller white flowers; it comes from Turkey and Lebanon. H 20cm (8in) S 5cm (2in). Hardy/Z3–6.

RANUNCULUS
Buttercup, crowfoot

This is a widely distributed genus of about 400 species of mainly deciduous, sometimes evergreen, tuberous, fibrous-rooted or rhizomatous perennials, annuals and biennials. The name is derived from the Latin word *rana* (frog) because many of the species grow in damp places.

Cultivation Grow in full sun or light shade. Plant the tubers in late winter indoors or in spring outdoors, placing them 5cm (2in) deep and 8cm (3in) apart (claws facing downwards) in borders or containers. They like plenty of moisture while they are in growth, although too much will cause the leaves to turn yellow. Make sure the compost (soil mix) or soil is fast draining.

Propagation Divide tuberous species in spring or autumn. Sow seed of *R. asiaticus* in autumn for flowering in late spring.

Pests and diseases Slugs, snails, aphids and mildew.

Ranunculus asiaticus
Persian buttercup

This colourful plant originated in the eastern Mediterranean, north-eastern Africa and south-western Asia. It produces single or double, peony-type flowers, 5cm (2in) across, in white and a range of colours including red, pink, orange and yellow. The flowering time varies according to cultivation. As a conservatory plant it will flower in late spring, but outside in the garden it will flower in summer. H 25cm (10in) S 20cm (8in). Half-hardy/Z8–10.

Ranunculus asiaticus 'Mount Vernon'

Schizostylis coccinea 'Jennifer'

Schizostylis coccinea 'Sunrise'

SCHIZOSTYLIS
Kaffir lily

The genus takes its name from the Greek words *schizo* (to cut, to divide) and *stilis* (style), because the style is divided into 3 distinct branches. It is a genus of only one species of virtually evergreen rhizomatous plants, which live in damp places in southern Africa. The flowers are like small gladioli, with 6–10 flowers on each stem, and 2 flowers open at a time. They make excellent cut flowers.

Cultivation They thrive in moderately fertile, moist but well-drained soil in full sun. In spring plant the rhizomes, at least 3 to a group, 8cm (3in) deep and 15–20cm (6–8in) apart, in a sunny, sheltered border where the soil will remain moist throughout the growing period. Apply a mulch in winter. The protection and warmth of a south-facing wall is ideal. Leave undisturbed. They make a lovely association with small coloured grasses, such as *Festuca glauca* (blue fescue) or *Uncinia rubra*. They can also be grown in containers.
Propagation Divide rhizomes in spring.
Pests and diseases None.

Schizostylis coccinea **'Jennifer'**
This is a robust cultivar derived from a species originally found in Lesotho and Swaziland in southern Africa where it thrives by streams and riverbanks. Spikes of beautiful cup-shaped, mid-pink flowers are borne on slender stems, like small gladioli. These are a truly welcome sight in autumn. H 60cm (24in) S 30cm (1ft). Borderline hardy/Z6–9.

Schizostylis coccinea **'Major'**
This robust cultivar produces spikes of striking, large, cup-shaped red flowers on stiff stems in autumn. H 60cm (24in) S 30cm (12in), Borderline hardy/Z6–9.

Schizostylis coccinea **'Sunrise'**
This cultivar produces spikes of cup-shaped, salmon-pink flowers, which are borne on slender stems, like small gladioli. They appear in autumn. In good, damp but well drained conditions they should clump up well to provide useful colour in the autumn border. H 60cm (24in) S 30cm (12in). Borderline hardy/Z6–9.

Schizostylis coccinea 'Major'

Bulbs with red flowers

Anemone 'The Governor'	Fritillaria imperalis 'Rubra'
Begonia 'Flamboyant'	Hedychium coccineum
Canna 'Roi Humbert'	Hippeastrum 'Red Lion'
Canna 'President'	Hyacinthus orientalis
Canna 'Rosemond Coles'	'Hollyhock'
Crocosmia 'Fire Bird'	Lilium 'Red Carpet'
Crocosmia 'Lucifer'	Lilium speciosum var. rubrum
Dahlia 'Arabian Night'	Nerine bowdenii 'Cordora'
Dahlia 'Dark Desire'	Schizostylis coccinea 'Major'
Dahlia 'Doris Day'	Tulipa 'Apeldoorn'
Dahlia 'Geerings Indian	Tulipa 'Little Princess'
Summer'	Tulipa 'Madame Lefeber'
Dahlia 'Ragged Robin'	Tulipa 'Mona Lisa'
Dahlia 'Tally Ho'	Tulipa 'Red Riding Hood'

Scilla peruviana

SCILLA
Squill

This is a genus of about 90 species of bulbs found in a variety of locations in Europe, Asia and southern Africa. It is closely related to the genera *Chionodoxa* and *Puschkinia*.

Cultivation Grow in full sun or partial shade. In early autumn plant the bulbs 8–10cm (3–4in) deep in borders or containers.
Propagation Divide clumps of established bulbs when dormant in summer.
Pests and diseases Viruses.

Scilla bifolia
This species is native to central and southern Europe and Turkey. In early spring it produces spikes of up to 10 starry, blue to purple-blue flowers. They are excellent for naturalizing and will do well under deciduous shrubs. H 15cm (6in) S 5cm (2in). Hardy/Z1–8.

Scilla bithynica
Turkish squill
The species comes from north-western Turkey and Bulgaria, where it grows in damp meadows, woods and scrub. In early to mid-spring spikes of 6–12 star-shaped, blue flowers, 2cm (¼in) across, are borne above strap-like leaves. Plant among shrubs in borders or in partially shaded grassy areas among small trees and shrubs where they will flower with *Anemone blanda* and *Crocus*. H 10–15cm (4–6in) S 8cm (3in). Hardy/Z1–8.

Scilla liliohyacinthus
Originally from south-western France and Spain, this is a small, clump-forming perennial with relatively large, lily-like bulbs, flowering in late spring with dense, conical racemes of 5–20 star-shaped, bright blue flowers. It prefers cool conditions. H 15–25cm (5–10in) S 8cm (3in). Hardy/Z3–9.

Scilla mischtschenkoana 'Tubergeniana'
This species comes from southern Russia and Iran. It flowers in late winter and early spring, producing spikes of 2–6 starry, pale blue flowers. Bulbs should be planted at the front of a sunny border or with other bulbs in containers. They also look lovely grown informally in fine grass alongside cyclamen and *Galanthus nivalis* (snowdrop). H 10–15cm (4–6in) S 5cm (2in). Hardy/Z1–8.

Scilla peruviana
This species is not native to Peru, as the specific name suggests, but from Portugal, Spain, Italy and North Africa. It is virtually evergreen, with new basal leaves developing in autumn as the old ones fade. In early summer the bloom appears, gorgeous conical heads of 50–100 star-shaped, purplish-blue flowers. It is definitely a show-stopper and worthy of being grown in a container and raised up on a sunny wall so that all can enjoy its beauty. Provide a cool winter refuge away from frost. It is only borderline hardy, so if grown in a border, choose the shelter of a south-facing wall in well-drained soil. There is a white form, *S. peruviana* f. *alba*. H 15–30cm (6–12in) S 20cm (8in). Borderline hardy/Z8–10.

Scilla siberica
Siberian squill
This species is native to southern Russia and Turkey, where it grows among rocks, scrub and woods. It produces spikes of 4–5 bell-shaped, nodding, bright blue flowers, about 1cm (½in) across. They should be planted at the front of a sunny border or with other bulbs in containers, flowering alongside *Anemone blanda* and *Crocus*. They also look charming grown informally in grass, where they establish quickly to form large clumps. Here crocus, early daffodils and anemones might also be planted. *S. siberica* 'Spring Beauty' has a darker blue flower. H 15cm (6in) S 5cm (2in). Hardy/Z1–8.

Scilla siberica

Sinningia 'Hollywood'

SINNINGIA
Gloxinia

The genus was named in honour of Wilhelm Sinning (1794–1874), who was head gardener at the University of Bonn. It embraces about 40 species of tuberous perennials and low-growing shrubs from Central and South America. The best known plant in the genus is the florists' gloxinia. It is thought that the name gloxinia was given by a Belgian nurseryman, Louis Van Houtte, who named a special new cultivar that had bright carmine, white-edged, drooping petals after his wife, Gloxinia Mina. Another theory is that it was named after Benjamin Peter Gloxin. Modern cultivars are mainly from *S. speciosa* and *S. guttata*.

Cultivation Grow in light or partial shade indoors. In spring plant the tubers on the surface of the compost (soil mix) and keep barely moist until growth is noticed. Plant one tuber in a 13cm (5in) diameter pot. Never expose the plants to direct sunlight. Apply a dilute liquid feed during the growing and flowering season. As the foliage dies down, reduce watering, and keep tubers dry in winter.

Propagation Sow seed in fine compost in late winter. Take cuttings from young shoots.

Pests and diseases Leafhoppers and western flower thrips.

Sinningia 'Etoile de Feu'
(syn. *Gloxinia* 'Etoile de Feu')
This sinningia produces wide, trumpet-shaped, carmine-pink flowers with wavy paler margins all summer long. Grow it as a houseplant. H 25cm (10in) S 45cm (18in). Tender/Z10.

Sinningia 'Hollywood'
(syn. *Gloxinia* 'Hollywood')
It produces wide, trumpet-shaped, sumptuous, violet flowers, which are sometimes edged with silver and will flower through the summer. H 25cm (10in) S 45cm (18in). Tender/Z10.

Sinningia 'Mont Blanc'
(syn. *Gloxinia* 'Mont Blanc')
The pure white, trumpet-shaped flowers appear above velvety leaves. This excellent houseplant will continue to flower through the summer. H 25cm (10in) S 45cm (18in). Tender/Z10.

STERNBERGIA
Autumn daffodil

This genus of 8 species of dwarf bulb was named after the Austrian botanist Count Kaspar von Sternberg (1761–1838). Found on stony hillsides, scrub and pine forests in southern Europe, Turkey and Central Asia, they are similar to crocuses but have 6, not 3, stamens and grow from bulbs rather than from corms. Like the crocus, some species are autumn-flowering and some flower in spring. All parts are poisonous.

Cultivation. Grow in full sun. As soon as they are available in late summer (so that they do not dry out too much) plant the bulbs 15cm (6in) deep near the front of a sunny border beneath a wall. They establish best in alkaline soils. They will increase by bulb division, but do not disturb until the clump fails to flower.

Propagation Separate offsets when dormant in late summer.

Pests and diseases Prone to narcissus viruses, narcissus bulb flies and eelworms.

Sternbergia lutea
Mount Etna lily, golden crocus
The species comes originally from among the rocks, scrub and pine woods of southern Europe, from Spain to Afghanistan. Yellow, goblet-shaped flowers, 4cm (1½in) across, appear in autumn at the same time as the dark green, strap-like leaves. H 15cm (6in) S 8cm (3in). Borderline hardy/Z6–9.

Sinningia 'Etoile de feu'

Sternbergia lutea

Tigridia pavonia

Trillium grandiflorum 'Flore Pleno'

TIGRIDIA
Tiger flower

This genus includes 23 species of bulbs from seasonally dry lands in Mexico and Guatemala. The genus is named after the Latin word *tigris* (tiger), a reference to the local jaguars with their spotted coats, like the central marking on the flowers. Its brilliant colouring and distinctive markings have made it a favourite plant for hybridizing.

Cultivation Grow in full sun. In spring plant the bulbs 10cm (4in) deep in a sunny sheltered border. They need lifting before winter frosts. Overwinter in dry sand, at a temperature of 10°C (50°F), and replant in spring. They make good outdoor container plants when planted in a soil-based compost (soil mix). They associate well with bronze-foliage plants.

Propagation Buy offsets when dormant. Sow seed at 13–16°C (55–61°F) in spring.

Pests and diseases Prone to viruses.

Tigridia pavonia
Peacock flower

Native to Mexico, this bulb produces a succession of orange, yellow, white, pink or red flowers, each 10–15cm (4–6in) across, with intricate and beautifully contrasting central markings. They flower through the summer. H 1.5m (5ft), though more often 50cm (20in) in cultivation in Europe, S 10cm (4in). Tender/Z8–10.

TRILLIUM
Trinity flower, wake robin, wood lily

This genus includes about 30 species of rhizomatous plants, mainly from higher altitude woodland in North America. They have a distinctive whorl of 3 broad leaves, out of which grows a flower consisting of 3 green sepals and 3 beautiful petals, hence the genus name, which is based on the Latin *tri*- (three).

Cultivation Trilliums require deep or partial shade and deep moist soil, preferably neutral to acid. In autumn or early spring plant the rhizomes 10cm (4in) deep. They spoil if they are allowed to dry out before planting, so obtain stock that has been transported in moist peat. They will take a while to recover in their new conditions, but once established they should be left undisturbed to create a bold group.

Propagation Can be grown from seed but plants take 7 years to reach flowering size. Divide rhizomes in autumn or early spring, making sure that each new section has at least one growing point.

Pests and diseases Slugs and snails may damage the leaves.

Trillium grandiflorum f. roseum

This comes from woods beside streams in eastern North America. In late spring and early summer this cultivar bears pale pink, cup-shaped flowers on top of the dark green leaves. The flowers open wide and have large, slightly wavy petals, 8cm (3in) wide, which grow darker as they age. It looks lovely beside the unfurling fronds of young ferns. *T. grandiflorum* 'Flore Pleno' AGM is a double white form. H 40cm (16in) S 30–40cm (12–16in). Hardy/Z5–9.

Trillium luteum
Yellow wake robin

The species grows in rich woodland areas of south-eastern North America where in spring sweetly fragrant, golden-yellow or bronze-green flowers are borne erect on top of mid-green leaves, heavily marked with paler green. The narrow flower petals are about 9cm (3¹/₂in) long.

Bluebells and lily-of-the-valley make perfect planting partners. H 40cm (16in) S 30–40cm (12–16in). Hardy/Z5–9.

Trillium undulatum
Painted trillium, painted wood lily

This rhizomatous perennial, from hemlock and spruce forests of eastern North America, has funnel-shaped flowers composed of 3 wavy, white or pink petals with a frill of red-edged, green sepals. The petals have a red stripe at the base. The single flowers appear from mid- to late spring and are carried above oval, blue-green leaves. It thrives in moist, acid soil. H 10–20cm (4–8in) S 30cm (12in). Hardy/Z5–9.

Trillium grandiflorum f. roseum

Triteleia ixioides

TRITELEIA
Californian hyacinth

This genus is composed of about 15 species of corms. Closely related to *Brodiaea*, it is mainly found in grass and woodland in the west of the United States. Its name is derived from the Greek *tri* (three) and *telos* (end), a reference to the stigma being three-lobed. It makes a good cut flower and can be dried.

Cultivation In autumn plant the corms 8cm (3in) deep in a sunny herbaceous border where they would enjoy the same conditions as autumn-flowering nerines. Alternatively, plant them in containers in a soil-based compost (soil mix) and stand them on a sunny sheltered patio, mixing them with later flowering lilies in a large container. Keep dry and sheltered in winter.

Propagation Sow seed at 13–16°C (55–61°F) as soon as ripe or in early spring. Separate corms when dormant.

Pests and diseases None.

Triteleia ixioides 'Starlight'

T. ixioides (syn. *Brodiaea ixioides, B. lutea*) from which this cultivar was developed is native to western North America, in California and southern Oregon. In early and midsummer its strong stems bear loose heads, 12cm (4¹/₂in) across, of up to 25 starry yellow flowers. It is pretty in a sunny border or raised up in a container where the blooms can be enjoyed for up to 6 weeks. H 25cm (10in) S 10cm (4in). Borderline hardy/Z7–10.

Triteleia laxa 'Koningin Fabiola'

The cultivar is derived from the species *T. laxa* (syn. *Brodiaea laxa*), which originates in western North America, in California and southern Oregon. In early summer its stems bear loose umbels, 15cm (6in) across, of up to 25 purple-blue flowers, each 5cm (2in) long. It is an attractive plant to mass in a border or in a large container. It is also good as a cut flower. H 25cm (10in) S 10cm (4in). Borderline hardy/Z7–10.

TRITONIA

The name derives from the Greek word *triton* (weathercock), a clue to the strange habit of the stamens in some of the species, which change directions. It is a genus of 28 species of corms, closely related to *Crocosmia* and mainly found on grassy or stony hillsides of South Africa and Swaziland.

Cultivation They like light, sandy soil and a sheltered position in full sun. In autumn plant the corms 8cm (3in) deep in a sunny, well-drained border. Provide a winter mulch. Alternatively, plant them in containers in a soil-based compost (soil mix) and stand on a sunny sheltered patio. Keep dry and frost-free in winter.

Propagation Sow seed at 13–16°C (55–61°F) as soon as ripe. Separate corms when dormant.

Pests and diseases None.

Tritonia crocata

This species is native to Western Cape and Eastern Cape, South Africa. In summer it produces spikes of up to 10 cup-shaped, orange or pink flowers, with transparent margins. There are several interesting cultivars, including *T. crocata* 'Princess Beatrix', which has brilliant orange-red flowers. H 15–35cm (6–14in) S 20cm (8in). Half-hardy/Z7–10.

Tritonia laxifolia

This is a smaller species of the plant found in Eastern Cape, South Africa, as well as in Tanzania, Malawi and Zambia. It produces colourful spikes of 10–12 cup-shaped, salmon-pink, orange to brick-red flowers in late summer to early autumn. H 20cm (8in) S 20cm (8in). Half-hardy/Z7–10.

Tritonia crocata

Bulbs with blue flowers

Agapanthus 'Ben Hope'	*Crocus* 'Blue Pearl'
Agapanthus 'Blue Giant'	*Hyacinthoides non-scripta*
Agapanthus 'Blue Moon'	*Hyacinthus orientalis* 'Blue
Allium caeruleum	Delft'
Anemone blanda	*Iris* 'Sapphire Beauty'
Anemone 'Lord Lieutenant'	*Scilla peruviana*
Camassia quamash	*Scilla siberica*
Chionodoxa sardensis	*Triteleia laxa* 'Koningin Fabiola'

Tulbaghia violacea var. robustior

Tulbaghia sinnleri syn. T. fragrans

TULBAGHIA
Society garlic

This genus was named after Ryk Tulbagh (d.1771), who was governor of the Cape of Good Hope. It contains about 26 species of deciduous or semi-evergreen, clump-forming perennials, growing from bulbs or fleshy rhizomes, all native to South Africa.

Cultivation They like well-drained soil and a sheltered position in full sun. In areas that are not frost-free, tulbaghias are best planted in a container in soil-based potting compost (soil mix) so that they can be moved out to a sunny position once all risk of frost has passed in the late spring. Keep almost dry and frost free in winter.

Propagation Sow seed in a cold frame as soon as it is ripe, or in spring. It germinates easily and the seedlings soon reach flowering size. Alternatively, divide in spring.
Pests and diseases Outdoors none, although aphids may be a problem under glass.

Tulbaghia acutiloba
This species grows from a bulb that is native to the Eastern Cape and Transvaal in South Africa. The leaves are grey-green, erect and narrow. The scented white flowers are borne continually on small stems throughout the summer. They appear like miniature daffodils with tiny orange trumpets. H 12cm (5in) S 8cm (3in). Borderline hardy/Z7–10.

Tulbaghia 'Fairy Star'
This is an interspecific cross between *T. violacea* and *T. cominsii*, which has resulted in a slightly less robust plant but with a very pretty pale lilac-pink, open flowerhead. The leaves are grey-green, erect and narrow. The flowers are borne from midsummer until early autumn. H 30cm (12in) S 30cm (12in). Borderline hardy/Z7–10.

Tulbaghia leucantha
This small but unusual and rather variable species is native to South Africa. It produces dainty flowers, which appear like miniature daffodils with tiny, rusty orange trumpets and pale lilac petals on small stems throughout the summer. H 20cm (8in) S 8cm (3in). Half-hardy/Z8–10.

Tulbaghia natalensis
This species grows from a bulb that is native to north-east Transvaal and KwaZulu/Natal in

South Africa. The leaves are grey-green, erect and narrow. The pale lilac flowers are borne on small stems throughout the summer. H 20cm (8in) S 8cm (3in). Borderline hardy/Z7–10.

Tulbaghia simmleri
syn. *T. fragrans*
From early to midsummer delicate umbels of light to deep purple flowers appear on tall slender stems. They are commonly known as sweet garlic or pink agapanthus. H 60cm (24in) S 25cm (10in). Borderline hardy/Z7–10.

Tulbaghia violacea
This species grows from a bulb-like rhizome found in the Eastern Cape and Transvaal. The leaves are grey-green, erect and narrow. The flowers are borne on tall stems from midsummer until early autumn. They appear as delicate umbels of lilac flowers smelling of garlic. H 45–60cm (18–24in) S 25cm (10in). Borderline hardy/Z7–10.

Tulbaghia violacea var. robustior
From midsummer to early autumn the delicate lilac-purple flowers of this species appear on the tall slender stems. They have the common characteristic of smelling of garlic. H 45–60cm (18–24in) S 25cm (10in). Borderline hardy/Z7–10.

Tulbaghia violacea 'Silver Lace'
This is similar to the species but has slightly larger flowers and an attractive cream stripe in the leaves. It is also slightly more tender. H 35 (14in) S 25cm (10in). Borderline hardy/Z7–10.

Tulbaghia violacea

Bulbs with lilac or purple flowers

Allium cristophii	*Hyacinthus orientalis*
Allium 'Globemaster'	'Amethyst'
Allium 'Purple Sensation'	*Iris* 'George'
Allium schubertii	*Iris* 'Pauline'
Crocus 'Pickwick'	*Sinningia* 'Hollywood'
Crocus tommasinianus	*Tulbaghia simmleri*
'Whitewell Purple'	*Tulbaghia violacea*
Dahlia 'Belle of the Ball'	*Tulipa* 'Blue Heron'
Dahlia 'Purple Gem'	*Tulipa* 'Blue Parrot'

TULIPA
Tulip

This is one of the best known of all bulb groups, loved for its range of flamboyant colours, including red, orange, yellow, pink, mauve, purple and near-black, as well as white. True blue is the one colour that is missing. The genus is made up of about 100 species, which are found on hot, dry hillsides of temperate Europe, the Middle East and, particularly Central Asia, often growing on alkaline soils.

Over the last 400 years thousands of cultivars have been raised. The name comes from the Turkish word *tulbend* (turban), perhaps reflecting the shape and colour range of the flowers. In 1554 Ghislain de Busbecq (1522–91), then ambassador of the Holy Roman Empire to Süleyman the Magnificent, confused the name with the word *tulipam*, hence the name of the *Tulipa* genus today.

Usually the flowers are held singly, but some plants are multiheaded, as is the case with the species *T. tarda*, which may have 2 to 3 flowers. Occasionally the flowers are double, like those of the cultivars 'Peach Blossom' and 'Angélique'. Sometimes the petals are fringed, for example in 'Blue Heron', and sometimes they are quite crinkled, as in the Parrot tulips.

Most cultivars reach 40cm (16in) or more when in flower, but there are many dwarf cultivars and smaller species, which are ideal for the front of the border. All tulips are excellent for pots and window boxes, and the bulbs are quite small so they do not take up too much planting space. Tulips make extremely good cut flowers. Note that all parts may cause mild stomach ache if ingested, and contact with any part may aggravate skin allergies in some people.

Cultivation Tulips like a site in full sun. They should be planted to a depth of twice the height of the bulb, which usually means around 10cm (4in) deep for the dwarfer forms and 15cm (6in) or more for the taller cultivars, which will have larger bulbs. On lighter soils these depths can be increased. Deadhead after flowering. Remove the old stems and leaves once they have withered.

The bulbs can be lifted for the summer dormancy period or left in the ground where the Darwin, Kaufmanniana, Greigii and Triumph hybrids in particular will form good clumps if they are left alone. Lift if required and ripen in a greenhouse. Store in a dry place out of direct sunlight for planting again in autumn. Choose only the biggest bulbs to replant in the borders. The smaller ones can be grown on in a nursery bed. An annual potash-rich fertilizer or sulphate of potash is beneficial and should be applied in late winter before the first shoots appear. Tulips are good container plants in a soil-based compost (soil mix); however, they may not flower as well after the first year, so remove and replant.

Propagation Separate offsets of species and cultivars after lifting in summer and grow on. Seed sown from the species takes 4–7 years to produce flowers. Sow seed in autumn in containers in a cold frame or cold greenhouse.

Pests and diseases Slugs, stem and bulb eelworms, tulip fire, bulb rots and viruses.

Single Early Group (Division 1)

These have single, cup-shaped flowers in early to mid-spring. They are suitable for borders and containers. All are hardy/Z3–8.

Tulipa 'Apricot Beauty'

Tulipa 'Oranje Nassau'

Tulipa 'Apricot Beauty'

This Single Early is one of the best of all tulips for its soft apricot, tangerine-flushed colouring. Flowering in mid-spring, it looks excellent planted with pink-cupped daffodils, such as *Narcissus* 'Rainbow' or 'Salome', carpeted with *Tanacetum parthenium* 'Aureum' (golden feverfew) and backed by the vivid light green colouring of *Philadelphus coronarius* 'Aureus'. It is also stunning in a container with simple white pansies. H 45cm (18in). Hardy/Z3–8.

Tulipa 'Yokohama'

Bred in 1961, this has stood the test of time and proved to be a very good tulip with its cheerful bright yellow colouring. It resists all kinds of bad weather and lasts for a long time. It is an unusual Single Early tulip in that it has tapered flowers. H 30cm (12in). Hardy/Z3–8.

Double Early Group (Division 2)

These tulips have double, bowl-shaped flowers in mid-spring, often margined or flecked with an additional colour. They are suitable for borders and containers. All are hardy/Z3–8.

Tulipa 'Abba'

This short, sturdy tulip bears large red flowers with a deep scarlet flame. It flowers in mid-spring. Plant in a border with violas and *Bellis* (daisy). It is striking when planted in a container with *Muscari* (grape hyacinth). H 25cm (10in). Hardy/Z3–8.

Tulipa 'Kareol'

This short, sturdy tulip bears large yellow flowers. It blooms from early to mid-spring. Plant in a border with blue violas and red or white *Bellis* (daisy). It is also lovely planted with *Muscari* (grape hyacinth). H 25cm (10in). Hardy/Z3–8.

Tulipa 'Monte Carlo'

This short, sturdy tulip bears wonderful yellow flowers from early to mid-spring. Plant in a border with violas and *Bellis* (daisy). It associates beautifully with *Muscari* (grape hyacinth). H 30cm (12in). Hardy/Z3–8.

Tulipa 'Oranje Nassau'

This short, sturdy tulip bears large orange flowers from early to mid-spring. Plant in a border with violas, hyacinths and blue *Muscari* (grape hyacinth). It is excellent in containers. H 25cm (10in). Hardy/Z3–8.

Tulipa 'Peach Blossom'

This short, sturdy tulip bears large rose-pink flowers from early to mid-spring. Plant in a border with blue violas, pink *Bellis* (daisy) and blue *Muscari* (grape hyacinth). Excellent for containers and baskets. H 25cm (10in). Hardy/Z3–8.

Tulipa 'Peach Blossom'

Tulipa 'Attila'

Tulipa 'Negrita'

Triumph Group (Division 3)

The single cup-shaped flowers are produced from mid- to late spring. They are suitable for borders and containers. All are hardy/Z3–8.

Tulipa 'Attila'

This Triumph tulip bears light purple flowers. Flowering in mid-spring, it looks good among pale dwarf wallflowers in a border or in a large container. H 50cm (20in). Hardy/Z3–8.

Tulipa 'Golden Melody'

One of the Triumph hybrids, this has large golden-yellow flowers, which hold their petals for a long time. In borders they might be planted beside grey-leaved plants such as *Senecio cineraria*. It flowers in mid-spring and will survive well if left in the soil all year round. H 55cm (22in). Hardy/Z3–8.

Tulipa 'Lustige Witwe' (syn. *T.* 'Merry Widow')

This Triumph hybrid bears large, single, cherry-pink flowers, edged in white. It is a late-spring-flowering tulip, which lasts a long time in flower. It can be planted to good effect with *Lunaria annua* (honesty), a flowering rosemary bush or other grey-leaved plants. H 35cm (14in). Hardy/Z3–8.

Tulipa 'Negrita'

This Triumph hybrid flowers from mid- to late spring. The large beetroot purple flowers retain their poise for two weeks or more. It mixes well with the red or yellow Apeldoorn tulips or with purple-leaved *Heuchera*. It will survive well left in border soil and multiply to form good clumps. Alternatively, plant in containers with pale blue pansies. H 55cm (22in). Hardy/Z3–8.

Tulipa 'New Design'

The variegated-leaved hybrid, which has a white edge to the leaves, looks stylish. The light pink petals deepen to a rosy pink around the edge. Plant in a group where you can enjoy them with the sun behind them: they look glorious backlit. They flower in mid-spring and are good partners for other silver-leaved foliage plants, while a carpet of snow white *Bellis* (daisy) would be the perfect accompaniment in a container. H 30cm (12in). Hardy/Z3–8.

Tulipa 'Prinses Irene'

This Triumph hybrid has unusual orange flowers that are streaked with purple. It flowers in mid-spring and looks especially effective planted among dwarf, orange wallflowers in beds and borders. It also associates well with black violas or pansies. H 35cm (14in). Hardy/Z3–8.

Tulipa 'Shirley'

The flowers of this Triumph hybrid are a combination of white with a mauve-purple edge, which becomes more defined with age. It flowers from mid- to late spring and is excellent planted with tall *Fritillaria persica* or *T.* 'Queen of Night', with which it shares a similar colouring on the edges of the petals. H 50cm (20in). Hardy/Z3–8.

Tulipa 'Striped Bellona'

This Triumph hybrid, which flowers in mid-spring, has utterly stunning striped red and yellow flowers. It looks showy in the border and is just as good in a medium or large container. H 50cm (20in). Hardy/Z3–8.

Darwin Hybrid Group (Division 4)

The large, single, oval flowers are carried at the top of tall, sturdy, erect stems, making them excellent for cutting. Among this group are some of the very best and most reliable of all border tulips. All are hardy/Z3–8.

Tulipa 'Apeldoorn'

This Darwin hybrid flowers from mid- to late spring, and the large scarlet flowers retain their petals for a long period. This tulip looks beautiful with lime-green foliage. It will survive well left in border soil and multiply to form good clumps. Alternatively, plant in large containers. H 55cm (22in). Hardy/Z3–8.

Tulipa 'Apeldoorn's Elite'

A Darwin hybrid, this flowers from mid- to late spring. The large scarlet flowers are edged with yellow. It will survive well left in border soil and multiply to form good clumps. It is also suitable for large containers. H 55cm (22in). Hardy/Z3–8.

Tulipa 'Golden Melody'

Tulipa 'Prinses Irene'

Tulipa 'Apeldoorn'

Tulipa '**Beauty of Apeldoorn**'
This Darwin hybrid flowers from mid- to late spring. The large yellow flowers are flushed with orange, and this tulip looks beautiful associated with yellows, lime-green and blues. It will survive well left in border soil and multiply to form good clumps. It is also suitable for containers. H 55cm (22in). Hardy/Z3–8.

Tulipa '**Gordon Cooper**'
This Darwin hybrid is strong growing and bears pink flowers. It associates well with rose-coloured wallflowers and blue polyanthus. It flowers in mid-spring and will survive well if left in the soil all year round. H 60cm (24in). Hardy/Z3–8.

Tulipa '**Yellow Apeldoorn**'
This Darwin hybrid flowers from mid- to late spring. The large golden-yellow flowers make an excellent show and are reliable, like other 'Apeldoorn' relations. This tulip looks beautiful with purple-leaved *Heuchera*. It will survive well left in border soil and multiply to form good clumps. Alternatively, plant in large containers. H 55cm (22in). Hardy/Z3–8.

Single Late Group (Division 5)
The flowers, which are cupped or goblet-shaped, are borne in late spring. Sometimes several to the stem, the flowers may be white to yellow, pink, red or almost black. Darwin and Cottage tulips belong in this group. All are hardy/Z3–8.

Tulipa 'Beauty of Apeldoorn'

Tulipa '**Esther**'
This is one of the prettiest of the all-pink Single Late tulips. It flowers in late spring and is excellent planted with blue forget-me-nots or blue pansies; alternatively, plant it with the slightly later flowering *T.* 'Queen of Night'. H 50cm (20in). Hardy/Z3–8.

Tulipa '**Ile de France**'
This is an impressive rich cardinal red tulip, which was introduced in 1968. It is very robust by nature and stands up well to windy and inclement weather. It looks equally good planted in containers, borders and beds. H 50cm (20in). Hardy/Z3–8.

Tulipa '**Paul Scherer**'
This is a luscious, almost black tulip with a velvety maroon-black colouring just like blackberries. It is a good choice for borders, where it is especially impressive as it catches the sun, as well as for containers. Plant close to dark blue or black bicolour pansies. H 50cm (20in). Hardy/Z3–8.

Tulipa 'Yellow Apeldoorn'

Tulipa 'Esther'

Tulipa 'Paul Scherer'

Tulipa 'Queen of Night'

Tulipa 'Mona Lisa'

Tulipa 'West Point'

Tulipa 'Queen of Night'

This is a stunning dark purple tulip that flowers in late spring and looks beautiful beneath an arch of yellow laburnum flowers or against a backdrop of pale blue wisteria. Blue, pink or white forget-me-nots make an ideal partner in a border display or in a container. H 60cm (24in). Hardy/Z3–8.

Tulipa 'Swan Wings'

This is a tall tulip with elegant white flowers. The petals are delicately fringed. It flowers from mid- to late spring and is ideal for a border display or in a large container. Plant with black pansies or *Tanacetum parthenium* 'Aureum' (golden feverfew). H 55cm (22in). Hardy/Z3–8.

Lily-flowered Group (Division 6)

The petals of the slender flowers are often pointed and curve backwards. These tulips are late flowering and can be susceptible to wind damage. All are hardy/Z3–8.

Tulipa 'Ballerina'

A Lily-flowered hybrid, this is one of the most arresting of all tulips, with its scented, vibrant orange flowers. Flowering in mid-spring, it is excellent planted with other orange flowers or plants with bronze foliage. In containers combine it with deep blue pansies. H 55cm (22in). Hardy/Z3–8.

Tulipa 'Mona Lisa'

In mid- to late spring this large Lily-flowered hybrid bears yellow flowers that are streaked with a reddish raspberry-pink. This is a dramatic tulip for a sheltered spot. It is perfect beside bronze-coloured foliage or underplanted with yellow wallflowers or pansies. H 55cm (22in). Hardy/Z3–8.

Tulipa 'Pieter de Leur'

This is a cardinal-red tulip with blood-red shading at the tips and an ivory white base. It is a striking choice for containers, borders and beds, where it associates well with lime-green foliage or yellow bedding plants. H 25cm (10in). Hardy/Z3–8.

Tulipa 'West Point'

This late-spring-flowering Lily-flowered hybrid has distinctive primrose-yellow flowers, which look especially charming near blue forget-me-nots or purple wallflowers. H 50cm (20in). Hardy/Z3–8.

Tulipa 'White Triumphator'

This elegant late-spring-flowering Lily-flowered hybrid has distinctive pure white flowers, which look especially charming in borders underplanted with blue or white forget-me-nots or in association with white *Syringa* (lilac). H 60cm (24in). Hardy/Z3–8.

Fringed Group (Division 7)

The petals of the cup-shaped flowers are fringed at the edges, and sometimes a different colour may appear. The flowers are borne in late spring. All are hardy/Z3–8.

Tulipa 'Blue Heron'

This Fringed tulip bears large, violet-purple flowers with lilac-fringed petals. It is a strong-growing tulip, flowering in late spring. In borders it can be underplanted with grey-leaved plants or, for a more exciting combination, place it close to *Tanacetum parthenium* 'Aureum' (golden feverfew), which will really make it come alive. It is also an excellent bulb for planting in containers. H 60cm (24in). Hardy/Z3–8.

Tulipa 'Hamilton'

This tulip bears large yellow flowers, which are dramatically fringed. It is a strong-growing tulip that flowers in late spring. Grow it in a border or in a container and enjoy a great show of colour at the end of the tulip season. H 60cm (24in). Hardy/Z3–8.

Tulipa 'Pieter de Leur'

Tulipa 'Hamilton'

Viridiflora Group (Division 8)

The flowers are touched with various amounts of green, a feature that makes these tulips highly desirable. The flowers appear in late spring. All are hardy/Z3–8.

Tulipa 'Spring Green'

The flowers of this Viridiflora hybrid are an unusual creamy white with broad green stripes on the petals. Flowering in late spring, it looks delightful against bright green or green-grey foliage in the border or in a container with pansies. H 40cm (16in). Hardy/Z3–8.

Rembrandt Group (Division 9)

The cup-shaped flowers, which appear in late spring, are white, yellow or red with black, brown, bronze, purple, red or pink stripes or feathers. These tulips are good cut flowers. This type of tulip is depicted in paintings by Dutch Old Masters. Because the markings are actually caused by a virus, few are produced commercially nowadays. All are hardy/Z3–8.

Parrot Group (Division 10)

The cup-shaped flowers have twisted petals that are irregularly cut and banded with colours. Even in tight bud these tulips look amazing, then, as the petals unfurl, the full glorious shape and colours are revealed. As a result they are extremely flamboyant and a good choice if you want drama in your garden. The flowers appear in late spring. All are hardy/Z3–8.

Tulipa 'Spring Green'

Tulipa 'Apricot Parrot'

This is one of the most beautiful tulips, with its large pale apricot flowers feathered with tangerine and orange. Flowering in late spring, they are suitable planting partners for *Tanacetum parthenium* 'Aureum' (golden feverfew) or purple *Heuchera*. It also makes a great container plant grown with orange or purple wallflowers. H 45cm (18in). Hardy/Z3–8.

Tulipa 'Black Parrot'

Flowering in late spring, this handsome tulip is typical of the Parrot group. It has large black flowers, which open wide, but it is stunning even in bud, when the crinkled edges of the petals make fascinating patterns. Suitable partners include *Tanacetum parthenium* 'Aureum' (golden feverfew) and purple *Heuchera*. It also makes a great container planting combined with white and black pansies. H 45cm (18in). Hardy/Z3–8.

Tulipa 'Blue Parrot'

Tulipa 'Blue Parrot'

This tulip has single, large lilac-blue flowers, and irregular crimping along the edge of the petals. It flowers in late spring. In borders it can be planted with pink or blue forget-me-nots, and in containers pink, lavender or violet-blue pansies are perfect companions. H 60cm (24in). Hardy/Z3–8.

Tulipa 'Fantasy'

A Parrot group hybrid, flowering in late spring, this tulip has large pink flowers, crested with green, with irregular crimping along the edges of the petals. It is sensuous in bud, especially when the petals start to unfurl. Plant behind dark-leaved *Heuchera*. H 55cm (22in). Hardy/Z3–8.

Double Late Group (Division 11)

These tulips bear fully double, bowl-shaped flowers in late spring. The petals are often margined or flamed with an additional colour. They are suitable for borders and containers. All are hardy/Z3–8.

Tulipa 'Angélique'

This Double Late tulip, which flowers from mid- to late spring, bears large rose-pink flowers. It is a star performer and one of the most popular of all tulips. It looks beautiful planted in borders with pansies, pink forget-me-nots, arabis or aubrieta. In a container it is a good companion for lavender-blue pansies. H 45cm (18in). Hardy/Z3–8.

Tulipa 'Apricot Parrot'

Tulipa 'Fantasy'

Tulipa 'Angélique'

Tulipa 'Montreux'

Tulipa 'Chopin'

Tulipa 'Montreux'

This is a Double Late tulip, flowering from mid- to late spring, that bears fragrant, primrose-yellow flowers. It looks striking planted in borders with blue or white forget-me-nots, arabis or aubrieta. In a container it is a good companion for lavender-blue pansies. H 45cm (18in). Hardy/Z3–8.

Tulipa 'Peaches and Cream'

This Double Late tulip bears fragrant, creamy white flowers with a pink flush from mid- to late spring. It looks striking planted in borders with forget-me-nots, arabis or aubrieta, and in a container underplanted with pastel-coloured pansies. H 45cm (18in). Hardy/Z3–8.

Tulipa 'Tacoma'

This Double Late tulip bears large, fragrant, white flowers from mid- to late spring. It looks striking planted in borders with forget-me-nots, arabis or aubrieta, and in a container it would look stylish underplanted with black and white pansies. H 45cm (18in). Hardy/Z3–8.

Tulipa 'Wirosa'

This Double Late tulip bears large, fragrant, red and white flowers from mid- to late spring. It looks striking planted in borders with white or blue forget-me-nots, and in a container it would make an eye-catching partnership with black or white pansies. H 35cm (14in). Hardy/Z3–8.

Kaufmanniana Group (Division 12)

The group includes the species *T. kaufmanniana*, which is native to Central Asia, and its hybrids. These are small, sturdy tulips, which usually flower early in spring or in mid-spring. They often have bicoloured flowers, which open flat in sunshine, and are sometimes spotted bronze, red or purple on the foliage. They are suitable for borders and containers. All are hardy/Z3–8.

Tulipa 'Chopin'

In early spring the large, single, yellow flowers are streaked with red, while the leaves have attractive mottled markings. This tulip looks beautiful associated with primroses and dwarf daffodils. The bulbs will continue to flower well in future seasons. They are also perfect for containers, underplanted with rich blue violas. H 25cm (10in). Hardy/Z3–8.

Tulipa 'Heart's Delight'

Like many of the Kaufmanniana hybrids, this has irregularly striped leaves. It is a small tulip, and the white edges of the dark pink petals create a pretty feathering effect. It is excellent planted beside blue primulas, violas or dwarf daffodils, or plant it near the deep wine-red foliage of *Ajuga reptans* 'Burgundy Glow'. It flowers in early spring and will survive well if left in the ground all year round. H 25cm (10in). Hardy/Z3–8.

Tulipa 'Tacoma'

Tulipa 'Heart's Delight'

Tulipa 'Shakespeare'

Tulipa 'Shakespeare'

This small, elegant and early-flowering tulip has comparatively long flowers, which are salmon-pink, flushed with orange and yellow. In a border they can be planted beside primroses and dwarf daffodils; in a container *Muscari* (grape hyacinths) or *Anemone blanda* would be perfect partners. H 25cm (10in). Hardy/Z3–8.

Tulipa 'Stresa'

This small but showy early-spring-flowering tulip has red flowers with broad yellow edges to the petals. It creates a stunning display in borders, where it associates well with primroses and dwarf daffodils. The bulbs can be left in the ground all year and will

continue to flower well in future seasons. H 25cm (10in). Hardy/Z3–8.

Fosteriana Group (Division 13)

This group includes the species *T. fosteriana* and its hybrids, which include crosses with those of this species and *T. kaufmanniana* and *T. greigii*. They have many similarities to Kaufmanniana and Greigii tulips, but the flowers of Fosteriana tulips are taller and larger. The leaves are sometimes marked with red or purple. They are suitable for borders and containers. All are hardy/Z3–8.

Tulipa 'Concerto'

The white flowers open in mid-spring and as a small group make an attractive and refreshing display alongside other whites, creams or soft yellows. H 20cm (8in). Hardy/Z3–8.

Tulipa 'Madame Lefeber' (syn. *T.* 'Red Emperor')

This is a popular cultivar with showy red flowers, which open in the sun to reveal a yellow base. The flowers are borne in mid-spring and are perfect beside black, blue or yellow pansies or violas. Left in the border it will naturalize well. H 40cm (16in). Hardy/Z3–8.

Tulipa 'Orange Emperor'

This is a popular cultivar of *T. fosteriana*, a species that is native to Central Asia. The orange

Tulipa 'Concerto'

flowers are showy, opening in the sun to reveal a yellow base. The flowers appear in mid-spring and are perfect beside bronze-coloured foliage or yellow wallflowers or pansies. Left in the border it will naturalize well. H 40cm (16in). Hardy/Z3–8.

Greigii Group (Division 14)

This group includes the species *T. greigii* and its hybrids, which include crosses with those of this species and *T. kaufmanniana*. They have single, bowl-shaped flowers in early to mid-spring. They are usually yellow to red, sometimes flamed. The blue-grey leaves have wavy margins and are sometimes marked with maroon. They are suitable for borders and containers. All are hardy/Z3–8.

Tulipa 'Cape Cod'

This is a sturdy tulip with large, orange-edged, yellow flowers and interesting purple-striped foliage. The flowers appear in mid-spring. H 30cm (12in). Hardy/Z3–8.

Tulipa 'Pinocchio'

This cultivar has leaves with purple markings. It flowers in mid-spring, having red flowers edged with white. It is good for naturalizing in borders. H 25cm (10in). Hardy/Z3–8.

Tulipa 'Plaisir'

This is a carmine-red tulip with lemon-yellow feathering at the edge of the petals. The leaves are heavily mottled. It is a good choice for containers and borders. H 25cm (10in). Hardy/Z3–8.

Tulipa 'Madame Lefeber'

Tulipa 'Plaisir'

Tulipa 'Quebec'

This tulip provides an outstanding show in mid-spring, when its multiflowering heads sometimes carry 3–5 blooms on each stem. The scarlet-edged flowers are pale chartreuse. The leaves are less obviously striped than those of other tulips in this group. Plant alongside polyanthus or violas. It is excellent for a tub or patio planter. H 35cm (14in). Hardy/Z3–8.

Tulipa 'Red Riding Hood'

This Greigii hybrid is one of the best-known tulips, with large scarlet flowers and outstanding purple-striped foliage. Flowering in mid-spring, it is a good partner for violas and dwarf daffodils. It is also excellent for a medium container. H 30cm (12in). Hardy/Z3–8.

Tulipa 'Toronto'

This popular Greigii hybrid produces several pretty pink flowers on each stem and characteristic purple-striped foliage. Flowering in mid-spring, it is a good partner for primroses and dwarf daffodils, and a carpet of black violas would provide the perfect contrast in a container. H 35cm (14in). Hardy/Z3–8.

Miscellaneous Group (Division 15)

The group includes species tulips and selected forms and hybrids that are not in the other divisions. All are hardy/Z3–8.

Tulipa clusiana

This species tulip originates in an area extending from Iran to the western Himalayas. It flowers from early to mid-spring. The slim, white flowers have a distinctive dark pink stripe on the outside, with purple markings inside and purple stamens. Plant near the front of a border with aubrieta or arabis for partners where the bulbs will flower happily for years if left undisturbed. H 30cm (12in). Hardy/Z3–8.

Tulipa clusiana 'Lady Jane'

This is a delightful dwarf cultivar. The outer petals are a combination of rose-pink and white, and the inner ones are purely white. It flowers in mid-spring and is the perfect companion for pink or white *Bellis* (daisy). It is also ideal for hanging baskets and other small to medium containers. H 15cm (6in). Hardy/Z3–8.

Tulipa 'Honky Tonk'

This is a little jewel, with soft yellow flowers delicately flushed with pink. It flowers from mid- to late spring and is excellent planted with little violas in a rock garden or in a small container. H 15cm (6in). Hardy/Z3–8.

Tulipa humilis Violacea Group

The species from which the cultivars developed is native to Turkey and Iran. Although it is one of the shortest tulips, the

Tulipa kolpakowskiana

violet-pink flowers, with blue-black basal markings, make a strong statement, particularly near the front of a border with aubrieta or violas. The flowers appear in early spring, and plants will survive well if left in the soil all year round. H 8cm (3in). Hardy/Z3–8.

Tulipa kolpakowskiana

This species, which originates in Central Asia, has small, elegant yellow flowers, which fade to pale orange, flushed violet-grey on the outside. The flowers, which appear in late spring, are held on curved stems. This is an easy tulip to grow at the front of a border or in a small container. Creamy little violas would make suitable planting partners. H 20cm (8in). Hardy/Z3–8.

Tulipa linifolia

This is a popular species, which is native to Central Asia. It flowers

in late spring, producing bright red flowers and narrow leaves. Little violas would make a suitable planting partner in a rock garden or in a small container. H 15cm (6in). Hardy/Z3–8.

Tulipa linifolia Batalinii Group 'Bright Gem'

A short, late-flowering cultivar, closely related to the species tulip (see above), it flowers in late spring and has bronze-yellow flowers. It is ideal for small baskets, wall pots or any other small container. H 15cm (6in). Hardy/Z3–8.

Tulipa 'Little Princess'

The orange-red flowers open wide to reveal black centres. This little tulip, which flowers from mid- to late spring, looks striking in a painted wire basket or other small container, underplanted with black violas. H 10cm (4in). Hardy/Z3–8.

Tulipa linifolia

Bulbs that are good as cut flowers	
Agapanthus (many)	*Gladiolus* (many)
Allium cristophii	*Hippeastrum* (many)
Allium giganteum	*Iris xiphium* (many)
Allium 'Purple Sensation'	*Lilium* (many)
Anemone coronaria	*Muscari* (many)
Eucomis (many)	*Narcissus* (many)
Dahlia (many)	*Nerine* (many)
Freesia (many)	*Tulipa* (many)
Fritillaria imperialis	*Triteleia laxa* 'Koningin Fabiola'

Tulipa tarda planted with *T. urumiensis*

Tulipa saxatilis

This species tulip from Crete flowers in mid-spring. The delicate lilac-pink petals have a strongly contrasting yellow centre. Its glossy leaves appear in late winter. Choose a sunny spot and plant close to pastel-coloured or dark purple plants. H 15cm (6in). Hardy/Z3–8.

Tulipa saxatilis Bakeri Group 'Lilac Wonder'

Closely related to the species *T. saxatilis* this small Bakeri Group cultivar is slightly darker. It is excellent planted around the edge of small containers where it will soften the rim. Plant with *Milium effusum* 'Aureum' (Bowles' golden grass) or *Tanacetum parthenium* 'Aureum' (golden feverfew). H 15cm (6in). Hardy/Z3–8.

Tulipa sylvestris

This short species tulip is native to open woodlands of Italy, Sicily and Sardinia but has become naturalized further north in Europe, including in the Netherlands and Britain. The delicate yellow flowers appear in mid-spring. Try planting it in borders or grass in light shade. H 25cm (10in). Hardy/Z3–8.

Tulipa tarda

This is a short species tulip, originally from Central Asia, which flowers from mid- to late spring. The rather floppy flowers are white and yellow, and each bulb might produce more than one flowering stem. It is ideal for planting at the front of hanging baskets or other small to medium containers. H 10cm (4in). Hardy/Z3–8.

Tulipa saxatilis

Tulipa 'Tinka'

This short cultivar flowers from mid- to late spring. It has red flowers edged in yellow, the whole effect being delicate rather than strident. It is ideal for a hanging basket or other small to medium container. H 10cm (4in). Hardy/Z3–8.

Tulipa turkestanica

This short species tulip is native to Central Asia, and it is one of the first tulips to flower, appearing in late winter or early spring. Its white petals are distinctly pointed, and each has a yellow base. Choose a sheltered, sunny site and plant at the front of a border or in a medium container. H 25–30cm (10–12in). Hardy/Z3–8.

Tulipa urumiensis

This dwarf species tulip, which probably originated in western Iran, flowers from mid- to late spring. It bears several small yellow flowers, which are green-bronze on the outside, and is worth being seen at close quarters at the front of a border or raised bed. Like *T. tarda*, it is ideal for the front of a hanging basket or other small to medium container. The two can be combined for subtle but interesting results. H 10cm (4in). Hardy/Z3–8.

Tulipa saxatilis 'Lilac Wonder'

Tulipa turkestanica

VELTHEIMIA

Named after a German patron of botany, August Ferdinand Graf von Veltheim (1741–1801), this is a genus of only two species of perennial bulbs, which are found growing on rocky and grassy hillsides in South Africa. They are cultivated for their beautiful spring flowers and make excellent houseplants.

Cultivation Plant in autumn with the neck of the bulb just above the soil surface. In frost-prone areas treat as a houseplant and plant in a small pot using a soil-based compost (soil mix) with added sharp sand. Place in a sunny position and begin to water as soon as growth begins, giving a fortnightly low-nitrogen liquid feed. Keep just moist once the leaves have faded and the bulb is dormant.

Propagation Sow seed at 19–24°C (66–75°F) in autumn. Remove offsets in late summer.

Pests and diseases None.

Veltheimia bracteata
(syn. V. viridifolia)

This is a robust perennial bulb, native to South Africa, which flowers in spring. It bears thick, wavy, dark green leaves and dense racemes of up to 60 pendent, tubular, pinkish-purple flowers on stout, erect, yellow-spotted purple stems. Sometimes the flowers are red or yellowish-red. It makes a spectacular display indoors, which

can be repeated year after year. H 45cm (16in) S 30cm (12in). Tender/Z10.

VERATRUM

This is a genus of about 45 species of large, vigorous perennials growing from poisonous black rhizomes, which give rise to its Latin name, from *vere* (truly) and *ater* (black). It grows in damp meadows and open woodland of the northern hemisphere. Its pleated, heavily veined, mid- to dark green leaves are particularly distinctive.

Cultivation Grow in a moist, shady site in a mixed border or in a woodland or wild garden. Provide shelter from drying winds. All parts are highly toxic if ingested.

Propagation Sow seed in a cold frame as soon as it is ripe, or in spring. Divide in autumn or early spring.

Pests and diseases Slugs and snails may be a problem.

Veratrum album
False hellebore, white hellebore

Native to Europe, North Africa and north Asia, this species has pleated basal leaves to 30cm (12in) long and a few stem leaves. It flowers in early and midsummer, bearing numerous star-shaped, greenish-white to white flowers on erect, freely branched panicles to 60cm (24in) long. H 1.8m (6ft) S 60cm (24in). Hardy/Z7–9.

Veratrum nigrum

This species, which is native to Europe and Russia, China and Korea, has long, pleated, basal leaves, to 35cm (14in) long. It flowers in mid- and late summer, bearing numerous star-shaped, almost black flowers on erect, freely branched panicles to 45cm (18in) long. They have an unpleasant scent. H 60–120cm (2–4ft) S 60cm (24in). Hardy/Z7–9.

WATSONIA
Bugle lily

The genus is named in honour of Sir William Watson (1715–87), an English apothecary, physician and naturalist who is known for his research into electricity. It is a genus of about 60 species of corms, usually found on grassy slopes and plateaux of South Africa and Madagascar, and the plants are not dissimilar to gladioli.

Cultivation Grow in light, sandy soil, in a sheltered position in full sun. In autumn or spring plant the corms 15cm (6in) deep in a sheltered sunny border; plants need the protection of a winter mulch. They enjoy the same conditions as autumn-flowering nerines and, like them, are best left undisturbed to form good clumps. Alternatively, plant them in soil-based compost (potting mix) in a large, deep container standing on a sunny, sheltered patio; or plunge the pot in the open border in summer. Overwinter in a frost-free environment.

Propagation Sow seed at 13–18°C (55–64°F) in autumn. Separate corms when dormant, and pot them up in a sandy compost. Keep them dry during the winter and start watering the young plants in the spring.

Pests and diseases None.

Watsonia angusta

This evergreen species is native to South Africa, blooming in late spring or early summer. The long flower spikes bear up to 20 graceful, pale orange flowers, each about 4cm (1½in) long. H 60–90cm (24–36in) S 10cm (4in). Half-hardy/Z9–10.

Watsonia angusta

Watsonia marginata

This clump-forming species is native to Western Cape in South Africa. The narrow leaves, to 45cm (18in) long, are arranged in a fan-like formation. In late spring to early summer the flower spikes are covered with fragrant pink flowers, each to 5cm (2in) long. H 1–1.5m (3–5ft) S 15cm (6in). Tender/Z10.

Watsonia 'Tresco Dwarf Pink'

This is a pretty cultivar producing spikes of shell-pink flowers in late spring or early summer. It was bred in southwest Scotland. H 30cm (12in). Tender/Z10.

Veltheimia bracteata

Veratrum album

Watsonia 'Tresco Dwarf Pink'

ZANTEDESCHIA
Arum lily, calla lily

This genus, which is named in honour of Giovanni Zantedeschi (1773–1846), an Italian botanist and physician, includes about 6 species of rhizomatous plants, usually found in moist soil around lakes or swamps in southern and eastern Africa. They are evergreen in warmer climates but deciduous in cooler areas. The flowers are good for cutting.
Cultivation Grow in consistently damp soil in a sheltered site in full sun. It prefers acidic to mildly acidic soil. In spring plant the rhizomes 15cm (6in) deep in soil-based compost (soil mix) in deep containers, 30–45cm (12–18in) apart, or in a sunny, sheltered border where the protection of a winter mulch is important. Alternatively, plant one tuber to a pot and plunge the container into an open border or beside water for the summer months. It is vital that the tubers are kept moist during the growing period. Bring containers under shelter in winter and repot in spring. *Z. aethiopica* 'Crowborough' can be grown as an aquatic plant in a planting basket, 25–30cm (10–12in) across, in heavy loam soil and placed in water to 30cm (12in) deep. Retrieve for winter months and keep sheltered and frost-free.
Propagation Divide in spring.
Pests and diseases Fungi and aphids.

Zantedeschia aethiopica 'Crowborough'
The species from which this cultivar originates is widely naturalized in tropical and temperate regions of South Africa. Large, white, funnel-shaped spathes are carried above the glossy leaves. It flowers from early to midsummer. H 90cm (36in) S 60cm (24in). Borderline hardy/Z8–10.

Zantedeschia aethiopica 'Green Goddess'
A succession of green spathes, with a central white area splashed with green, appear in summer above deep green, arrow-shaped leaves. This is a curious plant, which will appeal to anyone with a keen eye for design or flower arranging. It is a little more susceptible to frost than *Z. aethiopica* 'Crowborough'. H 75cm (30in) S 60cm (24in). Borderline hardy/Z9–10.

Zantedeschia 'Anneke'
This cultivar, which is partly derived from *Z. elliottiana*, produces large, claret-red, funnel-shaped spathes. The leaves are mottled. It makes a striking contribution in the midsummer garden in borders, as a marginal aquatic or in a container. H 50cm (24in) S 10cm (4in). Tender/Z9–10.

Zantedeschia 'Black Magic'
This cultivar, partly derived from *Z. elliottiana*, produces large, funnel-shaped spathes, which are a rich yellow with a black mark at the throat. The leaves are mottled. Try planting in black containers for the midsummer garden. H 60–90cm (24–36in) S 10cm (4in). Tender/Z9–10.

Zantedeschia 'Cameo'
This cultivar, partly derived from *Z. elliottiana*, produces large, salmon-pink, funnel-shaped spathes, which have a contrasting black mark at the throat. The leaves are mottled. It makes an attractive choice for the midsummer garden, in borders, as a marginal aquatic or in a container. H 50cm (24in) S 10cm (4in). Tender/Z9–10.

Zantedeschia 'Flame'
Although the colouring may vary, this cultivar generally produces funnel-shaped spathes which open yellow with a red edge, maturing through shades of orange to a glowing red flame. The leaves are dark green with white spots. H 40–65cm (16-26in) S 60cm (24in). Tender/Z9–10.

Zantedeschia 'Pink Mist'
A succession of funnel-shaped spathes, which are white with a blush of pink, makes this a really attractive plant, flowering in summer above deep green, arrow-shaped leaves. H 75cm (30in) S 60cm (24in). Borderline hardy/Z9–10.

Zantedeschia 'Picasso'
A succession of sensational funnel-shaped spathes, which are dark purple with white rims, make this a striking plant. It flowers in summer above dark green, arrow-shaped leaves, which have lighter flecks. H 75cm (30in) S 60cm (24in). Borderline hardy/Z9–10.

Zantedeschia 'Pink Persuasion'
This cultivar, partly derived from *Z. elliottiana*, produces large pink, funnel-shaped spathes. The leaves are mottled. This makes a pretty plant in the midsummer garden in a border, as a marginal aquatic or in a container. H 50cm (24in) S 10cm (4in). Tender/Z9–10.

Zantedeschia rehmannii
Pink arum
This eye-catching species is native to eastern South Africa and Swaziland. The leaves are spotted light green or white, and in summer the flower stem carries a yellow spadix surrounded by a reddish-pink spathe, to 8cm (3in) long. The pink becomes more intense if the soil is acidic. Treat as a houseplant or as a container plant on the patio. H 40cm (16in) S 25cm (10in). Tender/Z9–10.

Zantedeschia 'Flame'

Zantedeschia 'Schwarzwalder'
A succession of funnel-shaped, almost black spathes makes this a really striking plant. It flowers in summer above deep green, arrow-shaped leaves, which have lighter flecks. H 75cm (30in) S 60cm (24in). Borderline hardy/Z9–10.

Zantedeschia 'Solfatare'
This cultivar, partly derived from *Z. elliottiana*, produces large, funnel-shaped spathes, which are a rich yellow with a black blush. The leaves are heavily mottled. It makes an impressive container plant. H 60–90cm (24–36in) S 10cm (4in). Tender/Z9–10.

Zantedeschia aethiopica 'Crowborough'

Calendar of care

Most bulbs are relatively easy plants to look after and many will give years of pleasure with very little extra need for care and attention. Snowdrops and aconites, little cyclamen and most of the early daffodils, scillas, grape hyacinths and bluebells will continue without stint with only the occasional need to divide. There are others, however, which need rather more care, simply because they originate from warm climates where there is no threat of winter frosts. In these circumstances, the bulbs either have to be planted in a sunny sheltered site, in very well-drained conditions where winter cold will have a minimal effect with the help of a thick mulch of ashes or grit, or they need to be lifted before the winter starts and kept either dry in frost-free temperatures or in containers in the shelter of a heated greenhouse. Feeding and the need for moisture are common to all plants although some have greater need than others. Planted in the right positions with regard to sun or shade, and with either free-draining or moisture retentive soil, is half the battle. Trilliums need moist shade, nerines need sunny, freely drained soil. Choose your plants with care and reap the rich rewards.

Irises and alliums create a worthwhile partnership, enjoying a sunny border, both similar in height, yet providing a valuable contrast in flower shape.

Winter

Many of the summer- and autumn-flowering bulbs are available to buy at this time of year, including low-growing to medium begonias, *Anemone coronaria*, freesias and taller dahlias, lilies, crinums, nerines, chasmanthe and gladioli. Of these, lilies can be purchased in both autumn and late winter. They are perfectly hardy, and as long as soil conditions allow deep digging to take place, they can be planted at either time.

Most of the bulbs, corms, tubers and rhizomes that are offered for sale in late winter are tender plants, which come from warmer climates where there are no winter frosts. They should be planted in spring, so that when the foliage emerges, all risk of frost has passed. It is possible, however, to cheat the season, because some tubers and corms, such as begonias and dahlias, can be started into growth in pots in late winter, under the protection of glass, so they are ready to plant out in early summer. This method leads to earlier blooms and therefore a long flowering season.

Start dahlias into growth in pots in late winter, under the protection of glass, ready to plant out in early summer.

Galanthus (snowdrop) can be bought in late winter in pots or as loose clumps of plants with the leaves still attached to the bulbs. These are known as snowdrops "in the green". Plant them directly into borders or grassland, where they will establish and flower for years to come.

Bringing on

Cannas, begonias and dahlias are available in a wonderful array of colours and can be started into growth in late winter or early spring so that they produce a mass of flowers throughout summer. Cannas and dahlias should be planted into, and begonias should be placed on top of, barely moist compost (soil mix) and kept in a light, cool to warm place until growth begins at the roots. Increase the available moisture once leaves begin to emerge.

Planting in borders or containers

In mild spells, when the ground can be well dug, plant lilies in the border, either singly or in groups of three or more. Alternatively, plant them in deep containers. They thrive on well-drained soil, so add a layer of grit beneath the bulbs in both borders and containers.

Watering

This is a time when attention to watering is crucial, especially with container-grown plants. Moisture is necessary to bulbs at all stages of growth, and it is important to check that the compost (soil mix) is moist in all pots, troughs, window boxes and hanging baskets from autumn right through to spring. Pots and troughs will probably fare best, but window boxes and hanging baskets tend to dry out quickly. Lack of moisture in late autumn and early winter will inhibit root growth, and lack of water in late winter, when the leaves and buds are emerging, is also detrimental. Keep an eye on the compost and water as necessary. Do not, however, be tempted to water if frost threatens, as bulbs will not appreciate having their roots in wet, frozen conditions. It is much better to ignore any bright sunny days when nights are likely to be frosty, and water only on overcast days when the nights will be milder.

Feeding

This is not a major task at this time of year, although care should be given to any bulbs, tubers, rhizomes and corms in pots if you want to keep the plants for another display next season. Feed at flowering time or once thereafter, so that the foliage is kept healthy and the goodness can go back into the bulbs as the leaves die down. Border bulbs benefit from a general-purpose feed, which should be applied to the border in late winter or early spring. Many of the summer bulbs will still be in the greenhouse, so the best time to feed them will be when they are planted out.

Eranthis hyemalis (winter aconite) makes a welcome splash of yellow in late winter.

Protection against frost

All the hardy, autumn-planted bulbs that have been given homes in grassland or borders should not come to any harm in frosty weather. Those such as nerines and crinums, which may be considered borderline in colder areas, will benefit from a mulch of dry leaves. Bulbs and other plants that are in containers are at far greater risk. Hanging baskets should be taken off their brackets if temperatures drop below freezing for any prolonged length of time. A degree or two of frost overnight will not do any harm, but two or three nights and days of continued frost will pose greater problems. Place the baskets in the protection of a porch, garage or greenhouse. Pots and troughs should be given the protection of a house wall, where the temperatures will be less extreme, or put in a garage, porch or greenhouse. Sometimes they are too large and heavy to move easily, in which case they should be wrapped in a cloak of bubble wrap before the temperature

Galanthus (snowdrop) multiply persistently where they are growing in damp woodland, and will eventually spread to carpet vast areas. Plant them under shrubs and enjoy a similar, if scaled-down, effect.

Iris 'Pauline' has dark violet flowers with distinctive white markings on the falls. This Reticulata iris is sweetly scented. Plant in an individual pot or with winter greenery in a hanging basket.

drops to freezing. This will at least provide a little protection. Never water in frosty weather, when it is better to keep the compost (soil mix) on the dry side.

Deadheading

Removing dead flowerheads means that a plant's energy is not wasted on the production of seed at the expense of increasing the size of the bulb. However, if you want to increase from seed, you should allow the full cycle of growth to continue unabated. Many of the late winter bulbs and corms, including snowdrops, *Eranthis hyemalis* (winter aconite), *Crocus tommasinianus*, cyclamen and *Anemone blanda*, naturalize well by seed propagation.

Propagation

Collect seeds from winter aconites in late winter and early spring, and sprinkle them where you want them to flower, either in special propagation boxes or direct on border soil or grass. Divide clumps of snowdrops and *Leucojum vernum* (spring snowflake) and replant.

Pest watch

Squirrels and mice might dig up newly planted bulbs. Snails might attack early daffodils, while birds might eat crocus flowers.

Enjoy

Now is the time to enjoy the flowers on many winter bulbs, such as the many different kinds of snowdrops. *Galanthus nivalis* and all its relations, *Leucojum vernum*, commonly known as spring snowflakes, early daffodils such as *Narcissus* 'Rijnveld's Early Sensation' (syn. 'January Gold') and 'February Gold', and the early tulips. Enjoy the flowers on winter corms such as the dwarf *Iris danfordiae*, crocus, and also on tubers such as those of the winter aconites, *Anemone blanda* and *Cyclamen coum*.

Spring

Some of the summer-flowering bulbs that were available in late winter will still be on sale, but choose those that are still plump and firm and have not been dried out by over-exposure on the garden-centre shelves. As spring progresses, cannas, begonias and dahlias in growth will go on sale, but the choice of colour and size will be more restricted than if you had bought dormant tubers and rhizomes.

Bringing on

Cannas and dahlias should be planted into, and begonias placed on top of, barely moist compost (soil mix) and kept in a light, cool to warm place until growth begins at the roots. Increase moisture once leaves begin to emerge. Plant outside when all risk of frost has passed.

Planting in borders, grass or containers

Gladioli, *Anemone coronaria* (single De Caen hybrids and semi-double St Bridgid varieties), *Zantedeschia*

(arum lily), tigridia, sparaxis, crinums and lilies should be planted now. You might like to try a succession of anemones which flower about three months after planting.

Transplanting

Dichelostemmas, ornithogalums and lilies that were potted earlier and now have good root formation should be transplanted. Either transfer from the pot or simply bury the pot in the garden borders.

Galanthus (snowdrop) and *Eranthis hyemalis* (winter aconite) can be purchased in spring as growing plants with their leaves intact. They might be sold in pots or in loose groups after flowering, but whichever kind you obtain, they will successfully transplant and flower well the following season.

Lifting

The life-cycle of a bulb normally continues for at least six weeks after flowering has finished, so do not be tempted to lift and dry off bulbs,

Dahlia tubers are now showing sustained new growth. New shoots can be used for propagation material.

rhizomes and so on until well after this date. Do not mow grassy areas until six weeks after snowdrops, crocuses or daffodils have finished flowering, or the following year's blooms will be greatly inhibited.

Watering

This is essential for container-grown specimens, especially if other bedding plants have been added to the scheme. Take special care with hanging baskets, which tend to dry out quickly, and with window boxes, which often receive little rainfall. Border bulbs, corms and so forth will normally receive adequate natural rainfall, although in exceptionally dry seasons they may benefit from additional moisture.

Feeding

Feed at flowering time or once thereafter so that the foliage is kept healthy and the goodness can go back into the bulbs as the leaves die down. Grassland and border bulbs will benefit from a general-purpose

The sumptuous blue of *Muscari* (grape hyacinth) is set off perfectly by an underplanting of *Senecio cineraria* with all its light silvery foliage.

feed applied in late winter or early spring. Container-grown specimens will benefit from a liquid feed.

Protection against frost

Hardy bulbs are unlikely to suffer in frosty spring weather, but keep an eye on the temperature in your greenhouse where you might be bringing on cannas, begonias and dahlias. Keep the plants away from the glass, where temperatures drop fastest, and maintain the temperature above freezing. Keep the compost (soil mix) on the dry side.

Deadheading

Hyacinths, daffodils and tulips should be deadheaded to avoid energy being wasted on seed production, but if you want to propagate bulbs such as *Scilla siberica*, *Muscari armeniacum*, *Chionodoxa luciliae* and *C. forbesii*, allow the seedheads to develop. Collect the seed and sow in propagation boxes or allow them to self-seed in situ.

Tulipa 'Blue Parrot' is just one of the many Parrot tulips available, all exhibiting the fullness of flower that makes them so popular.

Do not worry about hardy spring-flowering bulbs such as tulips, hyacinths and daffodils being harmed by late spring frosts.

Propagation

Collect ripe seed from winter aconites and, in due course, from *Muscari armeniacum* (grape hyacinth) and scillas. Sow in propagation boxes or simply allow them to self-seed in situ.

Pest watch

Slugs and snails adore succulent growth and will attack the young foliage on tulips and alliums, lilies and daffodil flowers. General garden cleanliness is important in keeping the slug and snail population at bay, and some gardeners use chemicals against certain pests with varying degrees of success. Rabbits, mice and birds are a nightmare as far as many bulbous plants are concerned, greedily eating off all the new shoots or flowers. Rabbits, fortunately, won't touch daffodils. Buried wire fences can stop rabbits, but there is little you can do to frighten off birds, mice and squirrels.

Enjoy

This is a really wonderful season for bulbs and corms of all kinds, and there is a multitude of daffodils, tulips, hyacinths, *Erythronium* (dog's tooth violet), fritillaries, irises, *Leucojum* (snowflake), grape hyacinths and trilliums coming into flower in grasslands, borders and containers. While you are enjoying them all, now is the time to search out your favourite colours for planting next autumn.

Summer

Gladioli might still be on sale, and late plantings now will give colour in autumn. Purchases of growing dahlias and begonias, cannas and *Zantedeschia* (arum lily) will allow you to obtain lots of colour this summer, although the range of colours will be more restricted than with dry tubers, rhizomes and so forth purchased in late winter.

Bringing on
Late plantings of dahlias and begonias are still possible, and, given warmth and moisture, they will soon grow on and produce good plants for planting out once the roots are well developed.

Planting in borders, grass or containers
Gladioli and anemones (single De Caen hybrids and semi-double St Bridgid varieties) can still be planted, although they will be later to flower than if they were planted in spring. Anemones will flower about three months after planting, while gladioli might take up to four months.

Allium seedheads are just one of the many delights of summer. They can be enjoyed in the garden or used in dried flower arrangements.

You will need to deadhead begonia blooms regularly to encourage production of flowers.

Transplanting
This is a major task now. Once all risk of frost has passed, the dahlias, cannas and begonias that were started into growth earlier can be planted out in the garden. They will be suitable for sunny borders or containers. Add slow-release food granules or well-rotted manure to the prepared holes before planting.

Lifting
If you want to remove tulips and daffodil bulbs from the borders, now is the time to lift them carefully so that they can be dried off, cleaned, sorted, labelled and stored for use again in the autumn. The best time is when the leaves have withered but are still visible.

Watering
Depending on the weather, be prepared to water. Dahlias are thirsty plants, especially in the early stages of growth.

Feeding
Once the buds have formed on dahlias, begonias and cannas, they will benefit from a regular liquid feed during the summer.

Protection against frost
This should no longer be necessary.

Deadheading
Regular deadheading of begonias, dahlias and cannas will ensure longer flower production and bigger blooms. It will also make the plants look much tidier. Gladioli and lilies should be deadheaded to conserve energy for next year's display.

Propagation
In midsummer, seeds of *Fritillaria meleagris* (snake's head fritillary) should be collected when ripe and sown in a propagating box. In late summer, small black bulbils will form up the stems of some types of lily, including those derived from

Tall-growing lilies can be supported with a special metal stake and detachable hoop.

Lilium lancifolium (formerly *L. tigrinum*; tiger lily). These will eventually fall off and propagate themselves at the foot of the parent plant, or they can be collected and planted in a propagating box.

Mowing grasslands where bulbs have flowered earlier

Normally it is best to leave growth intact for at least six weeks before mowing, or the lifecycle of the bulbs will not be completed and next year's flowering will be seriously impaired. Grassed areas with late-flowering daffodils and camassias should not be mown until midsummer.

Staking

All tall-growing lilies, gladioli and dahlias will need support. Single canes or special metal-hooped supports are adequate for lilies and gladioli, but dahlias, which grow much wider and have many strong branches, will need greater support, either from a metal stake and wider circle, substantial peasticks or from three or four stakes surrounding the plant and linked by string.

Pest watch

Slugs, snails and earwigs think dahlias are wonderful fodder. Look out for vine weevil damage to begonia tubers. The grubs can be killed by beneficial nematodes, which are watered on in late summer, or by using a systemic insecticide.

Enjoy

In early summer, rich purple is still present in the flowerheads of alliums, while gorgeous blue is possible with tall camassias, which emerge from the borders and grasslands. Later blues are rarer, but they are still possible with freesias, anemones and triteleia. The mid- to late summer range of tubers, rhizomes, bulbs and corms is dazzling. Dahlias and gladioli are available in dozens of brilliant hues, ranging from red, yellow, orange, pink and purple to white, while begonias and cannas light up the border with fiery yellows, oranges and reds. Kniphofias add another tier to the drama, and with their long tapering racemes provide a rich source of colour.

The seeds of *Fritillaria meleagris* (snake's head fritillary) will be ready for collection in midsummer. They should be sown in a propagating box.

Autumn

The autumn months bring a deluge of dry bulbs into garden centres and stores, some pre-packaged in groups of three, five and sometimes ten at a time, while others, such as the common types of daffodil, tulip and hyacinth, are sold loose so that they can be picked up in any quantity. The pre-packs can be more expensive, but the range is usually far greater. Buy early if you want to obtain special named varieties. Look out for some of your favourite colours in tulips, pick out dwarf daffodils for pots and baskets, and buy hyacinths for scent.

Bringing on
Some genera, such as calochortus and dichelostemma, are best planted in pots and kept in a frost-free potting shed, ready for transplanting or plunging into the garden the following summer.

Planting direct in borders, grass or containers
Autumn-flowering colchicums and *Lilium candidum* (Madonna lily) should be planted as soon as they are

Continue to deadhead the flowers of begonias, cannas and dahlias.

available. All the late winter- and spring-flowering varieties, including daffodils, tulips and hyacinths, should be planted direct into borders, grasslands or containers as soon as convenient, so they can form good roots in autumn and early winter. Summer-flowering lilies should also be planted now, although some will also be available in late winter.

Lifting
Tender specimens, such as begonias, dahlias, cannas and gladioli, should be lifted, dried, cleaned, labelled and stored for the winter in frost-free conditions, ready for planting the following year.

Watering
This will not be necessary for border or grass-grown plants, but take care with containers, such as hanging baskets and window boxes, which are apt to dry out quickly and may receive little rainfall.

Protection against frost
Dahlias can be left outside until blackened by the first frost, but then they should be lifted and kept frost-free or left in situ and mulched.

Deadheading
Continue to deadhead cannas, begonias and dahlias so that they still provide welcome colour for as long as the weather allows. The first frosts might vary, in some years striking in early autumn while in others it might be several weeks later.

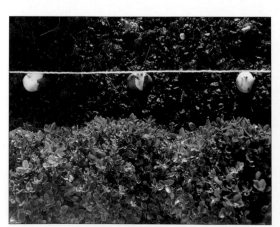

Bulbs, such as these tulips, can be planted in formal lines using taut lengths of string as a guide. Space the tulip bulbs at 15–20cm (6–8in) intervals underneath the string.

So many different varieties of bulb are available to buy and plant now, there is bound to be something to suit everyone. Just make sure that the bulbs are plump and firm and reject any that are not perfect.

Dark-leaved cannas still make an impact in the late autumn border but they are best lifted before the first frosts.

Propagation

On replanting daffodils and tulips lifted in early summer, the main large bulb can be replanted to create a flowering clump, while smaller bulbs and corms can be planted out in rows, ready to bulk up in size for flowering in two or three years' time.

Pest watch

Earwigs, slugs and snails will still take their toll on growing plants. Look out for vine weevil damage to begonia tubers. The grubs can be killed by beneficial nematodes or by using a systemic insecticide, which is watered on in late summer. Mice and squirrels might try to dig up newly planted bulbs and corms. Be sure to firm in the soil around them.

Enjoy

This is the time to enjoy the glory of all the dahlia, begonia and canna flowers, which will bloom well until the first frosts sadly curtail the show. Late gladioli and sprays of schizostylis will also give pleasure now, as well as the glorious funnel-shaped blooms of pink or white crinums. Frilly pink nerines will come into bloom, and it is always surprising to see such vivid pink flowers at this time of year.

Much shorter specimens will also be in flower now, including the goblet shaped colchicums, either white or lilac, yellow sternbergias, and the delicate pink or white flowers of tiny autumn-flowering *Cyclamen hederifolium*.

Once autumn frosts have blackened dahlia foliage, it is time to cut down the stems and lift the tubers or mulch.

Suppliers

United Kingdom

The African Garden
David Fenwick
96 Wasdale Gardens
Plymouth
Devon PL6 8TW
Tel: 01752 301402
www.theafricangarden.com
*The garden is dedicated to the
conservation and culture of Southern
African bulbs, including agapanthus,
and holds the NCCPG National Plant
Reference Collections of crocosmia with
chasmanthe, tulbaghia, eucomis
with galtonia, freesia and amaryllis.*

Avon Bulbs
Chris Ireland Jones
Burnt House Farm
Mid Lambrook
South Petherton
Somerset TA13 5HE
Tel: 01460 242177
www.avonbulbs.com
Extensive list. Mail order only.

The Beth Chatto Gardens Ltd
Elmstead Market
Colchester
Essex CO7 7DB
Tel: 01206 822007
www.bethchatto.co.uk
*Extensive list including agapanthus,
allium, croscosmia, gladiolus, nerine.
Garden, nursery and mail order.*

Blackmore and Langdon Ltd.
Pensford
Bristol BS39 4JL
Tel: 01275 332300
www.blackmore-langdon.com
*Plants available from nursery and mail
order. Specialists in begonias.*

Bloms Bulbs
Primrose Nurseries
Melchbourne
Beds MK44 1ZZ
Tel: 01234 709099
www.blomsbulbs.com
Extensive list. Mail order only.

Border Belles
Old Branxton Cottages
Innerwick
Nr Dunbar
East Lothian
Scotland EH42 1QT
Tel: 01368 840325
www.borderbelles.com
*Anemone, erythronium, kniphofia,
fritillaria, trillium. Mail order only.*

Bressingham Gardens
Bressingham
Diss
Norfolk IP22 2AG
Tel: 01379 688282
www.bressinghamgardens.com
*Many bulbs including alliums, anemones,
crocosmias and trillium. Nursery, garden
and mail order.*

Broadleigh Gardens
Bishops Hull
Taunton
Somerset, TA4 1AE
Tel: 01283 286231
www.broadleighbulbs.co.uk
*Extensive list. Mail order. Viewing
9.00–16.00 Monday–Friday.*

Buckland Plants
Whinnieliggate
Kirkcudbright
Scotland DG6 4XP
Tel: 01557 331323
www.bucklandplants.co.uk
*Anemone, crocosmia, erythronium,
lilium, trillium. Mail order.*

Cambo
Kingsbarns
St Andrews
Fife KY16 8QD
Tel: 01333 450313
www.camboestate.com
*Mail order sale of galanthus, aconites
and Leucojum vernum "in the green".*

Edulis
Paul Barney
The Walled Garden
Bare Court Farm
Tidmarsh Lane
Pangbourne
Reading
Berkshire RG8 8SG
Tel: 01635 578113
www.edulis.co.uk
*Specializes in hedychiums, eucomis,
cannas and agapanthus. Mail order or by
appointment only.*

Elm Tree Nursery
Sidbury
Sidmouth
Devon EX10 OQG
Tel: 01395 597790
elmtreecyclamen@btopenworld.com
Hardy cyclamen. Mail order only.

Fir Trees Pelargonium Nursery
Stokesley
Middlesbrough,
Cleveland TS9 5LD
Tel: 01642 713066
*Specializes in pelargonium species and
cultivars including P. schottii. Open
1 April–31 August, seven days a week.*

Narcissus

Hart Canna
27 Guildford Road West
Farnborough
Hampshire GU14 6PS
Tel: 01252 514421
www.hartcanna.com
*Canna. Mail order only. National
collection of canna can be visited by
appointment.*

Jacques Amand
Clamp Hill
Stanmore
Middlesex HA7 3JS
Tel: 020 8420 7110
www.jacquesarmand.com
Extensive list. Mail order only.

Kobakoba
2 High Street
Ashcott
Bridgwater
Somerset TA79PL
Tel: 01458 210700
www.kobakoba.co.uk
*Hedychium and other zingiberaceae.
Mail order.*

Marwood Hill Gardens
Barnstable
Devon EX31 4EB
Tel: 01271 342528
malcolm.pharaoh@supanet.com
www.marwoodhillgarden.co.uk
*Tulbaghia, kniphofia. Nursery open
11.00–16.30, seven days a week.*

Pennard Plants
3 The Gardens
East Pennard
Shepton Mallet

Somerset BA4 6TU
Tel: 01749 860039
www.pennardplants.com
*Agapanthus, kniphofias, crocosmias and
South African bulbous plants.*

Shipton Bulbs
Y Felin
Henllan Amgoed
Whitland
Carmarthenshire SA34 OSL
Tel: 01994 240125
www.bluebellbulbs.co.uk
*Mainly sales of bulbs which are either
native or naturalize well, many of them
late winter or spring flowering. Garden
can be visited, but phone first.*

Pine Cottage Plants
Pine Cottage
Fourways
Eggesford
Nr Chumleigh
Devon EX18 7QZ
Tel: 01769 580076
www.pcplants.co.uk
*UK National Collection of Agapanthus.
Sells many cultivars, as well as dierama,
hedychium and crocosmia. Garden open
last two weeks in July and first three
weeks in August; other times by
appointment.*

Pitcairn Alpines
Scotts Park
Pitcairngreen
Perth PH1 3LT
Tel: 01738 583213
www.pitcairnalpines.co.uk
*Anemones, erythroniums and fritillaria.
Mail order only.*

Canna (top) and zantedeschia (bottom)

Walker Bulbs at Taylors
Washway House Farm
Holbeach
Spalding
Lincs PE12 7PP
Tel: 01406 426216
www.taylors-bulbs.com
*Extensive list including award-winning
narcissus and lilium. Mail order.*

Derry Watkins
Greenways Lane
Cold Ashton
Chippenham
Wilts SN14 8LA
Tel: 01225 891686
www.specialplants.net
*Mail order. Open Wednesdays in July and
August and through NGS.*

World Bulbs
PO Box 2911
Aldridge
WS9 OWB
Tel: 01922 453396
www.worldbulbs.com
Bulb and seed catalogues.

Tulip

Muscari

The Netherlands

B & B Quality Bulbs
De Gouw 41e
1602 DN Enkhuizen
www.qualitybulbs.com

Th. Langeveld B.V.
Vennestraat 8
2161 LE Lisse
Tel: +31 (0) 252 431943
www.langeveld.com

Tulip World B.V.
Grasweg 71
1031 HX Amsterdam
Tel: +31 20 6944171
www.tulipworld.com

From top left clockwise: begonia, dahlia, anemone and ranunculus

United States of America

Aaron's Bulb Farm
PO Box 800
Summer
GA 31789
Tel: (800) 913 9347
www.aaronscanna-amaryllis.com
Wide range of amaryllis, and canna.

Bloms Bulbs Inc.
491-233 Glen Eagle Square
Glen Mills
PA 19342
Tel: (866)-7-TULIPS
www.blombulbs.com

The Bulb Crate
2560 Deerfield Road
Riverwoods
IL 60015
Tel: (847) 317-1414
www.thebulbcrate.com

D. J. Enterprises
4768 Boylston Highway
Horse Shoe
NC 28742
Tel: (828) 891-5467
www.djgrowglad.com
*Grower of gladiolus bulbs, lily, canna
and iris in the mountains of western
North Carolina.*

Flowers and Greens
35717 Lasiandra Lane
Davis
CA 95616
Tel: (530) 756 9238
www.buy-alstroemeria.com

Gardener's Supply Company
128 Intervale Road
Burlington
VE 05401
Tel: (888) 833 1412
www.gardeners.com

John Scheepers Inc.
23 Tulip Drive
PO Box 638
Bantam
CT 06750
Tel: (860) 567 0838
www.johnscheepers.com

Langeveld Bulbs Inc.
PO Box 2105
Lakewood
NJ 08701
Tel: (732) 367 2000
www.langveld.com

The Lily Pad
3403 Steamboat Island Rd NW
PMB 374
Olympia
WA 98502
Tel: (360) 866-0291
www.lilypadbulbs.com
Many different species of lilies.

Chasmanthe (top), freesia (bottom left) and gladioli (bottom right)

From top left clockwise: hyacinth, camassia, scilla, bluebell and muscari

Nature Hills Nursery Inc.
3334 North 88th Plaza
Omaha
NB 68134
Tel: (888) 864 7763
www.naturehills.com
Anemones, begonia, lilies and other bulbs.

Odyssey Bulbs
PO Box 38
Berrien Springs
Michigan 49103
Tel: (877) 220 1657
www.odysseybulbs.com
Specializes in unusual and rare bulbs.

Van Bourgondien
PO Box 2000
Virginia Beach
VA 23450-2000
Tel: (800) 327-4268
www.dutchbulbs.com
Sells a variety of Dutch bulbs, including tulips, lilies, gladioli and daffodils.

White Flower Farm
PO Box 50
Litchfield
CT 06759
Tel: (800) 503 9624
www.whitefarm.com

Wooden Shoe Tulip Farm
33814 S. Meridian Road
OR 97071
Tel: (800) 711-2006
www.woodenshoe.com
Specializes in tulips and daffodils. Visitors welcome.

Canada

Art's Nursery Ltd
8940 192nd Street
Surrey
BC V4N 3W8
Tel: (604) 882-1201
www.artnursery.com
Specializes in dahlias.

Lilies in the Valley
RR No. 1
Rosseau
Ontario POC 1JO
Tel: (705) 732-2224
www.lilies.ca
Sells 214 varieties of lilies, including orientals, asiatics, hybrids and tiger lilies.

Crinum (top), lilies (middle) and tulips (bottom)

Australia

Brenda Lyon Specialty Bulbs
'Falkirk'
2070 Edith Road
Oberon
NSW 2787
Tel: (02) 6336 1282
www.ozdaffodils.com
Daffodil specialist with over 2,000 varieties. Visit the farm last two weeks in September.

Broersen Bulbs Pty Ltd
365–367 Monbulk Road
Silvan
Victoria 3795
Tel: (03) 9737 9202
www.broersen.com.au
Alliums, anemones, freesias, iris, lilies and many other bulbs by mail order.

Bulbs Direct
PO Box 30
Leopold
Victoria 3224
Tel: (03) 5250 5132
www.bulbsdirect.com.au
Mail order service. Over 400 varieties of bulb.

Hancock's Daffodils
PO Box 4120
Langwarrin
Victoria 3910
Tel: 0500 532337
www.daffodilbulbs.com
Tulips, daffodils, alliums, freesias, iris and many other bulbs by mail order.

Patchwork Nursery
PO Box 50
The Patch
Victoria 3792
Tel: (03) 9756 7277
www.nurseriesonline.com.au
Specializes in alliums.

Timothy Drewitt Bulb Nurseries
8–10 Henderson Hill Road
Silvan
Victoria 3795
Tel: (03) 9737 9827
www.nurseriesonline.com.au
Specializes in rare and unusual daffodil bulbs.

Van Dieman Quality Bulbs
365 Lighthouse Road
Wynyard
TAS 7325
Tel: (03) 6442 2012
www.vdqbulbs.com.au

Iris

Index

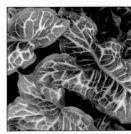

Arum italicum 'Marmoratum'

Canna 'Rosemond Coles'

Crocus 'Blue Pearl'

Cyclamen persicum

Fritillaria imperialis 'Maxima Lutea'

Dahlia 'Hayley Jane'

Plant Hardiness Zones

Plant entries in this book have been given zone numbers, and these zones relate to their hardiness. The zonal system used, shown below, was developed by the Agricultural Research Service of the U.S. Department of Agriculture. According to this system, there are 11 zones, based on the average annual minimum temperature in a particular geographical zone. When a range of zones is given for a plant, the smaller number indicates the northernmost zone in which a plant can survive the winter and the higher number gives the most southerly area in which it will perform consistently.

As with any system, this one is not hard and fast. It is simply a rough indicator, as many factors other than temperature also play an important part where hardiness is concerned. These factors include altitude, wind exposure, proximity to water, soil type, the presence of snow or existence of shade, night temperature, and the amount of water received by a plant. These kinds of factors can easily alter a plant's hardiness by as much as two zones.

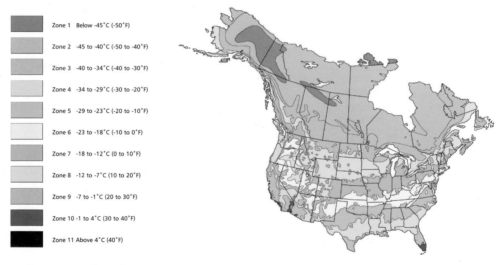

Zone 1 Below -45°C (-50°F)

Zone 2 -45 to -40°C (-50 to -40°F)

Zone 3 -40 to -34°C (-40 to -30°F)

Zone 4 -34 to -29°C (-30 to -20°F)

Zone 5 -29 to -23°C (-20 to -10°F)

Zone 6 -23 to -18°C (-10 to 0°F)

Zone 7 -18 to -12°C (0 to 10°F)

Zone 8 -12 to -7°C (10 to 20°F)

Zone 9 -7 to -1°C (20 to 30°F)

Zone 10 -1 to 4°C (30 to 40°F)

Zone 11 Above 4°C (40°F)

Acknowledgements

Author's acknowledgements
I am indebted to John D. Taylor C.B.E., John D. Taylor II and John Walkers of O.A. Taylor and Sons Ltd of Holbeach for their support and technical advice. I would like to thank Michelle Garrett, Jonathan Buckley and, particularly, Peter Anderson for their expertise as photographers, capturing many glorious scenes both here in my garden at Stevington, Bedfordshire, as well as other locations. As always it is a pleasure to work with such a dedicated team. I would also like to thank my editor Caroline Davison, helped by Sarah Uttridge and Molly Perham, for their enthusiasm and guidance. As always, I wish to thank my husband Simon for his unfailing help and encouragement.

Publisher's acknowledgements
The publishers would like to thank the following gardens, which are photographed in this book: Beth Chatto Gardens, Chenies Manor, The Coppice, East Lambrook, Great Dixter, Kew Gardens, Lamport Hall, RHS Rosemoor, RHS Wisley, The Savill Garden, Upper Mill Cottage. Unless listed below photographs are © Anness Publishing Ltd.

t = top; b = bottom; c= centre; r =right; l = left. **Mary Evans Picture Library**: 13t, 14t, 15t; **Garden Picture Library**: 164tl (John Glover), 164tc (Howard Rice), 164br (Mark Bolton), 165tl (J S Sira), 167tc (Chris Burrows), 177tr (Brian Carter), 177br (Geoff Dann), 191tr (Densey Clyne); 191br (Clive Nichols), 191tl (Howard Rice), 191bl (John Glover), 191br (J. S. Sira), 195tr (Howard Rice), 197tl (Juliette Wade), 197tc (David England), 199tl (James Guilliam), 199tc (Chris Burrows), 199bl (Philippe Bonduel), 217br (Philippe Bonduel), 220tr (Sunniva Harte), 220br (John Glover), 221tl (Neil Holmes), 221bl (Chris Burrows), 223br (Sunniva Harte), 224tl (Philippe Bonduel), 225tl (Chris Burrows), 225br (John Glover), 226tl (Sunniva Harte), 226tc (Howard Rice), 226bl (Dennis Davis), 237tr (John Glover); **Garden World Images**: 163tl, 163b, 167tl, 168br, 169tr, 169bl, 169br, 173tl, 173tr, 175tc, 175bc, 176tr, 198br, 208bl, 213bl, 215bl, 216bl, 217tr, 217bl, 218br, 220tl, 220bc, 236bl; **Holt Studios**: 48bl, 49tr, 51bl, 51br, 52tl, 52tc; **Science Photo Library**: 12bl, 12tr, 48tr, 48bc, 49br, 50tl, 51tl, 52br, 157bl, 187tc, 187br.